Geometric Computing for Perception Action Systems

Springer Science+Business Media, LLC

Eduardo Bayro Corrochano

Geometric Computing for Perception Action Systems

Concepts, Algorithms, and Scientific Applications

With 73 Illustrations

Springer

Eduardo Bayro Corrochano
Centro de Investigaciòn y Estudios Avanzados
del I.P.N., Unidad de Guadalajara
Computer Science Department
Prolongaciòn Lòpez Mateos Sur 590
Guadalajara, Jalisco 45090
Mexico
edb@gdl.cinvestav.mx

Library of Congress Cataloging-in-Publication Data
Bayro Corrochano, Eduardo.
Geometric computing for perception action systems: concepts, algorithms, and scientific applications/Eduardo Bayro Corrochano.
p. cm.
Includes bibliographical references and index.
ISBN 978-1-4612-6535-1 ISBN 978-1-4613-0177-6 (eBook)
DOI 10.1007/978-1-4613-0177-6
1. Machine learning. 2. Clifford algebras. 3. Geometry—Data processing. I. Title.
Q325.5.B38. 2001
006.3'1—dc21 2001018391

Printed on acid-free paper.

Production managed by Frank McGuckin; manufacturing supervised by Joe Quatela.
Camera-ready copy prepared from the author's TeX files using Springer's svsing2e.sty macro.

9 8 7 6 5 4 3 2 1

ISBN 978-1-4612-6535-1 SPIN 10789868

Preface

Despite great advances in computer hardware over the last three decades, concomitant efforts to build intelligent machines have not as yet produced satisfactory autonomous systems. The complexity of involved cognitive tasks is, to a great degree, still not clear enough. Biologically, creatures interact with their environment in order to survive, evolve, and reproduce. Their activity is triggered by different needs and goals which must be satisfied. As soon as a creature feels nourished and secure, its internal activity may switch to a higher cognitive level so as to satisfy other, more sophisticated needs for building up intelligence. The brain, which can be imagined as a geometric engine, is responsible for these behaviors. The hypothesis underlying geometric interpretation of brain function assumes that a "mapping" process takes place between external stimuli and the brain, which triggers information processing, and that both of these tasks invoke the properties of higher-order geometric representation. It is this interaction between external and internal worlds which brings about perception—and then action—in some finite cycle of interaction with the environment. In other words, afferent and efferent activities, controlled by the brain and the nervous system, support the development of behavioral capabilities. We believe this type of "learning by experience" can be reproduced in robotics, using internal geometric representations as the foundation for computer cognition.

In mathematical terms, one can formalize the relationship between the external physical signals of world objects and the corresponding internal signals that are created to represent those objects. This is done by using extrinsic vectors to represent data from the outside world and intrinsic vectors to depict internal representation. We should consider, however, that external and internal worlds may each use different reference-coordinate systems. If we interpret the acquisition of knowledge as a distributed process, we can imagine various domains of geometric representation, with different vectorial bases obeying different metrics. All of which begs the question: How is it possible that nature has acquired such tremendous representation and processing power for dealing with such complex representations through evolution? Some researchers claim that internal vectorial representations whose reference frames are intrinsic to the creature are covariant for perception analysis and contravariant for action synthesis, and that therefore geometric mapping between external and internal vectorial spaces is implemented by a neural network that functions as a metric tensor. Clifford algebra, when interpreted geometrically, appears to provide an alternative to this type of tensor analysis, since it is essentially a coordinate-free, or invariant, system, and, unlike tensor calculus, it also includes spinor theory. Presently, the most frequently used approach for neural computation is matrix algebra, but there are numerous examples to show that geometric algebra is capable of unmasking certain invariants that would be otherwise obscured using matrix computations.

If we are interested in building artificial-intelligent machines, then we must first consider which algebraic system will allow the machines to deal successfully with the high complexity of any particular cognitive task. The following is a brief review and critique of current approaches in the design of PAC systems. (In the context of our discussion here, we shall use the acronym PAC [for perception–action cycle] to describe the intelligent systems we hope to model mathematically.) The primary question for autonomous systems is how to model mathematically the processes of representation and learning. Until the mid-1980s, the study of representation and learning was essentially considered to be the purview of specialists in neurocomputing, but in recent years researchers from other fields have expanded their study of this question as well. Indeed, some of the most important recent developments have come out of the fields of signal theory, computer vision, and robotics. Although these individual advances appear promising, each discipline remains separate in its approach and there is still no mechanism that would allow these advances to be combined into one unified concept. For example, the linear algebra of real and complex numbers is not really sufficient for the linear modeling of transformations of higher-grade geometric objects (such as lines, planes, and volumes). Linear algebra and projective geometry continue to be two separate fields, and neither system allows for the exploration of symmetries of higher-order entities. Similarly, early attempts to model 3D motion using quaternions, as in the case of 3D kinematics in computer vision and robotics, have had some success, but this technique may not be used in conjunction with other mathematical systems. The use of dual quaternions also is promising, but has not been explored enough for the tasks of 2D and 3D kinematics and dynamics. Lie group theory has been used successfully in image processing for the generalization of the wavelet transform or filter steerability; however, this technique would gain more power if it could be used within a geometric framework. Cayley-Grassmann algebra, with its operations of meet and join, offers an elegant computational system for the algebra of incidence in computer vision; however, used by itself, it lacks the key concepts of duality, inner product, and spinors. When researchers use these and other systems, they quickly lose themselves in the design of the PAC system because, used separately, such systems either require exceedingly complex algebraic formulations or obscure the underlying geometry of the problem, as is the case with the use of classical matrix calculus. Clearly, what is needed for the development of PAC systems is a fusion of these disciplines that would employ a coordinate-free and algebraicly enriched mathematical system using higher-order vectors or multivectors. Accordingly, we have taken up the challenge of applying geometric algebra to the development of PAC systems.

Historically, Clifford algebra in its geometric interpretation has constituted the general framework for the embedding and development of ideas of multilinear algebra, multivariable analysis, and the representation theory of Lie groups and Lie algebras. This trend toward geometric algebra started in 300 B.C. with the synthetic geometry of Euclid and has continued to evolve into the present. The analytic geometry of Descartes (1637), the complex algebra of Wessel and Gauss (1798), Hamilton algebra (1843), matrix algebra (Cayley, 1854), exterior algebra (Grassmann, 1844), Clifford algebra (1878), the tensor algebra of Ricci (1890), the differential forms of Cartan (1923), and the spin algebra of Pauli and Dirac (1928) have all contributed to a maturing geometric algebra framework. Geometric algebra offers a multivector concept for representation and a geometric product for multivector computation, which allow for a versatile higher-order representation and computation in domains of different dimensions and metric. Complex numbers, quaternions, and dual quaternions can all be represented in both rotor and motor bivector algebras. Moreover, double, or hyperbolic, numbers can also be found in geometric algebras of positive signature. Local analysis at tangent spaces, which requires differential operations to enhance the geometric symmetries of invariants, have been done successfully using Lie algebra and Lie theory. Since the Lie algebras are isomorphic with bivector algebras, such differential operations can be advantageously implemented for complex computations of differential geometry, as in the recognition of higher-order symmetries. Geometric algebra also offers certain advantages for working in the null cone space, as it gives us access to the multiparticle concept, thereby allowing us to deal with a variety of invariants useful for causality and space and time analysis. Projective geometry and multilinear algebra, too, are elegantly reconciled in Clifford algebra, providing the resulting algebra of incidence with the duality principle, inner product, and outer morphisms. Our initial attempts to use geometric algebra in cognitive systems have been successful, reinforcing our opinion that there is no need to abandon this framework in order to carry out different kinds of computations. For all of these reasons, we believe that the single unifying language of geometric algebra offers the strongest potential for building PAC systems: it allows us better to understand links between different fields, incorporate techniques from one field into another, reformulate old procedures, and find extensions by widening their sphere of applicability. Finally, geometric algebra helps to reduce the complexity of algebraic expressions, and as a result improves algorithms both in speed and accuracy.

Chapter Organization

The present volume illustrates the promise of geometric algebra for the design of PAC systems. We begin with basic theoretical concepts and then move on to a variety of practical applications in the field of cognitive systems.

Fundamental Concepts

Chapter 1 gives an outline of geometric algebra. After preliminary definitions, we discuss in some detail the geometric algebras of the two-dimensional and three-dimensional space.

Chapter 2 explains how geometric algebras may be used for solving problems in image analysis and robotics. First, using the 3D algebra of planar rotors, we model the motion of points and lines. Then, using the 4D algebra of motors, we model the 3D Euclidean transformation of points, lines, and planes—a procedure useful in 3D kinematics. (The effectiveness of motor algebra for representation will be illustrated in Chapter 7 by the computation of the direct and inverse kinematics of robot manipulators, and in Chapter 8 by the estimation of rigid motion using line observations.)

Chapter 3 shows that geometric algebra is a very elegant language for expressing all the ideas of projective geometry and linear algebra, as it provides us with a system in which real computer implementations are straightforwardly carried out. We also introduce the geometry of n-uncalibrated cameras and its practical connotations.

Chapter 4 examines Lie group theory, Lie algebra, and the algebra of incidence in the geometric algebra framework. First, we give the basics of manifolds, Lie groups, and Lie algebras, and then we reformulate Lie theory in the geometric algebra framework. The use of a universal geometric algebra generated by reciprocal frames allows us to embed Lie algebra within a bivector algebra framework. Working with bivectors, rather than with Lie algebra represented as matrixes, appears to be more beneficial for local geometric computations on the tangent space. The algebra of incidence is treated in the linear model of the n-dimensional affine plane. It is notable that in this framework we are able to compute the meet and join of geometric objects involving Euclidean rigid transformations.

Practical Applications

Chapter 5 applies geometric algebra to image processing. First, we explain the quaternionic Fourier transform and its main properties. Then, the Gabor complex and quaternionic filters are explained. Thereafter, we show the design of Lie operators using the null cone for detection of visual invariants. Finally, we present edge detection in color images using quaternion-based algebraic algorithms.

Chapter 6 uses geometric algebra techniques to presents the formation of 3D projective invariants for both points and lines in multiple images. The invariants are then tested as functions of bilinearities and trilinearities using simulated and real data. Finally, we apply this technique to a simple task of visually guided robotics and to a 3D shape and motion reconstruction using n-uncalibrated cameras.

Chapter 7 analyzes robot manipulator kinematics using motor algebra. Our approach allows us to represent the problem with geometric insight using motion models of points, lines, and planes. We also illustrate the computation of the inverse kinematics in the 3D affine plane, simultaneously applying the operations of meet and join and rigid transformations of points, lines, and planes.

Chapter 8 presents the estimation of rigid motion using line observations. To do this, we show the development of the extended Kalman filter within the geometric algebra framework. This recursive filter has the virtue that it estimates the translation and rotation transformations simultaneously. The key for the filter design is to work in the 4D geometric algebra called motor algebra and represent the motion of the measurement frames as a motion of lines. As an illustration, we estimate the existing transformation between a manipulator and an object. We also consider the topic of hand–eye calibration as a problem of axis lines in motion, once again using the language of motor algebra.

Chapter 9 presents the generalization of feedforward neural networks in a Clifford, or geometric, algebra framework. The application of neural networks working in different geometric algebras is shown. The efficiency of the geometric neural nets indicates a step forward in the design of algorithms for multidimensional artificial learning. Finally, the generalization of the support-vector machines in the geometric algebra is given.

This book is addressed to a broad audience of cyberneticists, computer scientists, engineers, applied physicists, and applied mathematicians. The preliminary chapters should be accessible even for undergraduate students. Readers should use the first three chapters to become familiar with the basic mathematical concepts of computing with multivectors. Readers working in signal and image processing should read Chapters 4 and 5. Chapters 3 and 6 are dedicated to computer vision. Robotics topics are treated in Chapter 7. Readers interested in estimation and neuralcomputing should refer to Chapters 8 and 9. The first four chapters and Chapter 6 contain training exercises designed to stimulate readers to develop their skills in the calculus of geometric algebra. The author is convinced that the reader will find working within a geometric algebra framework to be a liberating experience. It is hoped that one result will be to accelerate the design and implementation of algorithms for real-time cognitive or PAC systems.

Eduardo José Bayro Corrochano would like to thank the Deutsche Forschungsgemeinschaft project SO 320-2-1, the Center for Research in Mathematics (CIMAT, Guanajuato, Mexico), and the Consejo Nacional de Ciencia y Tecnología (REDII–CONACYT, Mexico) for their support of this project. I am also very grateful to David Hestenes and Garret Sobczyk, Joan Lasenby, Kostas Daniilidis, Thomas Bülow, and my former students Vladimir Banarer, Detlev Kähler, Yiwen Zhang, and Bodo Rosenhahn for fruitful discussions and technical cooperation. Their generous help, creative suggestions, and criticism were decisive for the completion of the chapters. Finally, Ruth Steinberg helped to clean up my stilted English prose and bring consistency to the writing, for which I am most grateful.

Guadalajara, Mexico
January 2001

Eduardo Jose Bayro Corrochano

Contents

A todos los niños desnutridos de Latinoamérica que viven sin recibir cariño, educación y nunca gozarán de la libertad de acceder a la ciencia.

Part I

FUNDAMENTAL CONCEPTS

1. Mathematical Preliminaries

1.1 Introduction

Geometric algebra is a coordinate-free approach to geometry based on the algebras of Grassmann[38] and Clifford [20]. The geometric approach to Clifford algebra adopted in this book was pioneered in the 1960s by David Hestenes [51], who has since worked on developing his version of Clifford algebra—which will be referred to as *geometric algebra* in this volume—into a unifying language for mathematics and physics [47, 48]. Hestenes also presented a study of projective geometry using Clifford algebra [49]. The introductory sections of this chapter will present the basic definitions of geometric algebra. In the text, we denote scalars with lowercase letters, matrices with uppercase letters, and we use bold lowercase for both vectors in three dimensions and the bivector parts of spinors. Spinors and dual quaternions in four dimensions are denoted by bold uppercase letters.

1.2 Geometric Product and Multivectors

Geometric algebra is defined in a space whose elements are called *multivectors*; a general multivector is a linear combination of different types of objects, for example, scalars and vectors. In addition to vector addition and scalar multiplication, geometric algebra employs a non-commutative product, the geometric or Clifford product, which is associative and distributive for addition. The existence of such a product and the calculus associated with geometric algebra give the system tremendous power. A further distinguishing feature of this graded algebra is that any multivector squares to a scalar. The *geometric product* of two vectors $\boldsymbol{a}$ and $\boldsymbol{b}$ is written $\boldsymbol{ab}$ and can be expressed as the sum of its symmetric and anti-symmetric parts,

$$\boldsymbol{ab} = \boldsymbol{a}\cdot\boldsymbol{b} + \boldsymbol{a}\wedge\boldsymbol{b}, \tag{1.1}$$

where the inner product $\boldsymbol{a}\cdot\boldsymbol{b}$ and the outer product $\boldsymbol{a}\wedge\boldsymbol{b}$ are defined by

$$\boldsymbol{a}\cdot\boldsymbol{b} \quad = \quad \frac{1}{2}(\boldsymbol{ab} + \boldsymbol{ba}) \tag{1.2}$$

$$a \wedge b = \frac{1}{2}(ab - ba). \tag{1.3}$$

The inner product of two vectors is the standard *scalar* or *dot* product which results in a scalar. The outer, or wedge, product of two vectors is a new quantity we call a *bivector*. We think of a bivector as a directed area in the plane containing $\boldsymbol{a}$ and $\boldsymbol{b}$, formed by sweeping $\boldsymbol{a}$ along $\boldsymbol{b}$ (see Fig. 1.1.a).

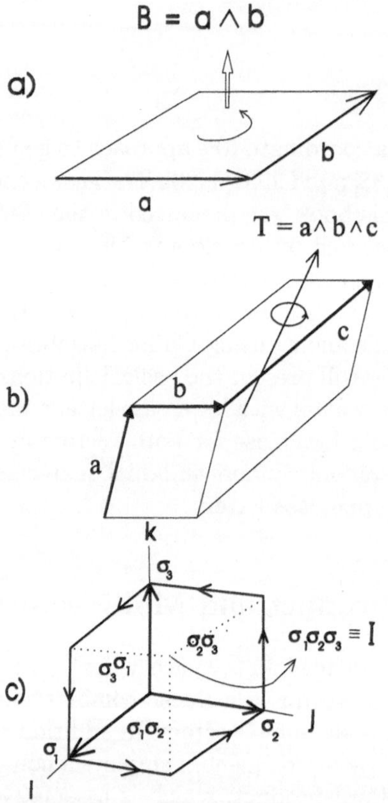

FIGURE 1.1. Representation of (a) bivector $\boldsymbol{B}$, (b) trivector $\boldsymbol{T}$, and (c) 3D basis

Thus, $\boldsymbol{b}\wedge\boldsymbol{a}$ will have the opposite orientation from $\boldsymbol{a}\wedge\boldsymbol{b}$, making the outer product anti-commutative, as given in equation (1.3). The outer product is immediately generalizable to higher dimensions. For example, $(\boldsymbol{a}\wedge\boldsymbol{b})\wedge\boldsymbol{c}$, a *trivector*, is interpreted as the oriented volume formed by sweeping the area $\boldsymbol{a}\wedge\boldsymbol{b}$ along vector $\boldsymbol{c}$ (see Fig. 1.1.b). The outer product of k linear independent vectors is a *k-blade*, and such a quantity is said to have *grade k*. A multivector is *homogeneous* if it contains terms of only a single grade. Thus, a k-vector is a homogeneous multivector of grade k as a linear combination of linear independent k-blades. Using geometric algebra, we can easily manipulate multivectors, which then allows us to keep track of objects of different grade simultaneously.

Any two, paired multivectors can be multiplied using the geometric product. Consider two homogeneous multivectors $\boldsymbol{A}_r$ and $\boldsymbol{B}_s$ of grades r and s, respectively. The geometric product of $\boldsymbol{A}_r$ and $\boldsymbol{B}_s$ can be written as

$$\boldsymbol{A}_r\boldsymbol{B}_s = \langle\boldsymbol{AB}\rangle_{r+s} + \langle\boldsymbol{AB}\rangle_{r+s-2} + \ldots + \langle\boldsymbol{AB}\rangle_{|r-s|} \tag{1.4}$$

where $\langle\boldsymbol{AB}\rangle_t$ denotes the t-grade part of multivector $\boldsymbol{A}_r\boldsymbol{B}_s$—for example, $\boldsymbol{ab} = \langle\boldsymbol{ab}\rangle_0 + \langle\boldsymbol{ab}\rangle_2 = \boldsymbol{a}\cdot\boldsymbol{b} + \boldsymbol{a}\wedge\boldsymbol{b}$. Note that $\langle\boldsymbol{AB}\rangle_0$ corresponds to a full contraction, or inner product , and that $\langle\boldsymbol{AB}\rangle_{|r-s|}$ is a generalized contraction, or generalized inner product. Since the elements of $\boldsymbol{A}_r\boldsymbol{B}_s$ are of different grade, $\boldsymbol{A}_r\boldsymbol{B}_s$ is thus an *inhomogeneous multivector* . In the following sections, expressions of grade 0 will be written ignoring their subindex, that is, $\langle\boldsymbol{ab}\rangle_0 = \langle\boldsymbol{ab}\rangle$.

1.3 The Geometric Algebra of the n-D space

An n-dimensional vector space can be spanned by using the orthonormal basis of vectors $\{\sigma_i\}$, $i = 1, ..., n$, such that $\sigma_i \cdot \sigma_j = \delta_{ij}$. This leads to a basis which spans the linear vector space of its corresponding entire geometric algebra $\mathcal{G}_n$. Thus,

$$1, \{\sigma_i\}, \{\sigma_i \wedge \sigma_j\}, \{\sigma_i \wedge \sigma_j \wedge \sigma_k\}, \ldots, I \equiv \sigma_1 \wedge \sigma_2 \wedge \ldots \wedge \sigma_n. \tag{1.5}$$

The dimension of the linear space is 2^n. In $\mathcal{G}_n$ we can find multivectors of grade 0 (scalars), grade 1 (vectors), grade 2 (bivectors), grade 3 (trivectors), and so on, up to grade n.

The multivector $I = \sigma_1 \wedge \sigma_2 \wedge \ldots \wedge \sigma_n$ is called the unit pseudoscalar, or unit *hypervolume*. Depending on the algebraic properties we want to enforce in a geometric algebra $\mathcal{G}_n$, we select basis vectors which square according to $\sigma_i^2 > 0$, < 0, or $=0$, which gives us the dimensions of the maximal involved subspaces with positive, negative, and zero *signatures*. Thus, the signature of $\mathcal{G}_n$ will be uniquely specified by $\mathcal{G}_{p,q,r}$, where p, q, and r stand for the numbers for basis vectors which square to $+1$, -1 and 0, respectively.

The multivector basis elements of even grade span a subalgebra of $\mathcal{G}_{p,q,r}$, which we will denote by $\mathcal{G}^+_{p,q,r}$, and the multivector basis elements of odd grade span the linear space $\mathcal{G}^-_{p,q,r}$, which does not actually constitute an algebra.

1.3.1 Dual blades and duality in the geometric product

In the multivector basis of a geometric algebra there is a dual relationship among individual multivector basis components. This relationship is the result of the geometric product between a t-blade $\boldsymbol{A}_t$ and the unit pseudoscalar I, as follows:

$$\begin{aligned} \boldsymbol{A}^* &= I\boldsymbol{A} \\ \langle \boldsymbol{A}^* \rangle_{n-t} &= \langle \boldsymbol{A} \rangle_t \langle I \rangle_n, \end{aligned} \tag{1.6}$$

where $\boldsymbol{A}^*$ represents the dual of $\boldsymbol{A}$. As simple examples of that dual relationship in $\mathcal{G}_{3,0,0}$, the duals of vectors $\{\sigma_i\}$ are the bivectors $\sigma_i \wedge \sigma_j = I\sigma_k$, and the duals of scalars are the trivectors. In subsequent chapters, we will denote the dual of a multivector using the notation Dual[.], for example, $\text{Dual}[\boldsymbol{a}_t] = < I_n \boldsymbol{a}_t >_{n-t} = I\boldsymbol{a}$.

Since the multivector basis of some grade spans a subspace of the geometric algebra, its dual multivector basis will span the dual subspace. The duality relates the dual subspaces, and, moreover, in addition to the signature of I, it also indicates whether this duality represents complex numbers ($I^2 = -1$), double numbers ($I^2 = 1$) or dual numbers ($I^2 = 0$).

The concept of duality can be also seen in the dual relation between the outer and the inner products. This relation, known as the Hodge dual [70] , involves the hypervolume or pseudoscalar as follows:

$$\boldsymbol{A} \cdot \boldsymbol{B} = \boldsymbol{A}^* \wedge \boldsymbol{B} = (I\boldsymbol{A}) \wedge \boldsymbol{B}, \tag{1.7}$$

where $\boldsymbol{A}\,\boldsymbol{B}$ are k-blades and $\boldsymbol{A}^* = I\boldsymbol{A}$ is the dual of $\boldsymbol{A}$. The Hodge dual depends not only on the metric but also on the orientation of the pseudoscalar. This equation is very useful for the simplification of complex equations, when we want to express an inner product in terms of the outer product, as in the case of the algebra of incidence in projective geometry.

1.3.2 Reversion and magnitude of multivectors

The *reversion* of a k-blade $\boldsymbol{A} = \sigma_1 \wedge \sigma_2 \wedge \sigma_3 \ldots \wedge \sigma_k$ reverses the order of its multivector basis components:

$$\widetilde{\boldsymbol{A}} = (-1)^{k-1} \sigma_k \ldots \wedge \sigma_3 \wedge \sigma_2 \wedge \sigma_1. \tag{1.8}$$

Here, the sign indicates the reversion of odd or even blades. The reversion of a multivector $\boldsymbol{M}$ is computed taking the reversion of its blades:

$$\widetilde{\boldsymbol{M}} = < \widetilde{\boldsymbol{M}} >_0 + < \widetilde{\boldsymbol{M}} >_1 + < \widetilde{\boldsymbol{M}} >_2 + \ldots + < \widetilde{\boldsymbol{M}} >_n. \tag{1.9}$$

The reversion operation for multivectors over the geometric product and addition fulfills

$$\widetilde{AB} = \widetilde{B}\widetilde{A},$$
$$(\widetilde{A+B}) = \widetilde{A} + \widetilde{B},$$
$$< \widetilde{A} >_0 = < A >_0 . \tag{1.10}$$

The computation of the *magnitude* or modulus of a blade can be done using the reversion operation, as follows:

$$||A|| = < \widetilde{A}A >_0^{\frac{1}{2}} = || < A >_k ||^2. \tag{1.11}$$

Accordingly, the magnitude of a multivector M reads

$$\begin{aligned} ||M|| &= < \widetilde{M}M >_0^{\frac{1}{2}} \\ &= (|| < M >_0 ||^2 + || < M >_1 ||^2 \\ &\quad + || < M >_2 ||^2 + ... + || < M >_n ||^2)^{\frac{1}{2}}. \end{aligned} \tag{1.12}$$

1.4 Geometric Algebra of General Complex Numbers

The most general complex numbers [59, 110] can be categorized into three different systems: ordinary complex numbers, double numbers, and dual numbers. In general, a complex number can be represented as a *composed number* $\mathbf{a} = b + \omega c$ using the algebraic operator ω, in which $\omega^2 = -1$ in the case of complex numbers, $\omega^2 = 1$ in the case of double numbers, and $\omega^2 = 0$ in the case of dual numbers. For dual numbers, b represents the real term and c the dual term.

This chapter also requires the notion of a function of a dual variable, in which a differentiable real function $f : \mathcal{R} \rightarrow \mathcal{R}$ with a dual argument $\alpha + \omega\beta$, where $\alpha,\beta \in \mathcal{R}$, can be expanded using a Taylor series. Because $\omega^2 = \omega^3 = \omega^4 = ... = 0$, the function reads

$$\begin{aligned} f(\alpha + \omega\beta) &= f(\alpha) + \omega f'(\alpha)\beta + \omega^2 f''(\alpha)\frac{\beta^2}{2!} + ... \\ &= f(\alpha) + \omega f'(\alpha)\beta. \end{aligned} \tag{1.13}$$

A useful illustration of this expansion is the exponential function of a dual number,

$$e^{\alpha+\omega\beta} = e^{\alpha} + \omega e^{\alpha}\beta = e^{\alpha}(1 + \omega\beta). \tag{1.14}$$

In his seminal paper "Preliminary sketch of bi-quaternions" [19], Clifford introduced the use of dual numbers *the motors* or *bi-quaternions* to represent screw motion. Later, Study [104] used dual numbers to represent the relative position of two skew lines in space— that is, $\hat{\theta} = \theta + \omega d$, where $\hat{\theta}$ represents the dual angle, θ for the difference of the line orientation angles, and d for the distance between both lines.

The algebras of complex, double (hyperbolic), and dual numbers are isomorphic to certain geometric algebras. For these algebras we must choose the appropriate multivector basis, so that the unit pseudoscalar squares to 1 for the case of double numbers, to -1 for complex numbers, and to 0 for dual numbers. Note that the pseudoscalar for these numbers maintains its geometric interpretation as a unit hypervolume, and that, as is the case with ω, they are commutative with either vectors or bivectors, depending only upon the type of the geometric algebra used.

In the following sections, we will consider some examples of composed numbers in geometric algebra: complex numbers in the space $\mathcal{G}_{0,1,0}$, double numbers in the space $\mathcal{G}_{1,0,0}$, and dual complex numbers in the space $\mathcal{G}_{1,0,1}$. We shall describe complex and dual numbers for 2D, 3D, and 4D spaces in some detail. The dual numbers will be used later for the modeling of points, lines, and planes, as well as for the modeling of motion.

1.5 2D Geometric Algebras of the Plane

In this section we want to illustrate the application of different 2D geometric algebras for the modeling of group transformations on the plane. In doing so, we can also clearly see the geometric interpretation and the use of complex, double, and dual numbers for the cases of rotation, affine, and Lorentz transformations, respectively [88, 110]. We find these transformations in various tasks of image processing. For the modeling of the 2D space, we choose a geometric algebra which has $2^2 = 4$ elements, given by

$$\underbrace{1}_{scalar}, \quad \underbrace{\sigma_1, \sigma_2}_{vectors}, \quad \underbrace{\sigma_1\sigma_2}_{bivector} \equiv I. \tag{1.15}$$

The highest grade element for the 2D space, called the unit pseudoscalar $I \equiv \sigma_1\sigma_2$, is a bivector . According to the used vector basis, the signature of the geometric algebra will change, yielding complex, double, or dual numbers. Each of these cases is illustrated below.

In the geometric algebra $\mathcal{G}_{2,0,0}$, where $I = \sigma_1\sigma_2$ with $I^2 = -1$, we want to represent the rotation of the points (x,y) of the *Euclidean plane*. Here, a rotation of the point $\boldsymbol{z} = x\sigma_1 + y\sigma_2 = r(cos\alpha\sigma_1 + sin\alpha\sigma_2) \in \mathcal{G}_{2,0,0}$ can be computed as the geometric product of the vector and the complex number $e^{I\frac{\theta}{2}} = cos\frac{\theta}{2} + \sigma_1\sigma_2 sin\frac{\theta}{2} = (cos\frac{\theta}{2} + I sin\frac{\theta}{2}) \in \mathcal{G}^+_{2,0,0}$, or $\in$ Spin(2) (spin group), as follows:

$$\begin{aligned} \boldsymbol{z}' &= e^{-I\frac{\theta}{2}} \boldsymbol{z} e^{I\frac{\theta}{2}} \\ &= e^{-I\frac{\theta}{2}} r(cos\alpha\sigma_1 + sin\alpha\sigma_2) e^{I\frac{\theta}{2}} \\ &= (cos\frac{\theta}{2} + I sin\frac{\theta}{2})^{-1} r(cos\alpha\sigma_1 + sin\alpha\sigma_2)(cos\frac{\theta}{2} + I sin\frac{\theta}{2}) \\ &= r(cos(\alpha+\theta)\sigma_1 + sin(\alpha+\theta)\sigma_2). \end{aligned} \tag{1.16}$$

Fig. 1.2.b illustrates that each point of the 2D image of the die is rotated by θ. Note that this particular form for representing rotation, $e^{I\frac{\theta}{2}} = (cos\frac{\theta}{2}+Isin\frac{\theta}{2})$, can be generalized to higher dimensions (see the algebra of rotors in 3D space in the next section).

Let us now represent the points as dual numbers in the geometric algebra $\mathcal{G}_{1,0,1}$, where $I^2 = 0$. A 2D point can be represented in $\mathcal{G}_{1,0,1}$ as $\boldsymbol{z} = x\sigma_1 + y\sigma_2 = x(\sigma_1 + s\sigma_2)$, where $s = \frac{y}{x}$ is the slope. The shear transformation of this point can be computed by applying a unit shear dual number $e^{I\frac{\tau}{2}} = (1 + I\frac{\tau}{2}) \in \mathcal{G}_{1,0,1}$ as follows:

$$\begin{aligned} \boldsymbol{z}' &= e^{-I\frac{\tau}{2}}\boldsymbol{z}e^{I\frac{\tau}{2}} = (1 - I\frac{\tau}{2})(x(\sigma_1 + s\sigma_2))(1 + I\frac{\tau}{2}) \\ &= x(\sigma_1 + (s + \tau)\sigma_2). \end{aligned} \quad (1.17)$$

Note that the overall effect of this transformation is to shear the plane, where the points (x,y) lie parallel to the σ_2-axis through the shear τ with a shear angle of $tan^{-1}\tau$. Fig. 1.2.c depicts the effect of the shear transformation acting on the 2D image of the die.

By using the representation of the double number in $\mathcal{G}_{1,1,0}$, where $I^2 = 1$, we can implement the Lorentz transformation of the points. This transformation is commonly used in space-time algebra for special relativity computations and it has been suggested for use in psychophysics as well [28, 55]. In this context, a 2D point is associated with a double number $\boldsymbol{z} = t\sigma_1 + x\sigma_2 = \rho(cosh\alpha\sigma_1 + sinh\alpha\sigma_2) \in \mathcal{G}_{1,1,0}$. The lines $|t| = |x|$ divide the plane into two quadrants with $|t| > |x|$ and two quadrants with $|t| < |x|$. If we apply a 2D unit displacement vector $e^{I\frac{\beta}{2}} = a+Ib = (cosh\beta+Isinh\beta) \in \mathcal{G}_{1,1,0}$ from one of the quadrants, $|t| > |x|$, to an arbitrary point $\boldsymbol{z} = t + Ix$, we get

$$\begin{aligned} \boldsymbol{z}' &= e^{-I\frac{\beta}{2}}\boldsymbol{z}e^{I\frac{\theta}{2}} \\ &= e^{-I\frac{\beta}{2}}\rho(cosh\alpha\sigma_1 + sinh\alpha\sigma_2)e^{I\frac{\theta}{2}} \\ &= (cosh\frac{\beta}{2} + Isinh\frac{\beta}{2})^{-1}(\rho(cosh\alpha\sigma_1 + sinh\alpha\sigma_2))(cosh\frac{\beta}{2} + Isinh\frac{\beta}{2}) \\ &= \rho(cosh(\alpha + \beta)\sigma_1 + sinh(\alpha + \beta)\sigma_2). \end{aligned} \quad (1.18)$$

The point is displaced along a particular hyperbolic path through the interval $\rho\beta$ in $|t| < |x|$. Fig. 1.2.d illustrates the effect of the Lorentz transformation acting on the 2D image of the die.

1.6 Geometric Algebra of Euclidean 3D Space

For the case of embedding Euclidean 3D space, we choose the geometric algebra $\mathcal{G}_{3,0,0}$, which has $2^3 = 8$ elements given by

$$\underbrace{1}_{scalar},\ \underbrace{\{\sigma_1, \sigma_2, \sigma_3\}}_{vectors},\ \underbrace{\{\sigma_1\sigma_2, \sigma_2\sigma_3, \sigma_3\sigma_1\}}_{bivectors},\ \underbrace{\{\sigma_1\sigma_2\sigma_3\} \equiv I}_{trivector}. \quad (1.19)$$

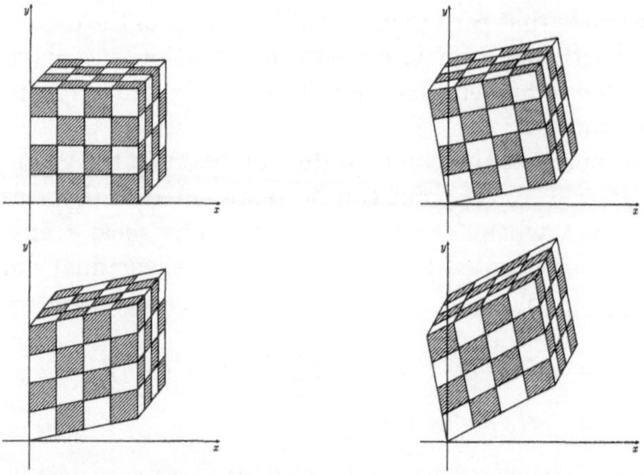

FIGURE 1.2. Effects of 2D transformations: (a) original cube, (b) cube after rotation, (c) after shear transformation, and (d) after Lorentz transformation

The highest-grade algebraic element for the 3D space is a trivector called a unit pseudoscalar $I \equiv \sigma_1\sigma_2\sigma_3$, which squares to -1 and which commutes with the scalars and bivectors in the 3D space. In the algebra of three-dimensional space we can construct a trivector $\boldsymbol{a}\wedge\boldsymbol{b}\wedge\boldsymbol{c} = \lambda I$, where the vectors $\boldsymbol{a}$, $\boldsymbol{b}$, and $\boldsymbol{c}$ are in general position and $\lambda \in \mathcal{R}$. Note that no 4-vectors exist since there is no possibility of sweeping the volume element $\boldsymbol{a}\wedge\boldsymbol{b}\wedge\boldsymbol{c}$ over a fourth dimension.

Multiplication of the three basis vectors σ_1, σ_2, and σ_3 by I results in the three basis bivectors $\sigma_1\sigma_2 = I\sigma_3$, $\sigma_2\sigma_3 = I\sigma_1$, and $\sigma_3\sigma_1 = I\sigma_2$. These simple bivectors rotate vectors in their own plane by 90°, for example, $(\sigma_1\sigma_2)\sigma_2 = \sigma_1$, $(\sigma_2\sigma_3)\sigma_2 = -\sigma_3$, etc. Identifying the unit vectors $\boldsymbol{i}$, $\boldsymbol{j}$, $\boldsymbol{k}$ of quaternion algebra with $I\sigma_1, -I\sigma_2, I\sigma_3$ allows us to write the famous Hamilton relations $\boldsymbol{i}^2 = \boldsymbol{j}^2 = \boldsymbol{k}^2 = \boldsymbol{ijk} = -1$. Since the $\boldsymbol{i}, \boldsymbol{j}, \boldsymbol{k}$ are really bivectors, it comes as no surprise that they represent 90° rotations in orthogonal directions and provide a system well suited for the representation of general 3D rotations (see Fig. 1.1.c).

1.6.1 The algebra of rotors

In geometric algebra a *rotor* (short name for rotator), $\boldsymbol{R}$, is an even-grade element of the Euclidean algebra of 3D-space. If Q= $\{r_0, r_1, r_2, r_3\} \in \mathcal{G}_{3,0,0}$ represents a unit quaternion, then the rotor which performs the same rotation is simply given by

$$\boldsymbol{R} = \underbrace{r_0}_{scalar} + \underbrace{r_1(I\sigma_1) - r_2(I\sigma_2) + r_3(I\sigma_3)}_{bivectors}. \tag{1.20}$$

The rotor algebra $\mathcal{G}^+_{3,0,0}$ is therefore a subset of the Euclidean geometric algebra of three-dimensional space.

Consider in $\mathcal{G}_{3,0,0}$ two nonparallel vectors $\boldsymbol{a}$ and $\boldsymbol{b}$ which are referred to the same origin. In general, a rotation operation of a vector $\boldsymbol{a}$ toward the vector $\boldsymbol{b}$ can be performed by two *reflections*, respective to the unit vector axes $\boldsymbol{n}$ and $\boldsymbol{m}$ (see Fig. 1.3). The components of the first reflection are

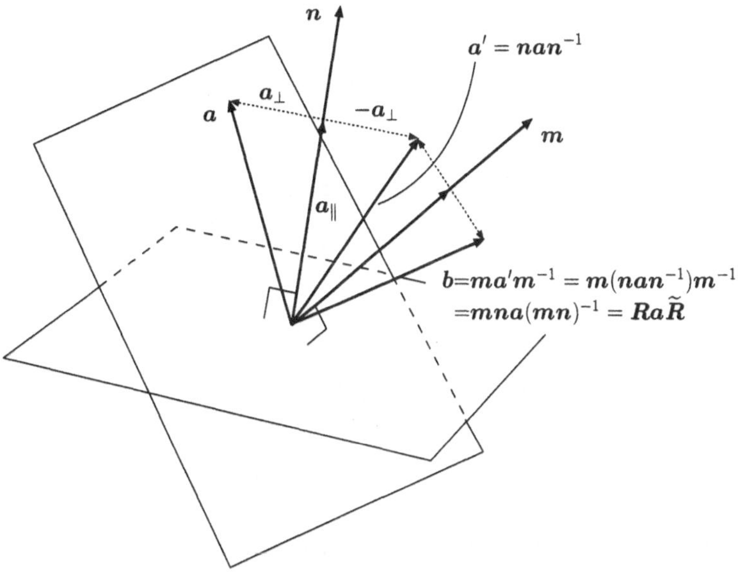

FIGURE 1.3. Rotor in the 3D space formed by a pair of reflections

$$\boldsymbol{a}_{\|} = |\boldsymbol{a}|cos(\alpha)\frac{\boldsymbol{n}}{|\boldsymbol{n}|} = |\boldsymbol{a}||\boldsymbol{n}|cos(\alpha)\frac{\boldsymbol{n}}{|\boldsymbol{n}|^2} = (\boldsymbol{a}\cdot\boldsymbol{n})\boldsymbol{n}^{-1} \tag{1.21}$$

$$\begin{aligned}\boldsymbol{a}_{\perp} &= \boldsymbol{a}-\boldsymbol{a}_{\|} = \boldsymbol{a}-(\boldsymbol{a}\cdot\boldsymbol{n})\boldsymbol{n}^{-1} = (\boldsymbol{a}\boldsymbol{n}-\boldsymbol{a}\cdot\boldsymbol{n})\boldsymbol{n}^{-1}\\ &= (\boldsymbol{a}\wedge\boldsymbol{n})\boldsymbol{n}^{-1},\end{aligned} \tag{1.22}$$

so the vector $\boldsymbol{a}$ after the first reflection becomes

$$\begin{aligned}\boldsymbol{a}' &= \boldsymbol{a}_{\|}-\boldsymbol{a}_{\perp} = (\boldsymbol{a}\cdot\boldsymbol{n})\boldsymbol{n}^{-1}-(\boldsymbol{a}\wedge\boldsymbol{n})\boldsymbol{n}^{-1} = (\boldsymbol{a}\cdot\boldsymbol{n}-\boldsymbol{a}\wedge\boldsymbol{n})\boldsymbol{n}^{-1}\\ &= (\boldsymbol{n}\cdot\boldsymbol{a}+\boldsymbol{n}\wedge\boldsymbol{a})\boldsymbol{n}^{-1} = \boldsymbol{n}\boldsymbol{a}\boldsymbol{n}^{-1}.\end{aligned} \tag{1.23}$$

The second reflection respective to the axis unit $\boldsymbol{m}$ completes the vector rotation of $\boldsymbol{a}$ toward $\boldsymbol{b}$, as follows:

$$\begin{aligned}\boldsymbol{b} &= \boldsymbol{m}(\boldsymbol{a}')\boldsymbol{m}^{-1} = \boldsymbol{m}(\boldsymbol{n}\boldsymbol{a}\boldsymbol{n}^{-1})\boldsymbol{m}^{-1} = \boldsymbol{m}\boldsymbol{n}\boldsymbol{a}\boldsymbol{n}^{-1}\boldsymbol{m}^{-1} = (\boldsymbol{m}\boldsymbol{n})\boldsymbol{a}(\boldsymbol{m}\boldsymbol{n})^{-1}\\ &= \boldsymbol{R}\boldsymbol{a}\boldsymbol{R}^{-1} = \boldsymbol{R}\boldsymbol{a}\tilde{\boldsymbol{R}}.\end{aligned} \tag{1.24}$$

The rotor $\boldsymbol{R}$ composed by these two reflections performs a rotation that is two times greater than the angle between $\boldsymbol{m}$ and $\boldsymbol{n}$.

According to equations (1.9–1.12), the reversion and magnitude of a rotor $\boldsymbol{R}$ are, respectively, given by

$$\begin{aligned} \tilde{\boldsymbol{R}} &= r_0 - r_1\sigma_2\sigma_3 - r_2\sigma_3\sigma_1 - r_3\sigma_1\sigma_2 = r_0 - \boldsymbol{r} \\ ||\boldsymbol{R}||^2 &= \boldsymbol{R}\tilde{\boldsymbol{R}}. \end{aligned} \tag{1.25}$$

This implies that the unique multiplicative inverse of $\boldsymbol{R}$ is given by

$$\boldsymbol{R}^{-1} = \tilde{\boldsymbol{R}} \parallel \boldsymbol{R} \parallel^{-2}. \tag{1.26}$$

If a rotor $\boldsymbol{R}$ satisfies the equation

$$\boldsymbol{R}\tilde{\boldsymbol{R}} = \parallel \boldsymbol{R} \parallel^2 = r_0^2 - \boldsymbol{r}\cdot\boldsymbol{r} = 1, \tag{1.27}$$

then we say that this rotor is a unit rotor and its multiplicative inverse is simply $\boldsymbol{R}^{-1} = \tilde{\boldsymbol{R}}$, as denoted previously in equation (1.24).

Equation(1.24) shows that the unit rotor corresponds to the geometric product of two unit vectors,

$$\boldsymbol{R} = \boldsymbol{m}\boldsymbol{n} = \boldsymbol{m}\cdot\boldsymbol{n} + \boldsymbol{m}\wedge\boldsymbol{n}. \tag{1.28}$$

The components of equation (1.28) correspond to the scalar and bivector terms of an equivalent quaternion in $\mathcal{G}_{3,0,0}$, and thus $\boldsymbol{R} \in \mathcal{G}^+_{3,0,0}$. This even subalgebra corresponds to the algebra of rotors.

Considering the scalar and the bivector terms of the rotor of equation (1.28), we can further write the Euler representation of a 3D rotation with angle θ in the left-hand sense, as follows:

$$\begin{aligned} \boldsymbol{R} &= r_0 + \boldsymbol{r} = r_0 + r_1\sigma_2\sigma_3 + r_2\sigma_3\sigma_1 + r_3\sigma_1\sigma_2 \\ &= a_c + a_s\bar{\boldsymbol{r}}_n = cos(\frac{\theta}{2}) + sin(\frac{\theta}{2})\bar{\boldsymbol{r}}_n = e^{\frac{\theta}{2}\bar{\boldsymbol{r}}_n}, \end{aligned} \tag{1.29}$$

where $\bar{\boldsymbol{r}}_n$ is the unitary rotation axis-vector spanned by the bivector basis $\sigma_2\sigma_3$, $\sigma_3\sigma_1$, and $\sigma_1\sigma_2$, and the scalars a_c and $a_s \in \mathcal{R}$.

The transformation of a rotor $\boldsymbol{p} \mapsto \mathbf{Rp\tilde{R}} = \boldsymbol{p}'$ is a very general way of handling rotations which works for multivectors of any grade and in spaces of any dimension. In contrast to quaternion calculus, rotors combine in a straightforward manner—i.e., a rotor $\boldsymbol{R}_1$ followed by a rotor $\boldsymbol{R}_2$ is equivalent to a total rotor $\boldsymbol{R}$ where $\boldsymbol{R} = \boldsymbol{R}_2\boldsymbol{R}_1$.

For the rotation of a vector $\boldsymbol{p}$ in the right-hand sense, we simply adopt the rotor with the minus sign to agree with the standard right-hand rule for the direction of the rotation:

$$\begin{aligned} \boldsymbol{R} &= e^{-\frac{\bar{\boldsymbol{r}}_\theta}{2}} = e^{-\frac{\theta}{2}\bar{\boldsymbol{r}}_n} \\ &= cos(\theta/2) - sin(\theta/2)\bar{\boldsymbol{r}}_n. \end{aligned} \tag{1.30}$$

This rotation operation is depicted in Fig. 1.4. The rotated vector $\boldsymbol{p}'$ is given by

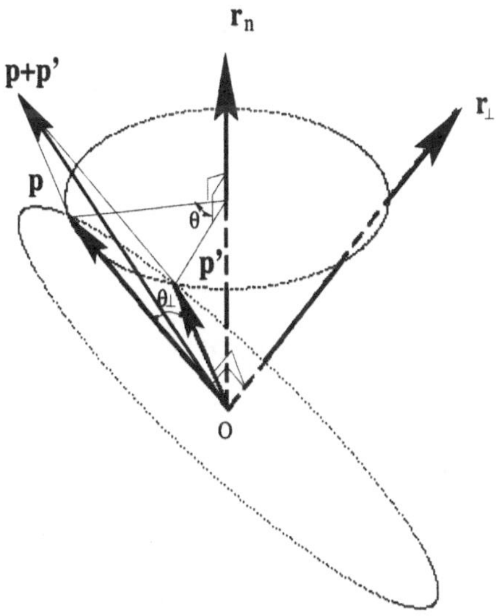

FIGURE 1.4. Geometric interpretation of rotation

$$\boldsymbol{p}' = \boldsymbol{R}\boldsymbol{p}\tilde{\boldsymbol{R}} = \Big(cos(\theta/2) - sin(\theta/2)\bar{\boldsymbol{r}}_n\Big)\boldsymbol{p}\Big(cos(\theta/2) + sin(\theta/2)\bar{\boldsymbol{r}}_n\Big). \quad (1.31)$$

Since the rotation path from $\boldsymbol{p}$ and $\boldsymbol{p}'$ is not necessarily unique, neither is the rotor $\boldsymbol{R}$ unique. The shortest path determined by the endpoints $\boldsymbol{p}$ and $\boldsymbol{p}'$ lies on a great circle of a sphere with radius $\| \boldsymbol{p} \|$, and this is called *orthogonal rotation*. The rotor itself is called *orthogonal rotor* $\boldsymbol{R}_\perp$ and it can be calculated using the unit vectors $\frac{\boldsymbol{p}'+\boldsymbol{p}}{\|\boldsymbol{p}'+\boldsymbol{p}\|}$ and $\frac{\boldsymbol{p}}{\|\boldsymbol{p}\|}$, as follows:

$$\begin{aligned} \boldsymbol{R}_\perp &= -\frac{(\boldsymbol{p}'+\boldsymbol{p})\boldsymbol{p}}{\| \boldsymbol{p}'+\boldsymbol{p} \| \cdot \| \boldsymbol{p} \|} = -\frac{(\boldsymbol{p}'+\boldsymbol{p})\cdot\boldsymbol{p} + (\boldsymbol{p}'+\boldsymbol{p})\wedge\boldsymbol{p}}{\| \boldsymbol{p}'+\boldsymbol{p} \| \cdot \| \boldsymbol{p} \|} \\ &= -\frac{(\boldsymbol{p}'+\boldsymbol{p})\cdot\boldsymbol{p}}{\| \boldsymbol{p}'+\boldsymbol{p} \| \cdot \| \boldsymbol{p} \|} - \frac{-\boldsymbol{p}\wedge(\boldsymbol{p}'+\boldsymbol{p})}{\| \boldsymbol{p}'+\boldsymbol{p} \| \cdot \| \boldsymbol{p} \|} \\ &= \boldsymbol{r}_{\perp 0} + \boldsymbol{r}_\perp = cos(\theta_\perp/2) - sin(\theta_\perp/2)\boldsymbol{r}_{n,\perp}, \end{aligned} \quad (1.32)$$

where the rotation axis bivector $\boldsymbol{r}_\perp$, or the unit rotation axis bivector $\boldsymbol{r}_{n,\perp}$, are perpendicular to both $\boldsymbol{p}$ and $\boldsymbol{p}'$ and the angle $\theta_\perp/2$ is the angle between the vectors $\boldsymbol{p}$ and $\boldsymbol{p}'+\boldsymbol{p}$.

1.6.2 Quaternionic representations and functions

Rotors are isomorphic with quaternions. In signal analysis quaternions have been used quite often in an operational sense. In contrast, rotors were introduced for geometric operations. In this subsection we will provide some definitions for quaternions which will be useful for the analysis and processing of signals in Chapter 6.

The polar representation of a quaternion $\boldsymbol{q} = r + x\boldsymbol{i} + y\boldsymbol{j} + z\boldsymbol{k} \in G^+_{3,0,0}$ is given when the quaternion, seen as a Lie group, is expressed in terms of the Lie algebra of bivectors:

$$\boldsymbol{q} = |\boldsymbol{q}| e^{\sigma_2\sigma_3\phi} e^{\sigma_1\sigma_2\psi} e^{\sigma_1\sigma_3\theta} = |\boldsymbol{q}| e^{\boldsymbol{i}\phi} e^{\boldsymbol{k}\psi} e^{\boldsymbol{j}\theta}, \tag{1.33}$$

in which $(\phi, \theta, \psi) \in [-\pi, \pi[\times[-\frac{\pi}{2}, \frac{\pi}{2}[\times, \pi[- \times [-\frac{\pi}{4}, \frac{\pi}{4}]$.

For a unit quaternion $\boldsymbol{q} = q_0 + q_x i + q_y j + q_z k$, $|\boldsymbol{q}|$=1, its phase can be evaluated first by computing $\psi = -\frac{arcsin(2(q_x q_y - q_0 q_z))}{2}$ and then by checking that it adheres to the following rules:

- If $\psi \in]-\frac{\pi}{4}, \frac{\pi}{4}[$, then $\phi = \frac{arg(\boldsymbol{q}\mathcal{T}_j(\bar{\boldsymbol{q}}))}{2}$ and $\theta = \frac{arg(\mathcal{T}_i(\bar{\boldsymbol{q}})\boldsymbol{q})}{2}$.
- If $\psi = \pm\frac{\pi}{4}$, then select either ϕ=0 and $\theta = \frac{arg(\mathcal{T}_k(\bar{\boldsymbol{q}})\boldsymbol{q})}{2}$ or θ=0 and $\phi = \frac{arg(\boldsymbol{q}\mathcal{T}_k(\bar{\boldsymbol{q}}))}{2}$.
- If $e^{\boldsymbol{i}\phi} e^{\boldsymbol{k}\psi} e^{\boldsymbol{j}\theta} = -\boldsymbol{q}$ and $\phi \geq 0$, then $\phi \to \phi - \pi$.
- If $e^{\boldsymbol{i}\phi} e^{\boldsymbol{k}\psi} e^{\boldsymbol{j}\theta} = -\boldsymbol{q}$ and $\phi < 0$, then $\phi \to \phi + \pi$.

The reader can find the details of the development of these rules in [15].

The concept of quaternionic Hermitian function is very useful for the computation of the inverse quaternionic Fourier transform using the quaternionic analytic signal, as we will see in Chapter 6. As an extension of the Hermitian function $f : \mathbb{R} \to \mathbb{C}$ with $f(x) = f^*(-x)$ for every $x \in \mathbb{R}$, we regard $f : \mathbb{R}^2 \to \mathbb{H}$ as a quaternionic Hermitian function if it fulfills the following non-trivial involution rules [21]:

$$\begin{aligned} f(-x, y) &= -jf(x, y)j = \mathcal{T}_j(f(x, y)), \\ f(x, -y) &= -if(x, y)i = \mathcal{T}_i(f(x, y)), \\ f(-x, -y) &= -if(-x, y)i = -i(-jf(x, y)j)i = (-i - j)f(x, y)(ji) \\ &= -kf(x, y)k = \mathcal{T}_k(f(x, y)). \end{aligned} \tag{1.34}$$

1.7 4D Geometric Algebra for 3D Kinematics

Usually, problems of robotics are treated in algebraic systems of 2D and 3D space. In the case of 3D rigid motion, or Euclidean transformation, we are confronted with a nonlinear mapping; however, if we employ homogeneous coordinates in 4D geometric algebra we can linearize the rigid motion in 3D Euclidean space. That is why we choose three basis vectors which square to one and a fourth vector which squares to zero—to provide dual copies of the multivectors of the 3D space. In other words, we extend the Euclidean geometric algebra $\mathcal{G}_{3,0,0}$ to the special or degenerated geometric algebra $\mathcal{G}_{3,0,1}$, which is spanned via the following basis:

$$\underbrace{1}_{scalar}, \underbrace{\gamma_k}_{4\ vectors}, \underbrace{\gamma_2\gamma_3, \gamma_3\gamma_1, \gamma_1\gamma_2, \gamma_4\gamma_1, \gamma_4\gamma_2, \gamma_4\gamma_3}_{6\ bivectors}, \underbrace{I\gamma_k}_{4\ pseudovectors}, \underbrace{I}_{unit\ pseudoscalar} \quad (1.35)$$

where $\gamma_4^2 = 0$, $\gamma_k^2 = +1$ for k=1, 2, 3. The unit pseudoscalar is $I = \gamma_1\gamma_2\gamma_3\gamma_4$, with

$$I^2 = (\gamma_1\gamma_2\gamma_3\gamma_4)(\gamma_1\gamma_2\gamma_3\gamma_4) = -(\gamma_3\gamma_4)(\gamma_3\gamma_4) = 0. \quad (1.36)$$

In Chapter 2 the motor algebra $\mathcal{G}_{3,0,1}^+$, which is the even subalgebra of $\mathcal{G}_{3,0,1}$, will be utilized to obtain linear 4D models of the 3D motion of points, lines, and planes.

1.8 4D Geometric Algebra for Projective 3D Space

To this point, we have dealt with transformations in three-dimensional space. When we use homogeneous coordinates, we increase the dimension of the vector space by one. As a result, the transformation of 3D motion becomes linear. Let us now model the projective 3D space P^3. This space corresponds to the homogeneous extended space R^4. In real applications it is important to regard the signature of the modeled space to facilitate the computations. In the case of the modeling of the projective plane using homogeneous coordinates, we adopt $\mathcal{G}_{3,0,0}$ of the ordinary space, E^3, which has the standard Euclidean signature. For the four-dimensional space R^4 we are forced to adopt the same signature as in the case of the Euclidean space. This geometric algebra $\mathcal{G}_{1,3,0}$ is spanned with the following basis:

$$\underbrace{1}_{scalar}, \underbrace{\gamma_k}_{4\ vectors}, \underbrace{\gamma_2\gamma_3, \gamma_3\gamma_1, \gamma_1\gamma_2, \gamma_4\gamma_1, \gamma_4\gamma_2, \gamma_4\gamma_3}_{6\ bivectors}, \underbrace{I\gamma_k}_{4\ pseudovectors}, \underbrace{I}_{unit\ pseudoscalar} \quad (1.37)$$

where $\gamma_4^2 = +1$, $\gamma_k^2 = -1$ for k=1,2,3. The unit pseudoscalar is $I = \gamma_1\gamma_2\gamma_3\gamma_4$, with

$$I^2 = (\gamma_1\gamma_2\gamma_3\gamma_4)(\gamma_1\gamma_2\gamma_3\gamma_4) = -(\gamma_3\gamma_4)(\gamma_3\gamma_4) = -1. \quad (1.38)$$

The geometric algebras $\mathcal{G}_{3,0,0}$ and $\mathcal{G}_{1,3,0}$ will be used in Chapter 7 for the geometric modeling of the image plane and the visual 3D space. In space-time algebra the fourth basis vector γ_4 of $\mathcal{G}_{1,3,0}$ is selected as the time axis for applications of the *projective split* [64]. This helps to associate multivectors of the 4D space with multivectors of the 3D space. The role and use of the projective split for a variety of problems involving the algebra of incidence will also be discussed in Chapter 7.

1.9 Conclusion

This chapter gives an outline of geometric algebra. In particular, it explains the geometric product and the meaning of multivectors. The geometric approach adopted is a version of Clifford algebra and it is used in the whole book as unifying language for the design of artificial perception action systems. The chapter presents the geometric algebras of the plane and 3D space, where we can find the planar and 3D quaternions. Finally we introduce 4D geometric algebras useful for computations involving dual quaternions (motors) or projective geometry. The chapter offers various exercises, so that the reader can start to learn to compute in Clifford algebra in an easy manner.

1.10 Exercises

1.1. Given $\boldsymbol{a} = \gamma_2 + 2\gamma_1\gamma_2$, $\boldsymbol{b} = \gamma_1 + 2\gamma_2$, and $\boldsymbol{c} = 3\gamma_1\gamma_2 \in \mathcal{G}_{2,0,0}$, compute $\boldsymbol{ab}$, $\boldsymbol{ba}$, and $\boldsymbol{bac}$.

1.2. Given the coordinates (2,5), (5,7), and (6,0) for the corners of a triangle, compute $\in \mathcal{G}_{2,0,0}$, the triangle's area, using multivectors.

1.3. Given $\boldsymbol{a} = \gamma_1 - 2\gamma_2$, $\boldsymbol{b} = \gamma_1 + \gamma_2$, and $\boldsymbol{v} = 5\gamma_1 - \gamma_2 \in \mathcal{G}_{2,0,0}$, compute α and β for $\boldsymbol{r} = \alpha\boldsymbol{a} + \beta\boldsymbol{b}$.

1.4. Given $\boldsymbol{a} = 8\gamma_1 - \gamma_2$ and $\boldsymbol{b} = 2\gamma_1 + 2\gamma_2 \in \mathcal{G}_{2,0,0}$, compute $\boldsymbol{a}_{||}$ and $\boldsymbol{b}_c$.

1.5. For each $\boldsymbol{x} \in \mathcal{G}_{2,0,0}$, prove $\boldsymbol{x}\bar{\boldsymbol{x}} = \bar{\boldsymbol{x}}\boldsymbol{x}$ and compute the inverse $\boldsymbol{x}^{-1}$ when $\boldsymbol{x}\bar{\boldsymbol{x}} \neq 0$.

1.6. Prove, using multivectors in $\mathcal{G}_{2,0,0}$, the following sinus identity:

$$\frac{sin\alpha}{a} = \frac{sin\beta}{b} = \frac{sin\gamma}{c}.$$

1.7. Show in $\mathcal{G}_{3,0,0}$ that the pseudoscalar I commutes with γ_1, γ_2, and γ_3. Compute the volume of a parallelepiped spanned by the vectors $\boldsymbol{a} = 3\gamma_1 - 4\gamma_2 + 4\gamma_3$, $\boldsymbol{b} = 2\gamma_1 + 4\gamma_2 - 2\gamma 3$, and $\boldsymbol{c} = 4\gamma_1 - 2\gamma_2 - 3\gamma 3$.

1.8. Compute $\boldsymbol{AB}$ in $\mathcal{G}_{3,0,0}$ if $\boldsymbol{A} = 3\gamma_1\gamma_2 + 6\gamma_2\gamma_3$ and $\boldsymbol{B} = \boldsymbol{a}\wedge\boldsymbol{b}$ where $\boldsymbol{a} = 3\gamma_1 - 4\gamma_2 + 5\gamma_3$ and $\boldsymbol{b} = 2\gamma_1 + 4\gamma_2 - 2\gamma_3$.

1.9. Given in $\mathcal{G}_{3,0,0}$ the vector $\boldsymbol{a} = 3\gamma_1 + 5\gamma_2 + 6\gamma_3$ and the bivector $\boldsymbol{B} = 3\gamma_2\gamma_3 + 6\gamma_3\gamma_1 + 2\gamma_1\gamma_2$, compute the parallel and orthogonal projections of $\boldsymbol{a}$ with respect to the plane $\boldsymbol{B}$. Then compute the cross-product of these projected components and interpret geometrically the dual relationship of the result with respect to $\boldsymbol{B}$.

1.10. Show in $\mathcal{G}_{3,0,0}$ that the geometric product of the bivector $\boldsymbol{A}$ and any vector $\boldsymbol{x}$ can be decomposed as follows:

$$\boldsymbol{A}\boldsymbol{x} = \boldsymbol{A}\cdot\boldsymbol{x} + \frac{1}{2}(\boldsymbol{A}\boldsymbol{x} - \boldsymbol{x}\boldsymbol{A}) + \boldsymbol{A}\wedge\boldsymbol{x}.$$

1.11. Given $\boldsymbol{x} = 1 + \boldsymbol{a} + \boldsymbol{B}$, where $\boldsymbol{a} \in R^3$ and $\boldsymbol{B} \in \bigwedge^2 R^3$, and given the outer inverse of $\boldsymbol{x}$ is $\boldsymbol{x}^{\wedge(-1)} = 1 - \boldsymbol{a} - \boldsymbol{B} + \alpha\boldsymbol{a}\wedge\boldsymbol{B}$, where $\alpha \in R$.
(a) Compute α. (*Hint*: Use the power series or $\boldsymbol{x}\wedge\boldsymbol{x}^{\wedge(-1)} = 1$; the outer square root of $\boldsymbol{x}$ is $\boldsymbol{x}^{\wedge(\frac{1}{2})} = 1 + \frac{1}{2}\boldsymbol{a} + \frac{1}{2}\boldsymbol{B} + \beta\boldsymbol{a}\wedge\boldsymbol{B}$, where $\beta \in R$.)
(b) Compute β. (*Hint*: $\boldsymbol{x}^{\wedge(\frac{1}{2})}\wedge\boldsymbol{x}^{(\frac{1}{2})} = \boldsymbol{x}$.).
(c) Give a geometric interpretation of the outer inverse and of the outer square root and suggest their applications.

1.12. Using CLICAL [69] in $\mathcal{G}_{3,0,0}$, rotate the vector $\boldsymbol{r} = 2\gamma_1 + 3\gamma_2 + 2\gamma_3$ about the axis $\boldsymbol{n} = 1.4\gamma_1 + 1.9\gamma_2$ with angle $\theta = |\boldsymbol{n}|$. Since $|\theta| \leq \phi$, the rotation is well defined.

1.13. Two consecutive rotations in $\mathcal{G}_{3,0,0}$, one about the axis $\boldsymbol{a}$ with the angle $\alpha = |\boldsymbol{a}|$ and another about the axis $\boldsymbol{b}$ with the angle $\beta = |\boldsymbol{b}|$, are equivalent to the rotation about an axis **c**. Prove this statement using the Rodriguez formula,

$$\boldsymbol{c}' = \frac{\boldsymbol{a}' + \boldsymbol{b}' - \boldsymbol{a}' \times \boldsymbol{b}'}{1 - \boldsymbol{a}'\boldsymbol{b}'},$$

where $\boldsymbol{a}' = \frac{\boldsymbol{a}}{\alpha}tan(\frac{\alpha}{2})$ and $\alpha = |\boldsymbol{a}|$. (*Hint*: Compare the scalar and bivector terms of $e^{I\frac{\boldsymbol{c}}{2}} = e^{I\frac{\boldsymbol{b}}{2}}e^{I\frac{\boldsymbol{a}}{2}}$.)

1.14. Using the vectors $\boldsymbol{a}$ and $\boldsymbol{b}$ of $\mathcal{G}_{3,0,0}$, prove that the rotation of $\boldsymbol{a}$ to $\boldsymbol{b}$ can be represented by the rotor

$$\boldsymbol{R} = (\boldsymbol{a}\boldsymbol{b})^{\frac{1}{2}} = \frac{(\boldsymbol{a}+\boldsymbol{b})\boldsymbol{b}}{|\boldsymbol{a}+\boldsymbol{b}|} = \frac{\boldsymbol{a}(\boldsymbol{b}+\boldsymbol{a})}{|\boldsymbol{b}+\boldsymbol{a}|}.$$

Since the norm $|\boldsymbol{a}+\boldsymbol{b}| = [2(1+\boldsymbol{a}\cdot\boldsymbol{b})]^{\frac{1}{2}}$ is not relevant, you can write $\boldsymbol{R}$ as follows:

$$\boldsymbol{R} \doteq (\boldsymbol{a}+\boldsymbol{b})\boldsymbol{b} = \boldsymbol{a}(\boldsymbol{b}+\boldsymbol{a}) = 1 + \boldsymbol{a}\boldsymbol{b}.$$

Also prove this equation. You can interpret the symbol $\doteq$ as a projective identity or an identity up to a scalar factor. (*Hint*: Each rotation can be represented by two reflections.)

2. Kinematics of the 2D and 3D Spaces

2.1 Introduction

This chapter presents the geometric algebra framework for dealing with 3D kinematics. The reader will see the usefulness of this mathematical approach for applications in computer vision and kinematics. We start with an introduction to 4D geometric algebra for 3D kinematics. Then we reformulate, using 3D and 4D geometric algebras, the classic model for the 3D motion of vectors. Finally, we compare both models, that is, the one using 3D Euclidean geometric algebra and our model, which uses 4D motor algebra.

2.2 Motor Algebra

The word *motor* is an abbreviation of "moment and vector." Clifford introduced motors with the name bi-quaternions [19]. Motors are isomorphic to dual quaternions, with the necessary condition $I^2 = 0$. They can be found in the special 4D even subalgebra of $\mathcal{G}_{3,0,1}$ introduced in section 1.7. This even subalgebra is denominated by $\mathcal{G}^+_{3,0,1}$ and is only spanned via a bivector basis, as follows:

$$\underbrace{1}_{scalar}, \quad \underbrace{\gamma_2\gamma_3, \gamma_3\gamma_1, \gamma_1\gamma_2, \gamma_4\gamma_1, \gamma_4\gamma_2, \gamma_4\gamma_3,}_{6 \quad bivectors} \quad \underbrace{I}_{unit\ pseudoscalar} . \tag{2.1}$$

This kind of basis structure also allows us to represent spinors, which are composed of scalar and bivector terms. Motors, then, are also spinors, and as such, they represent a special kind of rotor. Because a Euclidean transformation includes both rotation and translation, we will show in the following subsection a spinor representation for both transformations in the definition of motors. But we must first show the relationship between motors and screw motion theory.

Note that the bivector terms of the basis correspond to the same basis for spanning 3D lines. Note also that the dual of a scalar is the pseudoscalar P and that the duals of the first three basis bivectors are actually the next three bivectors, that is, $(\gamma_2\gamma_3^*) = I\gamma_2\gamma_3 = \gamma_4\gamma_1$.

We said in section 1.6.1 that a rotor relates two vectors in 3D space. According to Clifford [19], a motor operation is necessary to convert the rotation axis of a rotor into the rotation axis of a second rotor. Each rotor can be geometrically represented as a rotation plane with the rotation axis normal to this plane. Fig. 2.1.a depicts a motor action in detail. Note that the involved rotor axes are represented as line axes. In the figure, we first orient one axis parallel to the other by applying the rotor $\boldsymbol{R}_s$. Then, we slide the rotated axis a distance d along the connecting axis, so that it ends up overlapping the axis of the second rotor. Altogether, this operation can be described as forming a *twist* about a screw with line axis $\boldsymbol{l}$, whose pitch relationship *pitch* equals $\frac{d}{\theta}$ for $\theta \neq 0$. A motor, then, is specified only by its direction and the position of the *screw-axis line*, twist angular magnitude, and pitch. Fig. 2.1.b shows an action of a motor on a real object. In this case, the motor relates the rotation-axis line of the initial position of the object to the rotation-axis line of its final position. Note that in both figures the angle and sliding distance indicate how rigid displacement takes place around and along a screw-axis line $\boldsymbol{l}$, respectively. A *degenerated motor* can only rotate and not slide along the line $\boldsymbol{l}$ as Fig. 2.1.c shows. In this case, therefore, the two axes are coplanar.

2.2.1 Motors, rotors, and translators in $\mathcal{G}^+_{3,0,1}$

Since a rigid motion consists of the rotation and translation transformations, it should be possible to split a motor multiplicatively in terms of these two spinor transformations, which we will call a rotor and a *translator*. In the following discussion, we will denote all bivector components of a spinor by bold lowercase letters. Let us now express this procedure algebraically. First of all, let us consider a simple rotor in its *Euler representation* for a rotation with an angle θ,

$$\begin{aligned} \boldsymbol{R} &= a_0 + a_1\gamma_2\gamma_3 + a_2\gamma_3\gamma_1 + a_3\gamma_1\gamma_2 \\ &= a_0 + \boldsymbol{a} \\ &= cos(\frac{\theta}{2}) + sin(\frac{\theta}{2})\boldsymbol{n} \\ &= a_c + a_s\boldsymbol{n}, \end{aligned} \tag{2.2}$$

where $\boldsymbol{n}$ is the unit 3D bivector of the rotation axis spanned by the bivector basis $\gamma_2\gamma_3$, $\gamma_3\gamma_1$, $\gamma_1\gamma_2$, and a_c, $a_s \in \mathcal{R}$. Now, dealing with the rotor of a screw motion, the rotation-axis vector should be represented as a screw-axis line. For that, we must relate the rotation axis to a reference coordinate system at the distance $\boldsymbol{t}_c$. A 3D translation in motor algebra is represented by a spinor $\boldsymbol{T}_c$ called a translator. If we apply a translator from the left to rotor $\boldsymbol{R}$, and then apply the translator's conjugate from the right, we get a modified rotor,

$$\boldsymbol{R}_s = \boldsymbol{T}_c\boldsymbol{R}\widetilde{\boldsymbol{T}}_c$$

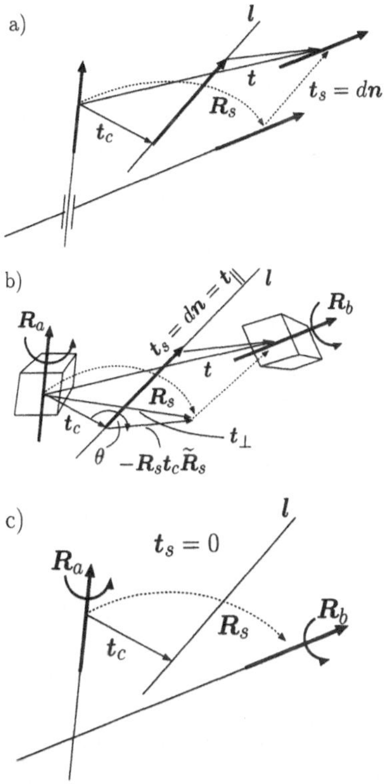

FIGURE 2.1. Screw motion about the line axis $\boldsymbol{l}$ ($\boldsymbol{t}_s$: longitudinal displacement by d and $\boldsymbol{R}_s$: rotation angle θ): (a) motor relating two axis lines, (b) motor applied to an object, (c) degenerated motor relating two coplanar rotors. (Note: indicated 3D vectors are represented as bivectors in text.)

$$
\begin{aligned}
&= (1+I\frac{\boldsymbol{t}_c}{2})(a_0+\boldsymbol{a})(1-I\frac{\boldsymbol{t}_c}{2}) \\
&= a_0+\boldsymbol{a}+Ia_0\frac{\boldsymbol{t}_c}{2}+I\frac{\boldsymbol{t}_c}{2}\boldsymbol{a}-Ia_0\frac{\boldsymbol{t}_c}{2}-I\boldsymbol{a}\frac{\boldsymbol{t}_c}{2} \\
&= a_0+\boldsymbol{a}+I(\frac{\boldsymbol{t}_c}{2}\boldsymbol{a}-\boldsymbol{a}\frac{\boldsymbol{t}_c}{2}) \\
&= a_0+\boldsymbol{a}+I(\boldsymbol{a}\wedge\boldsymbol{t}_c). \qquad (2.3)
\end{aligned}
$$

Here, $\boldsymbol{t}_c$ is the 3D vector of translation spanned by the bivector basis $\gamma_2\gamma_3$, $\gamma_3\gamma_1$, $\gamma_1\gamma_2$. Then, expressing the last equation in Euler terms, we get the spinor representation,

$$
\begin{aligned}
\boldsymbol{R}_s &= a_0+a_s\boldsymbol{n}+Ia_s\boldsymbol{n}\wedge\boldsymbol{t}_c \\
&= a_c+a_s(\boldsymbol{n}+I\boldsymbol{m}) \\
&= cos(\frac{\theta}{2})+sin(\frac{\theta}{2})(\boldsymbol{n}+I\boldsymbol{m})
\end{aligned}
$$

$$= \quad cos(\frac{\theta}{2}) + sin(\frac{\theta}{2})\boldsymbol{l}. \tag{2.4}$$

This result is indeed interesting because the new rotor $\boldsymbol{R}_s$ can now be applied with respect to an axis line $\boldsymbol{l}$ expressed in dual terms of direction $\boldsymbol{n}$ and moment $\boldsymbol{m} = \boldsymbol{n}\wedge\boldsymbol{t}_c$. Now, to define the motor finally, let us slide the distance $\boldsymbol{t}_s = d\boldsymbol{n}$ along the rotation-axis line $\boldsymbol{l}$. Since a motor is applied from the left and conjugated from the right, we should use the half of $\boldsymbol{t}_s$ in the spinor expression of $\boldsymbol{T}_s 1$ when we define the motor:

$$\begin{aligned}
\boldsymbol{M} &= \boldsymbol{T}_s\boldsymbol{R}_s = (1 + I\frac{\boldsymbol{t}_s}{2})(a_0 + \boldsymbol{a} + I\boldsymbol{a}\wedge\boldsymbol{t}_c) \\
&= (1 + I\frac{d\boldsymbol{n}}{2})(a_c + a_s\boldsymbol{n} + Ia_s\boldsymbol{n}\wedge\boldsymbol{t}_c) \\
&= a_c + a_s\boldsymbol{n} + Ia_s\boldsymbol{n}\wedge\boldsymbol{t}_c + I\frac{d}{2}a_c\boldsymbol{n} - I\frac{d}{2}a_s\boldsymbol{n}\boldsymbol{n} \\
&= (a_c - I\frac{d}{2}a_s) + (a_s + Ia_c\frac{d}{2})(\boldsymbol{n} + I\boldsymbol{n}\wedge\boldsymbol{t}_c) \\
&= (a_c - Ia_s\frac{d}{2}) + (a_s + Ia_c\frac{d}{2})\boldsymbol{l}.
\end{aligned} \tag{2.5}$$

Note that this expression of the motor makes explicit the unit line bivector of the screw-axis line $\boldsymbol{l}$.

Now let us express a motor using Euler representation. By substituting the constants $a_c = cos(\frac{\theta}{2})$ and $a_s = sin(\frac{\theta}{2})$ in the motor equation (2.5) and using the property of equation (1.13), we get

$$\begin{aligned}
\boldsymbol{M} &= \boldsymbol{T}_s\boldsymbol{R}_s = (cos(\frac{\theta}{2}) - Isin(\frac{\theta}{2})\frac{d}{2}) + (sin(\frac{\theta}{2}) + Icos(\frac{\theta}{2})\frac{d}{2})\boldsymbol{l} \\
&= cos(\frac{\theta}{2} + I\frac{d}{2}) + sin(\frac{\theta}{2} + I\frac{d}{2})\boldsymbol{l},
\end{aligned} \tag{2.6}$$

which is a dual-number representation of the spinor. Now, let us analyze the resultant expressions,

$$\begin{aligned}
\boldsymbol{R} &= cos(\frac{\theta}{2}) + sin(\frac{\theta}{2})\boldsymbol{n} \\
\boldsymbol{R}_s &= cos(\frac{\theta}{2}) + sin(\frac{\theta}{2})\boldsymbol{l} \\
\boldsymbol{M} &= cos(\frac{\theta}{2} + I\frac{d}{2}) + sin(\frac{\theta}{2} + I\frac{d}{2})\boldsymbol{l}.
\end{aligned} \tag{2.7}$$

We can see that the rotation axis $\boldsymbol{n}$ of the simple rotor $\boldsymbol{R}$ is changed to a rotation-axis line, so that $\boldsymbol{R}_s$ now rotates about an axis line. And in the motor expression, the information for sliding distance d is now made explicit in terms of dual arguments of the trigonometric functions. It is also interesting to note that the expression for the motor using dual angles simply extends the expression of $\boldsymbol{R}_s$.

If we expand the exponential function of the dual bivectors using a Taylor series, the result will follow the general expression $e^{\alpha+I\beta} = e^{\alpha} + Ie^{\alpha}\beta = e^{\alpha}(1+I\beta)$, which is a special case of equation (1.13). Once again, we obtain the motor expression as the spinor

$$e^{\boldsymbol{l}\frac{\theta}{2}+I\frac{\boldsymbol{t}_s}{2}} = (1+I\frac{\boldsymbol{t}_s}{2})e^{\boldsymbol{l}\frac{\theta}{2}} = \boldsymbol{T}_s\boldsymbol{R}_s, \tag{2.8}$$

where $I\frac{\boldsymbol{t}_s}{2} = I\frac{1}{2}(t_1\sigma_2\sigma_3 + t_2\sigma_3\sigma_1 + t_3\sigma_1\sigma_2) = \frac{1}{2}(t_1\sigma_4\sigma_1 + t_2\sigma_4\sigma_2 + t_3\sigma_4\sigma_3)$.

If we want to express the motor using only rotors in a dual spinor representation, we proceed as follows:

$$\begin{aligned} \boldsymbol{M} &= \boldsymbol{T}_s\boldsymbol{R}_s = (1+I\frac{\boldsymbol{t}_s}{2})\mathbf{R}_s \\ &= \boldsymbol{R}_s + I\frac{\boldsymbol{t}_s}{2}\boldsymbol{R}_s. \end{aligned} \tag{2.9}$$

Let us consider carefully the resultant dual part of the motor. This is the geometric product of the bivector $\boldsymbol{t}_s$ and the rotor $\boldsymbol{R}_s$. Since both are expressed in terms of the same bivector basis, their geometric product will be also expressed in this basis, which can be considered as a new rotor $\boldsymbol{R}'_s$. Thus, we can further write

$$\boldsymbol{M} = \boldsymbol{R}_s + I\frac{\boldsymbol{t}_s}{2}\boldsymbol{R}_s = \boldsymbol{R}_s + I\boldsymbol{R}'_s. \tag{2.10}$$

In this equation the line axes of the rotors are skewed (see Fig. 2.1.a). That means that they represent the general case of non-coplanar rotors. If the sliding distance $\boldsymbol{t}_s$ is zero, then the motor will degenerate to a rotor

$$\boldsymbol{M} = \boldsymbol{T}_s\boldsymbol{R}_s = (1+I\frac{\boldsymbol{t}_s}{2})\boldsymbol{R}_s = (1+I\frac{0}{2})\boldsymbol{R}_s = \boldsymbol{R}_s. \tag{2.11}$$

In this case, that is, when the two generating axis lines of the motor are coplanar, we get the so-called *degenerated motor* (see Fig. 2.1.c).

Finally, the bivector $\boldsymbol{t}_s$ can be expressed in terms of the rotors using previous results

$$\boldsymbol{R}'_s\widetilde{\boldsymbol{R}}_s = (\frac{\boldsymbol{t}_s}{2}\boldsymbol{R}_s)\widetilde{\boldsymbol{R}}_s; \tag{2.12}$$

therefore,

$$\boldsymbol{t}_s = 2\boldsymbol{R}'_s\widetilde{\boldsymbol{R}}_s. \tag{2.13}$$

Fig. 2.1 shows that the 3D vector $\boldsymbol{t}$, expressed in the bivector basis, is referred to the rotation axis of the rotor, and that $\boldsymbol{t}_s$ is a bivector along the motor-axis line. Thus, $\boldsymbol{t}$, considered here as a bivector, can be computed in terms of the bivectors $\boldsymbol{t}_c$ and $\boldsymbol{t}_s$, as follows:

$$\begin{aligned}\boldsymbol{t} &= \boldsymbol{t}_{\perp} + \boldsymbol{t}_{\parallel} \\ \boldsymbol{t} &= (\boldsymbol{t}_c - \boldsymbol{R}_s\boldsymbol{t}_c\widetilde{\boldsymbol{R}}_s) + (\boldsymbol{t}\cdot\boldsymbol{n})\boldsymbol{n} = (\boldsymbol{t}_c - \boldsymbol{R}_s\boldsymbol{t}_c\widetilde{\boldsymbol{R}}_s) + d\boldsymbol{n} \\ &= \boldsymbol{t}_c - \boldsymbol{R}_s\boldsymbol{t}_c\widetilde{\boldsymbol{R}}_s + \boldsymbol{t}_s \\ &= \boldsymbol{t}_c - \boldsymbol{R}_s\boldsymbol{t}_c\widetilde{\boldsymbol{R}}_s + 2\boldsymbol{R}'_s\widetilde{\boldsymbol{R}}_s. \end{aligned} \tag{2.14}$$

So far, we have analyzed the motor from a geometrical point of view. Next, we will look at the motor's relevant algebraic properties.

2.2.2 Properties of motors

A general motor can be expressed as

$$\boldsymbol{M}_{\alpha} = \alpha\boldsymbol{M}, \tag{2.15}$$

where $\alpha \in \mathcal{R}$ and $\boldsymbol{M}$ is a unit motor, as explained in the previous sections. In this section, we will employ unit motors. The norm of a motor $\boldsymbol{M}$ is defined as follows:

$$\begin{aligned}|\boldsymbol{M}| &= \boldsymbol{M}\widetilde{\boldsymbol{M}} = \boldsymbol{T}_s\boldsymbol{R}_s\widetilde{\boldsymbol{R}}_s\widetilde{\boldsymbol{T}}_s = (1 + I\frac{\boldsymbol{t}_s}{2})\boldsymbol{R}_s\widetilde{\boldsymbol{R}}_s(1 - I\frac{\boldsymbol{t}_s}{2}) \\ &= 1 + I\frac{\boldsymbol{t}_s}{2} - I\frac{\boldsymbol{t}_s}{2} = 1,\end{aligned} \tag{2.16}$$

where $\widetilde{\boldsymbol{M}}$ is the conjugate motor and 1 is the identity of the motor multiplication. Now, using equation (2.10) and considering the unit motor magnitude, we find two useful properties, expressed by

$$\begin{aligned}|\boldsymbol{M}| &= \boldsymbol{M}\widetilde{\boldsymbol{M}} = (\boldsymbol{R}_s + I\boldsymbol{R}'_s)(\widetilde{\boldsymbol{R}}_s + I\widetilde{\boldsymbol{R}}'_s) \\ &= \boldsymbol{R}_s\widetilde{\boldsymbol{R}}_s + I(\widetilde{\boldsymbol{R}}_s\boldsymbol{R}'_s + \widetilde{\boldsymbol{R}}'_s\boldsymbol{R}_s) = 1.\end{aligned} \tag{2.17}$$

These equations require the following constraints:

$$\boldsymbol{R}_s\widetilde{\boldsymbol{R}}_s = 1 \tag{2.18}$$

$$\widetilde{\boldsymbol{R}}_s\boldsymbol{R}'_s + \widetilde{\boldsymbol{R}}'_s\boldsymbol{R}_s = 0. \tag{2.19}$$

Now we can show that the combination of two rigid motions can be expressed using two consecutive motors. The resultant motor describes the overall displacement, namely,

$$\begin{aligned}\boldsymbol{M}_c &= \boldsymbol{M}_a\boldsymbol{M}_b = (\boldsymbol{R}_{s_a} + I\boldsymbol{R}'_{s_a})(\boldsymbol{R}_{s_b} + I\boldsymbol{R}'_{s_b}) \\ &= \boldsymbol{R}_{s_a}\boldsymbol{R}_{s_b} + I(\boldsymbol{R}_{s_a}\boldsymbol{R}'_{s_b} + \boldsymbol{R}'_{s_a}\boldsymbol{R}_{s_b}) \\ &= \boldsymbol{R}_{s_c} + I\boldsymbol{R}'_{s_c}.\end{aligned} \tag{2.20}$$

Note that, on the one hand, pure rotations combine multiplicatively, and, on the other hand, the dual parts containing the translation combine additively.

Using equation (2.10), let us express a motor in terms of dual spinors:

$$\begin{aligned} \boldsymbol{M} &= \boldsymbol{T}_s\boldsymbol{R}_s = \boldsymbol{R}_s + I\boldsymbol{R}_s' \\ &= (a_0 + a_1\gamma_2\gamma_3 + a_2\gamma_3\gamma_2 + a_3\gamma_2\gamma_1) + \\ &\qquad I(b_0 + b_1\gamma_2\gamma_3 + b_2\gamma_3\gamma_2 + b_3\gamma_2\gamma_1) \\ &= (a_0 + \boldsymbol{a}) + I(b_0 + \boldsymbol{b}). \end{aligned} \tag{2.21}$$

We can use another notation to enhance the components of the real and dual parts of the motor, as follows:

$$\boldsymbol{M} = (a_0, \boldsymbol{a}) + I(b_0, \boldsymbol{b}). \tag{2.22}$$

Here, each term within the brackets consists of a scalar part and a 3D bivector.

A motor expressed in terms of a translator and a rotor is manipulated similarly as in the case of a rotor, from the left and its conjugate from the right. These left and right operations, called *motor reflections*, are used to build an automorphism equivalent to the screw. Yet, by conjugating only the rotor or only the translator for the second reflection, we can derive different types of automorphisms.

By changing the sign of the scalar and bivector in the real and dual parts of the motor, we get the following variations:

$$\begin{aligned} \boldsymbol{M} &= (a_0 + \boldsymbol{a}) + I(b_0 + \boldsymbol{b}) = \boldsymbol{T}_s\boldsymbol{R}_s \\ \widetilde{\boldsymbol{M}} &= (a_0 - \boldsymbol{a}) + I(b_0 - \boldsymbol{b}) = \widetilde{\boldsymbol{R}}_s\widetilde{\boldsymbol{T}}_s \\ \bar{\boldsymbol{M}} &= (a_0 + \boldsymbol{a}) - I(b_0 + \boldsymbol{b}) = \boldsymbol{R}_s\widetilde{\boldsymbol{T}}_s \\ \widetilde{\bar{\boldsymbol{M}}} &= (a_0 - \boldsymbol{a}) - I(b_0 - \boldsymbol{b}) = \widetilde{\boldsymbol{R}}_s\boldsymbol{T}_s. \end{aligned} \tag{2.23}$$

The first, second, and fourth versions will be used for modeling the motion of points, lines, and planes, respectively.

Using equation (2.23), it is now a straightforward matter to compute the expressions for the individual components:

$$\begin{aligned} a_0 &= \frac{1}{4}(\boldsymbol{M} + \widetilde{\boldsymbol{M}} + \bar{\boldsymbol{M}} + \widetilde{\bar{\boldsymbol{M}}}) \\ Ib_0 &= \frac{1}{4}(\boldsymbol{M} + \widetilde{\boldsymbol{M}} - \bar{\boldsymbol{M}} - \widetilde{\bar{\boldsymbol{M}}}) \\ \boldsymbol{a} &= \frac{1}{4}(\boldsymbol{M} - \widetilde{\boldsymbol{M}} + \bar{\boldsymbol{M}} - \widetilde{\bar{\boldsymbol{M}}}) \\ I\boldsymbol{b} &= \frac{1}{4}(\boldsymbol{M} - \widetilde{\boldsymbol{M}} - \bar{\boldsymbol{M}} + \widetilde{\bar{\boldsymbol{M}}}). \end{aligned} \tag{2.24}$$

2.3 Representation of Points, Lines, and Planes Using 3D Geometric Algebra

The modeling of points, lines, and planes in 3D Euclidean space will be done using the Euclidean geometric algebra $\mathcal{G}_{3,0,0}$, where the pseudoscalar $I^2 = -1$. A point in 3D space represents a position and thus can be simply spanned using the vector basis of $\mathcal{G}_{3,0,0}$:

$$\boldsymbol{x} = x\sigma_1 + y\sigma_2 + z\sigma_3, \tag{2.25}$$

where x, y, $z \in \mathcal{R}$.

In classical vector calculus, a line is described by a position vector $\boldsymbol{x}$ that touches any point of the line and by a vector $\boldsymbol{n}$ for the line direction, that is, $\boldsymbol{l} = \boldsymbol{x} + \alpha\boldsymbol{n}$, where $\alpha \in \mathcal{R}$. In geometric algebra we employ a multivector concept, and we can thus compactly represent in $\mathcal{G}_{3,0,0}$ any line, using a vector $\boldsymbol{n}$ for its direction and a bivector $\boldsymbol{m}$ for the orientation of the plane within which the line lies. Thus,

$$\boldsymbol{l} = \boldsymbol{n} + \boldsymbol{x}\wedge\boldsymbol{n} = \boldsymbol{n} + \boldsymbol{m}. \tag{2.26}$$

Note that the moment bivector $\boldsymbol{m}$ is computed as the outer product of the position vector $\boldsymbol{x}$ and the the line direction vector $\boldsymbol{n}$. We can also compute $\boldsymbol{m}$ as the dual of a vector, that is, $I\boldsymbol{x} \times \boldsymbol{n} = \boldsymbol{m}$.

The representation of the plane is even more striking. The plane is a geometric entity one grade higher than the line, so we would expect that the multivector representation of the plane would be a natural multivector grade extension from that of the line. In classical vector calculus, a plane is described in terms of *Hesse distance*, which represents the distance from the origin to the plane, and a vector which indicates the plane orientation, that is, $\{d, \boldsymbol{n}\}$. Note that this description is composed of two separate attributes. Once again, using geometric algebra we can express the plane more compactly and with clearer geometric sense. In $\mathcal{G}_{3,0,0}$, for example, the extension of the line expression to a plane would be expressed in terms of a bivector $\boldsymbol{n}$ and a trivector Id,

$$\boldsymbol{h} = \boldsymbol{n} + \boldsymbol{x}\wedge\boldsymbol{n} = \boldsymbol{n} + Id, \tag{2.27}$$

where the bivector $\boldsymbol{n}$ indicates the plane orientation, and the outer product of the position vector $\boldsymbol{x}$ and the bivector $\boldsymbol{n}$ builds a trivector which can be expressed using Hesse distance, a scalar value, and the unit pseudoscalar I. Note that the trivector represents a volume, whereas the scalar$d$ represents the Hesse distance. Fig. 2.2 compares the different representations of points, lines, and planes using classical vector calculus, Euclidean geometric algebra for $\mathcal{G}_{3,0,0}$, and motor algebra for $\mathcal{G}^+_{3,0,1}$.

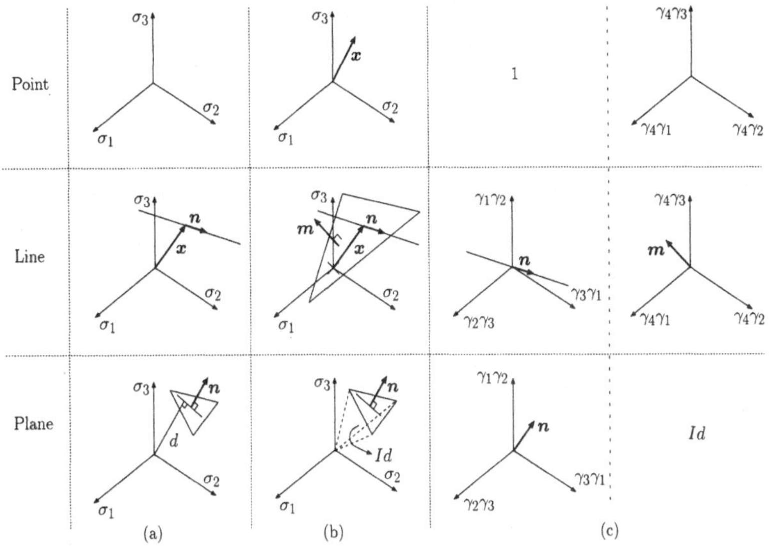

FIGURE 2.2. Representations of (a) points, (b) lines, and (c) planes using vector calculus, $\mathcal{G}_{3,0,0}$, and $\mathcal{G}_{3,0,1}$

2.4 Representation of Points, Lines, and Planes Using Motor Algebra

In this section we will model points, lines, and planes in 4D space using the special algebra of the motors $\mathcal{G}^+_{3,0,1}$, which spans in 4D the line space using a bivector basis.

For the case of the point representation, we proceed by embedding a 3D point on the hyperplane $X_4 = 1$, so that the equation of the point $\boldsymbol{X} \in \mathcal{G}^+_{3,0,1}$ reads

$$\begin{aligned} \boldsymbol{X} &= 1 + x_1\gamma_4\gamma_1 + x_2\gamma_4\gamma_2 + x_3\gamma_4\gamma_3 \\ &= 1 + I(x_1\gamma_2\gamma_3 + x_2\gamma_3\gamma_1 + x_3\gamma_1\gamma_2) \\ &= 1 + I\boldsymbol{x}, \end{aligned} \tag{2.28}$$

or $\boldsymbol{X} = (1,0) + I(0,\boldsymbol{x})$. We can see that in this expression the real part consists of the scalar 1 and the dual part of a 3D bivector.

Since we are working in the algebra $\mathcal{G}^+_{3,0,1}$ spanned only by bivectors and scalars, we see that this special geometric algebra is the most appropriate system for line modeling. Unlike the line representation, the point and the plane are in some sense asymmetric representations with respect to the scalar and bivector parts. Let us now rewrite the line equation (2.26) of $\mathcal{G}_{3,0,0}$ in the degenerated geometric algebra $\mathcal{G}^+_{3,0,1}$. We can express the vector and the dual vector of equation (2.26) in $\mathcal{G}^+_{3,0,1}$ as a bivector and a dual bivector. Since the product of the unit pseudoscalar $I = \gamma_1\gamma_2\gamma_3\gamma_4$ and any dual bivectors built from the basis $\{\gamma_4\gamma_1, \gamma_4\gamma_2, \gamma_4\gamma_3\}$ is zero, we must select the bivector basis $\{\gamma_2\gamma_3, \gamma_3\gamma_1, \gamma_1\gamma_2\}$ for representing the line

$$\boldsymbol{L} = \boldsymbol{n} + I\boldsymbol{m}. \tag{2.29}$$

In this case, the bivectors for the line direction and the moment are computed using two bivector points, $\boldsymbol{x}_1$ and $\boldsymbol{x}_2$, lying on the line, as follows:

$$\begin{aligned}
\boldsymbol{n} &= (\boldsymbol{x}_2 - \boldsymbol{x}_1) = (x_{21} - x_{11})\gamma_2\gamma_3 + (x_{22} - x_{12})\gamma_3\gamma_1 + (x_{23} - x_{13})\gamma_1\gamma_2 \\
&= L_{n_1}\gamma_2\gamma_3 + L_{n_1}\gamma_3\gamma_1 + L_{n_3}\gamma_1\gamma_2 \\
\boldsymbol{m} &= \boldsymbol{x}_1 \times \boldsymbol{x}_2 \\
&= (x_{12}x_{23} - x_{13}x_{22})\gamma_2\gamma_3 + (x_{13}x_{21} - x_{11}x_{23})\gamma_3\gamma_1 + \ldots + \\
&\qquad +(x_{11}x_{22} - x_{12}x_{21})\gamma_1\gamma_2 \\
&= L_{m_1}\gamma_2\gamma_3 + L_{m_2}\gamma_3\gamma_1 + L_{m_3}\gamma_1\gamma_2.
\end{aligned} \tag{2.30}$$

This line representation using dual numbers is easy to understand and to manipulate algebraically, and it is fully equivalent to the representation in terms of *Plücker coordinates.* Using bracket notation, the line equation becomes $\boldsymbol{L} \equiv (0, \boldsymbol{n}) + I(0, \boldsymbol{m})$, where $\boldsymbol{n}$ and $\boldsymbol{m}$ are spanned with a 3D bivector basis.

For the equation of the plane, we proceed in a similar manner as for equation (2.27). We represent the orientation of the plane via the bivector $\boldsymbol{n}$ and the outer product between a bivector touching the plane and its orientation $\boldsymbol{n}$. This outer product results in a quatrivector, which we can express as the Hesse distance $d = (\boldsymbol{x} \cdot \boldsymbol{n})$ multiplied by the unit pseudoscalar,

$$\boldsymbol{H} = \boldsymbol{n} + \boldsymbol{x} \wedge \boldsymbol{n} = \boldsymbol{n} + I(\boldsymbol{x} \cdot \boldsymbol{n}) = \boldsymbol{n} + Id, \tag{2.31}$$

or $\boldsymbol{H} = (0, \boldsymbol{n}) + I(d, 0)$. Note that the plane equation is the dual of the point equation

$$\boldsymbol{H} = (d + I\boldsymbol{n})^* = (I\boldsymbol{n})^* + (d)^* = \boldsymbol{n} + Id, \tag{2.32}$$

where the plane orientation is given by the unit bivector $\boldsymbol{n}$ and the Hesse distance d by the scalar 1.

2.5 Representation of Points, Lines, and Planes Using 4D Geometric Algebra

We can also represent point, lines, and planes using the entire 4D geometric algebra $\mathcal{G}_{3,0,1}$. As opposite to the previous representations which use only bivectors, this representation will also use vectors and the trivectors basis. The point expressed in terms of trivectors is given by

$$\boldsymbol{X} = \gamma_1\gamma_2\gamma_3 + x_1\gamma_1\gamma_2\gamma_3\gamma_4 + x_2\gamma_3\gamma_1\gamma_4 + x_3\gamma_1\gamma_2\gamma_4. \tag{2.33}$$

The equation of the line using bivectors basis is exactly the same as that for equation (2.29):

$$\begin{aligned} \boldsymbol{L} &= L_{n_1}\gamma_2\gamma_3 + L_{n_1}\gamma_3\gamma_1 + L_{n_3}\gamma_1\gamma_2 + L_{m_1}\gamma_4\gamma_1 + L_{m_2}\gamma_4\gamma_2 + L_{m_3}\gamma_4\gamma_3 \\ &= L_{n_1}\gamma_2\gamma_3 + L_{n_1}\gamma_3\gamma_1 + L_{n_3}\gamma_1\gamma_2 + I(L_{m_1}\gamma_2\gamma_3 + L_{m_2}\gamma_3\gamma_1 + L_{m_3}\gamma_1\gamma_2) \\ &= \boldsymbol{n} + I\boldsymbol{m}. \end{aligned} \tag{2.34}$$

The equation of the plane is spanned using basis vectors in terms of the normal of the plane and the Hessian distance:

$$\boldsymbol{H} = \boldsymbol{n}_x\gamma_1 + \boldsymbol{n}_y\gamma_2 + \boldsymbol{n}_z\gamma_3 + d\gamma_4. \tag{2.35}$$

Note that in this equation the multivector basis of the point and plane have been swapped. This equation corresponds to the dual of point equation (2.33) and makes use of a vector as the dual of each trivector:

$$\begin{aligned} \boldsymbol{H} &= (d\gamma_1\gamma_2\gamma_3 + n_x\gamma_2\gamma_3\gamma_4 + n_y\gamma_3\gamma_1\gamma_4 + n_z\gamma_1\gamma_2\gamma_4)^* \\ &= d(\gamma_1\gamma_2\gamma_3)^* + n_x(\gamma_2\gamma_3\gamma_4)^* + n_y(\gamma_3\gamma_1\gamma_4)^* + n_z(\gamma_1\gamma_2\gamma_4)^* \\ &= n_x\gamma_1 + n_y\gamma_2 + n_z\gamma_3 + d\gamma_4. \end{aligned} \tag{2.36}$$

Note that the dual operation is actually not carried out via the pseudoscalar $I = \gamma_1\gamma_2\gamma_3\gamma_4$ because this will lead to the square of γ_4, which equals zero. In order to explain the relation between equation (2.33) and equation (2.35), we are simply relating in the dual sense each basis vector with a basis trivector. Since equations (2.28) and (2.31) are the duals of equations (2.33) and (2.35), we can reconsider Fig. 2.2.c, now using a trivector coordinate basis for depicting the point equation (2.33), and similarly, Fig. 2.2.a, now using a vector coordinate basis for the plane equation (2.35).

The following sections are concerned with the modeling of the motion of basic geometric entities in 3D and 4D space. By comparing these motion models, we will show the power of geometric algebra in the representation and linearizing of the translation transformation achieved in 4D geometric algebra.

2.6 Motion of Points, Lines, and Planes in 3D Geometric Algebra

The 3D motion of a point $\boldsymbol{x}$ in $\mathcal{G}_{3,0,0}$ is given by the following equation:

$$\boldsymbol{x}' = \boldsymbol{R}\boldsymbol{x}\tilde{\boldsymbol{R}} + \boldsymbol{t}. \tag{2.37}$$

Using equation (2.26), the motion equation of the line can be expressed as follows:

$$\begin{aligned}
\boldsymbol{l}' &= \boldsymbol{n}' + \boldsymbol{m}' = \boldsymbol{n}' + \boldsymbol{x}' \wedge \boldsymbol{n}' \\
&= \boldsymbol{R}\boldsymbol{n}\tilde{\boldsymbol{R}} + (\boldsymbol{R}\boldsymbol{x}\tilde{\boldsymbol{R}} + \boldsymbol{t}) \wedge (\boldsymbol{R}\boldsymbol{n}\tilde{\boldsymbol{R}}) \\
&= \boldsymbol{R}\boldsymbol{n}\tilde{\boldsymbol{R}} + \boldsymbol{R}\boldsymbol{x}\tilde{\boldsymbol{R}} \wedge \boldsymbol{R}\boldsymbol{n}\tilde{\boldsymbol{R}} + \boldsymbol{t} \wedge \boldsymbol{R}\boldsymbol{n}\tilde{\boldsymbol{R}} \\
&= \boldsymbol{R}\boldsymbol{n}\tilde{\boldsymbol{R}} + \boldsymbol{R}\boldsymbol{x}\tilde{\boldsymbol{R}} \wedge \boldsymbol{R}\boldsymbol{n}\tilde{\boldsymbol{R}} + \frac{\boldsymbol{t}}{2}\boldsymbol{R}\boldsymbol{n}\tilde{\boldsymbol{R}} - \boldsymbol{R}\boldsymbol{n}\tilde{\boldsymbol{R}}\frac{\boldsymbol{t}}{2} \\
&= \boldsymbol{R}\boldsymbol{n}\tilde{\boldsymbol{R}} + \boldsymbol{R}\boldsymbol{n}\frac{\boldsymbol{t}}{2}\tilde{\boldsymbol{R}} + \frac{\boldsymbol{t}}{2}\boldsymbol{R}\boldsymbol{n}\tilde{\boldsymbol{R}} + \boldsymbol{R}\boldsymbol{m}\tilde{\boldsymbol{R}},
\end{aligned} \tag{2.38}$$

where $\boldsymbol{x}'$ stands for the rotated and shifted position vector, $\boldsymbol{n}'$ stands for the rotated orientation vector, and $\boldsymbol{m}'$ for the new line moment.

The model of the motion of the plane in $\mathcal{G}_{3,0,0}$ can be expressed in terms of the multivector Hesse equation (2.27), as follows:

$$\begin{aligned}
\boldsymbol{h}' &= \boldsymbol{n}' + Id' = \boldsymbol{n}' + \boldsymbol{x}' \wedge \boldsymbol{n}' \\
&= \boldsymbol{R}\boldsymbol{n}\tilde{\boldsymbol{R}} + (\boldsymbol{R}\boldsymbol{x}\tilde{\boldsymbol{R}} + \boldsymbol{t}) \wedge (\boldsymbol{R}\boldsymbol{n}\tilde{\boldsymbol{R}}) \\
&= \boldsymbol{R}\boldsymbol{n}\tilde{\boldsymbol{R}} + \boldsymbol{R}\boldsymbol{x}\tilde{\boldsymbol{R}} \wedge \boldsymbol{R}\boldsymbol{n}\tilde{\boldsymbol{R}} + \boldsymbol{t} \wedge \boldsymbol{R}\boldsymbol{n}\tilde{\boldsymbol{R}} \\
&= \boldsymbol{R}\boldsymbol{n}\tilde{\boldsymbol{R}} + \boldsymbol{t} \wedge \boldsymbol{R}\boldsymbol{n}\tilde{\boldsymbol{R}} + \boldsymbol{R}\boldsymbol{x} \wedge \boldsymbol{n}\tilde{\boldsymbol{R}} \\
&= \boldsymbol{R}\boldsymbol{n}\tilde{\boldsymbol{R}} + \boldsymbol{t} \wedge \boldsymbol{R}\boldsymbol{n}\tilde{\boldsymbol{R}} + \boldsymbol{R}(Id)\tilde{\boldsymbol{R}} \\
&= \boldsymbol{R}\boldsymbol{n}\tilde{\boldsymbol{R}} + \boldsymbol{t}^* \cdot \boldsymbol{R}\boldsymbol{n}\tilde{\boldsymbol{R}} + Id \\
&= \boldsymbol{R}\boldsymbol{n}\tilde{\boldsymbol{R}} + I(\boldsymbol{t} \cdot \boldsymbol{R}\boldsymbol{n}\tilde{\boldsymbol{R}} + d),
\end{aligned} \tag{2.39}$$

where $\boldsymbol{n}'$ stands for the rotated bivector plane orientation, $\boldsymbol{x}'$ stands for the rotated and shifted position vector, and d' for the new Hesse distance. Here, we use the concept of duality to claim that $\boldsymbol{t} \wedge \boldsymbol{R}\boldsymbol{n}\tilde{\boldsymbol{R}} = \boldsymbol{t}^* \cdot \boldsymbol{R}\boldsymbol{n}\tilde{\boldsymbol{R}} = (I\boldsymbol{t}) \cdot \boldsymbol{R}\boldsymbol{n}\tilde{\boldsymbol{R}}$.

2.7 Motion of Points, Lines, and Planes Using Motor Algebra

The modeling of the 3D motion of geometric primitives using the motor algebra $\mathcal{G}^+_{3,0,1}$ takes place in a 4D space where rotation and translation are multiplicative operators that are applied as multiplicative operators, and the result is that the 3D general motion becomes linear. Having created a linear model, we can then compute simultaneously the unknown rotation and translation. This will be useful for the case of the hand-eye problem, or when we apply the motor extended Kalman filter (see Chapter 8).

For the modeling of the point motion, we use the point representation of equation (2.28) and the motor relations given in equation (2.23), with $I^2 = 0$:

$$\begin{aligned}
\boldsymbol{X}' &= 1 + I\boldsymbol{x}' = \boldsymbol{M}\boldsymbol{X}\widetilde{\overline{\boldsymbol{M}}} = \boldsymbol{M}(1 + I\boldsymbol{x})\widetilde{\overline{\boldsymbol{M}}} \\
&= \boldsymbol{T}_s\boldsymbol{R}_s(1 + I\boldsymbol{x})\tilde{\boldsymbol{R}}_s\boldsymbol{T}_s \\
&= (1 + I\frac{\boldsymbol{t}_s}{2})\boldsymbol{R}_s(1 + I\boldsymbol{x})\tilde{\boldsymbol{R}}_s(1 + I\frac{\boldsymbol{t}_s}{2})
\end{aligned}$$

$$\begin{aligned} &= (1+I\frac{t_s}{2})(1+I\boldsymbol{R}_s\boldsymbol{x}\tilde{\boldsymbol{R}}_s)(1+I\frac{t_s}{2}) \\ &= 1+I\frac{t_s}{2}+I\boldsymbol{R}_s\boldsymbol{x}\tilde{\boldsymbol{R}}_s+I\frac{t_s}{2} \\ &= 1+I(\boldsymbol{R}_s\boldsymbol{x}\tilde{\boldsymbol{R}}_s+\boldsymbol{t}_s). \end{aligned} \tag{2.40}$$

Note that the dual part of this equation in 4D space is fully equivalent to equation (2.37), which is in 3D space .

The motion of a 3D line or screw motion can be seen as the rotation of the line about the axis line $\boldsymbol{L}_s$ and its translation along this axis line, as depicted in Fig. 2.3. Note that in the figure the line $\boldsymbol{L}_s$ is shifted a distance $\boldsymbol{t}_c$ from

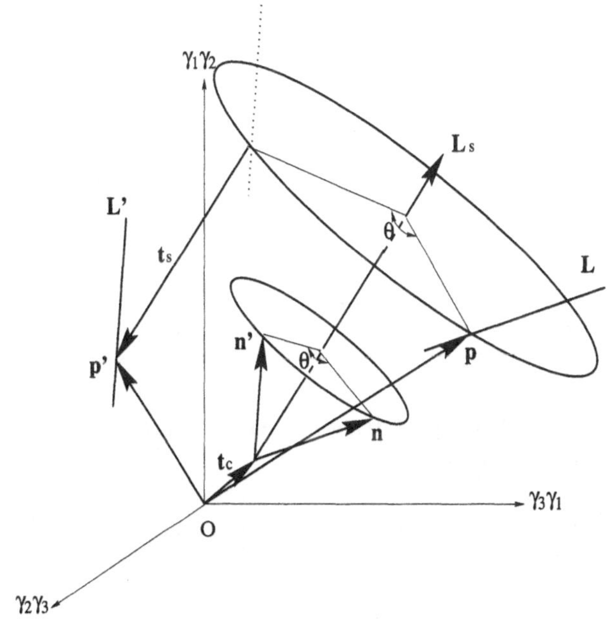

FIGURE 2.3. The screw motion of a line

the origin. Now, using line equation (2.29) we can express the motion of a 3D line as follows:

$$\boldsymbol{L}'=\boldsymbol{n}'+I\boldsymbol{m}'=\boldsymbol{M}(\boldsymbol{L})\tilde{\boldsymbol{M}}=\boldsymbol{T}_s\boldsymbol{R}_s(\boldsymbol{n}+I\boldsymbol{m})\tilde{\boldsymbol{R}}_s\tilde{\boldsymbol{T}}_s. \tag{2.41}$$

This equation can be further expressed purely in terms of rotors, as follows:

$$\begin{aligned} \boldsymbol{L}' &= (1+I\frac{\boldsymbol{t}_s}{\boldsymbol{2}})\boldsymbol{R}_s(\boldsymbol{n}+I\boldsymbol{m})\tilde{\boldsymbol{R}}_s(1-I\frac{\boldsymbol{t}_s}{2}) \\ &= (1+I\frac{\boldsymbol{t}_s}{\boldsymbol{2}})(\boldsymbol{R}_s\boldsymbol{n}\tilde{\boldsymbol{R}}_s+I\boldsymbol{R}_s\boldsymbol{m}\tilde{\boldsymbol{R}}_s-I\boldsymbol{R}_s\boldsymbol{n}\tilde{\boldsymbol{R}}_s\frac{\boldsymbol{t}_s}{2}) \\ &= \boldsymbol{R}_s\boldsymbol{n}\tilde{\boldsymbol{R}}_s+I(-\boldsymbol{R}_s\boldsymbol{n}\tilde{\boldsymbol{R}}_s\frac{\boldsymbol{t}_s}{2}+\frac{\boldsymbol{t}_s}{2}\boldsymbol{R}_s\boldsymbol{n}\tilde{\boldsymbol{R}}_s+\boldsymbol{R}_s\boldsymbol{m}\tilde{\boldsymbol{R}}_s) \end{aligned}$$

$$= \boldsymbol{R}_s \boldsymbol{n} \tilde{\boldsymbol{R}}_s + I(\boldsymbol{R}_s \boldsymbol{n} \tilde{\boldsymbol{R}}_s{}' + \boldsymbol{R}_s' \boldsymbol{n} \tilde{\boldsymbol{R}}_s + \boldsymbol{R}_s \boldsymbol{m} \tilde{\boldsymbol{R}}_s.) \qquad (2.42)$$

Note that in this equation, before we merge the bivector $\frac{\boldsymbol{t}_s}{2}$ with the rotor $\boldsymbol{R}_s$ or $\tilde{\boldsymbol{R}}_s$, the real and the dual parts are fully equivalent with the elements of line equation (2.38) of $\mathcal{G}_{3,0,0}$.

Equation (2.42)is very useful as a linear algorithm to estimate simultaneous rotation and translation, as in the case of hand-eye calibration [7] or for the algorithm for the motor extended Kalman filter presented in Chapter 8 .

The transformation of a plane under a rigid motion in $\mathcal{G}^+_{3,0,1}$ can be seen as the motion of the dual of the point. Thus, equation (2.31) can be utlized to express the motion equation of the plane:

$$\begin{aligned}
\boldsymbol{H}' &= \boldsymbol{n}' + Id' = \boldsymbol{M}\boldsymbol{H}\tilde{\tilde{\boldsymbol{M}}} = \boldsymbol{M}(\boldsymbol{n} + Id)\tilde{\tilde{\boldsymbol{M}}} \\
&= \boldsymbol{T}_s \boldsymbol{R}_s(\boldsymbol{n} + Id)\tilde{\boldsymbol{R}}_s \boldsymbol{T}_s \\
&= (1 + I\frac{\boldsymbol{t}_s}{\boldsymbol{2}})(\boldsymbol{R}_s \boldsymbol{n} \tilde{\boldsymbol{R}}_s + Id)(1 + I\frac{\boldsymbol{t}_s}{\boldsymbol{2}}) \\
&= \boldsymbol{R}_s \boldsymbol{n} \tilde{\boldsymbol{R}}_s + I(\boldsymbol{R}_s \boldsymbol{n} \tilde{\boldsymbol{R}}_s \frac{\boldsymbol{t}_s}{2} + \frac{\boldsymbol{t}_s}{2} \boldsymbol{R}_s \boldsymbol{n} \tilde{\boldsymbol{R}}_s + d) \\
&= \boldsymbol{R}_s \boldsymbol{n} \tilde{\boldsymbol{R}}_s + I(\boldsymbol{t}_s \cdot (\boldsymbol{R}_s \boldsymbol{n} \tilde{\boldsymbol{R}}_s) + d). \qquad (2.43)
\end{aligned}$$

Note that the real part and the dual part of this expression are fully equivalent to the bivector and trivector parts of equation (2.39) in $\mathcal{G}_{3,0,0}$.

2.8 Motion of Points, Lines, and Planes Using 4D Geometric Algebra

For the modeling of the motion of points, lines, and planes in $\mathcal{G}_{3,0,1}$, only the automorphism equivalent of the screw and its conjugate are required.

The motion of the point is given by

$$\begin{aligned}
\boldsymbol{X}' &= \boldsymbol{M}\boldsymbol{X}\tilde{\boldsymbol{M}} = \boldsymbol{T}_s \boldsymbol{R}_s(\boldsymbol{X})\tilde{\boldsymbol{R}}_s \tilde{\boldsymbol{T}}_s \\
&= (1 + I\frac{\boldsymbol{t}_s}{2})\boldsymbol{R}_s(\gamma_1\gamma_2\gamma_3 + I\boldsymbol{x})\tilde{\boldsymbol{R}}_s(1 - I\frac{\boldsymbol{t}_s}{2}) \\
&= (1 + \gamma_4\frac{\boldsymbol{t}}{2})(\gamma_1\gamma_2\gamma_3 + I\boldsymbol{R}_s \boldsymbol{x} \tilde{\boldsymbol{R}}_s)(1 - \gamma_4\frac{\boldsymbol{t}}{2}) \\
&= \gamma_1\gamma_2\gamma_3 + I\frac{\boldsymbol{t}}{2} + I\boldsymbol{R}_s \boldsymbol{x} \tilde{\boldsymbol{R}}_s + I\frac{\boldsymbol{t}_s}{2} \\
&= \gamma_1\gamma_2\gamma_3 + I(\boldsymbol{R}_s \boldsymbol{x} \tilde{\boldsymbol{R}}_s + \boldsymbol{t}_s), \qquad (2.44)
\end{aligned}$$

where $\boldsymbol{t}_s = t_x\gamma_2\gamma_3 + t_y\gamma_3\gamma_1 + t_z\gamma_1\gamma_2$, $\boldsymbol{x} = x_x\gamma_1 + x_y\gamma_2 + x_z\gamma_3$, and $\boldsymbol{t} = t_x\gamma_1 + t_y\gamma_2 + t_z\gamma_3$. Note that the dual part of this equation in 4D space is fully equivalent to equation (2.37) in 3D space.

The equation of the motion of the line is exactly the same as equation (2.42).

The motion of the plane is given by

$$\begin{aligned}
\boldsymbol{H}' &= \boldsymbol{n}' + \gamma_4 d' = n'_x\gamma_1 + n'_y\gamma_2 + n'_z\gamma_3 + d'\gamma_4 = \boldsymbol{M}\boldsymbol{H}\tilde{\boldsymbol{M}} = \boldsymbol{M}(\boldsymbol{n} + \gamma_4 d)\tilde{\boldsymbol{M}} \\
&= \boldsymbol{T}_s\boldsymbol{R}_s(\boldsymbol{n} + \gamma_4)\tilde{\boldsymbol{R}}_s\tilde{\boldsymbol{T}}_s = (1 + I\frac{\boldsymbol{t}_s}{\mathbf{2}})(\boldsymbol{R}_s\boldsymbol{n}\tilde{\boldsymbol{R}}_s + \gamma_4 d)(1 - I\frac{\boldsymbol{t}_s}{\mathbf{2}}) \\
&= \boldsymbol{R}_s\boldsymbol{n}\tilde{\boldsymbol{R}}_s + I\frac{\boldsymbol{t}_s}{\mathbf{2}}\boldsymbol{R}_s\boldsymbol{n}\tilde{\boldsymbol{R}}_s - \boldsymbol{R}_s\boldsymbol{n}\tilde{\boldsymbol{R}}_s I\frac{\boldsymbol{t}_s}{\mathbf{2}} + \gamma_4 d \\
&= \boldsymbol{R}_s\boldsymbol{n}\tilde{\boldsymbol{R}}_s + I(\frac{\boldsymbol{t}_s\boldsymbol{R}_s\boldsymbol{n}\tilde{\boldsymbol{R}}_s - \boldsymbol{R}_s\boldsymbol{n}\tilde{\boldsymbol{R}}_s\boldsymbol{t}_s}{\mathbf{2}}) + \gamma_4 d \\
&= \boldsymbol{R}_s\boldsymbol{n}\tilde{\boldsymbol{R}}_s + I(\boldsymbol{t}_s \wedge \boldsymbol{R}_s\boldsymbol{n}\tilde{\boldsymbol{R}}_s) + \gamma_4 d \\
&= \boldsymbol{n}' + \gamma_4(I_3\boldsymbol{t}_s)\wedge\boldsymbol{n}' + \gamma_4 d = \boldsymbol{n}' + \gamma_4(\boldsymbol{t}_s^* \cdot \boldsymbol{n}') + \gamma_4 d \\
&= \boldsymbol{n}' + \gamma_4(\boldsymbol{t} \cdot \boldsymbol{n}' + d)
\end{aligned} \tag{2.45}$$

The real and dual parts of this expression are equivalent in a higher dimension to the bivector and trivector parts of equation (2.39) in $\mathcal{G}_{3,0,0}$.

2.9 Incidence Relations Between Points, Lines, and Planes

The geometric relations between points, lines, and planes expressed in terms of incidence relations are very useful when we are dealing with the geometry of configurations and the relative motion of objects. Blaske introduced the basic relations of incidence using dual quaternions [14]. These relations can be also formulated for the representations of points, lines, and planes in the motor algebra $\mathcal{G}^+_{3,0,1}$ or in the 4D degenerated geometric algebra $\mathcal{G}_{3,0,1}$.

A point $\boldsymbol{P}$ lying on a line $\boldsymbol{L}$ fulfills the equation

$$\boldsymbol{P}^*\boldsymbol{L} + \boldsymbol{L}^*\boldsymbol{P} = 0, \tag{2.46}$$

where $\boldsymbol{P}^*$ and $\boldsymbol{L}^*$ are their conjugated respectively.

The distance d of a point relative to a plane $\boldsymbol{\Phi}$ is given by

$$\boldsymbol{P}^*\boldsymbol{\Phi} + \boldsymbol{\Phi}^*\boldsymbol{P} = d\gamma_1\gamma_2\gamma_3\gamma_4. \tag{2.47}$$

If $d = 0$, the point lies on the plane; if d is negative, it is behind the plane; and if d is positive, it is in front of the plane.

The intersection point $\boldsymbol{P}$ of a line $\boldsymbol{L}$ crossing a plane $\boldsymbol{\Phi}$ can be computed as

$$\boldsymbol{L}^*\boldsymbol{\Phi} + \boldsymbol{\Phi}^*\boldsymbol{L} = \boldsymbol{P}. \tag{2.48}$$

In this case, if the line is parallel to the plane, the equation equals zero.

Incidence relations are fundamental in projective geometry, we will study in more detail in Chapters 3 and 4.

2.9.1 Flags of points, lines, and planes

When dealing with geometric configurations as in object modeling or robot navigation planing, it is useful to resort to a type of *geometric indicator*, which allows us to detect whether a geometric condition is fulfilled or not. These kind of indicators are called flags, and they are expressions relating points, lines, and planes that have some common attributes. Flags generate varieties [91].

We can express a point touching a line as the equation of the so-called *point-line flag*:

$$\mathcal{F}_{PL} = \boldsymbol{P} + \boldsymbol{L}. \tag{2.49}$$

If $\boldsymbol{P}\boldsymbol{P}^*$=1 and $\boldsymbol{L}\boldsymbol{L}^*$=1, then $\mathcal{F}_{PL}\mathcal{F}^*_{PL}$=1.

If we have a point which touches a line and also a plane, and in which the orientation of the plane is parallel to the line, then we can represent the *line–plane flag* as

$$\mathcal{F}_{L\Phi} = \boldsymbol{L} + \boldsymbol{\Phi}. \tag{2.50}$$

In this equation, if $\boldsymbol{L}\boldsymbol{L}^*$=1 and $\boldsymbol{\Phi}\boldsymbol{\Phi}^*$=1, then $\mathcal{F}_{L\Phi}\mathcal{F}^*_{L\Phi}$=1.

Finally, if a point touches a line and a plane and the line has the same orientation as the normal to the plane, we can assign to this geometry the following *point-line-plane flag*:

$$\mathcal{F}_{PL\Phi} = \boldsymbol{P} + \boldsymbol{L} + \boldsymbol{\Phi}. \tag{2.51}$$

Here, if $\boldsymbol{P}\boldsymbol{P}^*$=1 , $\boldsymbol{L}\boldsymbol{L}^*$=1, and $\boldsymbol{\Phi}\boldsymbol{\Phi}^*$=1, then $\mathcal{F}_{PL\Phi}\mathcal{F}^*_{PL\Phi}$=1.

2.10 Conclusion

This chapter presents the Clifford or geometric algebra for computations in visually guided robotics. Looking for other suitable ways of representing algebraic relations of geometric primitives we consider the complex and dual numbers in the geometric algebra framework. It turns out that in this framework the algebra of motors is well suited to express the 3D kinematics. Doing that we can linearize the nonlinear 3D rigid motion transformation. In this chapter the geometric primitives points, lines, and planes are represented using the 3D Euclidean geometric algebra and the 4D motor algebra. Next the rigid motions of these geometric primitives are elegantly expressed using rotors, motors, and concepts of duality. In the algebra of motors we extend the 3D Euclidean space representation to a 4D space by means of a dual copy of scalars, vectors, and rotors or quaternions. Finally, we formulate incidence relations between points, lines, and planes using the motor algebra framework.

2.11 Exercises

2.1. Split the vector $\boldsymbol{v} = -2\gamma_1 + 7\gamma_2 + 10\gamma_3$ into the components $\boldsymbol{x} = 3\gamma_1 - 1.5\gamma_2$, $\boldsymbol{y} = 2\gamma_1 + 4\gamma_2 - 2\gamma_3$, and $\boldsymbol{z} = 5\gamma_1 + 3\gamma_2 + 3\gamma_3$. In other words, compute the coefficients α, β, γ of the equation $\boldsymbol{v} = \alpha\boldsymbol{x} + \beta\boldsymbol{y} + \gamma\boldsymbol{z}$. Draw in three dimensions the vectors and the volume $\boldsymbol{a}\wedge\boldsymbol{bc}$.

2.2. The outer square root of a multivector $\boldsymbol{M}$ is $\boldsymbol{x}$, which is the solution of the equation $\boldsymbol{M} = \boldsymbol{x}\wedge\boldsymbol{x}$. If $\boldsymbol{M} = \alpha + \boldsymbol{a}$, where $\alpha \in R$, we can write $\boldsymbol{x} = \sqrt{(}\alpha)(1 + \frac{\boldsymbol{a}}{\alpha})^{\frac{1}{2}}$. This equation can be expanded using the following series:

$$(1 + \frac{\boldsymbol{a}}{\alpha})^{\frac{1}{2}} = 1 + \frac{1}{2}\frac{\boldsymbol{a}}{\alpha} + \frac{\frac{1}{2}(\frac{1}{2} - 1)}{2} \cdot \frac{\boldsymbol{a}\wedge\boldsymbol{a}}{\alpha^2} + \frac{\frac{1}{2}(\frac{1}{2} - 1)(\frac{1}{2} - 2)}{3!} \cdot \frac{\boldsymbol{a}\wedge\boldsymbol{a}\wedge\boldsymbol{a}}{\alpha^3} + ...$$

The quantity of the elements of this series should be at least equal to the dimension of the considered geometric algebra. Generate a program file for CLICAL to compute the outer square root of $\boldsymbol{M}$, where Re($\boldsymbol{M}$)>0. Give any $\boldsymbol{M}$ and verify the identity $\boldsymbol{x}\wedge\boldsymbol{x} = \boldsymbol{M}$.

2.3. Rotate in 4D Euclidean space, using CLICAL [69], the vector $\boldsymbol{v} = \gamma_1 + gj + gk$, first related to the plane $\gamma_1\gamma_2$ by the angle $\frac{\phi}{4}$, and then related to the plane $\sigma_4\gamma_2$ by the angle $\frac{\phi}{5}$.

2.4. Given $\boldsymbol{a} = 2\gamma_1 + 4\gamma_2 + 5\gamma_3$, $\boldsymbol{b} = 5\gamma_1 + 3\gamma_2 + 3\gamma_3$, $\boldsymbol{A} = \boldsymbol{a}\gamma_1\gamma_2\gamma_3$, and $\boldsymbol{B} = \boldsymbol{b}\gamma_1\gamma_2\gamma_3$, compute the bivectors $\frac{1}{2}(1+\sigma_1\sigma_2\sigma_3\sigma_4)\boldsymbol{A}$ and $\frac{1}{2}(1-\sigma_1\sigma_2\sigma_3\sigma_4)\boldsymbol{B}$ and show that they commute.

2.5. Given the bivector $\boldsymbol{B} = \alpha\gamma_1\gamma_2 + \beta\sigma_4\sigma_3$, compute $\boldsymbol{B}\cdot\boldsymbol{B}$, $\boldsymbol{B}\wedge\boldsymbol{B}$, and $\boldsymbol{B}\times\boldsymbol{B}$ and explain what kinds of multivectors result.

2.6. For this problem, use the same multivectors $\boldsymbol{A}$ and $\boldsymbol{B}$ that you used in exercise 2.4. Given $\boldsymbol{C} = \frac{1}{2}(1+\gamma_1\gamma_2\gamma_3\sigma_4)\boldsymbol{A} + \frac{1}{2}(1-\gamma_1\gamma_2\gamma_3\sigma_4)\boldsymbol{B}$, express exp($\boldsymbol{C}$) using $a = |\boldsymbol{a}|$ and $b = |\boldsymbol{b}|$. What are the rotation angles generated by exp($\boldsymbol{C}$)?

2.7. Given in $\mathcal{G}_{3,0,0}$ the points $\boldsymbol{a} = 0.5\gamma_1 + 2.0\gamma_2 + 1.3\gamma_3$, $\boldsymbol{b} = 1.5\gamma_1 + 1.2\gamma_2 + 2.3\gamma_3$, and $\boldsymbol{c} = 0.7\gamma_1 + 1.2\gamma_2 - 0.3\gamma_3$, compute the line $\boldsymbol{l}$ crossing $\boldsymbol{a}$ and $\boldsymbol{b}$, and the plane ϕ tangent to the points $\boldsymbol{a}$, $\boldsymbol{a}$, and $\boldsymbol{c}$.

2.8. Using the software packet CLIFFORD 4.0 [1] and point $\boldsymbol{a}$, line $\boldsymbol{l}$, and plane $\boldsymbol{\phi}$ from exercise 2.7, compute new values for the point, line, and plane after undergoing a rigid motion given by the translation $\boldsymbol{t} = 1.0\gamma_1 - 2.7\gamma_2 + 5.3\gamma_3$. Also compute the rotor $\boldsymbol{R} = cos(\frac{\theta}{2}) + sin(\frac{\theta}{2})\boldsymbol{n}$, where $\theta = \frac{\pi}{6}$ and $\boldsymbol{n}$ is the unit 3D bivector of the rotation axis given by $\boldsymbol{n} = 0.7\sigma_2\sigma_3 + 1.2\sigma_3\sigma_1 + 0.9\sigma_1\sigma_2$.

2.9. Express point $\boldsymbol{a}$, line $\boldsymbol{l}$, and plane ϕ given in exercise 2.7 in the algebra of motors $\mathcal{G}^+_{3,0,1}$.

2.10. Using the software packet CLIFFORD 4.0 and the point, line, and plane given in exercise 2.9, compute their new values after undergoing the rigid motion given by the translator $\boldsymbol{T} = 1 + I\frac{1.0\gamma_2\gamma_3 - 2.7\gamma_3\gamma_1 + 5.3\gamma_1\gamma_2}{2}$ and the rotor $\boldsymbol{R}_s = cos(\frac{\theta}{2}) + sin(\frac{\theta}{2})\boldsymbol{l}$, where $\theta = \frac{\pi}{6}$ and $\boldsymbol{l}$ is the screw-axis line. Compare your results with the results of exercise 8.

2.11. Express the geometric objects of exercise 7 in the degenerated algebra $\mathcal{G}_{3,0,1}$: the point $\boldsymbol{a}$ using trivectors, the line $\boldsymbol{l}$ using bivectors and the plane ϕ using vectors.

2.12. Using the software packet CLIFFORD 4.0 and point $\boldsymbol{a}$, line **1**, and plane ϕ from exercise 2.11, compute new values for the point, line, and plane after undergoing the rigid motion given by the translator $\boldsymbol{T} = 1 + I\frac{1.0\gamma_2\gamma_3 - 2.7\gamma_3\gamma_1 + 5.3\gamma_1\gamma_2}{2}$. Also compute the rotor $\boldsymbol{R}_s = cos(\frac{\theta}{2}) + sin(\frac{\theta}{2})\boldsymbol{l}$, where $\theta = \frac{\pi}{6}$ and $\boldsymbol{l}$ is the screw-axis line. Compare your results with the results of exercises 2.8 and 2.10.

2.13. Prove the Rodriguez formula for 3D rigid motion using motor algebra. Compare you results with the results from exercise 1.12. Why is the motor algebra expression superior?

2.14. In the degenerated algebra $\mathcal{G}_{3,0,1}$, choose a point $\boldsymbol{P}$ using trivectors and a line $\boldsymbol{L}$ using bivectors, and prove that the following expression,

$$\boldsymbol{P}^*\mathbf{L} + \boldsymbol{L}^*\boldsymbol{P},$$

equals zero if the point lies on the line. Prove the same equation using representations of the point and line in the motor algebra $\mathcal{G}^+_{3,0,1}$.

2.15. In the degenerated algebra $\mathcal{G}_{3,0,1}$ for the point $\boldsymbol{P}$ using trivectors, and the plane $\boldsymbol{\Phi}$ using vectors, show that the following expression,

$$\boldsymbol{P}^*\boldsymbol{\Phi} + \boldsymbol{\Phi}^*\boldsymbol{P} = d\gamma_1\gamma_2\gamma_3\gamma_4$$

will describe a particular geometric configuration, depending upon the value of d. If d=0, the point lies on the plane; if $d \neq 0$, d indicates the distance of the point to the plane; and if d is negative, the point is behind the plane. Using CLIFFORD 4.0 and some points of the 3D space, check this equation. Check the equation again using the representations of the point and plane in the motor algebra $\mathcal{G}^+_{3,0,1}$.

2.16. In the degenerated algebra $\mathcal{G}_{3,0,1}$ for the line $\boldsymbol{L}$ using bivectors, the plane $\boldsymbol{\Phi}$ using vectors show that the following expression,

$$L^*\boldsymbol{\Phi} + L^*\boldsymbol{\Phi},$$

will describe a particular geometric configuration. If this expression equals zero, the line lies on the plane or is parallel to it; if not, the equation yields the intersecting point. This equation can be seen as a kind of meet equation when using a degenerated algebra. Using CLIFFORD 4.0 and some points of 3D space, check the equation. Check the same equation using the representations of the line and plane in the motor algebra $\mathcal{G}^+_{3,0,1}$.

2.17. Flags are very useful when we are interested in relating geometrical points, lines, and planes. Show in the degenerated algebra $\mathcal{G}_{3,0,1}$ that the plane perpendicular to the line $\boldsymbol{L}$ passing through the point $\boldsymbol{P}$ is given by

$$\boldsymbol{\Phi}^{\perp} = \frac{1}{2}(\boldsymbol{P}\boldsymbol{L}^* - \boldsymbol{L}\boldsymbol{P}^*).$$

This equation is a kind of extension which relates the mapping of the flags

$$f_{PL} = \frac{1}{\sqrt{2}}(\boldsymbol{P} + \boldsymbol{L}) \rightarrow f_{P\Phi} = \frac{1}{\sqrt{2}}(\boldsymbol{P} + \boldsymbol{\Phi}^{\perp}).$$

The inverse of this mapping relates the plane to the line perpendicular to the plane passing through the point. That is,

$$\boldsymbol{L}^{\perp} = \frac{1}{2}(\boldsymbol{\Phi}\boldsymbol{P}^* - \boldsymbol{P}\boldsymbol{\Phi}^*).$$

Check that $(\boldsymbol{L}^{\perp})^{\perp} = \boldsymbol{L}$.

3. Lie Algebras and Algebra of Incidence Using the Null Cone and Affine Plane

3.1 Introduction

In this chapter we give the fundamentals of Lie algebra and the algebra of incidence using the computational frameworks of the null cone and the n-dimensional affine plane. Using Lie algebra within this computational framework has the advantage that it is easily accessible to the reader because there is a direct translation of the familiar matrix representations to representations using bivectors from geometric algebra. Generally speaking, Lie group theory is the appropriate tool for the study and analysis of the action of a group on a manifold. Since we are interested in purely geometric computations, the use of geometric algebra is appropriate for carrying out computations in a coordinate-free manner by using a bivector representation of the most important Lie algebras. We will represent Lie operators using bivectors for the computation of a variety of invariants. This chapter benefits of work done in colaboration with Sobczyk [11, 100].

It is usual to use a geometric algebra $\mathcal{G}_{p,q,0}$ with Minkowski metric for computations of projective geometry and algebra of incidence, and separately a degenerated algebra for the computation of rigid motion, for example, the motor algebra $\mathcal{G}^+_{3,0,1}$. In contrast, here we use the affine plane framework, which allows us to make computations involving both the algebra of incidence and Euclidean rigid transformations.

The organization of this chapter is as follows. Section 2 introduces the geometric algebra of reciprocal null cones. Section 3 explains the computational frameworks of the horosphere and affine plane. Section 4 examines the basic properties of the general linear group from the perspective of geometric algebra. Section 5 shows the computing of rigid motion in the affine plane. Section 6 studies the Lie group and Lie algebra of the affine plane. Section 7 presents the algebra of incidence in the n-dimensional affine plane. Concluding remarks are given in Section 8 and exercises are in Section 9.

3.2 Geometric Algebra of Reciprocal Null Cones

This section introduces the 2^{2n}-dimensional geometric algebra $\mathcal{G}_{n,n}$. This geometric algebra is best understood by considering the properties of two

2^n-dimensional *reciprocal Grassmann subalgebras.* These subalgebras are generated by the vector bases of the reciprocal null cones N and $\overline{N}$. Let us start by explaining the meaning of null cones.

3.2.1 Reciprocal null cones

The *reciprocal null cones* N and $\overline{N}$ are real linear n-dimensional vector spaces whose vectors square to null— that is, for $\boldsymbol{x} \in N$, $\boldsymbol{x}^2$=0 and for $\overline{\boldsymbol{x}} \in \overline{N}$, $\overline{\boldsymbol{x}}^2$=0. In that regard, an associative geometric multiplication also equals zero—namely, for $\boldsymbol{x}$, $\boldsymbol{y}, \boldsymbol{z} \in N$,

$$\boldsymbol{z}^2 = (\boldsymbol{x}+\boldsymbol{y})^2 = (\boldsymbol{x}+\boldsymbol{y})(\boldsymbol{x}+\boldsymbol{y}) = \boldsymbol{x}^2 + \boldsymbol{x}\boldsymbol{y} + \boldsymbol{y}\boldsymbol{x} + \boldsymbol{y}^2 = \boldsymbol{x}\boldsymbol{y} + \boldsymbol{y}\boldsymbol{x} = 0. \quad (3.1)$$

This result indicates that the symmetric part of geometric product of two vectors is simply zero. Thus, the geometric product of two vectors will be equal to the outer product:

$$\boldsymbol{x}\boldsymbol{y} = \boldsymbol{x}\cdot\boldsymbol{y} + \boldsymbol{x}\wedge\boldsymbol{y} = \frac{1}{2}(\boldsymbol{x}\boldsymbol{y}+\boldsymbol{y}\boldsymbol{x}) + \frac{1}{2}(\boldsymbol{x}\boldsymbol{y}-\boldsymbol{y}\boldsymbol{x}) = \frac{1}{2}(\boldsymbol{x}\boldsymbol{y}-\boldsymbol{y}\boldsymbol{x}) = \boldsymbol{x}\wedge\boldsymbol{y}. \quad (3.2)$$

Similarly, for the vectors in the reciprocal null cone,

$$\overline{\boldsymbol{x}\boldsymbol{y}} = \overline{\boldsymbol{x}}\cdot\overline{\boldsymbol{y}} + \overline{\boldsymbol{x}}\wedge\overline{\boldsymbol{y}} = \frac{1}{2}(\overline{\boldsymbol{x}\boldsymbol{y}}+\overline{\boldsymbol{y}\boldsymbol{x}}) + \frac{1}{2}(\overline{\boldsymbol{x}\boldsymbol{y}}-\overline{\boldsymbol{y}\boldsymbol{x}}) = \frac{1}{2}(\overline{\boldsymbol{x}\boldsymbol{y}}-\overline{\boldsymbol{y}\boldsymbol{x}}) = \overline{\boldsymbol{x}}\wedge\overline{\boldsymbol{y}}. \quad (3.3)$$

The *reciprocal vector bases* $\{e\}$ and $\{\overline{e}\}$ span the reciprocal null cones:

$$N = span\{e_1, ..., e_n\} \qquad \overline{N} = span\{\overline{e}_1, ..., \overline{e}_n\}. \quad (3.4)$$

The *neutral pseudo-Euclidean space* $I\!R^{n,n}$ is the linear space spanned by the null cones:

$$I\!R^{n,n} = span\{N, \overline{N}\} = \{\boldsymbol{x}+\overline{\boldsymbol{x}} | \boldsymbol{x} \in N, \overline{\boldsymbol{x}} \in \overline{N}\}. \quad (3.5)$$

The reciprocal vector bases satisfy the following defining *inner product* relations:

$$e_i \cdot \overline{e}_j = \overline{e}_j \cdot e_i = \delta_{ij} \quad (3.6)$$

and

$$e_i \cdot e_j = 0 \qquad \overline{e}_i \cdot \overline{e}_j = 0, \quad (3.7)$$

for all i, j = 1, 2, ... , n. The inner product relations of equations (3.6) and (3.7) tell us that the reciprocal basis vectors e_i and $\overline{e}_i$ are all null vectors and are mutually orthogonal. Because of equation (3.6), the reciprocal vector bases are said to be dual, because they satisfy the relationship $\{e\}\cdot\{\overline{e}\}$=id, where id stands for the identity.

The outer product defining relations are

$$e_i \wedge e_j = e_i e_j = -e_j e_i \qquad \bar{e}_i \wedge \bar{e}_j = \bar{e}_i \bar{e}_j = -\bar{e}_j \bar{e}_i. \tag{3.8}$$

Note that the geometric product of two vectors equals the outer product only when both belong either to the null cone N or to the reciprocal cone $\overline{N}$. This is no longer true for arbitrary $\boldsymbol{x}$, $\boldsymbol{y} \in I\!R^{n,n}$ owing to the dual relationship of the reciprocal bases expressed by equations (3.7) and (3.8).

3.2.2 The universal geometric algebra $\mathcal{G}_{n,n}$

The vector bases of the reciprocal null cones N and $\overline{N}$ generate the 2^n-dimensional subalgebra $\mathcal{G}_N = gen\{e_1, ..., e_n\}$ and the 2^n-dimensional reciprocal subalgebra $\mathcal{G}_{\overline{N}} = gen\{\bar{e}_1, ..., \bar{e}_n\}$, which have the structure of Grassman algebras.

The geometric algebra $\mathcal{G}_{n,n}$ is built by the direct product of these 2^n-dimensional Grassmann subalgebras:

$$G_{n,n} = \mathcal{G}_N \otimes \mathcal{G}_{\overline{N}} = gen\{e_1, ..., e_n, \bar{e}_1, ..., \bar{e}_n\}. \tag{3.9}$$

When n is countably infinite, we call $\mathcal{G}_{\infty,\infty}$ the *universal geometric algebra.* The universal algebra $\mathcal{G}_{\infty,\infty}$ contains all of the algebras $\mathcal{G}_{n,n}$ as subalgebras.

The reciprocal bases $\{e\} \in N$ and $\{\bar{e}\} \in \bar{N}$ are also called *dual*, because they fulfill equation (3.6)—$\{e\} \cdot \{\bar{e}\}$=id. They generate the k-vector bases of $\mathcal{G}_{n,n}$,

$$\Big\{1, \{e\}, \{\bar{e}\}, \{e_i e_j\}, \{\bar{e}_i \bar{e}_j\}, \{e_i \bar{e}_j\}, \{e_i e_j \bar{e}_k\}, ..., \{e_{j_1} ... \bar{e}_{j_i} \bar{e}_{j_l} \ldots e_{j_k}\}, I, \bar{I}\Big\} \tag{3.10}$$

consisting of scalars, vectors, bivectors, trivectors, ... , and the dual pseudoscalars $I = e_1 \wedge e_2 \wedge e_3 ... \wedge e_n$ and $\bar{I} = \bar{e}_1 \wedge \bar{e}_2 \wedge \bar{e}_3 ... \wedge \bar{e}_n$ which satisfy $I\bar{I} = 1$. Note that the $\binom{2n}{k}$-dimensional bases of k-vectors $\{e_{j_1} ... \bar{e}_{j_i} \bar{e}_{j_l} \ldots e_{j_k}\}$ for the $\binom{2n}{k}$ sets of indices $1 \leq j_1 < j_2 < \ldots < j_k \leq 2n$ are generated by different combinations of e's and $\bar{e}$'s.

3.2.3 The standard bases of $\mathcal{G}_{n,n}$

In the previous subsections, we have discussed in some detail the *orthogonal null vector bases* $\{e_i, \bar{e}_i\}$ of the geometric algebra $\mathcal{G}_{n,n}$. Using these orthogonal null vector bases, we can construct new *orthonormal* bases $\{\sigma, \eta\}$ of $\mathcal{G}_{n,n}$,

$$\begin{aligned} \sigma_i &= \frac{1}{\sqrt{2}}(e_i + \bar{e}_i) \\ \eta_i &= \frac{1}{\sqrt{2}}(e_i - \bar{e}_i), \end{aligned} \tag{3.11}$$

for i=1, 2, 3, ... , n. According the properties of equations (3.6 to 3.8), these bases vectors for $i \neq j$ satisfy

$$\sigma_i{}^2 = 1,\ \sigma_i \cdot \sigma_j = \delta_{i,j},\ \sigma_i\sigma_j = -\sigma_j\sigma_i$$
$$\eta_i{}^2 = -1,\ \eta_i \cdot \eta_j = -\delta_{i,j},\ \eta_i \cdot \eta_j = -\eta_j\ \eta_i$$
$$\eta_i\sigma_j = -\sigma_j\eta_i,\ \eta_i \cdot \sigma_j = 0. \tag{3.12}$$

The basis $\{\sigma\}$ spans a real Euclidean vector space $I\!R^n$ and generates the geometric subalgebra $G_{n,0}$, whereas $\{\eta\}$ spans an anti-Euclidean space $R^{0,n}$ and generates the geometric subalgebra $G_{0,n}$. We can now express the geometric algebra $\mathcal{G}_{n,n}$ as the direct product of these geometric subalgebras:

$$\mathcal{G}_{n,n} = \mathcal{G}_{n,0} \otimes \mathcal{G}_{0,n} = gen\{\sigma_1, ..., \sigma_n, \eta_1, ..., \eta_n\}. \tag{3.13}$$

The dual pseudoscalars are given by $I = \sigma_1 \wedge \sigma_2 \wedge \sigma_3 ... \sigma_n$ and $\bar{I} = \eta_1 \wedge \eta_2 \wedge \eta_3 .. \wedge \eta_n$, which satisfy $I\bar{I} = 1$.

3.2.4 Representations and operations using bivector matrices

In this subsection, we use a notation which extends the familiar addition and multiplication of matrices of real numbers to matrices consisting of vectors and bivectors. The notation is somewhat similar to the Einstein summation convention of tensor calculus, and it can be used to directly express the close relationships that exist between Clifford algebra and matrix algebra [100].

We begin by writing the *Witte basis* of null vector $\{\mathbf{e}\}$ and the corresponding reciprocal basis $\{\bar{\mathbf{e}}\}$ of $\mathcal{G}_{n,n}$ in *row form* and *column form*, respectively:

$$\{e\} = (\, e_1 \quad e_2 \quad \cdot \quad \cdot \quad e_n\,), \qquad \{\bar{e}\} = \begin{pmatrix} \bar{e}_1 \\ \bar{e}_2 \\ \cdot \\ \cdot \\ \bar{e}_n \end{pmatrix}. \tag{3.14}$$

Taking advantage of the usual matrix multiplication between a *row* and a *column* and the properties of the geometric product, we get

$$\{\bar{e}\}\{e\} = \{\bar{e}\} \cdot \{e\} + \{\bar{e}\}\wedge\{e\} = \mathrm{I} + \begin{pmatrix} \bar{e}_1 \wedge e_1 & \bar{e}_1 \wedge e_2 & \dots & \bar{e}_1 \wedge e_n \\ \bar{e}_2 \wedge e_1 & \bar{e}_2 \wedge e_2 & \dots & \bar{e}_2 \wedge e_n \\ \dots & \dots & \dots & \dots \\ \dots & \dots & \dots & \dots \\ \bar{e}_n \wedge e_1 & \bar{e}_n \wedge e_2 & \dots & \bar{e}_n \wedge e_n \end{pmatrix} \tag{3.15}$$

where I is the $n \times n$ identity matrix. Similarly,

$$\{e\}\{\bar{e}\} = \{e\} \cdot \{\bar{e}\} + \{e\}\wedge\{\bar{e}\} = \sum_{i=1}^{n} e_i \cdot \bar{e}_i + \sum_{i=1}^{n} e_i \wedge \bar{e}_i \tag{3.16}$$

$$= n + \sum_{i=1}^{n} e_i \wedge \bar{e}_i. \tag{3.17}$$

In terms of the null cone bases, a vector $\boldsymbol{x} \in N$ is given by

$$\boldsymbol{x} = \{e\}\boldsymbol{x}_{\{e\}} = (e_1, e_2, ..., e_n) \begin{pmatrix} x_1 \\ x_2 \\ \cdot \\ \cdot \\ x_n \end{pmatrix} \tag{3.18}$$

$$= (e_1, e_2, ..., e_n) \begin{pmatrix} \bar{e}_1 \cdot \boldsymbol{x} \\ \bar{e}_2 \cdot \boldsymbol{x} \\ \cdot \\ \cdot \\ \bar{e}_n \cdot \boldsymbol{x} \end{pmatrix} = \{e\}(\{\bar{e}\} \cdot \boldsymbol{x}) = \sum_{i=1}^{n} x_i e_i. \tag{3.19}$$

The vectors $\boldsymbol{x} \in N$ behave like column vectors, and the vectors $\overline{\boldsymbol{x}} \in \overline{N}$ like row vectors. This property makes it possible to define the transpose of the vector $\boldsymbol{x}$ as follows:

$$\boldsymbol{x}^T = (\{e\}x_{\{e\}})^T = x_e^T\{\bar{e}\} = (x_1 x_2 ... x_n) \begin{pmatrix} \bar{e}_1 \\ \bar{e}_2 \\ \cdot \\ \cdot \\ \bar{e}_n \end{pmatrix}. \tag{3.20}$$

Note that using the transpose operation it is possible to move between the null cones N and $\overline{N}$.

3.2.5 Bivector representation of linear operators

One important application of the bivector matrix representation is the representation of a linear operator $f \in End(\mathcal{N})$. Recalling the basic Clifford algebra identity

$$(\boldsymbol{a} \wedge \boldsymbol{b}) \cdot \boldsymbol{x} = (\boldsymbol{b} \cdot \boldsymbol{x})\boldsymbol{a} - (\boldsymbol{a} \cdot \boldsymbol{x})\boldsymbol{b} \tag{3.21}$$

between the bivector $\boldsymbol{a} \wedge \boldsymbol{b}$ and the vector $\boldsymbol{x}$, we can use the reciprocal bases to express the vector $\boldsymbol{x}$ in the form

$$\boldsymbol{x} = \{e\}\boldsymbol{x}_{\{e\}} = (\{e\} \wedge \{\bar{e}\}) \cdot \boldsymbol{x}, \tag{3.22}$$

where $\boldsymbol{x}_{\{e\}}$ represents the *column vector* components of $\boldsymbol{x}$:

$$\boldsymbol{x}_{\{e\}} = \begin{pmatrix} x_1 \\ x_2 \\ \cdot \\ \cdot \\ x_n \end{pmatrix} = \begin{pmatrix} \bar{e}_1 \cdot \boldsymbol{x} \\ \bar{e}_2 \cdot \boldsymbol{x} \\ \cdot \\ \cdot \\ \bar{e}_n \cdot \boldsymbol{x} \end{pmatrix} = \{\bar{e}\} \cdot \boldsymbol{x}. \tag{3.23}$$

This is the *key idea* to the bivector representation of a linear operator. Let $f \in End(\mathcal{N})$, and we then have the following relationships:

$$\begin{aligned} f(\boldsymbol{x}) &= f(\{e\}\boldsymbol{x}_{\{e\}}) = \{e\}\mathcal{F}\boldsymbol{x}_{\{e\}} = \Big((\{e\}\mathcal{F})\wedge\{\bar{e}\}\Big)\cdot\boldsymbol{x} \\ &= F\cdot\boldsymbol{x}, \end{aligned} \tag{3.24}$$

where the bivector $F \in \mathcal{G}$ is defined by

$$F = (\{e\}\mathcal{F})\wedge\{\bar{e}\} = \sum_{i=1}^{n}\sum_{j=1}^{n} f_{ij}e_i\wedge\bar{e}_j = \{e\}\wedge(\mathcal{F}\{\bar{e}\}). \tag{3.25}$$

Thus, a linear operator $f \in End(\mathcal{N})$ can now be pictured as a linear mapping $f : \mathcal{N} \to \mathcal{N}$ of the null cone $\mathcal{N}$ onto itself. Furthermore, it can be represented in the bivector form $f(\boldsymbol{x}) = F\cdot\boldsymbol{x}$, where $F = (\{e\}\mathcal{F})\wedge\{\bar{e}\}$ is a bivector in the enveloping geometric algebra $\mathcal{G}$. As an example, we can show for the linear operator T its representation as a bivector matrix:

$$\begin{aligned} T &= \begin{bmatrix} t_{11} & t_{12} & t_{13} & t_{14} \\ t_{21} & t_{22} & t_{23} & t_{24} \\ t_{31} & t_{32} & t_{33} & t_{34} \\ t_{41} & t_{42} & t_{43} & t_{44} \end{bmatrix} \\ &\equiv \begin{bmatrix} t_{11}e_1\wedge\bar{e}_1 & t_{12}e_1\wedge\bar{e}_2 & t_{13}e_1\wedge\bar{e}_3 & t_{14}e_1\wedge\bar{e}_4 \\ t_{21}e_2\wedge\bar{e}_1 & t_{22}e_2\wedge\bar{e}_2 & t_{23}e_2\wedge\bar{e}_3 & t_{24}e_2\wedge\bar{e}_4 \\ t_{31}e_3\wedge\bar{e}_1 & t_{32}e_3\wedge\bar{e}_2 & t_{33}e_3\wedge\bar{e}_3 & t_{34}e_3\wedge\bar{e}_4 \\ t_{41}e_4\wedge\bar{e}_1 & t_{42}e_4\wedge\bar{e}_2 & t_{43}e_4\wedge\bar{e}_3 & t_{44}e_4\wedge\bar{e}_4 \end{bmatrix}. \end{aligned} \tag{3.26}$$

Now, by considering $f, g \in gl(\mathcal{N})$ in the bivector form $f(\boldsymbol{x}) = F\cdot\boldsymbol{x}$ and $g(\boldsymbol{x}) = G\cdot\boldsymbol{x}$, and by calculating the commutator $[f, g]$, we find

$$[f, g](\boldsymbol{x}) = F\cdot(G\cdot\boldsymbol{x}) - G\cdot(F\cdot\boldsymbol{x}) = (F\times G)\cdot\boldsymbol{x}, \tag{3.27}$$

where the *commutator product of bivectors* $F\times G$ is defined by $F\times G = \frac{1}{2}[FG - GF]$. Thus the Lie bracket of the linear operators f and g becomes the commutator product of their respective bivectors F and G.

3.3 Horosphere and n-Dimensional Affine Plane

This section explains briefly the meaning of the computational frameworks the horosphere and the n-dimensional affine plane, which are useful in the study of conformal transformations [84]. This kind of transformation preserves angles between tangent vectors at each point. A common conformal transformation is the one defined by any analytic function in the complex plane. Conformal transformations also exist in the *pseudo-Euclidean* space $\mathbb{R}^{p,q}$. Since conformal transformations are nonlinear transformations, it will be desirable to linearize them. One way to do so is by moving up from the affine plane $\mathcal{A}_e(\mathbb{R}^{p,q})$ to the (p, q)-horosphere $\mathcal{H}_e^{p,q}(R^{p+1,q+1})$.

The *n-dimensional affine plane* $\mathcal{A}_e(\mathbb{R}^{p,q})$ is a homogenous representation of the points $\boldsymbol{x} \in \mathbb{R}^{p,q}$. It extends the $\mathbb{R}^{p,q}$ to a projective space with signature $\mathbb{R}^{p,q,1}$ using a null vector $\boldsymbol{e}$ as follows:

$$\boldsymbol{x}_h = \boldsymbol{x} + e \in \mathcal{A}_e(\mathbb{R}^{p,q}). \tag{3.28}$$

The (p, q)- horosphere is normally defined by

$$\mathcal{H}_e^{p,q}(R^{p+1,q+1}) = \{\frac{1}{2}\boldsymbol{x}_h\bar{e}\boldsymbol{x}_h | \boldsymbol{x}_h \in \mathcal{A}_e(\mathbb{R}^{p,q})\} \in R^{p+1,q+1}, \tag{3.29}$$

where the space $\mathbb{R}^{p,q}$ has been extended to $\mathbb{R}^{p+1,q+1}$ in order to have available two null vectors, $e = e_{n+1}$ and $\bar{e} = \bar{e}_{n+1}$. The conformal representation $\boldsymbol{x}_c$ of both a point $\boldsymbol{x} \in R^{p,q}$ and a point $\boldsymbol{x}_h \in \mathcal{A}_e(\mathbb{R}^{p,q})$ is given by

$$\begin{aligned} \boldsymbol{x}_c &= \frac{1}{2}\boldsymbol{x}_h\bar{e}\boldsymbol{x}_h = \frac{1}{2}[(\boldsymbol{x}_h \cdot \bar{e})\boldsymbol{x}_h + (\boldsymbol{x}_h \wedge \bar{e})\boldsymbol{x}_h] = \boldsymbol{x}_h - \frac{1}{2}\boldsymbol{x}_h^2\bar{e} = \boldsymbol{x} - \frac{1}{2}\boldsymbol{x}_h^2\bar{e} + e \\ &= exp(\frac{1}{2}\boldsymbol{x}\bar{e})\ e\ exp(-\frac{1}{2}\boldsymbol{x}\bar{e}). \end{aligned} \tag{3.30}$$

This equation tells us that all points on $\mathcal{H}_e^{p,q}$ can be obtained by a simple rotation of e with respect to the plane indicated by the bivector $\boldsymbol{x}\bar{e}$.

The points of the horosphere can be projected down into the affine plane by applying the simple formula,

$$\boldsymbol{x}_h = (\boldsymbol{x}_c \wedge \bar{e}) \cdot e, \tag{3.31}$$

and into the space $\mathbb{R}^{p,q}$ by using

$$\boldsymbol{x} = (\boldsymbol{x}_c \wedge \bar{e} \wedge e) \cdot (\bar{e} \wedge e). \tag{3.32}$$

Fig. 3.1 depicts

$$\begin{aligned} \mathcal{A}_e^2 &= \{\boldsymbol{x}_h | \boldsymbol{x}_h = \boldsymbol{x} + e, \boldsymbol{x} \in \mathbb{R}^2\}, \\ \mathcal{H}_e^2 &= \{\boldsymbol{x}_c = \frac{1}{2}\boldsymbol{x}_h\bar{e}\boldsymbol{x}_h | \boldsymbol{x}_h \in \mathcal{A}_e^2\}. \end{aligned} \tag{3.33}$$

Since $\boldsymbol{x} \in \mathbb{R}^2 = span\{\sigma_1, \sigma_2\}$, $e = \frac{1}{2}(\sigma + \eta)$, and $\bar{e} = \sigma - \eta$, any point on the horosphere in these terms is given by

$$\boldsymbol{x}_c = \boldsymbol{x} - \frac{1}{2}\boldsymbol{x}^2\bar{e} + e = \boldsymbol{x} - \frac{1}{2}(\boldsymbol{x}^2 - 1)\sigma + \frac{1}{2}(\boldsymbol{x}^2 + 1)\eta = \boldsymbol{x} + x_3\sigma + x_4\eta. \tag{3.34}$$

In order to be able to depict the horosphere in 3D, in the Fig. 3.1 we have ignored the coordinate x_3, considering instead the condition that η is orthogonal to σ_1, σ_2. In Section 3.7, we will use the frameworks of the n-dimensional affine plane and horosphere for computations of incidence algebra.

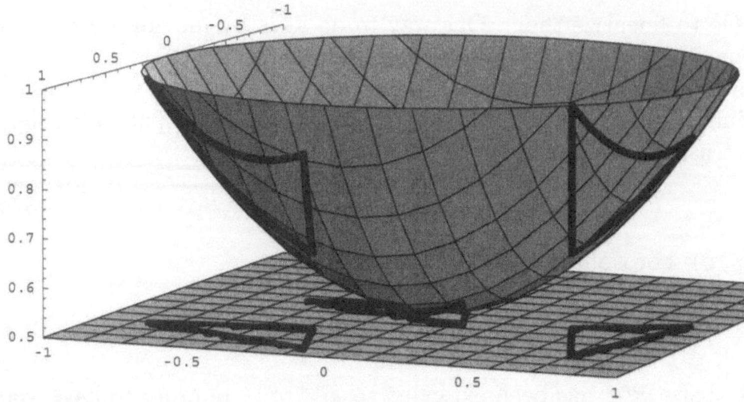

FIGURE 3.1. Horosphere of R^2 with triangles of the 2D affine plane projected into the horosphere

3.4 The General Linear Group

The general linear group $GL(\mathcal{N})$ is defined to be the subset of all *endomorphisms* $f \in End(\mathcal{N})$, with the property that $f \in GL(\mathcal{N})$ if and only if $\det(f) \neq 0$ [13]. The determinant of f is defined in the algebra $\mathcal{G}_N$ by

$$f(e_1)\wedge f(e_2)\wedge \ldots \wedge f(e_n) = \det(\mathcal{F})e_1\wedge e_2\wedge \ldots \wedge e_n, \tag{3.35}$$

where $\det(\mathcal{F})$ is just the ordinary determinant of the matrix of f with respect to the basis $\{\boldsymbol{e}\}$. Choosing the basis $\{\boldsymbol{e}\}$ makes explicit the isomorphism between the general linear groups $GL(\mathcal{N})$ and $GL(n, \mathcal{C})$. The latter corresponds to the general linear group of all complex $n \times n$ matrices $\mathcal{F}$ with $\det \mathcal{F} \neq 0$. The theory of Lie groups and their corresponding Lie algebras can be considered to be largely the study of the group-manifold $GL(n, \mathcal{C})$, since any Lie group is isomorphic to a subgroup of $GL(n, \mathcal{C})$ [34, p. 501].

Since we have referred to $GL(\mathcal{N})$ as a *manifold*, we must be careful to give it the structure of an n^2-dimensional topological metric space. We define the inner product $< f, g >$ of $f, g \in GL(\mathcal{N})$ to be the usual hermitian positive definite inner product

$$< f, g >= \sum_{j=1}^{n}\sum_{i=1}^{n} \overline{f_{ij}} g_{ij},$$

where $f_{ij}, g_{ij} \in \boldsymbol{C}$ are the components of the matrices $\mathcal{F}$ and $\mathcal{G}$ of f and g, respectively, with respect to the basis $\{\boldsymbol{e}\}$. The positive definite norm $|f|$ of $f \in GL(\mathcal{N})$ is defined by

$$|f|^2 =< f, f >= \sum_{j=1}^{n}\sum_{i=1}^{n} \overline{f_{ij}} f_{ij}$$

and is clearly zero if and only if $f = 0$.

The crucial relationship between a Lie group and its corresponding Lie algebra is almost an immediate consequence of the properties of the exponential of a linear operator $f \in End(\mathcal{N})$. The *exponential mapping* may be directly defined by the usual Taylor series

$$e^f = \sum_{i=0}^{\infty} \frac{f^i}{i!},$$

where convergence is with respect to the norm $|f|$. Note that $f^0 = 1$ is the identity operator on $\mathcal{N}$, and that f^k is the composition of f with itself k times.

The logarithm of a linear operator, $\theta_f = \log(f)$, exists and is well defined for any $f \in GL(\mathcal{N})$. The logarithm can also be defined in terms of an infinite series, or more directly, in terms of the *spectral form* of f [98]. Since the logarithm is the inverse function of the exponential function, we can write $f = e^{\theta_f}$ for any $f \in GL(\mathcal{N})$. The logarithmic form $f = e^{\theta_f}$ of $f \in GL(\mathcal{N})$ is useful for defining the *one-parameter group* $\{f_t\}$ of the operator $f \in GL(\mathcal{N})$,

$$f_t(\boldsymbol{x}) = e^{t\theta_f}\boldsymbol{x}. \tag{3.36}$$

The one parameter group $\{f_t\}$ is *continuously connected to the identity* in the sense that $f_0(\boldsymbol{x}) = \boldsymbol{x}$, and $f_1(\boldsymbol{x}) = f(\boldsymbol{x})$. Note that

$$f_0'(\boldsymbol{x}) = \theta_f e^{t\theta_f}|_{t=0}(\boldsymbol{x}) = \theta_f(\boldsymbol{x}), \tag{3.37}$$

so θ_f is *tangent* to f_t at the identity. The reason that $\{f_t\}$ is called a one-parameter group is because it satisfies the basic additive property

$$f_s\, f_t = e^{t\theta_f}e^{s\theta_f} = e^{(s+t)\theta_f} = f_{s+t}. \tag{3.38}$$

Since each linear operator $f \in End(\mathcal{N})$ can be represented according to equation(3.24) in the bivector form $f(x) = F \cdot \boldsymbol{x}$, we can express the one-parameter group $g_t x = e^{tf}x$ of the skew-symmetric transformation $f(x) = F \cdot x$ in the form

$$g_t x = e^{tf}x \equiv e^{\frac{t}{2}F}xe^{-\frac{t}{2}F}. \tag{3.39}$$

This equation can be proved by showing that the terms of the Taylor series expansion of both sides of equation (3.39) are identical at $t = 0$.

We begin with

$$e^{tf}x \doteq e^{\frac{t}{2}F}xe^{-\frac{t}{2}F}. \tag{3.40}$$

Clearly, for $t = 0$, we have

$$e^{0f}x = e^{0F}xe^{0F} = x.$$

Next, taking the first derivative of both sides of equation (3.40), we get

$$e^{tf}fx \doteq \frac{1}{2}Fe^{\frac{t}{2}F}xe^{-\frac{t}{2}F} - \frac{1}{2}Fe^{\frac{t}{2}F}xe^{-\frac{t}{2}F} = e^{\frac{t}{2}F}(F\cdot x)e^{-\frac{t}{2}F}. \tag{3.41}$$

Setting t equal to zero gives the identity $f(x) = F \cdot x$.

Taking the derivative of both sides of (3.41) gives

$$e^{tf}f^2x \doteq \frac{1}{2}Fe^{\frac{t}{2}F}(F\cdot x)e^{-\frac{t}{2}F} - \frac{1}{2}Fe^{\frac{t}{2}F}(F\cdot x)e^{-\frac{t}{2}F} = e^{\frac{t}{2}F}[F\cdot(F\cdot x)]e^{-\frac{t}{2}F},$$

and setting t equal to zero gives the identity $f^2(x) = F\cdot(F\cdot x)$. Continuing to take successive derivatives of (3.40) gives

$$e^{tf}f^k(x) \doteq e^{\frac{t}{2}F}(F^k : x)e^{-\frac{t}{2}F}, \tag{3.42}$$

where $F^k : x$ is defined recursively by $F^1 : x = F \cdot x$ and

$$F^k : x = F\cdot(F^{k-1} : x). \tag{3.43}$$

Finally, setting t equal to zero in equation (3.42) gives the identity

$$f^k(x) = F^k : x.$$

Equation (3.43) is interesting because it expresses the powers of a linear operator in terms of "powers" of its defining bivector. It is clear that each bivector defines a unique skew-symmetric linear operator, and conversely, that each skew-symmetric linear operator defines a unique bivector (see equation (3.24)). Thus, the study of the structure of a bivector is determined by and uniquely determines the corresponding structure of the corresponding linear operator. The the proof of the above theorem is attributable to Marcel Riesz [87].

3.4.1 The general linear algebra $gl(\mathcal{N})$ of the general linear Lie group $GL(\mathcal{N})$

We can now define the *general linear Lie algebra* $gl(\mathcal{N})$ of the general linear Lie group $GL(\mathcal{N})$. As a set, $gl(\mathcal{N}) \equiv End(\mathcal{N})$, which is just the set of all *tangent operators* $\theta_f = \log(f) \in End(\mathcal{N})$ to the one-parameter groups $f_t = e^{t\theta_f}$ defined for each $f \in GL(\mathcal{N})$. But to complete the definition of $gl(\mathcal{N})$, we must specify the algebraic operations of addition and multiplication which allow $End(\mathcal{N})$ to be seen as the Lie algebra $gl(\mathcal{N})$. Addition requires only the ordinary addition of linear operators, but multiplication is defined by the *Lie bracket* $[\theta_f, \theta_g]$ for $\theta_f, \theta_g \in gl(\mathcal{N})$. We will give an analytic definition of the Lie bracket [74, p. 3] which directly ties it to the group structure of $GL(\mathcal{N})$

$$[\theta_f, \theta_g] = \frac{d}{d(t^2)} f_t g_t f_{-t} g_{-t}|_{t=0} = \frac{1}{2t}\frac{d}{dt} f_t g_t f_{-t} g_{-t}|_{t=0},$$

Evaluating the Lie bracket by using the Taylor series expansions,

$$
\begin{aligned}
[\theta_f, \theta_g] &= \frac{1}{2t}\frac{d}{dt}(f_t g_t f_{-t} g_{-t})\big|_{t=0} \\
&= \frac{1}{2t}(\theta_f f_t g_t f_{-t} g_{-t} + f_t \theta_g g_t f_{-t} g_{-t} - f_t g_t \theta_f f_{-t} g_{-t} - f_t g_t f_{-t} \theta_g g_{-t}) \\
&= (\frac{1}{2t} f_t(\theta_f g_t - g_t \theta_f) f_{-t} g_{-t})|_{t=0} + (\frac{1}{2t} f_t g_t (\theta_g f_{-t} - f_{-t}\theta_g) g_{-t})|_{t=0} \\
&= \frac{1}{2}(\theta_f \theta_g - \theta_g \theta_f) + \frac{1}{2}(-\theta_g \theta_f + \theta_f \theta_g) \\
&= \theta_f \theta_g - \theta_g \theta_f, \qquad (3.44)
\end{aligned}
$$

we find that

$$
g_t = 1 + t\theta_g + \ldots, \quad \text{and} \quad f_{-t} = 1 - t\theta_f + \ldots .
$$

We have thus demonstrated that the Lie bracket, defined analytically above, reduces simply to the commutator product of the linear operators θ_f and θ_g in $gl(\mathcal{N})$. As such, it is not difficult to show that it satisfies the famous *Jacobi identity*, which is equivalent to the distributive law

$$
[\theta_f, [\theta_g, \theta_h]] = [[\theta_f, \theta_g], \theta_h] + [\theta_g, [\theta_f, \theta_h]]. \qquad (3.45)
$$

When we choose a particular basis $\{e\}$ of $\mathcal{N}$, the isomorphism between the general linear Lie algebra $gl(n, \mathcal{C})$ and $gl(\mathcal{N})$ becomes explicit, and the Lie bracket of linear operators just becomes the Lie bracket of $n \times n$ matrices,

$$
[f, g]\{e\} = fg\{e\} - gf\{e\} = \{e\}(\mathcal{F}\mathcal{G} - \mathcal{G}\mathcal{F}) = \{e\}[\mathcal{F}, \mathcal{G}], \qquad (3.46)
$$

where $[\mathcal{F}, \mathcal{G}]$ are the commutator products of the matrices $\mathcal{F}$ and $\mathcal{G}$. Alternatively, using the bivector representation of equation (3.24), the Lie bracket of linear operators is expressed in terms of the Lie bracket of the bivectors of the operators (3.27).

3.4.2 The orthogonal groups

The simplest well-known example of an *orthogonal group* is $SO(2)$, which is a subgroup of the general linear group $GL(\mathcal{N}^2)$. As a matrix group, it is generated by all 2×2 matrices of the form

$$
X_\theta = \begin{pmatrix} \cos\theta & -\sin\theta \\ \sin\theta & \cos\theta \end{pmatrix}. \qquad (3.47)
$$

The matrix X_θ generates a counterclockwise rotation in the xy-plane through the angle θ. Using (3.24), we get the corresponding bivector representation

$$
\boldsymbol{X}_\theta = \cos(\theta) e_1 \wedge \bar{e}_1 - \sin(\theta) e_1 \wedge \bar{e}_2 + \sin(\theta) e_2 \wedge \bar{e}_1 + \cos(\theta) e_2 \wedge \bar{e}_2. \qquad (3.48)
$$

For matrices $X_{\theta_1}, X_{\theta_2} \in SO(2)$, the group operation is ordinary matrix multiplication, $X_{\theta_2}X_{\theta_1} = X_{\theta_1+\theta_2}$. For the bivector representation $\boldsymbol{X}_{\theta_1}, \boldsymbol{X}_{\theta_2} \in SO(2)$, the group operation is defined by its *generalized dot product*, that is, for $\boldsymbol{x} \in \mathcal{N}^2$,

$$(\boldsymbol{X}_{\theta_1} : \boldsymbol{X}_{\theta_2}) \equiv \boldsymbol{X}_{\theta_2} \cdot (\boldsymbol{X}_{\theta_1} \cdot \boldsymbol{x}) = \boldsymbol{X}_{\theta_1+\theta_2} \cdot \boldsymbol{x}. \tag{3.49}$$

Note that the bivectors $\boldsymbol{X}_\theta$ are in $\mathcal{G}^2_{n,n}$.

Taking the derivatives of X_θ and $\boldsymbol{X}_\theta$ with respect to θ and evaluating at $\theta = 0$ gives the corresponding generators of the associated Lie algebra $so(2)$. As a matrix Lie algebra under the bracket operation of matricies, we find the generator

$$\frac{dX_\theta}{d\theta}|_{\theta\to 0} = \begin{pmatrix} 0 & -1 \\ 1 & 0 \end{pmatrix}. \tag{3.50}$$

As a bivector Lie algebra under the bracket operation of bivectors, we use equation (3.48) to find the bivector generator

$$\boldsymbol{B} = \frac{d\boldsymbol{X}_\theta}{d\theta}|_{\theta\to 0} = -\boldsymbol{e}_1\wedge\overline{\boldsymbol{e}}_2 + \boldsymbol{e}_2\wedge\overline{\boldsymbol{e}}_1 = -\sigma_{12} + \eta_{12}. \tag{3.51}$$

The *spinor group* $Spin(2)$ is defined by taking the exponential of the bivector (see equation (3.51)),

$$Spin(2) = \{\exp(\frac{1}{2}\theta\boldsymbol{B})| \ \ \theta \in \mathbb{R}\}.$$

According to Sobczyk [99], the exponential $\exp(\frac{1}{2}\theta\boldsymbol{B})$ can be calculated by noting that the bivector $\boldsymbol{B}$ satisfies the *minimal polynomial*

$$\boldsymbol{B}^3 + 4\boldsymbol{B} = \boldsymbol{B}(\boldsymbol{B} - 2i)(\boldsymbol{B} + 2i) = 0,$$

which implies the decomposition

$$\boldsymbol{B} = 0p_1 + 2ip_2 - 2ip_3,$$

where the mutually annihiliating idempotents are defined by

$$p_1 = \frac{\boldsymbol{B}^2 + 4}{4}, \ \ p_2 = -\frac{1}{8}\boldsymbol{B}(\boldsymbol{B} + 2i), \ \ p_3 = -\frac{1}{8}\boldsymbol{B}(\boldsymbol{B} - 2i).$$

Using this decomposition, we find that

$$\begin{aligned} \exp(\frac{1}{2}\theta\boldsymbol{B}) &= \exp(\frac{0\cdot\theta}{2})p_1 + \exp(i\theta)p_2 + \exp(-i\theta)p_3 \\ &= p_1 + \cos(\theta)(p_2 + p_3) + \sin(\theta)i(p_2 - p_3) \\ &= p_1 + \cos(\theta)(p_2 + p_3) + \frac{\boldsymbol{B}}{2}\sin(\theta). \end{aligned} \tag{3.52}$$

The group action of the *spinor group* $Spin(2)$ is given by

$$\boldsymbol{x}' = \exp(\frac{1}{2}\theta \boldsymbol{B})\boldsymbol{x}\exp(-\frac{1}{2}\theta \boldsymbol{B}),$$

where $\boldsymbol{x} = \{\boldsymbol{e}\}x_{\{\boldsymbol{e}\}} = x_1\boldsymbol{e}_1 + x_2\boldsymbol{e}_2$. We say that $Spin(2)$ is a "double covering" of the orthogonal group $SO(2)$ because the spinors $\pm\exp(\frac{1}{2}\theta\boldsymbol{B})$ represent the same group element. Note that now we can formulate the easy rule for the composition of two group elements, $\exp(\frac{1}{2}\theta_1\boldsymbol{B})$ and $\exp(\frac{1}{2}\theta_2\boldsymbol{B})$,

$$\exp(\frac{1}{2}\theta_1\boldsymbol{B})\exp(\frac{1}{2}\theta_2\boldsymbol{B}) = \exp(\frac{1}{2}(\theta_1+\theta_2)\boldsymbol{B}).$$

If we are only interested in the group $SO(2)$, a more natural place to carry out the calculations is in the Euclidean space $\mathbb{R}^2$. We project the null cone $\mathcal{N}^2$ down to $\mathbb{R}^2$ by using the reciprocal pseudoscalars I_2 and $\overline{I_2}$ defined by

$$I_2 = \sigma_1\sigma_2 \quad \text{and} \quad \overline{I_2} = (2-\sqrt{2})^2(\bar{e}_2+\sigma_2)(\bar{e}_1+\sigma_1).$$

Thus, for $\boldsymbol{x} = \{e\}\boldsymbol{x}_{\{e\}} = x_1e_1 + x_2e_2 \in \mathcal{N}^2$, the projection $\boldsymbol{x}' = P_I(\boldsymbol{x})$ gives

$$\boldsymbol{x}' = P_I(\boldsymbol{x}) = (\boldsymbol{x}\cdot\overline{I})\cdot I = x_1\sigma_1 + x_2\sigma_2 \in \mathbb{R}^2.$$

Note that this projection is invertible, in the sense that we can find $P_{I'}$ such that $\boldsymbol{x} = P_{I'}(\boldsymbol{x}')$. The projection $P_{I'}$ is specified by

$$\boldsymbol{x} = P_{I'}(\boldsymbol{x}') = (\boldsymbol{x}'\cdot\overline{I})\cdot I' = x_1e_1 + x_2e_2,$$

where $\overline{I}$ is defined as before and where $I' = e_1e_2$.

In $\mathbb{R}^2$ the generator of rotations is the simple bivector $\sigma_2\sigma_1$. This bivector can be obtained from the bivector (3.51) in $spin(2,2)$ by the simple projection

$$P_I(\boldsymbol{B}) = I_2^{-1}I_2\cdot\boldsymbol{B} = \sigma_2\sigma_1 = -I_2$$

onto the Lie algebra $so(2)$. For $\boldsymbol{x}' = x_1\sigma_1 + x_2\sigma_2 \in \mathbb{R}^2$, the equivalent rotation is given by

$$\boldsymbol{y}' = \exp(\frac{1}{2}\theta\sigma_2\sigma_1)\boldsymbol{x}'\exp(-\frac{1}{2}\theta\sigma_2\sigma_1).$$

The above ideas can be immediately generalized to the general Lie group $GL(\mathcal{N}^n)$ of null cone $\mathcal{N}^n$ and the orthogonal subgroups $SO(p,q)$ where $p+q = n$. The orthogonal group $SO(p,q)$ acts on the space $\mathbb{R}^{p,q}$. Thus, if we wish to work in this Lie group or in the corresponding Lie algebra, we first project the null cone $\mathcal{N}^n$ onto $\mathbb{R}^{p,q}$ by using the reciprocal vector basis elements, then carry out the rotation, and finally return to the null cone by using the inverse projection.

3.5 Computing Rigid Motion in the Affine Plane

A rotation in the affine n-plane $\mathcal{A}_e^n = \mathcal{A}_e(\mathbb{R}^n)$, just as in the Euclidean space $\mathbb{R}^n$, is the product of two reflections through two intersecting hyperplanes. If the normal unit vectors to these hyperplanes are m and n, respectively, then the versor of the rotation is given by

$$R = mn = e^{\frac{\theta}{2}B} = \cos(\frac{\theta}{2}) + B\sin(\frac{\theta}{2}), \tag{3.53}$$

where B is the unit bivector defining the plane of the rotation.

A translation of the vector $x_h \in \mathcal{A}_e^n$, along the vector $t \in \mathbb{R}^n$, to the vector $x'_h = x_h + t \in \mathcal{A}_e^n$, is effected by the versor

$$T = \exp(\frac{1}{2}t\bar{e}) = 1 + \frac{1}{2}t\bar{e} \tag{3.54}$$

when it is followed by the projection $P_A(x') \equiv (x \wedge \bar{e}) \cdot e$, which brings the horosphere *back* into the affine plane. Thus, for $x_h \in \mathcal{A}_e^n$, we get

$$\begin{aligned} x' &= TxT^{-1} = \exp(\frac{1}{2}t\bar{e})x_h\exp(-\frac{1}{2}t\bar{e}) \\ &= (1 + \frac{1}{2}t\bar{e})x_h(1 - \frac{1}{2}t\bar{e}) = x_h + \frac{1}{2}t\bar{e}x_h - \frac{1}{2}x_h t\bar{e} - \frac{1}{4}t\bar{e}x_h t\bar{e} \\ &= x_h + t + t\cdot(\bar{e}\wedge x^h) - \frac{1}{2}t^2\bar{e} \\ &= x_h + t - (t\cdot x_h + \frac{1}{2}t^2)\bar{e}. \end{aligned} \tag{3.55}$$

Applying P_A to this result, we get the expected translated vector

$$x'_h = P_A(x') = P_A[x_h + t - (t\cdot x_h + \frac{1}{2}t^2)\bar{e}] = x_h + t. \tag{3.56}$$

The advantage of carrying out translations in the affine plane rather than in the horosphere is that the affine plane is basically still a linear model of Euclidean space, whereas the horosphere is a more complicated *nonlinear* model.

Combining the versors for a rotation and a translation, we get the expression for the versor $M = TR$ of a rigid motion. For $x_h \in \mathcal{A}_e^n$, we then find that

$$x'_h = P_A[Mx_hM^{-1}] = P_A[TRx_hR^{-1}T^{-1}]. \tag{3.57}$$

Equivalently, we will often write $M^{-1} \equiv \widetilde{M}$, expressing M^{-1} in terms of the operation of *conjugation.* Whenever a calculation involves a translation, we must always apply the projection P_A to guarantee that our end-result will be in the affine plane. The above calculations can be checked with the Clifford algebra calculator CLICAL 4.0 [69]. Comparisons can also be made to the corresponding calculations made by Hestenes and Li [67] on the horosphere.

3.6 The Lie Algebra of the Affine Plane

The Lie algebra of the neutral affine plane $\mathcal{A}_{e_3}(\mathcal{N}^2)$ is useful in the analysis of visual invariants [55], so we will begin with its treatment here. The well-known matrix representation of the Lie group of affine transformations in the plane has six independent parameters, or degrees of freedom, and consists of all matrices of the form

$$g(A, \boldsymbol{v}) = \begin{bmatrix} a_{11} & a_{12} & a \\ a_{21} & a_{22} & b \\ 0 & 0 & 1 \end{bmatrix}, \tag{3.58}$$

where $\det g(A, \boldsymbol{v}) = \det A \neq 0$.

The one-parameter subgroups are generated by the matrices

$$\begin{aligned} T_x &= \begin{bmatrix} 1 & 0 & x \\ 0 & 1 & 0 \\ 0 & 0 & 1 \end{bmatrix}, & T_y &= \begin{bmatrix} 1 & 0 & 0 \\ 0 & 1 & y \\ 0 & 0 & 1 \end{bmatrix}, \\ D_u &= \begin{bmatrix} e^u & 0 & 0 \\ 0 & e^u & 0 \\ 0 & 0 & 1 \end{bmatrix}, & R_\theta &= \begin{bmatrix} cos(\theta) & -sin(\theta) & 0 \\ sin(\theta) & cos(\theta) & 0 \\ 0 & 0 & 1 \end{bmatrix}, \\ S_v &= \begin{bmatrix} e^v & 0 & 0 \\ 0 & e^{-v} & 0 \\ 0 & 0 & 1 \end{bmatrix}, & H_\phi &= \begin{bmatrix} cosh(\phi) & sinh(\phi) & 0 \\ sinh(\phi) & cosh(\phi) & 0 \\ 0 & 0 & 1 \end{bmatrix}. \end{aligned} \tag{3.59}$$

Using equation (3.37), we obtain the matrix representation of the Lie algebra basis generators by taking the derivative of equation (3.59) and evaluating the parameter at zero:

$$\begin{aligned} \mathcal{L}_x &= \begin{pmatrix} 0 & 0 & 1 \\ 0 & 0 & 0 \\ 0 & 0 & 0 \end{pmatrix}, & \mathcal{L}_y &= \begin{pmatrix} 0 & 0 & 0 \\ 0 & 0 & 1 \\ 0 & 0 & 0 \end{pmatrix}, \\ \mathcal{L}_s &= \begin{pmatrix} 1 & 0 & 0 \\ 0 & 1 & 0 \\ 0 & 0 & 0 \end{pmatrix}, & \mathcal{L}_r &= \begin{pmatrix} 0 & -1 & 0 \\ 1 & 0 & 0 \\ 0 & 0 & 0 \end{pmatrix}, \\ \mathcal{L}_b &= \begin{pmatrix} 1 & 0 & 0 \\ 0 & -1 & 0 \\ 0 & 0 & 0 \end{pmatrix}, & \mathcal{L}_B &= \begin{pmatrix} 0 & 1 & 0 \\ 1 & 0 & 0 \\ 0 & 0 & 0 \end{pmatrix}. \end{aligned} \tag{3.60}$$

The above matrix Lie group and matrix Lie algebra can be directly translated into the corresponding Lie group and Lie algebra of the affine plane $\mathcal{A}_{e_3}(\mathcal{N}^2)$. Each of the matrix generators in (3.59) and (3.60) can be replaced by its corresponding bivector representation (3.24). For example, the bivector representations of the generators of the Lie algebra are

$$\begin{aligned}
\mathcal{L}_x &= bivector(\mathcal{L}_x) = e_1 \wedge \bar{e}_3, \\
\mathcal{L}_y &= bivector(\mathcal{L}_y) = e_2 \wedge \bar{e}_3, \\
\mathcal{L}_s &= bivector(\mathcal{L}_s) = e_1 \wedge \bar{e}_1 + e_2 \wedge \bar{e}_2, \\
\mathcal{L}_r &= bivector(\mathcal{L}_r) = e_2 \wedge \bar{e}_1 - e_1 \wedge \bar{e}_2, \\
\mathcal{L}_b &= bivector(\mathcal{L}_b) = e_1 \wedge \bar{e}_1 - e_2 \wedge \bar{e}_2, \\
\mathcal{L}_B &= bivector(\mathcal{L}_\phi) = e_1 \wedge \bar{e}_2 + e_2 \wedge \bar{e}_1.
\end{aligned} \tag{3.61}$$

Expanding these bivector generators in the standard basis (3.11), we get

$$\begin{aligned}
\mathcal{L}_x &= \tfrac{1}{2}\sigma_1\sigma_3 - \tfrac{1}{2}\sigma_1\eta_3 - \tfrac{1}{2}\sigma_3\eta_1 - \tfrac{1}{2}\eta_1\eta_3, \\
\mathcal{L}_y &= \tfrac{1}{2}\sigma_2\sigma_3 - \tfrac{1}{2}\sigma_2\eta_3 - \tfrac{1}{2}a_3\eta_2 - \tfrac{1}{2}\eta_2\eta_3, \\
\mathcal{L}_s &= -\sigma_1\eta_1 - \sigma_2\eta_2, \\
\mathcal{L}_r &= -\sigma_1\sigma_2 + \eta_1\eta_2, \\
\mathcal{L}_b &= -\sigma_1\eta_1 + \sigma_2\eta_2, \\
\mathcal{L}_B &= -\sigma_1\eta_2 - \sigma_2\eta_1.
\end{aligned} \tag{3.62}$$

Let us see how the Lie algebra of the affine plane can be represented as a Lie algebra of vector fields over the null cone $\mathcal{N}^3$. The *vector derivative* or *gradient* $\partial_{\boldsymbol{x}} = \frac{\partial}{\partial \boldsymbol{x}}$ at the point $\boldsymbol{x} = xe_1 + ye_2 + ze_3 \in \mathcal{N}^3$ is defined by requiring $\boldsymbol{a} \cdot \partial_{\boldsymbol{x}}$ to be the *directional derivative* in the direction of $\boldsymbol{a}$. It follows that $\boldsymbol{a} \cdot \partial_{\boldsymbol{x}} \boldsymbol{x} = \boldsymbol{a}$. We also have

$$\partial_{\boldsymbol{x}} \boldsymbol{x} = \partial_{\boldsymbol{x}} \cdot \boldsymbol{x} + \partial_{\boldsymbol{x}} \wedge \boldsymbol{x} = 3 + \sum_{i=1}^{3} \bar{e}_i \wedge e_i,$$

where e and $\bar{e}$ are reciprocal bases for the reciprocal null cones $\mathcal{N}^3$ and $\overline{\mathcal{N}^3}$.

Now, let $\boldsymbol{a} = \boldsymbol{a}(\boldsymbol{x})$ and $\boldsymbol{b} = \boldsymbol{b}(\boldsymbol{x})$ be vector fields in $\mathcal{N}^3$. The Lie bracket $[\boldsymbol{a}, \boldsymbol{b}]$ is defined by

$$[\boldsymbol{a}, \boldsymbol{b}] = \boldsymbol{a} \cdot \partial_{\boldsymbol{x}} \boldsymbol{b} - \boldsymbol{b} \cdot \partial_{\boldsymbol{x}} \boldsymbol{a}.$$

Since in $\mathcal{N}^3$, $\partial_{\boldsymbol{x}} \wedge \partial_{\boldsymbol{x}} = 0$, we have the important integrability condition that

$$(\boldsymbol{a} \wedge \boldsymbol{b}) \cdot (\partial_{\boldsymbol{x}} \wedge \partial_{\boldsymbol{x}}) = [\boldsymbol{a}, \boldsymbol{b}] \cdot \partial_{\boldsymbol{x}} - [\boldsymbol{a} \cdot \partial_{\boldsymbol{x}}, \boldsymbol{b} \cdot \partial_{\boldsymbol{x}}] = 0,$$

where

$$[\boldsymbol{a} \cdot \partial_{\boldsymbol{x}}, \boldsymbol{b} \cdot \partial_{\boldsymbol{x}}] = \boldsymbol{a} \cdot \partial_{\boldsymbol{x}} \boldsymbol{b} \cdot \partial_{\boldsymbol{x}} - \boldsymbol{b} \cdot \partial_{\boldsymbol{x}} \boldsymbol{a} \cdot \partial_{\boldsymbol{x}}$$

is the Lie bracket or commutator product of the partial derivatives $\boldsymbol{a} \cdot \partial_{\boldsymbol{x}}$ and $\boldsymbol{b} \cdot \partial_{\boldsymbol{x}}$. It follows from this identity that

$$[\boldsymbol{a}, \boldsymbol{b}] \cdot \partial_{\boldsymbol{x}} = [\boldsymbol{a} \cdot \partial_{\boldsymbol{x}}, \boldsymbol{b} \cdot \partial_{\boldsymbol{x}}],$$

which relates the Lie bracket of the vector fields $[\boldsymbol{a}, \boldsymbol{b}]$ to the standard Lie bracket of the partial derivatives $[\boldsymbol{a} \cdot \partial_{\boldsymbol{x}}, \boldsymbol{b} \cdot \partial_{\boldsymbol{x}}]$.

Let us consider in detail the translation of the Lie algebra of the affine plane to the null-vector formulation in the null cone $\mathcal{N}^2$. Recall that the two-dimensional affine plane $\mathcal{A}_e(\mathcal{N}^2)$ in $\mathcal{N}^3$ is defined by

$$\mathcal{A}_e(\mathcal{N}) = \{\boldsymbol{x} \in \mathcal{N}^3 | \ \boldsymbol{x} = xe_1 + ye_2 + e_3\}. \tag{3.63}$$

We have already seen that the Lie algebra of the affine plane can be defined by a Lie algebra of matrices, or by an equivalent Lie algebra of bivectors. We now define this same Lie algebra as a Lie algebra of partial derivatives or as a Lie algebra of vector fields. We have the following correspondences:

$$\mathcal{L}_x = \frac{\partial}{\partial x} = e_1 \cdot \partial_{\boldsymbol{x}} = \boldsymbol{\mathcal{L}}_x \cdot (\boldsymbol{x} \wedge \partial_{\boldsymbol{x}}) \leftrightarrow \mathcal{L}_x \boldsymbol{x} = \boldsymbol{\mathcal{L}}_x \cdot \boldsymbol{x} = e_1 = L_x, \tag{3.64}$$

where $\boldsymbol{\mathcal{L}}_x = e_1 \wedge \bar{e}_3$;

$$\mathcal{L}_y = \frac{\partial}{\partial y} = e_2 \cdot \partial_{\boldsymbol{x}} = \boldsymbol{\mathcal{L}}_y \cdot (\boldsymbol{x} \wedge \partial_{\boldsymbol{x}}) \leftrightarrow \mathcal{L}_y \boldsymbol{x} = \boldsymbol{\mathcal{L}}_y \cdot \boldsymbol{x} = e_2 = L_y, \tag{3.65}$$

where $\boldsymbol{\mathcal{L}}_y = e_2 \wedge \bar{e}_3$;

$$\begin{aligned} \mathcal{L}_s &= x\frac{\partial}{\partial x} + y\frac{\partial}{\partial y} = (\boldsymbol{x} - e_3) \cdot \partial_{\boldsymbol{x}} = \boldsymbol{\mathcal{L}}_s \cdot (\boldsymbol{x} \wedge \partial_{\boldsymbol{x}}) \\ &\leftrightarrow \mathcal{L}_s \boldsymbol{x} = \boldsymbol{\mathcal{L}}_s \cdot \boldsymbol{x} = xe_1 + ye_2 = \boldsymbol{x} - e_3 = L_s, \end{aligned} \tag{3.66}$$

where $\boldsymbol{\mathcal{L}}_s = e_1 \wedge \bar{e}_1 + e_2 \wedge \bar{e}_2$;

$$\mathcal{L}_r = -y\frac{\partial}{\partial x} + x\frac{\partial}{\partial y} = \boldsymbol{\mathcal{L}}_r \cdot (\boldsymbol{x} \wedge \partial_{\boldsymbol{x}}) \leftrightarrow \mathcal{L}_r \boldsymbol{x} = \boldsymbol{\mathcal{L}}_r \cdot \boldsymbol{x} = L_r, \tag{3.67}$$

where $\boldsymbol{\mathcal{L}}_r = e_2 \wedge \bar{e}_1 - e_1 \wedge \bar{e}_2$;

$$\mathcal{L}_b = x\frac{\partial}{\partial x} - y\frac{\partial}{\partial y} = \boldsymbol{\mathcal{L}}_b \cdot (\boldsymbol{x} \wedge \partial_{\boldsymbol{x}}) \leftrightarrow \mathcal{L}_b \boldsymbol{x} = \boldsymbol{\mathcal{L}}_b \cdot \boldsymbol{x} = L_b, \tag{3.68}$$

where $\boldsymbol{\mathcal{L}}_b = e_1 \wedge \bar{e}_1 - e_2 \wedge \bar{e}_2$; and

$$\mathcal{L}_B = y\frac{\partial}{\partial x} + x\frac{\partial}{\partial y} = \boldsymbol{\mathcal{L}}_B \cdot (\boldsymbol{x} \wedge \partial_{\boldsymbol{x}}) \leftrightarrow \mathcal{L}_B \boldsymbol{x} = \boldsymbol{\mathcal{L}}_B \cdot \boldsymbol{x} = L_B, \tag{3.69}$$

where $\boldsymbol{\mathcal{L}}_B = e_1 \wedge \bar{e}_2 + e_2 \wedge \bar{e}_1$.

Thus, the Lie algebra of the affine plane is generated by the bivectors

$$\mathcal{M}_{bivectors} = \{\boldsymbol{\mathcal{L}}_x, \boldsymbol{\mathcal{L}}_y, \boldsymbol{\mathcal{L}}_s, \boldsymbol{\mathcal{L}}_r, \boldsymbol{\mathcal{L}}_b, \boldsymbol{\mathcal{L}}_B\}, \tag{3.70}$$

or, equivalently, by the vector fields of the form

$$\begin{aligned}\mathcal{M}_{vectorfields} &= \{\boldsymbol{\mathcal{L}}_x \cdot \boldsymbol{x}, \boldsymbol{\mathcal{L}}_y \cdot \boldsymbol{x}, \boldsymbol{\mathcal{L}}_s \cdot \boldsymbol{x}, \boldsymbol{\mathcal{L}}_r \cdot \boldsymbol{x}, \boldsymbol{\mathcal{L}}_b \cdot \boldsymbol{x}, \boldsymbol{\mathcal{L}}_B \cdot \boldsymbol{x}\} \\ &= \{L_x, L_y, L_s, L_r, L_b, L_B\}, \end{aligned} \qquad (3.71)$$

where $\boldsymbol{\mathcal{L}} \cdot \boldsymbol{x}$ for $\boldsymbol{\mathcal{L}} \in \mathcal{M}_{bivectors}$.

The Lie bracket $[\boldsymbol{\mathcal{L}}_1 \cdot \boldsymbol{x}, \boldsymbol{\mathcal{L}}_2 \cdot \boldsymbol{x}]$ is given by

$$[\boldsymbol{\mathcal{L}}_1 \cdot \boldsymbol{x}, \boldsymbol{\mathcal{L}}_2 \cdot \boldsymbol{x}] = \boldsymbol{\mathcal{L}}_2 \cdot (\boldsymbol{\mathcal{L}}_1 \cdot \boldsymbol{x}) - \boldsymbol{\mathcal{L}}_1 \cdot (\boldsymbol{\mathcal{L}}_2 \cdot \boldsymbol{x}) = (\boldsymbol{\mathcal{L}}_2 \times \boldsymbol{\mathcal{L}}_1) \cdot \boldsymbol{x},$$

where $\boldsymbol{\mathcal{L}}_1 \times \boldsymbol{\mathcal{L}}_2 = \frac{1}{2}(\boldsymbol{\mathcal{L}}_1\boldsymbol{\mathcal{L}}_2 - \boldsymbol{\mathcal{L}}_2\boldsymbol{\mathcal{L}}_1)$ is the commutator product of the bivectors $\boldsymbol{\mathcal{L}}_1, \boldsymbol{\mathcal{L}}_2 \in \mathcal{M}$.

The Lie algebra of the affine plane is useful for the analysis of motion in the image plane [55]. The vector fields of this Lie algebra are tangent to the flows or integral curves of their group action on the manifold and are presented in Fig. 3.2 as real images.

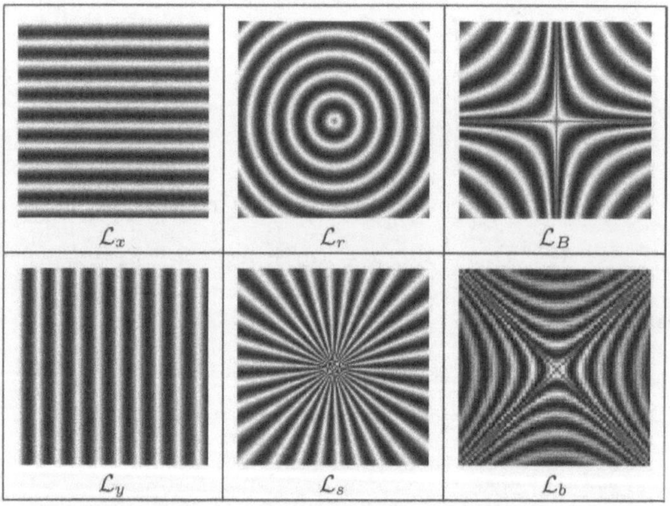

FIGURE 3.2. Lie algebra basis in the form of real images

We have found the generators

$\mathcal{L}_x = \frac{\partial}{\partial x}$	$\mathcal{L}_r = -y\frac{\partial}{\partial x} + x\frac{\partial}{\partial y}$	$\mathcal{L}_B = x\frac{\partial}{\partial x} - y\frac{\partial}{\partial y}$
$\mathcal{L}_y = \frac{\partial}{\partial y}$	$\mathcal{L}_s = x\frac{\partial}{\partial x} + y\frac{\partial}{\partial y}$	$\mathcal{L}_b = y\frac{\partial}{\partial x} + x\frac{\partial}{\partial y}$

(3.72)

of the Lie algebra of the affine plane $\mathcal{A}_{e_3}(\mathcal{N}^2)$ as vector fields along integral curves. Taking the commutator products of these infinitesimal differential generators gives the following multiplication Table 3.1 for this Lie algebra.

Using Table 3.1, we can verify the Jacobi identity for $\mathcal{L}_x, \mathcal{L}_s$, and $\mathcal{L}_b$, getting

$[\cdot,\cdot]$	$\mathcal{L}_x$	$\mathcal{L}_y$	$\mathcal{L}_s$	$\mathcal{L}_r$	$\mathcal{L}_b$	$\mathcal{L}_B$
$\mathcal{L}_x$	0	0	$\mathcal{L}_x$	$\mathcal{L}_y$	$\mathcal{L}_x$	$\mathcal{L}_y$
$\mathcal{L}_y$	0	0	$\mathcal{L}_y$	$-\mathcal{L}_x$	$-\mathcal{L}_y$	$\mathcal{L}_x$
$\mathcal{L}_s$	$-\mathcal{L}_x$	$-\mathcal{L}_y$	0	0	0	0
$\mathcal{L}_r$	$-\mathcal{L}_y$	$\mathcal{L}_x$	0	0	$-2\mathcal{L}_B$	$2\mathcal{L}_b$
$\mathcal{L}_b$	$-\mathcal{L}_x$	$\mathcal{L}_y$	0	$2\mathcal{L}_B$	0	$2\mathcal{L}_r$
$\mathcal{L}_B$	$-\mathcal{L}_y$	$-\mathcal{L}_x$	0	$-2\mathcal{L}_b$	$-2\mathcal{L}_r$	0

TABLE 3.1. Lie algebra of the affine plane

$$
\begin{array}{ccccccl}
[\mathcal{L}_x[\mathcal{L}_s\mathcal{L}_b]] & + & [\mathcal{L}_s[\mathcal{L}_b\mathcal{L}_x]] & + & [\mathcal{L}_b[\mathcal{L}_x\mathcal{L}_s]] & = & \\
[\mathcal{L}_x 0] & - & [\mathcal{L}_s\mathcal{L}_y] & + & [\mathcal{L}_b\mathcal{L}_x] & = & \\
0 & + & \mathcal{L}_y & - & \mathcal{L}_y & = & 0.
\end{array}
\tag{3.73}
$$

Or, equivalently, using CLICAL and the bivector representation for $\boldsymbol{\mathcal{L}}_x, \boldsymbol{\mathcal{L}}_r$, and $\boldsymbol{\mathcal{L}}_b$, we calculate

$$
\begin{array}{ccccccl}
[\boldsymbol{\mathcal{L}}_x[\boldsymbol{\mathcal{L}}_r\boldsymbol{\mathcal{L}}_b]] & + & [\boldsymbol{\mathcal{L}}_r[\boldsymbol{\mathcal{L}}_b\boldsymbol{\mathcal{L}}_x]] & + & [\boldsymbol{\mathcal{L}}_b[\boldsymbol{\mathcal{L}}_x\boldsymbol{\mathcal{L}}_r]] & = & \\
2\,[\boldsymbol{\mathcal{L}}_x\boldsymbol{\mathcal{L}}_B] & - & [\boldsymbol{\mathcal{L}}_r\boldsymbol{\mathcal{L}}_y] & + & [\boldsymbol{\mathcal{L}}_b\boldsymbol{\mathcal{L}}_y] & = & \\
2\boldsymbol{\mathcal{L}}_x & - & \boldsymbol{\mathcal{L}}_x & - & \boldsymbol{\mathcal{L}}_x & = & 0.
\end{array}
\tag{3.74}
$$

3.7 The Algebra of Incidence

In various applications in robotics, image analysis, and computer vision, the use of projective geometry and the algebra of incidence is extreme useful. Fortunately, these mathematical systems can be efficiently handled within the geometric algebra framework.

In projective geometry, points are represented using homogeneous coordinates of non-zero vectors in the $(n+1)$-dimensional Euclidean space $\mathbb{R}^{n+1}$. These can be seen as *projective rays* identified as points in the n-dimensional projective plane Π^n of $\mathbb{R}^{n+1}$. Furthermore, points, lines, planes, and higher-dimensional k-planes in Π^n are related with 1, 2, 3, and $(k+1)$-dimensional subspaces S^r of $\mathbb{R}^{n+1}$, where $k \leq n$. Since each k-subspace can be associated with a non-zero k-blade A_k of the geometric algebra $\mathcal{G}(\mathbb{R}^{n+1})$, it follows that the corresponding $(k-1)$-plane in Π^n can be named by the k-direction of the k-blade A_k.

The *meet* and *join* in Π^n are the principal operations of the algebra of incidence to compute the *intersection* and *union* of the k-planes. Suppose that the set of r points $a_1, a_2, \ldots, a_r \in \Pi^n$ and the set of s points $b_1, b_2, \ldots, b_s \in \Pi^n$ are both in general position (linearly independent vectors in $\mathbb{R}^{n+1}$), then the $(r-1)$-plane in Π^n is specified by the r-blade

$$A_r = a_1 \wedge a_2 \wedge \ldots \wedge a_r \neq 0, \tag{3.75}$$

and the $(s-1)$-plane by the s-blade

$$B_s = b_1 \wedge b_2 \wedge \ldots \wedge b_s \neq 0. \tag{3.76}$$

Considering the a's and b's to be the basis elements of respective subspaces $\mathcal{A}_r$ and $\mathcal{B}_s$, they can be sorted in such a way that

$$\mathcal{A}^r \cup \mathcal{B}^s = span\{a_1, a_2, \ldots a_s, b_{\lambda_1}, \ldots, b_{\lambda_k}\}. \tag{3.77}$$

Supposing that

$$B_s = b_{\lambda_1} \wedge \ldots \wedge b_{\lambda_k} \wedge b_{\alpha_1} \wedge \ldots \wedge b_{\alpha_{s-k}}, \tag{3.78}$$

it follows that the "meet" and "join" of the r-blade A_r and s-blade B_s are respectively given by

$$A_r \cup B_s = A_r \wedge b_{\lambda_1} \wedge \ldots \wedge b_{\lambda_k} \tag{3.79}$$

$$\mathcal{A}^r \cap \mathcal{B}^s = span\{b_{\alpha_1}, \ldots, b_{\alpha_{s-k}}\}. \tag{3.80}$$

Note that if the meet of A_r and $B_s = 0$, their join equals the wedge of the blades $A_r \cup B_s = A_r \wedge B_s$.

After the join of $\mathcal{A}^r$ and $\mathcal{B}^s$ has been computed, the $r+k$-blade

$$\overline{I}_{A_r \cup B_s} = \mathcal{A}^r \cup \mathcal{B}^s \tag{3.81}$$

can be used for computing the meet of the r- and s-blades A_r and B_s:

$$A_r \cap B_s = A_r \cdot (B_s \cdot I_{A_r \cup B_s}) = (I_{A_r \cup B_s} \cdot A_r) \cdot B_s. \tag{3.82}$$

This expression holds for the positive definite metric of $\mathbb{R}^{n+1}$. If we use any nondegenerated pseudo-Euclidean space $\mathbb{R}^{p,q}$, where $p+q=n+1$, we must use instead the reciprocal $r+k$-blade $\overline{I}_{A_r \cup B_s}$, for which the property $I_{A_r \cup B_s} \cdot \overline{I}_{A_r \cup B_s} \neq 0$ is satisfied. For this case, the meet equation reads

$$A_r \cap B_s = A_r \cdot (B_s \cdot \overline{I}_{A_r \cup B_s}) = (\overline{I}_{A_r \cup B_s} \cdot A_r) \cdot B_s. \tag{3.83}$$

Note that if the grade of the blade $A_r \cup B_s$ equals $n = p+q$, we can simply use the inverse of the pseudoscalar, so that $I \cdot \overline{I} = 1$.

In the case of the geometric algebra of the null cone $\mathcal{G}(N^{n+1})$, we define the following reciprocal $r+k$-blade for meet equation (3.83):

$$\overline{I}_{A_r \cup B_s} = \overline{a}_1 \wedge \overline{a}_2 \wedge \ldots \wedge \overline{a}_s \wedge \overline{b}_{\lambda_1} \wedge \ldots \wedge \overline{b}_{\lambda_k}. \tag{3.84}$$

A more complete discussion of these ideas can be found in [84, 100].

3.7.1 Incidence relations in the affine n-plane

This subsection presents incidence relations between points, lines, planes, and higher dimensional k-planes using the useful computational framework of the affine n-plane. Let us rewrite equation (3.28) in the larger pseudo-Euclidean space $\mathbb{R}^{n+1,1} = \mathbb{R}^n \oplus \mathbb{R}^{1,1}$, where $\mathbb{R}^{1,1} = span\{\sigma, \eta\}$:

$$\mathcal{A}_e(\mathbb{R}^n) = \{x_h = x + e|\ \ x \in \mathbb{R}^n\} \subset \mathbb{R}^{n+1,1}. \tag{3.85}$$

The null vector $e \in \mathbb{R}^{1,1}$ is given by $e = \frac{1}{2}(\sigma + \eta)$, and the reciprocal null vector $\overline{e} = \sigma_n - \eta_n$ fulfills the condition $e \cdot \overline{e} = 1$. Now, if we merge the n-affine plane $\mathcal{A}_e(\mathbb{R}^n)$ together with the plane at infinity, we obtain the projective plane Π^n. Each point $\boldsymbol{x} \in \mathcal{A}_e(\mathbb{R}^n)$ is called a *homogeneous representant* of the corresponding point in Π^n. Now points in the affine plane can be represented as rays in the projective space:

$$\mathcal{A}_e^{rays}(\mathbb{R}^n) = \{\boldsymbol{y}|\ \ \boldsymbol{y} \in \mathbb{R}^{n+1} \text{ and } \boldsymbol{y} \cdot \overline{e} \neq 0\ \} \subset \mathbb{R}^{n+1}. \tag{3.86}$$

Note that in this definition we consider $\boldsymbol{y} \cdot \overline{e} \neq 0$, because rays are directions and they remain the same if we multiply for a scalar. Accordingly, a homogeneous point of the n-affine plane can be uniquely computed from a ray as follows:

$$\frac{\boldsymbol{y}}{\boldsymbol{y} \cdot \overline{e}} \in \mathcal{A}_e(\mathbb{R}^n). \tag{3.87}$$

Now let us formulate useful incidence relations. If we consider k-points $a_1^h, a_2^h, \ldots, a_k^h \in \mathcal{A}_e^n$, where each $a_i^h = a_i + e$ for $a_i \in \mathbb{R}^n$, and then compute their the outer product, we get the $(k-1)$-plane A^h in Π^n:

$$\begin{aligned} A^h &= a_1^h \wedge a_2^h \wedge \ldots \wedge a_k^h = a_1^h \wedge (a_2^h - a_1^h) \wedge a_3^h \wedge \ldots \wedge a_k^h = \ldots \\ &= a_1^h \wedge (a_2^h - a_1^h) \wedge (a_3^h - a_2^h) \wedge \ldots \wedge (a_k^h - a_{k-1}^h) \\ &= a_1^h \wedge (a_2 - a_1) \wedge (a_3 - a_2) \wedge \ldots \wedge (a_k - a_{k-1}) \\ &= (a_1 + e) \wedge (a_2 - a_1) \wedge (a_3 - a_2) \wedge \ldots \wedge (a_k - a_{k-1}) \\ &= a_1 \wedge a_2 \wedge \ldots \wedge a_k + \\ &\qquad + e \wedge (a_2 - a_1) \wedge (a_3 - a_2) \wedge \ldots \wedge (a_k - a_{k-1}). \end{aligned} \tag{3.88}$$

This equation represents a $(k-1)$-plane in Π^n, but it also belongs to the affine n-plane $\mathcal{A}_e^n$ and thus contains important metrical information which can be extracted by taking the dot product from the left with $\overline{e}$:

$$\begin{aligned} \overline{e} \cdot A^h &= \overline{e} \cdot (a_1^h \wedge a_2^h \wedge \ldots \wedge a_k^h) \\ &= (a_2 - a_1) \wedge (a_3 - a_2) \wedge \ldots \wedge (a_k - a_{k-1}). \end{aligned} \tag{3.89}$$

Interestingly enough, this result, with a little modification, turns out to be the directed content of the $(k-1)$-simplex $A^h = a_1^h \wedge a_2^h \wedge \ldots \wedge a_k^h$ in the affine n-plane:

$$\begin{aligned} \frac{\bar{e}\cdot A^h}{(k-1)!} &= \frac{\bar{e}\cdot(a_1^h\wedge a_2^h\wedge\ldots\wedge a_k^h)}{(k-1)!} \\ &= \frac{(a_2-a_1)\wedge(a_3-a_2)\wedge\ldots\wedge(a_k-a_{k-1})}{(k-1)!}. \end{aligned} \tag{3.90}$$

3.7.2 Directed distances

Using our previous results, we can propose useful equations in the affine plane to relate points, lines, and planes metrically . The *directed distance* or *foot* from the $(k-1)$-plane $a_1^h\wedge\ldots\wedge a_k^h$ to the point b^h is given by

$$\begin{aligned} &d[a_1^h\wedge\ldots a_k^h, b^h] \equiv \\ &[\{\bar{e}\cdot(a_1^h\wedge\ldots\wedge a_k^h)\}\ (\bar{e}\cdot b^h)]^{-1}[\bar{e}\cdot(a_1^h\wedge\ldots\wedge a_k^h\wedge b^h)] \\ &= [a_2-a_1)\wedge\ldots\wedge(a_k-a_{k-1})]^{-1}[(a_2-a_1)\wedge\ldots\wedge(a_k-a_{k-1})\wedge(b-a_k)]. \end{aligned} \tag{3.91}$$

In the same sense, the equation of the directed distance between the two lines $a_1^h\wedge a_2^h$ and $b_1^h\wedge b_2^h$ in the affine n-plane reads

$$\begin{aligned} &d[a_1^h\wedge a_2^h, b_1^h\wedge b_2^h] \equiv \\ &\quad[\{\bar{e}\cdot(a_1^h\wedge a_2^h)\}\wedge\{\bar{e}\cdot(b_1^h\wedge b_2^h)\}]^{-1}[\bar{e}\cdot(a_1^h\wedge a_2^h\wedge b_1^h\wedge b_2^h)] \\ &\quad= [(a_2-a_1)\wedge(b_2-b_1)]^{-1}[(a_2-a_1)\wedge(b_1-a_2)\wedge(b_2-b_1)]. \end{aligned} \tag{3.92}$$

A general equation of the directed distance between the $(r-1)$-plane $A^h = a_1^h\wedge\ldots\wedge a_r^h$ and the $(s-1)$-plane $B^h = b_1^h\wedge\ldots\wedge b_s^h$ in the affine n-plane is similarly given by

$$\begin{aligned} &d[a_1^h\wedge\ldots\wedge a_r^h, b_1^h\wedge\ldots\wedge b_s^h] \equiv \\ &\{\bar{e}\cdot(a_1^h\wedge\ldots\wedge a_r^h)\}\wedge\{\bar{e}\cdot(b_1^h\wedge\ldots\wedge b_s^h)\}]^{-1}[\bar{e}\cdot(a_1^h\wedge\ldots\wedge a_r^h\wedge b_1^h\wedge\ldots\wedge b_s^h)] \\ &= [(a_2-a_1)\wedge\ldots\wedge(a_r-a_{r-1})\wedge(b_2-b_1)\wedge\ldots\wedge(b_s-b_{s-1})]^{-1} \\ &[(a_2-a_1)\wedge\ldots\wedge(a_r-a_{r-1})\wedge(b_1-a_r)\wedge(b_2-b_1)\wedge\ldots\wedge(b_s-b_{s-1})]. \end{aligned} \tag{3.93}$$

We have to be careful, because if $A^h\wedge B^h = 0$, the directed distance may or may not be equal to zero. If $(a_1^h\wedge\ldots\wedge a_r^h)\wedge(b_1^h\wedge\ldots\wedge b_{s-1}^h) \neq 0$, we can calculate the meet between the $(r-1)$-plane A^h and $(s-1)$-plane B^h,

$$\begin{aligned} p &= (a_1^h\wedge\ldots\wedge a_r^h)\cap(b_1^h\wedge\ldots\wedge b_s^h) \\ &= (a_1^h\wedge\ldots\wedge a_r^h)\cdot[(b_1^h\wedge\ldots\wedge b_s^h)\cdot\bar{I}_{A\cup B}], \end{aligned} \tag{3.94}$$

where

$$\bar{I}_{A\cup B} = \{\bar{e}\cdot[(a_1^h\wedge\ldots\wedge a_r^h)\wedge(b_1^h\wedge\ldots\wedge b_{s-1}^h)]\}\wedge\bar{e}.$$

It can happen that the point $p = A^h\cap B^h$ may not be in the affine n-plane, but the *normalized* point $p^h = \frac{p}{\bar{e}\cdot p}$ will either be in the affine plane or will be undefined. Finding the "normalized point" is not necessary in many calculations, but is required when the metric plays an important role or in the case of parallel hyperplanes, when it is used as an indicator.

3.7.3 Incidence relations in the affine 3-plane

This subsection presents some algebra of incidence relations for 3D Euclidean space represented in the affine 3-plane $\mathcal{A}_e^3$, with the pseudoscalar $I = \sigma_{123}e$ and the reciprocal pseudscalar $\overline{I} = \bar{e}\sigma_{321}$ satisfying the condition $I \cdot \overline{I} = 1$. Similar incidence relations were given by Blaschke [14] using dual quaternions, and later by Selig using the 4D degenerate geometric algebra $\mathcal{G}_{3,0,1}$ [93]. Unlike the formulas given by these authors, our formulas are generally valid in any dimension and are expressed completely in terms of the meet and join operations in the affine plane. Blaschke and Selig could not exploit the meet and join operations because they were using a geometric algebra with a degenerate metric.

The distance of a point b^h to the line $L^h = a_1^h \wedge a_2^h$ is the *magnitude* or *norm* of the directed distance,

$$|d| = \left|\left[\{\bar{e}\cdot(a_1^h\wedge a_2^h)\}\wedge\{(\bar{e}\cdot(b^h)\}\right]^{-1}\left[\bar{e}\cdot(a_1^h\wedge a_2^h\wedge b^h)\right]\right|. \tag{3.95}$$

The distance of a point b^h to the plane $A^h = a_1^h \wedge a_2^h \wedge a_3^h$ is

$$|d| = \left|\left[\{\bar{e}\cdot(a_1^h\wedge a_2^h\wedge a_3^h)\}\wedge\{(\bar{e}\cdot(b^h)\}\right]^{-1}\left[\bar{e}\cdot(a_1^h\wedge a_2^h\wedge a_3^h\wedge b^h)\right]\right|. \tag{3.96}$$

Let us analyze carefully the incidence relation between the lines $L_1^h = a_1^h \wedge a_2^h$ and $L_2^h = b_1^h \wedge b_2^h$, which are completely determined by their join $I_{L_1^h \cup L_2^h} = L_1^h \cup L_2^h$. The following formulas helps to test the incidence relations of the lines.

- If $I_{L_1^h \cup L_2^h}$ is a bivector, the lines coincide and $L_1^h = tL_2^h$ for some $t \in \mathbb{R}$.
- If $I_{L_1^h \cup L_2^h}$ is a 3-vector, the lines are either parallel or intersect in a common point. In this case,

$$p = L_1^h \cap L_2^h = L_1^h \cdot (L_2^h \cdot \overline{I}_{L_1^h \cup L_2^h}), \tag{3.97}$$

  where p is the result of the meet. If $\bar{e}\cdot p = 0$, the lines are parallel; otherwise, they intersect at the point $p_h = \frac{p}{\bar{e}\cdot p}$ in the affine 3-space$\mathcal{A}_e^3$.
- If $I_{L_1^h \cup L_2^h}$ is a 4-vector, the lines are skew. In this case, the distance is given by equation (3.93).

The incidence relation between a line $L^h = a_1^h \wedge a_2^h$ and a plane $B^h = b_1^h \wedge b_2^h \wedge b_3^h$ is also determined by their join, $L^h \cup B^h$. Clearly, if the join is a trivector, the line L^h lies in the plane B^h. The only other possibility is that their join is the pseudoscalar $I = \sigma_{123}e$. In this case,

$$p = L^h \cap B^h = L^h \cdot (B^h \cdot \overline{I}). \tag{3.98}$$

If $\bar{e} \cdot p = 0$, the line is parallel to the plane, with the directed distance determined by equation (3.94). Otherwise, their point of intersection in the affine plane is $p_h = \frac{p}{\bar{e} \cdot p}$.

Two planes, $A^h = a_1^h \wedge a_2^h \wedge a_3^h$ and $B^h = b_1^h \wedge b_2^h \wedge b_3^h$, in the affine plane $\mathcal{A}_e^3$ are either parallel, intersect in a line, or coincide. If their join is a trivector, that is, if $A^h = tB^h$ for some $t \in \mathbb{R}^*$, they obviously coincide. If they do not coincide, then their join is the pseudoscalar $I = \sigma_{123}e$. In this case, we calculate the meet as

$$L = A^h \cap B^h = (\bar{I} \cdot A^h) \cdot B^h. \tag{3.99}$$

If $\bar{e} \cdot L = 0$, the planes are parallel, with the directed distance determined by equation (3.94). Otherwise, L represents the line of intersection in the affine plane having the direction $\bar{e} \cdot L$.

The equivalent of the above incidence relations was given by Blaschke [14] using dual quaternions, and by Selig [91] utilizing a special or degenerate four-dimensional Clifford algebra. Whereas Blaschke uses only pure quaternions (bivectors) for his representation, Selig uses trivectors for points and vectors for planes. In contrast, in the affine 3-plane, points are always represented by vectors, lines by bivectors, and planes by trivectors. This offers a comprehensive and consistent interpretation which greatly simplifies the underlying conceptual framework. The following equations compares our equations (left side) with those of Blaschke and Selig (right side).

$$\textit{equation } (3.95) \equiv \frac{1}{2}(\tilde{p}l + \tilde{l}p) \tag{3.100}$$

$$\textit{equation } (3.96) \equiv \frac{1}{2}(\tilde{p}\pi + \tilde{\pi}p) \tag{3.101}$$

$$\textit{equation } (3.98) \equiv \frac{1}{2}(\tilde{l}\pi + \tilde{\pi}l), \tag{3.102}$$

3.7.4 Geometric constraints as flags

It is often necessary to check a geometric configuration during a rigid motion in Euclidean space, and simple geometric incidence relations can be used for this purpose. For example, a point p is on a line L if and only if

$$p \wedge L = 0. \tag{3.103}$$

Similarly, a point p is on a plane A if

$$p \wedge A = 0. \tag{3.104}$$

A line L will lie in plane A if

$$L \cap A = A. \tag{3.105}$$

Alternatively, the line L can meet the plane A in a single point p, in which case,

$$L \cap A = p,$$

or, if the line L is parallel to the plane A,

$$L \cap A = 0. \tag{3.106}$$

3.8 Conclusion

We have shown how geometric algebra can effectively be used to carry out analysis on a manifold, which is useful in robotics and image analysis. Geometric algebra offers a clear and concise geometric framework of multivectors in which calculations can be carried out. Since the elements and operations in geometric algebra are basis-free, computations are simpler and geometrically more transparent than in more traditional approaches.

Stereographic projection and its generalization to the conformal group and projective geometry have direct application to image analysis from one or more viewpoints. The key idea is that an image is first represented on the null cone, and then projected onto affine geometries or onto an n-dimensional affine plane, where the image analysis takes place. Since every Lie algebra can be represented by an appropriate bivector algebra in an affine geometry, it follows that a complete motion analysis should be possible using its bivector representation in geometric algebra. In Chapter 5 we will explore applications in robotics of the n-dimensional affine plane as a computing framework to both analyze rigid motion and to apply the algebra of incidence. In Chapter 6 we will employ Lie operators expressed in terms of bivectors to detect visual invariants.

3.9 Exercises

3.1. Prove that $\boldsymbol{x}_c = \frac{1}{2}\boldsymbol{x}_h \bar{e} \boldsymbol{x}_h = exp(\frac{1}{2}\boldsymbol{x}\bar{e})\ e\ exp(-\frac{1}{2}\boldsymbol{x}\bar{e})$, where $\boldsymbol{x}_c \in \mathcal{H}_e^{p,q}$, $x_h \in \mathcal{A}_e^{p,q}$, and $\boldsymbol{x} \in I\!R^n$.

3.2. The bases of the reciprocal null cones $\{e\} \in N$ and $\{\bar{e}\} \in N$ are called reciprocal or dual bases because they fulfill the relationship $\{e\} \cdot \{\bar{e}\} = id$, where id is an $n \times n$ identity matrix. The pseudoscalar of $\mathcal{G}(N)$ is $I = e_1 \wedge e_2 \wedge e_3 ... e_n$, and of $\mathcal{G}(\bar{N})$ is $\bar{I} = \bar{e}_1 \wedge \bar{e}_2 \wedge \bar{e}_3 ... \bar{e}_n$, both of which satisfy the condition $I \cdot \bar{I} = 1$. According to equation (3.18), we can express a second basis $\{a\} = \{e\}\mathcal{A} = \{e_1, e_2, e_3, ..., e_n\}A \in N$, where the matrix A is responsible for this change of basis. The hypervolume spanned by the basis $\{a\}$ is $\bigwedge_{i=1}^{n}\{a\} =$

$a_1 \wedge a_2 \wedge \ldots \wedge a_n = \det(\mathcal{A}) e_1 \wedge e_2 \wedge \ldots e_n = \det(\mathcal{A})\mathrm{I}$. The *bracket* of $\mathcal{A}$ is simply computed by taking the dot product of this hypervolume and the reciprocal pseudoscalar $\det(\mathcal{A}) = \bigwedge_{i=1}^{n}\{a\} \cdot \bar{I}$. Similar to the standard approach for obtaining a reciprocal basis, it is easy to see that the new reciprocal basis $\{\bar{a}\}$ can be computed by means of the equation

$$\bar{a}_i = (-1)^{i+1} \frac{(a_1 \wedge \ldots \wedge (1)_i \wedge \ldots \wedge a_n) \cdot \bar{I}}{[a_1\ a_2\ \ldots\ a_n]},$$

where a_i is left out of the wedge operation in position $(1)_i$. This expression guarantees that $\{\bar{a}\} \cdot \{a\} = id$. Find an expression for computing the inverse of the matrix $(\mathcal{A})$. (*Hint*: Use $\{\bar{a}\} = \mathcal{B}\{\bar{a}\}$.)

3.3. Projections from $\mathcal{G}_{3,3}$ to $\mathcal{G}_{3,0}$: Consider the Lie algebra $so(3)$ in $\mathcal{G}_{3,3}$:

$$\mathcal{L}_x = \begin{pmatrix} 0 & 1 & 0 \\ -1 & 0 & 0 \\ 0 & 0 & 0 \end{pmatrix}, \mathcal{L}_y = \begin{pmatrix} 0 & 0 & 1 \\ 0 & 0 & 0 \\ -1 & 0 & 0 \end{pmatrix}, \mathcal{L}_z = \begin{pmatrix} 0 & 0 & 0 \\ 0 & 0 & -1 \\ 0 & 1 & 0 \end{pmatrix}.$$

Using CLICAL, represent this Lie algebra in $\mathcal{G}_{3,3}$ using the bivector matrices $\boldsymbol{L}_x$, $\boldsymbol{L}_y$, and $\boldsymbol{L}_z$. Take their projections $P(\boldsymbol{L}_x) = I^{-1}(I \cdot \boldsymbol{L}_x)$, $P(\boldsymbol{L}_y) = I^{-1}(I \cdot \boldsymbol{L}_y)$, and $P(\boldsymbol{L}_z) = I^{-1}(I \cdot \boldsymbol{L}_z)$ using the Euclidean pseudoscalar $I = e_1 e_2 e_3$ and also using the reciprocal pseudoscalar $I = e_4 e_5 e_6$. Explain the dual relation of the results.

3.4. Using CLICAL, compute in the 2D affine plane $\mathcal{A}_e^2$ the new position of the point $\boldsymbol{x} = 4\sigma_1 + 2\sigma_2 \in \mathcal{A}(\mathbb{R}^2)$ after the translation $\boldsymbol{t} = 6\sigma_1 + 5\sigma_2 \in \mathcal{A}(\mathbb{R}^2)$.

3.5. Using CLICAL, compute in the 2D affine plane $\mathcal{A}_e^2$ the dilation of the point $\boldsymbol{x} = 3\sigma_1 + 5\sigma_2 \in \mathcal{A}(\mathbb{R}^2)$ for

$$\mathcal{D}_u = \begin{pmatrix} e^u & 0 & 0 \\ 0 & e^u & 0 \\ 0 & 0 & 1 \end{pmatrix} = \begin{pmatrix} 1.75 & 0 & 0 \\ 0 & 1.75 & 0 \\ 0 & 0 & 1 \end{pmatrix}.$$

3.6. Using CLICAL, compute in the geometric algebra of the null cone $\mathcal{G}(N^2)$ the new position of the point $x_0 = 2\sigma_1 + 3\sigma_2 \in \mathcal{A}(\mathbb{R}^2)$ after a rotation of $\theta = \frac{\pi}{6}$. Use equation (3.52) with the bivector of the spinor group $Spin(2)$ $\boldsymbol{B} = -e_1 \wedge \bar{e}_2 + -e_2 \wedge \bar{e}_1$. Note that the rotation is not computed with the exponential function but rather with a function depending on the mutually annihiliating idempotents.

3.7. Compute in the affine 2-plane $\mathcal{A}_e^2$, with the pseudoscalar $I = \sigma_1 \wedge \sigma_2 \wedge e$ and the reciprocal pseudoscalar $\bar{I} = \sigma_1 \wedge \sigma_2 \wedge \bar{e}$, the meet of the lines $L_1^h = a_1^h \wedge a_2^h$, and $L_2^h = b_1^h \wedge b_2^h$, where $a_1^h = 4\sigma_1 + e$, $a_2^h = 2\sigma_2 + e$, $b_1^h = e$, and $b_2^h = 2\sigma_1 + 3\sigma_2 + e$.

3.8. In the affine 2-plane $\mathcal{A}_e^2$, compute the intersecting point p^h of the lines L_1^h and L_3^h, where L_1^h is the line determined in problem 3.7 and L_3^h passes through the point $c_2^h = 4\sigma_1 + 3\sigma_2 + e$ and is orthogonal to the line L_1^h. (*Hint:* Consider the line $L_3^h = p^h \wedge c_2^h$ with the point $p^h = c_2^h + s\,i(a_1 - a_2)$ for $s \in \mathbb{R}$, where $i = \sigma_1\sigma_2$.) Note that $s \neq 0$ can be overlooked, because the line is uniquely defined by the 2-direction of the bivector $p^h \wedge c_2^h$ and not by its magnitude.

3.9. Theorem proving: Let a circle entered at the origin and $\boldsymbol{a}$ and $\boldsymbol{b}$ be the end points of the diameter. Take any point $\boldsymbol{c}$ on the circle and show in the 2-plane $\mathcal{A}_e^2$ that the lines $\boldsymbol{l}_{ac}$ and $\boldsymbol{l}_{cb}$ are perpendicular.

3.10. Theorem proving: Prove the theorem of Desargues's configuration in the 3D-projective plane Π^3. Consider that x_1, x_2, x_3 and y_1, y_2, y_3 are the vertices of two triangles in Π^3 and suppose that $(x_1 \wedge x_2) \cap (y_1 \wedge y_2) = z_3$, $(x_2 \wedge x_3) \cap (y_2 \wedge y_3) = z_1$, and $(x_3 \wedge x_1) \cap (y_3 \wedge y_1) = z_2$. You can claim that $c_1 \wedge c_2 \wedge c_3 = 0$ if and only if there is a point p such that $x_1 \wedge y_1 \wedge p = 0 = x_2 \wedge y_2 \wedge p = x_3 \wedge y_3 \wedge p$. (*Hint:* Express the point as linear combinations of a_1, b_1, a_2, b_2, and a_3, b_3. The other half of the proof follows by duality of the classical projective geometry.)

3.11. Theorem proving: Consider an arbitrary circumcircled triangle. From a point $\boldsymbol{d}$ on the circumcircle draw three perpendiculars to the triangle sides $\boldsymbol{bc}$, $\boldsymbol{ca}$, and $\boldsymbol{ab}$ to meet the circle at points $\boldsymbol{a}_1$, $\boldsymbol{b}_1$, and $\boldsymbol{c}_1$, respectively. Prove that the lines $\boldsymbol{l}_{aa_1}$, $\boldsymbol{l}_{bb_1}$, and $\boldsymbol{l}_{cc_1}$ are parallel. (*Hint:* In the affine 2-plane $\mathcal{A}_e^2$, interpret the geometry of your results according to the grade and the absolute value of the directed distances between the lines.)

3.12. Consider in the affine 3-plane $\mathcal{A}_e^3$ the points $a_1^h = 3\sigma_1 + 4\sigma_2 + 5\sigma_3 + e$, $a_2^h = 2\sigma_1 - 5\sigma_2 + 2\sigma_3 + e$, and $a_3^h = 1\sigma_1 + 6\sigma_2 + 4\sigma_3 + e$; the line $L_1^h = a_1^h \wedge a_2^h$; and the plane $\phi_1^h = a_1^h \wedge a_2^h \wedge a_3$. Compute, using the MAPLE packet CLIFFORD 4.0, for (a) one of the points, (b) the line, and (c) the plane, their new positions after the rigid motion. This is defined by a translation of $t_1^h = \sigma_1 + 2\sigma_2 + \sigma_3 + e$ and rotations about the three axes of $\theta_x = \frac{\pi}{5}$, $\theta_y = \frac{\pi}{3}$ and $\theta_z = \frac{\pi}{6}$. Recall that you compute the translation using the horosphere as an intermediate framework.

3.13. Consider in the affine 3-plane $\mathcal{A}_e^3$ the points $p_0^h = e$, $p_1^h = \sigma_2 + e$, $p_2^h = \sigma_1 + \sigma_2 + e$, $p_3^h = \sigma_1 + e$, $p_4^h = \sigma_1 + \sigma_3 + e$, $p_5^h = \sigma_1 + \sigma_2 + \sigma_3 + e$, $p_6^h = \sigma_2 + \sigma_3 + e$, and $p_7^h = \sigma_3 + e$; the lines $L_{01} = p_0^h \wedge p_1^h$, $L_{36} = p_3^h \wedge p_6^h$, and $L_{76} = p_7^h \wedge p_6^h$; and the planes $\phi_f = p_0^h \wedge p_1^h \wedge p_3^h$, $\phi_t = p_5^h \wedge p_6^h \wedge p_7^h$, and $\phi_r = p_2^h \wedge p_5^h \wedge p_6^h$. Compute, using CLIFFORD 4.0, the directed distances between p_7^h and ϕ_f, p_5^h and L_{36}, L_{01} and L_{36}, L_{36} and L_{76}, L_{01} and ϕ_t, L_{36} and ϕ_t, ϕ_f and ϕ_t, and ϕ_f and ϕ_r. Interpret the geometry of your results according to the grade and the absolute value of the directed distances.

4. Geometric Algebra of Computer Vision

4.1 Introduction

This chapter presents a mathematical approach based on *geometric algebra* for the computation of problems in computer vision. We will show that geometric algebra is a well-founded and elegant language for expressing and implementing those aspects of linear algebra and projective geometry that are useful for computer vision. Since geometric algebra offers both geometric insight and algebraic computational power, it is useful for tasks such as the computation of projective invariants, camera calibration, and the recovery of shape and motion. We will mainly focus on the geometry of multiple uncalibrated cameras.

The following section introduces 3D and 4D geometric algebras and formulates the aspects of projective geometry relevant for computer vision within the geometric algebra framework. Given this background, in subsections 4.2.4–4.2.5 we will look at the concepts of projective transformations and projective split. Section 4.3 presents the algebra of incidence, and Section 4.4 the algebra in projective space of points, lines, and planes. An analysis of monocular, binocular, and trinocular geometries is given in Section 4.5. Conclusions follow in the final section.

In this chapter vectors will be notated in boldface type (except for basis vectors) and multivectors will appear in bold italics. Lowercase letters are used to denote vectors in 3D Euclidean space, and uppercase letters to denote vectors in 4D projective space. We will also denote a geometric algebra $\mathcal{G}_{p,q,r}$, which refers to an n-dimensional geometric algebra in which p-basis vectors square to $+1$, q-basis vectors to -1, and r-basis vectors to 0, so that $p+q+r = n$.

4.2 The Geometric Algebras of 3D and 4D Spaces

The need for a mathematical framework to understand and process digital camera images of the 3D world prompted researchers in the late 1970s to use *projective geometry*. By using homogeneous coordinates, we were able to embed both 3D Euclidean visual space in the projective space P^3 or R^4, and the 2D Euclidean space of the image plane in the projective space P^2 or R^3. As a result, inherently nonlinear projective transformations from 3D space to the 2D image space now became linear, and points and directions could be differentiated rather than being represented by the same quantity. The use of projective geometry was indeed a step forward. However, there is still a need [50] for a mathematical system which reconciles projective geometry with multilinear algebra. Indeed, in most of the computer-vision literature these mathematical systems are divorced from one another. Depending on the problem at hand, researchers typically resort to different systems, for example, dual algebra [16] for incidence algebra and the Hamiltonian formulation for motion estimation [111]. Here, we suggest the use of a system which offers all of these mathematical facilities. Unlike matrix and tensor algebra, geometric algebra does not obscure the underlying geometry of the problem. We will, therefore, formulate the main aspects of such problems using geometric algebra, starting with the modeling of 3D visual space and the 2D image plane.

4.2.1 3D space and the 2D image plane

To introduce the basic geometric models in computer vision, we consider the imaging of a point $\mathbf{X} \in R^4$ into a point $\boldsymbol{x} \in R^3$. We will assume that the reader is familiar with the basic concepts of using homogeneous coordinates, which will be discussed in greater detail in later sections. The optical center C of the camera may be different from the origin of the world coordinate system O, as depicted in Fig. (4.1).

In the standard matrix representation, the mapping $P : \mathbf{X} \longrightarrow \boldsymbol{x}$ is expressed by the homogeneous transformation matrix

$$P = \begin{bmatrix} t_{11} & t_{12} & t_{13} & t_{14} \\ t_{21} & t_{22} & t_{23} & t_{14} \\ t_{31} & t_{32} & t_{33} & t_{34} \end{bmatrix}, \tag{4.1}$$

which may be decomposed into a product of three matrices,

$$P = KP_0M_0^c, \tag{4.2}$$

where P_0, K, and M_0^c will now be defined. P_0 is the 3×4 matrix,

$$\begin{bmatrix} 1 & 0 & 0 & 0 \\ 0 & 1 & 0 & 0 \\ 0 & 0 & 1 & 0 \end{bmatrix}, \tag{4.3}$$

which simply projects down from 4D to 3D and represents a projection from homogeneous coordinates of space to homogeneous coordinates of the image plane.

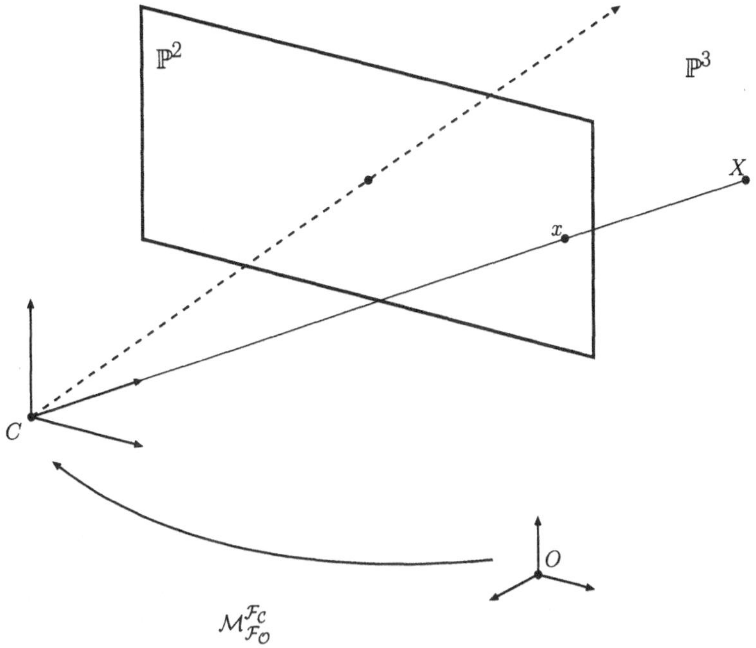

FIGURE 4.1. Pinhole camera model

M_0^c represents the 4×4 matrix containing the rotation and translation which takes the world frame $\mathcal{F}_0$ to the camera frame $\mathcal{F}_c$, and is given explicitly by

$$M_0^c = \begin{bmatrix} R & \boldsymbol{t} \\ \mathbf{0}^T & 1 \end{bmatrix}. \tag{4.4}$$

This Euclidean transformation is described by the *extrinsic parameters* of rotation (3×3 matrix R) and translation (3×1 vector $\boldsymbol{t}$). Finally, the 3×3 matrix K expresses the assumed camera model as an affine transformation between the camera plane and the image coordinate system, so that K is an upper triangular matrix. In the case of the perspective (or pinhole) camera, the matrix K, which we now call K_p, is given by

$$K_p = \begin{bmatrix} \alpha_u & \gamma & u_0 \\ 0 & \alpha_v & v_0 \\ 0 & 0 & 1 \end{bmatrix}. \tag{4.5}$$

The five parameters in K_p represent the camera parameters of scaling, shift, and rotation in the camera plane. In this case, the distance from the optical center to the image plane is finite. In later sections we will formulate the perspective camera in the geometric algebra framework.

One important task in computer vision is to estimate the matrix of intrinsic camera parameters K_p and the rigid motion given in M_0^c, in order to be able to reconstruct 3D data from image sequences.

4.2.2 The geometric algebra of 3D Euclidean space

The 3D space is spanned by three basis vectors $\{\sigma_1, \sigma_2, \sigma_3\}$, with $\sigma_i^2 = +1$ for all $i = 1, 2, 3$, and the 3D geometric algebra generated by these basis vectors has $2^3 = 8$ elements given by

$$\underbrace{1}_{scalar}, \underbrace{\{\sigma_1, \sigma_2, \sigma_3\}}_{vectors}, \underbrace{\{\sigma_1\sigma_2, \sigma_2\sigma_3, \sigma_3\sigma_1\}}_{bivectors}, \underbrace{\{\sigma_1\sigma_2\sigma_3\} \equiv I}_{trivector}. \tag{4.6}$$

Here, bivectors can be interpreted as oriented areas and trivectors as oriented volumes. Note that we will not use bold for these basis vectors. The highest-grade element is a trivector called the unit *pseudoscalar*. It can easily be verified that the pseudoscalar $\sigma_1\sigma_2\sigma_3$ squares to -1 and commutes with all multivectors (a multivector is a general linear combination of any of the elements in the algebra) in the 3D space. The unit pseudoscalar I is crucial when discussing duality. In a three-dimensionsal space we can construct a trivector $\boldsymbol{a} \wedge \boldsymbol{b} \wedge \boldsymbol{c}$, but no 4-vectors exist, since there is no possibility of sweeping the volume element $\boldsymbol{a} \wedge \boldsymbol{b} \wedge \boldsymbol{c}$ over a fourth dimension.

The three basis vectors $\{\sigma_i\}$ multiplied by I give the following basis bivectors:

$$I\sigma_1 = \sigma_2\sigma_3 \qquad I\sigma_2 = \sigma_3\sigma_1 \qquad I\sigma_3 = \sigma_1\sigma_2. \tag{4.7}$$

If we identify the $\boldsymbol{i}$, $\boldsymbol{j}$, $\boldsymbol{k}$ of the quaternion algebra with $\sigma_2\sigma_3$, $-\sigma_3\sigma_1$, and $\sigma_1\sigma_2$, we can recover the famous *Hamilton relations*:

$$\boldsymbol{i}^2 = \boldsymbol{j}^2 = \boldsymbol{k}^2 = \boldsymbol{ijk} = -1. \tag{4.8}$$

In geometric algebra a *rotor* $\boldsymbol{R}$ is an even-grade element of the algebra which satisfies the equation $\boldsymbol{R}\tilde{\boldsymbol{R}} = 1$. The relation between quaternions and rotors is as follows: if $\mathcal{Q} = \{q_0, q_1, q_2, q_3\}$ represents a *quaternion*, then the rotor which performs the same rotation is simply given by

$$\boldsymbol{R} = q_0 + q_1(I\sigma_1) - q_2(I\sigma_2) + q_3(I\sigma_3). \tag{4.9}$$

The quaternion algebra is therefore seen to be a subset of the geometric algebra of three-dimensional space.

4.2.3 A 4D geometric algebra for projective space

For the modeling of the image plane, we use $\mathcal{G}_{3,0,0}$, which has the standard *Euclidean signature*. We will show that if we choose to map between projective space and 3D Euclidean space via the projective split (see subsection 4.2.5), we are then forced to use the 4D geometric algebra $\mathcal{G}_{1,3,0}$ for $\mathcal{P}^3$. The Lorentzian metric we are using here has no adverse effects in the operations we outline in this chapter. However, we will briefly discuss in a later section how a $\{++++\}$ metric for our 4D space and a different split is being favored in recent research.

The Lorentzian 4D algebra has as its vector basis $\gamma_1, \gamma_2, \gamma_3, \gamma_4$, where $\gamma_4^2 = +1$ $and \gamma_k^2 = -1$ for $k = 1, 2, 3$. This then generates the following multivector basis:

$$\underbrace{1}_{scalar}, \underbrace{\gamma_k}_{4\ vectors}, \underbrace{\gamma_2\gamma_3, \gamma_3\gamma_1, \gamma_1\gamma_2, \gamma_4\gamma_1, \gamma_4\gamma_2, \gamma_4\gamma_3}_{6\ bivectors}, \underbrace{I\gamma_k}_{4\ trivectors}, \underbrace{I}_{pseudoscalar}. \tag{4.10}$$

The pseudoscalar is $I = \gamma_1\gamma_2\gamma_3\gamma_4$, with

$$I^2 = (\gamma_1\gamma_2\gamma_3\gamma_4)(\gamma_1\gamma_2\gamma_3\gamma_4) = -(\gamma_3\gamma_4)(\gamma_3\gamma_4) = -1. \tag{4.11}$$

The fourth basis vector, γ_4, can also be seen as a selected direction for the *projective split* [6] operation in 4D. We will see shortly that by carrying out the geometric product via γ_4, we can associate bivectors of our 4D space with vectors of our 3D space. The role and use of the projective split operation will be treated in more detail in a later section.

4.2.4 Projective transformations

Historically, the success of homogeneous coordinates has partly been due to their ability to represent a general displacement as a single 4×4 matrix and to linearize nonlinear transformations [32].

The following equation indicates how a projective transformation may be linearized by going up one dimension in the GA framework. In general, a point (x, y, z) in the 3D space is projected onto the image via a transformation of the form:

$$x' = \frac{\alpha_1 x + \beta_1 y + \delta_1 z + \epsilon_1}{\tilde{\alpha} x + \tilde{\beta} y + \tilde{\delta} z + \tilde{\epsilon}}, \quad y' = \frac{\alpha_2 x + \beta_2 y + \delta_2 z + \epsilon_2}{\tilde{\alpha} x + \tilde{\beta} y + \tilde{\delta} z + \tilde{\epsilon}}. \tag{4.12}$$

This transformation, which is expressed as the ratio of two linear transformations, is indeed nonlinear. In order to convert this nonlinear transformation in $\mathcal{E}^3$ into a linear transformation in R^4, we define a linear function $\underline{f}_p$ by mapping vectors onto vectors in R^4 such that the action of $\underline{f}_p$ on the basis vectors $\{\gamma_i\}$ is given by

$$\begin{aligned}
\underline{f}_p(\gamma_1) &= \alpha_1\gamma_1 + \alpha_2\gamma_2 + \alpha_3\gamma_3 + \tilde{\alpha}\gamma_4 \\
\underline{f}_p(\gamma_2) &= \beta_1\gamma_1 + \beta_2\gamma_2 + \beta_3\gamma_3 + \tilde{\beta}\gamma_4 \\
\underline{f}_p(\gamma_3) &= \delta_1\gamma_1 + \delta_2\gamma_2 + \delta_3\gamma_3 + \tilde{\delta}\gamma_4 \\
\underline{f}_p(\gamma_4) &= \epsilon_1\gamma_1 + \epsilon_2\gamma_2 + \epsilon_3\gamma_3 + \tilde{\epsilon}\gamma_4.
\end{aligned} \tag{4.13}$$

When we use homogeneous coordinates, a general point P in $\mathcal{E}^3$ given by $\boldsymbol{x} = x\sigma_1 + y\sigma_2 + z\sigma_3$ becomes the point $\mathbf{X} = (X\gamma_1 + Y\gamma_2 + Z\gamma_3 + W\gamma_4)$ in R^4, where $x = X/W$, $y = Y/W$, $andz = Z/W$. Now, using $\underline{f}_p$, the linear map of $\mathbf{X}$ onto $\mathbf{X}'$ is given by

$$\mathbf{X}' = \sum_{i=1}^{3}\{(\alpha_i X + \beta_i Y + \delta_i Z + \epsilon_i W)\gamma_i\} + (\tilde{\alpha}X + \tilde{\beta}Y + \tilde{\delta}Z + \tilde{\epsilon}W)\gamma_4. \quad (4.14)$$

The coordinates of the vector $\boldsymbol{x}' = x'\sigma_1 + y'\sigma_2 + z'\sigma_3$ in $\mathcal{E}^3$ which correspond to $\mathbf{X}'$ are given by

$$x' = \frac{\alpha_1 X + \beta_1 Y + \delta_1 Z + \epsilon_1 W}{\tilde{\alpha}X + \tilde{\beta}Y + \tilde{\delta}Z + \tilde{\epsilon}W} = \frac{\alpha_1 x + \beta_1 y + \delta_1 z + \epsilon_1}{\tilde{\alpha}x + \tilde{\beta}y + \tilde{\delta}z + \tilde{\epsilon}}, \quad (4.15)$$

and similarly,

$$y' = \frac{\alpha_2 x + \beta_2 y + \delta_2 z + \epsilon_2}{\tilde{\alpha}x + \tilde{\beta}y + \tilde{\delta}z + \tilde{\epsilon}}, \qquad z' = \frac{\alpha_3 x + \beta_3 y + \delta_3 z + \epsilon_3}{\tilde{\alpha}x + \tilde{\beta}y + \tilde{\delta}z + \tilde{\epsilon}}. \quad (4.16)$$

If the above represents projection from the world onto a camera image plane, we should take into account the focal length of the camera. This would require that $\alpha_3 = f\tilde{\alpha}$, $\beta_3 = f\tilde{\beta}$, etc. Thus, we can define $z' = f$ (focal length) independent of the point chosen. The nonlinear transformation in $\mathcal{E}^3$ then becomes a linear transformation, $\underline{f}_p$, in R^4. The linear function $\underline{f}_p$ can then be used to prove the invariant nature of various quantities under projective transformations [66].

4.2.5 The projective split

The idea of the *projective split* was introduced by Hestenes [50] in order to connect *projective geometry* and *metric geometry.* This is done by associating the even subalgebra of $\mathcal{G}_{n+1}$ with the geometric algebra of next lower dimension, $\mathcal{G}_n$. One can define a mapping between the spaces by choosing a preferred direction in $\mathcal{G}_{n+1}$, γ_{n+1}. Then, by taking the geometric product of a vector $\mathbf{X} \in \mathcal{G}_{n+1}$ and γ_{n+1},

$$\mathbf{X}\gamma_{n+1} = \mathbf{X}\cdot\gamma_{n+1} + \mathbf{X}\wedge\gamma_{n+1} = \mathbf{X}\cdot\gamma_{n+1}(1 + \frac{\mathbf{X}\wedge\gamma_{n+1}}{\mathbf{X}\cdot\gamma_{n+1}}), \quad (4.17)$$

the vector $\boldsymbol{x} \in \mathcal{G}_n$ can be associated with the bivector $\frac{\mathbf{X}\wedge\gamma_{n+1}}{\mathbf{X}\cdot\gamma_{n+1}} \in \mathcal{G}_{n+1}$. This result can be projectively interpreted as the pencil of all lines passing though the point γ_{n+1}. In physics, the projective split is called the *space-time split,* and it relates a space-time system $\mathcal{G}_4$ with a Minkowski metric to an observable system $\mathcal{G}_3$ with a Euclidean metric.

In computer vision, we are interested in relating elements of projective space with their associated elements in the Euclidean space of the image plane. Optical rays (bivectors) are mapped to points (vectors), optical planes (trivectors) are mapped to lines (bivectors), and optical volumes (4-vectors) to planes (trivector or pseudoscalar).

Suppose we choose γ_4 as a selected direction in R^4. We can then define a mapping which associates the bivectors $\gamma_i\gamma_4$, $i = 1,2,3$ in R^4 with the vectors σ_i, $i = 1,2,3$ in $\mathcal{E}^3$:

$$\sigma_1 \equiv \gamma_1\gamma_4, \quad \sigma_2 \equiv \gamma_2\gamma_4, \quad \sigma_3 \equiv \gamma_3\gamma_4. \tag{4.18}$$

Note that in order to preserve the Euclidean structure of the spatial vectors $\{\sigma_i\}$ (i.e. $\sigma_i^2 = +1$) we are forced to choose a non-Euclidean metric for the basis vectors in R^4. That is why we select the basis $\gamma_4^2 = +1$, $\gamma_i = -1$, $i = 1,2,3$ for $\mathcal{G}_{1,3,0}$. This is precisely the metric structure of Lorentzian space-time used in studies of relativistic physics. We note here that although we have chosen to relate our spaces via the projective split, it is possible to use a Euclidean metric $\{++++\}$ for our 4D space and define the split using reciprocal vectors [80]. It is becoming apparent that this is the preferred procedure since it generalizes nicely to splits from higher-dimensional spaces. However, for the problems discussed in this chapter, we encounter no problems by using the projective split.

Let us now see how we associate points via the projective split. For a vector $\mathbf{X} = X_1\gamma_1 + X_2\gamma_2 + X_3\gamma_3 + X_4\gamma_4$ in R^4 the projective split is obtained by taking the geometric product of $\mathbf{X}$ and γ_4:

$$\mathbf{X}\gamma_4 = \mathbf{X}\cdot\gamma_4 + \mathbf{X}\wedge\gamma_4 = X_4\left(1 + \frac{\mathbf{X}\wedge\gamma_4}{X_4}\right) \equiv X_4(1+\boldsymbol{x}). \tag{4.19}$$

According to equation (4.18), we can associate $\mathbf{X}\wedge\gamma_4/X_4$ in R^4 with the vector $\boldsymbol{x}$ in $\mathcal{E}^3$. Similarly, if we start with a vector $\boldsymbol{x} = x_1\sigma_1 + x_2\sigma_2 + x_3\sigma_3$ in $\mathcal{E}^3$, we represent it in R^4 by the vector $\mathbf{X} = X_1\gamma_1 + X_2\gamma_2 + X_3\gamma_3 + X_4\gamma_4$ such that

$$\begin{aligned} \boldsymbol{x} &= \frac{\mathbf{X}\wedge\gamma_4}{X_4} = \frac{X_1}{X_4}\gamma_1\gamma_4 + \frac{X_2}{X_4}\gamma_2\gamma_4 + \frac{X_3}{X_4}\gamma_3\gamma_4 \\ &= \frac{X_1}{X_4}\sigma_1 + \frac{X_2}{X_4}\sigma_2 + \frac{X_3}{X_4}\sigma_3, \end{aligned} \tag{4.20}$$

which implies $x_i = \frac{X_i}{X_4}$ for $i = 1,2,3$. This manner of representing $\boldsymbol{x}$ in a higher-dimensional space can therefore be seen to be equivalent to using *homogeneous coordinates* $\mathbf{X}$ for $\boldsymbol{x}$.

Let us now look at the representation of a line L in R^4. A line is given by the outer product of two vectors:

$$\begin{aligned} L &= \boldsymbol{A}\wedge\boldsymbol{B} \\ &= (L^{14}\gamma_1\gamma_4 + L^{24}\gamma_2\gamma_4 + L^{34}\gamma_3\gamma_4) + (L^{23}\gamma_2\gamma_3 + L^{31}\gamma_3\gamma_1 + L^{12}\gamma_1\gamma_2) \\ &= (L^{14}\gamma_1\gamma_4 + L^{24}\gamma_2\gamma_4 + L^{34}\gamma_3\gamma_4) - I(L^{23}\gamma_1\gamma_4 + L^{31}\gamma_2\gamma_4 + L^{12}\gamma_3\gamma_4) \\ &= \boldsymbol{n} - I\boldsymbol{m}. \end{aligned} \tag{4.21}$$

The six quantities $\{n_i, m_i\}$ $i = 1, 2, 3$ are precisely the Plücker coordinates of the line. The quantities $\{L^{14}, L^{24}, L^{34}\}$ are the coefficients of the *spatial part* of the bivector which represents the line direction $\boldsymbol{n}$. The quantities $\{L^{23}, L^{31}, L^{12}\}$ are the coefficients of the *non-spatial part* of the bivector which represents the *moment* of the line $\boldsymbol{m}$.

Let us now see how we can relate this line representation to an $\mathcal{E}^3$ representation via the projective split. We take a line L, joining points $\mathbf{A}$ and $\mathbf{B}$,

$$L = \mathbf{A} \wedge \mathbf{B} = \langle \mathbf{AB} \rangle_2 = \langle \mathbf{A}\gamma_4\gamma_4\mathbf{B} \rangle_2. \tag{4.22}$$

Here, the notation $\langle M \rangle_k$, tells us to take the grade-k part of the multivector M. Now, using our previous expansions of $\mathbf{X}\gamma_4$ in the projective split for vectors, we can write

$$L = (\mathbf{A}\cdot\gamma_4)(\mathbf{B}\cdot\gamma_4)\langle(1+\boldsymbol{a})(1-\boldsymbol{b})\rangle_2, \tag{4.23}$$

where $\boldsymbol{a} = \frac{\mathbf{A}\wedge\gamma_4}{\mathbf{A}\gamma_4}$ and $\boldsymbol{b} = \frac{\mathbf{B}\wedge\gamma_4}{\mathbf{B}\gamma_4}$ are the $\mathcal{E}^3$ representations of $\mathbf{A}$ and $\mathbf{B}$. Writing $A_4 = \mathbf{A}\cdot\gamma_4$ and $B_4 = \mathbf{B}\cdot\gamma_4$ then gives us

$$\begin{aligned} L &= A_4B_4\langle 1 + (\boldsymbol{a}-\boldsymbol{b}) - \boldsymbol{ab}\rangle_2 \\ &= A_4B_4\{(\boldsymbol{a}-\boldsymbol{b}) + \boldsymbol{a}\wedge\boldsymbol{b}\}. \end{aligned} \tag{4.24}$$

Let us now "normalize" the spatial and non-spatial parts of the above bivector:

$$\begin{aligned} L' &= \frac{L}{A_4B_4|\boldsymbol{a}-\boldsymbol{b}|} = \frac{(\boldsymbol{a}-\boldsymbol{b})}{|\boldsymbol{a}-\boldsymbol{b}|} + \frac{(\boldsymbol{a}\wedge\boldsymbol{b})}{|\boldsymbol{a}-\boldsymbol{b}|} \\ &= (n_x\sigma_1 + n_y\sigma_2 + n_z\sigma_3) + (m_x\sigma_2\sigma_3 + m_y\sigma_3\sigma_1 + m_z\sigma_1\sigma_2) \\ &= (n_x\sigma_1 + n_y\sigma_2 + n_z\sigma_3) + I_3(m_x\sigma_1 + m_y\sigma_2 + m_z\sigma_3) = \boldsymbol{n}' + I_3\boldsymbol{m}'. \end{aligned} \tag{4.25}$$

Here, $I_3 = \sigma_1\sigma_2\sigma_3 \equiv I_4$. Note that in $\mathcal{E}^3$ the line has two components, a vector representing the direction of the line and the dual of a vector (bivector) representing the moment of the line. This kind of representation completely encodes the position of the line in 3D space by specifying the plane in which the line lies and the perpendicular distance of the line from the origin.

4.3 The Algebra of Incidence

In this section we will discuss the use of geometric algebra for the *algebra of incidence* [49]. First, we will define the concept of the bracket; then, we will discuss *duality*; and, finally, we will show that the basic projective geometry operations of meet and join can be expressed easily in terms of standard operations within the geometric algebra. We also briefly discuss the linear algebra framework in GA, indicating how it can be used within projective geometry. One of the main reasons for moving to a projective space is so that lines, planes, etc., may be represented as real geometric objects and so that operations of intersection, etc., can be performed using simple manipulations (rather than sets of equations, as in the Euclidean space $\mathcal{E}^3$).

4.3.1 The bracket

In an n-D space any pseudoscalar will span a hypervolume of dimension n. Since, up to scale, there can only be one such hypervolume, all pseudoscalars P are multiples of the unit pseudoscalar I, such that $P = \alpha I$, with α being a scalar. We compute this scalar multiple by multiplying the pseudoscalar P and the inverse of I:

$$PI^{-1} = \alpha II^{-1} = \alpha \equiv [P]. \tag{4.26}$$

Thus, the *bracket* $[P]$ of the pseudoscalar P is its magnitude, arrived at by multiplication from the right by I^{-1}. This bracket is precisely the bracket of the Grassmann–Cayley algebra. The sign of the bracket does not depend on the signature of the space, and as a result it has been a useful quantity for nonmetrical applications of projective geometry.

The bracket of n vectors $\{\boldsymbol{x}_i\}$ is

$$\begin{aligned} [\boldsymbol{x}_1\boldsymbol{x}_2\boldsymbol{x}_3...\boldsymbol{x}_n] &= [\boldsymbol{x}_1\wedge\boldsymbol{x}_2\wedge\boldsymbol{x}_3\wedge...\wedge\boldsymbol{x}_n] \\ &= (\boldsymbol{x}_1\wedge\boldsymbol{x}_2\wedge\boldsymbol{x}_3\wedge...\wedge\boldsymbol{x}_n)I^{-1}. \end{aligned} \tag{4.27}$$

It can also be shown that this bracket expression is equivalent to the definition of the determinant of the matrix whose row vectors are the vectors $\boldsymbol{x}_i$.

To understand how we can express a bracket in projective space in terms of vectors in Euclidean space we can expand the pseudoscalar P using the projective split for vectors:

$$\begin{aligned} P &= \mathbf{X}_1\wedge\mathbf{X}_2\wedge\mathbf{X}_3\wedge\mathbf{X}_4 = \langle\mathbf{X}_1\gamma_4\gamma_4\mathbf{X}_2\mathbf{X}_3\gamma_4\gamma_4\mathbf{X}_4\rangle_4 \\ &= W_1W_2W_3W_4\langle(1+\boldsymbol{x}_1)(1-\boldsymbol{x}_2)(1+\boldsymbol{x}_3)(1-\boldsymbol{x}_4)\rangle_4, \end{aligned}$$

where $W_i = \mathbf{X}_i\cdot\gamma_4$ from equation (4.19). A pseudoscalar part is produced by taking the product of three spatial vectors (there are no spatial bivector$\times$spatial vector terms), such that

$$\begin{aligned} P &= W_1W_2W_3W_4\langle-\boldsymbol{x}_1\boldsymbol{x}_2\boldsymbol{x}_3-\boldsymbol{x}_1\boldsymbol{x}_3\boldsymbol{x}_4+\boldsymbol{x}_1\boldsymbol{x}_2\boldsymbol{x}_4+\boldsymbol{x}_2\boldsymbol{x}_3\boldsymbol{x}_4\rangle_4 \\ &= W_1W_2W_3W_4\langle(\boldsymbol{x}_2-\boldsymbol{x}_1)(\boldsymbol{x}_3-\boldsymbol{x}_1)(\boldsymbol{x}_4-\boldsymbol{x}_1)\rangle_4 \\ &= W_1W_2W_3W_4\{(\boldsymbol{x}_2-\boldsymbol{x}_1)\wedge(\boldsymbol{x}_3-\boldsymbol{x}_1)\wedge(\boldsymbol{x}_4-\boldsymbol{x}_1)\}. \end{aligned} \tag{4.28}$$

If $W_i = 1$, we can summarize the above relationships between the brackets of four points in R^4 and $\mathcal{E}^3$ as follows:

$$\begin{aligned} [\mathbf{X}_1\mathbf{X}_2\mathbf{X}_3\mathbf{X}_4] &= (\mathbf{X}_1\wedge\mathbf{X}_2\wedge\mathbf{X}_3\wedge\mathbf{X}_4){I_4}^{-1} \\ &\equiv \{(\boldsymbol{x}_2-\boldsymbol{x}_1)\wedge(\boldsymbol{x}_3-\boldsymbol{x}_1)\wedge(\boldsymbol{x}_4-\boldsymbol{x}_1)\}{I_3}^{-1}. \end{aligned} \tag{4.29}$$

4.3.2 The duality principle and meet and join operations

In order to introduce the concepts of *duality* which are so important in projective geometry, we must first define the dual A^* of an r-vector A as

$$A^* = AI^{-1}. \tag{4.30}$$

This notation, A^*, relates the ideas of duality to the notion of a *Hodge dual* in differential geometry. Note that, in general, I^{-1} might not necessarily commute with $\boldsymbol{A}$.

We see, therefore, that the dual of an r-vector is an $(n-r)$-vector. For example, in 3D space the dual of a vector ($r = 1$) is a plane or bivector ($n - r = 3 - 1 = 2$).

By using the ideas of duality, we are then able to relate the inner product to incidence operators in the following manner. In an n-D space, suppose we have an r-vector A and an s-vector B, where the dual of B is given by $B^* = BI^{-1} \equiv B \cdot I^{-1}$. Since $BI^{-1} = B \cdot I^{-1} + B \wedge I^{-1}$, we can replace the geometric product by the inner product alone (in this case, the outer product equals zero, and there can be no $(n+1)$-D vector). Now, using the identity

$$A_r \cdot (B_s \cdot C_t) = (A_r \wedge B_s) \cdot C_t \quad \text{for} \quad r + s \leq t, \tag{4.31}$$

we can write

$$A \cdot (BI^{-1}) = A \cdot (B \cdot I^{-1}) = (A \wedge B) \cdot I^{-1} = (A \wedge B) I^{-1}. \tag{4.32}$$

This expression can be rewritten using the definition of the dual as follows:

$$A \cdot B^* = (A \wedge B)^*. \tag{4.33}$$

This equation shows the relationship between the inner and outer products in terms of the duality operator. Now, if $r + s = n$, then $A \wedge B$ is of grade n and is therefore a pseudoscalar. Using equation (4.26), it follows that

$$\begin{aligned} A \cdot B^* &= (A \wedge B)^* = (A \wedge B) I^{-1} = ([A \wedge B] I) I^{-1} \\ &= [A \wedge B]. \end{aligned} \tag{4.34}$$

We see, therefore, that the bracket relates the inner and outer products to nonmetric quantities. It is via this route that the inner product, normally associated with a metric, can be used in a nonmetric theory such as projective geometry. It is also interesting to note that since duality is expressed as a simple multiplication by an element of the algebra, there is no need to introduce any special operators or any concept of a different space.

When we work with lines and planes, however, it will clearly be necessary to employ operations for computing the intersections, or *joins*, of geometric objects. For this, we will require a means of performing the set-theory operations of intersection, $\cap$, and union, $\cup$.

If in an n-dimensional geometric algebra the r-vector A and the s-vector B do not have a common subspace (null intersection), one can define the *join* of both vectors as follows:

$$J = A \cup B = A \wedge B, \tag{4.35}$$

so that the join is simply the outer product (an $r+s$ vector) of the two vectors. However, if A and B have common blades, the join would not simply be given by the wedge but by the subspace the two vectors span. The operation join J can be interpreted as a *common dividend of lowest grade* and is defined up to a scale factor. The join gives the pseudoscalar if $(r+s) \geq n$. We will use $\cup$ to represent the join only when the blades A and B have a common subspace; otherwise, we will use the ordinary exterior product, $\wedge$, to represent the join.

If there exists a k-vector C such that for A and B we can write $A = A'C$ and $B = B'C$ for some A' and B', then we can define the *intersection* or *meet* using the duality principle as follows:

$$(A \cap B)^* = A^* \cup B^*. \tag{4.36}$$

This is a beautiful result, telling us that the dual of the meet is given by the join of the duals. Since the dual of $A \cap B$ will be taken with respect to the *join* of A and B, we must be careful to specify which space we will use for the dual in equation (4.36). However, in most cases of practical interest this join will indeed cover the entire space, and therefore we will be able to obtain a more useful expression for the meet using equation (4.33). Thus,

$$A \cap B = ((A \cap B)^*)^* = (A^* \cup B^*)I = (A^* \wedge B^*)(I^{-1}I)I = (A^* \cdot B). \tag{4.37}$$

The above concepts are discussed further in [49].

4.3.3 Linear algebra

This subsection presents the geometric algebra approach to the basic concepts of linear algebra and is presented here for completeness. Although it will not be discussed in this chapter, the treatment of invariants [66] uses linear algebra and projective geometry to create geometric entities which are invariant under projective transformations.

A linear function f maps vectors to vectors in the same space. The extension of f to act linearly on multivectors is possible via the so-called *outermorphism* $\underline{f}$, which defines the action of f on r-blades thus:

$$\underline{f}(\boldsymbol{a}_1 \wedge \boldsymbol{a}_2 \wedge \ldots \wedge \boldsymbol{a}_r) = \underline{f}(\boldsymbol{a}_1) \wedge \underline{f}(\boldsymbol{a}_2) \wedge \ldots \wedge \underline{f}(\boldsymbol{a}_r). \tag{4.38}$$

The function $\underline{f}$ is called an outermorphism because $\underline{f}$ preserves the grade of any r-vector it acts upon. The action of $\underline{f}$ on general multivectors is then defined through linearity. The function $\underline{f}$ must therefore satisfy the following conditions:

$$\begin{aligned} \underline{f}(\boldsymbol{a}_1 \wedge \boldsymbol{a}_2) &= \underline{f}(\boldsymbol{a}_1) \wedge \underline{f}(\boldsymbol{a}_2) \\ \underline{f}(A_r) &= \langle \underline{f}(A_r) \rangle_r \\ \underline{f}(\alpha_1 \boldsymbol{a}_1 + \alpha_2 \boldsymbol{a}_2) &= \alpha_1 \underline{f}(\boldsymbol{a}_1) + \alpha_2 \underline{f}(\boldsymbol{a}_2). \end{aligned} \tag{4.39}$$

Accordingly, the outermorphism of a product of two linear functions is the product of the outermorphisms—that is, if $f(\boldsymbol{a}) = f_2(f_1(\boldsymbol{a}))$, we write $\underline{f} = \underline{f}_2 \underline{f}_1$. The *adjoint* $\overline{f}$ of a linear function $\underline{f}$ acting on the vectors $\boldsymbol{a}$ and $\boldsymbol{b}$ can be defined by the property

$$\underline{f}(\boldsymbol{a}) \cdot \boldsymbol{b} = \boldsymbol{a} \cdot \overline{f}(\boldsymbol{b}). \tag{4.40}$$

If $\underline{f} = \overline{f}$, the function is *self-adjoint* and can be represented by a symmetric matrix F ($F = F^T$).

Since the outermorphism preserves grade, the unit pseudoscalar must be mapped onto some multiple of itself; this multiple is called the *determinant* of $\underline{f}$. Thus,

$$\underline{f}(I) = \det(\underline{f}) I. \tag{4.41}$$

This is a particularly simple definition of the determinant, from which many properties of the determinants follow straightforwardly.

4.4 Algebra in Projective Space

Having introduced duality, defined the operations of meet and join, and given the geometric approach to linear algebra, we are now ready to carry out geometric computations using the algebra of incidence.

Consider three non-collinear points, P_1, P_2, P_3, represented by vectors $\boldsymbol{x}_1$, $\boldsymbol{x}_2$, $\boldsymbol{x}_3$ in $\mathcal{E}^3$ and by vectors $\mathbf{X}_1$, $\mathbf{X}_2$, $\mathbf{X}_3$ in R^4. The line L_{12} joining points P_1 and P_2 can be expressed in R^4 by the bivector

$$L_{12} = \mathbf{X}_1 \wedge \mathbf{X}_2. \tag{4.42}$$

Any point P, represented in R^4 by $\mathbf{X}$, on the line through P_1 and P_2, will satisfy the equation

$$\mathbf{X} \wedge L_{12} = \mathbf{X} \wedge \mathbf{X}_1 \wedge \mathbf{X}_2 = 0. \tag{4.43}$$

This is therefore the equation of the line in R^4. In general, such an equation is telling us that $\mathbf{X}$ belongs to the subspace spanned by $\mathbf{X}_1$ and $\mathbf{X}_2$—that is, that

$$\mathbf{X} = \alpha_1 \mathbf{X}_1 + \alpha_2 \mathbf{X}_2 \tag{4.44}$$

for some α_1, α_2. In computer vision we can use this equation as a geometric constraint to test whether a point $\mathbf{X}$ lies on L_{12}.

The plane Φ_{123} passing through points P_1, P_2, P_3 is expressed by the following trivector in R^4:

$$\Phi_{123} = \mathbf{X}_1 \wedge \mathbf{X}_2 \wedge \mathbf{X}_3. \tag{4.45}$$

In 3D space there are generally three types of intersections we wish to consider: the intersection of a line and a plane, a plane and a plane, and a line and a line. To compute these intersections, we will make use of the following general formula [47], which gives the inner product of an r-blade, $A_r = \boldsymbol{a}_1 \wedge \boldsymbol{a}_2 \wedge ... \wedge \boldsymbol{a}_r$, and an s-blade, $B_s = \boldsymbol{b}_1 \wedge \boldsymbol{b}_2 \wedge ... \wedge \boldsymbol{b}_s$ (for $s \leq r$):

$$\begin{aligned} B_s \cdot (\boldsymbol{a}_1 \wedge \boldsymbol{a}_2 \wedge ... \wedge \boldsymbol{a}_r) &= \\ &\sum_{\boldsymbol{j}} \epsilon(j_1 j_2 ... j_r) B_s \cdot (\boldsymbol{a}_{j_1} \wedge \boldsymbol{a}_{j_2} \wedge ... \wedge \boldsymbol{a}_{j_s}) \boldsymbol{a}_{j_s+1} \wedge ... \wedge \boldsymbol{a}_{j_r} \end{aligned} \tag{4.46}$$

In the equation, we sum over all the combinations $\boldsymbol{j} = (j_1, j_2, ..., j_r)$ such that no two j_k's are the same. If $\boldsymbol{j}$ is an even permutation of $(1, 2, 3, ..., r)$, then the expression $\epsilon(j_1 j_2 ... j_r) = +1$, and it is an odd permutation if $\epsilon(j_1 j_2 ... j_r)=$ - 1.

4.4.1 Intersection of a line and a plane

In the space R^4, consider the line $A = \mathbf{X}_1 \wedge \mathbf{X}_2$ intersecting the plane $\Phi = \mathbf{Y}_1 \wedge \mathbf{Y}_2 \wedge \mathbf{Y}_3$. We can compute the intersection point using a *meet* operation, as follows:

$$A \cap \Phi = (\mathbf{X}_1 \wedge \mathbf{X}_2) \cap (\mathbf{Y}_1 \wedge \mathbf{Y}_2 \wedge \mathbf{Y}_3) = A \cap \Phi = A^* \cdot \Phi. \tag{4.47}$$

Here, we have used equation (4.37), and we note that in this case the join covers the entire space.

Note also that the pseudoscalar I_4 in $\mathcal{G}_{1,3,0}$ for R^4 squares to -1, that it commutes with bivectors but anticommutes with vectors and trivectors, and that its inverse is given by $I_4{}^{-1} = -I_4$. Therefore, we can claim that

$$A^* \cdot \Phi = (AI^{-1}) \cdot \Phi = -(AI) \cdot \Phi. \tag{4.48}$$

Now, using equation (4.47), we can expand the meet, such that

$$\begin{aligned} A \cap \Phi &= -(AI) \cdot (\mathbf{Y}_1 \wedge \mathbf{Y}_2 \wedge \mathbf{Y}_3) \\ &= -\{(AI) \cdot (\mathbf{Y}_2 \wedge \mathbf{Y}_3)\} \mathbf{Y}_1 + \{(AI) \cdot (\mathbf{Y}_3 \wedge \mathbf{Y}_1)\} \mathbf{Y}_2 + \\ &\quad + \{(AI) \cdot (\mathbf{Y}_1 \wedge \mathbf{Y}_2)\} \mathbf{Y}_3. \end{aligned} \tag{4.49}$$

Noting that $(AI)\cdot(\mathbf{Y}_i\wedge\mathbf{Y}_j)$ is a scalar, we can evaluate equation 4.49 by taking scalar parts. For example, $(AI)\cdot(\mathbf{Y}_2\wedge\mathbf{Y}_3) = \langle I(\mathbf{X}_1\wedge\mathbf{X}_2)(\mathbf{Y}_2\wedge\mathbf{Y}_3)\rangle = I(\mathbf{X}_1\wedge\mathbf{X}_2\wedge\mathbf{Y}_2\wedge\mathbf{Y}_3)$. From the definition of the bracket given earlier, we can see that if $P = \mathbf{X}_1\wedge\mathbf{X}_2\wedge\mathbf{Y}_2\wedge\mathbf{Y}_3$, then $[P] = (\mathbf{X}_1\wedge\mathbf{X}_2\wedge\mathbf{Y}_2\wedge\mathbf{Y}_3)I_4{}^{-1}$. If we therefore write $[\mathbf{A}_1\mathbf{A}_2\mathbf{A}_3\mathbf{A}_4]$ as a shorthand for the magnitude of the pseudoscalar formed from the four vectors, then we can readily see that the meet reduces to

$$A\cap\Phi = [\mathbf{X}_1\mathbf{X}_2\mathbf{Y}_2\mathbf{Y}_3]\mathbf{Y}_1 + [\mathbf{X}_1\mathbf{X}_2\mathbf{Y}_3\mathbf{Y}_1]\mathbf{Y}_2 + [\mathbf{X}_1\mathbf{X}_2\mathbf{Y}_1\mathbf{Y}_2]\mathbf{Y}_3, \quad (4.50)$$

thus giving the intersection point (vector in R^4).

4.4.2 Intersection of two planes

The *line of intersection of two planes*, $\Phi_1 = \mathbf{X}_1\wedge\mathbf{X}_2\wedge\mathbf{X}_3$ and $\Phi_2 = \mathbf{Y}_1\wedge\mathbf{Y}_2\wedge\mathbf{Y}_3$, can be computed via the meet of Φ_1 and Φ_2:

$$\Phi_1\cap\Phi_2 = (\mathbf{X}_1\wedge\mathbf{X}_2\wedge\mathbf{X}_3)\cap(\mathbf{Y}_1\wedge\mathbf{Y}_2\wedge\mathbf{Y}_3). \quad (4.51)$$

As in the previous section, this expression can be expanded as

$$\begin{aligned}\Phi_1\cap\Phi_2 &= \Phi_1{}^*\cdot(\mathbf{Y}_1\wedge\mathbf{Y}_2\wedge\mathbf{Y}_3)\\ &= -\{(\Phi_1 I)\cdot\mathbf{Y}_1\}(\mathbf{Y}_2\wedge\mathbf{Y}_3) + \{(\Phi_1 I)\cdot\mathbf{Y}_2\}(\mathbf{Y}_3\wedge\mathbf{Y}_1) +\\ &\quad +\{(\Phi_1 I)\cdot\mathbf{Y}_3\}(\mathbf{Y}_1\wedge\mathbf{Y}_2).\end{aligned}$$

Once again, the join covers the entire space and so the dual is easily formed. Following the arguments of the previous section, we can show that $(\Phi_1 I)\cdot\mathbf{Y}_i \equiv -[\mathbf{X}_1\mathbf{X}_2\mathbf{X}_3\mathbf{Y}_i]$, so that the meet is

$$\begin{aligned}\Phi_1\cap\Phi_2 &= [\mathbf{X}_1\mathbf{X}_2\mathbf{X}_3\mathbf{Y}_1](\mathbf{Y}_2\wedge\mathbf{Y}_3) + [\mathbf{X}_1\mathbf{X}_2\mathbf{X}_3\mathbf{Y}_2](\mathbf{Y}_3\wedge\mathbf{Y}_1) +\\ &\quad +[\mathbf{X}_1\mathbf{X}_2\mathbf{X}_3\mathbf{Y}_3](\mathbf{Y}_1\wedge\mathbf{Y}_2), \quad (4.52)\end{aligned}$$

thus producing a line of intersection or bivector in R^4.

4.4.3 Intersection of two lines

Two lines will intersect only if they are coplanar. This means that their representations in R^4, $A = \mathbf{X}_1\wedge\mathbf{X}_2$, and $B = \mathbf{Y}_1\wedge\mathbf{Y}_2$ will satisfy the equation

$$A\wedge B = 0. \quad (4.53)$$

This fact suggests that the computation of the intersection should be carried out in the 2D Euclidean space which has an associated 3D projective counterpart R^3. In this plane, the intersection point is given by

$$\begin{aligned}A\cap B &= A^*\cdot B = -(AI_3)\cdot(\mathbf{Y}_1\wedge\mathbf{Y}_2)\\ &= -\{((AI_3)\cdot\mathbf{Y}_1)\mathbf{Y}_2 - ((AI_3)\cdot\mathbf{Y}_2)\mathbf{Y}_1\}, \quad (4.54)\end{aligned}$$

where I_3 is the pseudoscalar for R^3. Once again, we evaluate $((AI_3)\cdot\mathbf{Y}_i)$ by taking scalar parts:

$$(AI_3)\cdot\mathbf{Y}_i = \langle\mathbf{X}_1\mathbf{X}_2 I_3\mathbf{Y}_i\rangle = I_3\mathbf{X}_1\mathbf{X}_2\mathbf{Y}_i = -[\mathbf{X}_1\mathbf{X}_2\mathbf{Y}_i]. \tag{4.55}$$

The meet can therefore be written as

$$A\cap B = [\mathbf{X}_1\mathbf{X}_2\mathbf{Y}_1]\mathbf{Y}_2 - [\mathbf{X}_1\mathbf{X}_2\mathbf{Y}_2]\mathbf{Y}_1, \tag{4.56}$$

where the bracket $[\mathbf{A}_1\mathbf{A}_2\mathbf{A}_3]$ in R^3 is understood to mean $(\mathbf{A}_1\wedge\mathbf{A}_2\wedge\mathbf{A}_3)I_3{}^{-1}$. This equation is often an impractical means of performing the intersection of two lines. (See [80] for a method which creates a plane and intersects one of the lines with this plane; see also [30] for a discussion of what information can be gained when the lines do not intersect. See Chapter 3 for a complete treatment of the incidence relations between points, lines, and planes in the n-affine plane.)

4.4.4 Implementation of the algebra

In order to implement the expressions and procedures outlined so far in this chapter, we have used a computer algebra package written for MAPLE. The program can be found in [63] and works with geometric algebras of $\mathcal{G}_{1,3,0}$ and $\mathcal{G}_{3,0,0}$; a more general version of this program, which works with a user-defined metric on an n-D algebra, is in the public domain [3]. Using these packages, we are easily able to simulate the situation of several cameras (or one moving camera) looking at a world scene and to do so entirely in projective (4D) space. Much of the work described in subsequent sections has been tested in MAPLE.

4.5 Visual Geometry of n-Uncalibrated Cameras

In this section we will analyze the constraints relating the geometry of n-uncalibrated cameras. First, the pinhole camera model for one view will be defined in terms of lines and planes. Then, for two and three views, the epipolar geometry is defined in terms of bilinear and trilinear constraints. Since the constraints are based on the coplanarity of lines, we will only be able to define relationships expressed by a single tensor for up to four cameras. For more than four cameras, the constraints are linear combinations of bilinearities, trilinearities, and quadrilinearities.

4.5.1 Geometry of one view

We begin with the monocular case depicted in Fig. 4.2. Here, the image plane is defined by a vector basis of three arbitrary non-collinear points $\mathbf{A}_1$, $\mathbf{A}_2$,

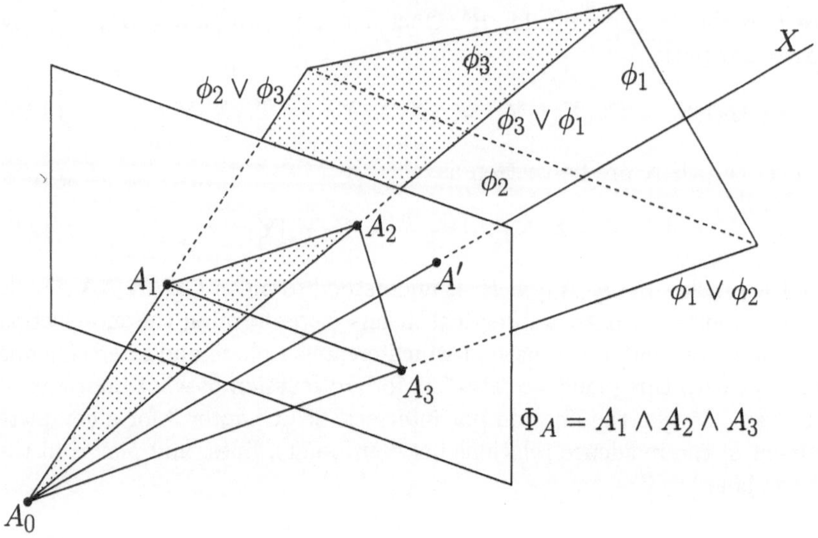

FIGURE 4.2. Projection into a single camera: the monocular case

and $\mathbf{A}_3$, with the optical center given by $\mathbf{A}_0$ (all vectors in R^4). Thus, $\{\mathbf{A}_i\}$ can be used as a coordinate basis for the image plane $\Phi_A = \mathbf{A}_1 \wedge \mathbf{A}_2 \wedge \mathbf{A}_3$, so that any point $\mathbf{A}'$ lying in Φ_A can be written as

$$\mathbf{A}' = \alpha_1 \mathbf{A}_1 + \alpha_2 \mathbf{A}_2 + \alpha_3 \mathbf{A}_3. \tag{4.57}$$

We are also able to define a bivector basis of the image plane $\{L_i^A\}$ spanning the lines in Φ_A:

$$L_1^A = \mathbf{A}_2 \wedge \mathbf{A}_3 \qquad L_2^A = \mathbf{A}_3 \wedge \mathbf{A}_1 \qquad L_3^A = \mathbf{A}_1 \wedge \mathbf{A}_2. \tag{4.58}$$

The bivectors $\{L_i^A\}$ together with the optical center allow us to define three planes, ϕ_i^A, as follows:

$$\begin{aligned} \phi_1^A &= \mathbf{A}_0 \wedge \mathbf{A}_2 \wedge \mathbf{A}_3 = \mathbf{A}_0 \wedge L_1^A \\ \phi_2^A &= \mathbf{A}_0 \wedge \mathbf{A}_3 \wedge \mathbf{A}_1 = \mathbf{A}_0 \wedge L_2^A \\ \phi_3^A &= \mathbf{A}_0 \wedge \mathbf{A}_1 \wedge \mathbf{A}_2 = \mathbf{A}_0 \wedge L_3^A. \end{aligned} \tag{4.59}$$

We will call the planes ϕ_j^A *optical planes*. Clearly, each is a trivector and can be written as

$$\phi_j^A = t_{j1}(I\gamma_1) + t_{j2}(I\gamma_2) + t_{j3}(I\gamma_3) + t_{j4}(I\gamma_4) \equiv t_{jk}(I\gamma_k) \tag{4.60}$$

since there are four basis trivectors in our 4D space. These optical planes also clearly intersect the image plane in the lines $\{L_j^A\}$. Furthermore, the intersections of the optical planes also define a bivector basis which spans the pencil of *optical rays* (rays passing through the optical center of the camera) in R^4. Thus,

$$\begin{aligned} L_{A1} &= \phi_2 \cap \phi_3 \equiv \mathbf{A}_0 \wedge \mathbf{A}_1 \\ L_{A2} &= \phi_3 \cap \phi_1 \equiv \mathbf{A}_0 \wedge \mathbf{A}_2 \\ L_{A3} &= \phi_1 \cap \phi_2 \equiv \mathbf{A}_0 \wedge \mathbf{A}_3, \end{aligned} \tag{4.61}$$

so that any optical ray resulting from projecting a world point $\mathbf{X}$ onto the image plane can be written as

$$\mathbf{A}_0 \wedge \mathbf{X} = x_j L_{Aj}.$$

We can now interpret the camera matrices, used so widely in computer vision applications, in terms of the quantities defined in this section.

The projection of any world point $\mathbf{X}$ onto the image plane is notated $\boldsymbol{x}$ and is given by the intersection of line $\mathbf{A}_0 \wedge \mathbf{X}$ with the plane Φ_A. Thus,

$$\boldsymbol{x} = (\mathbf{A}_0 \wedge \mathbf{X}) \cap (\mathbf{A}_1 \wedge \mathbf{A}_2 \wedge \mathbf{A}_3) = X_\mu \{(\mathbf{A}_0 \wedge \gamma_\mu) \cap (\mathbf{A}_1 \wedge \mathbf{A}_2 \wedge \mathbf{A}_3)\}, \tag{4.62}$$

where μ is summed over 1 to 4. We can now expand the meet given by equation (4.62) to get

$$\begin{aligned} \boldsymbol{x} = X_j \{ & [\mathbf{A}_0 \wedge \gamma_j \wedge \mathbf{A}_2 \wedge \mathbf{A}_3]\mathbf{A}_1 + [\mathbf{A}_0 \wedge \gamma_j \wedge \mathbf{A}_3 \wedge \mathbf{A}_1]\mathbf{A}_2 + \\ & [\mathbf{A}_0 \wedge \gamma_j \wedge \mathbf{A}_1 \wedge \mathbf{A}_2]\mathbf{A}_3 \}. \end{aligned} \tag{4.63}$$

Since $\boldsymbol{x} = x^k \mathbf{A}_k$, equation (4.63) implies that $\boldsymbol{x} = X_j P_{jk} \mathbf{A}_k$ and therefore that

$$x^k = P_{jk} X_j,$$

where

$$P_{jk} = [\mathbf{A}_0 \wedge \gamma_j \wedge L_k^A] \equiv [\phi_k \wedge \gamma_j] = -t_{kj}, \tag{4.64}$$

since $I\gamma_j \wedge \gamma_k = -I\delta_{jk}$. The matrix P takes $\mathbf{X}$ to $\boldsymbol{x}$ and is therefore the standard camera projection matrix. If we define a set of vectors $\{\phi_A^j\}$, $j = 1, 2, 3$, which are the duals of the planes $\{\phi_j^A\}$—that is, $\phi_A^j = \phi_j^A I^{-1}$—it is then easy to see that

$$\phi_A^j = -\phi_j^A I = I\phi_j^A = -[t_{j1}\gamma_1 + t_{j2}\gamma_2 + t_{j3}\gamma_3 + t_{j4}\gamma_4]. \tag{4.65}$$

Thus, we see that the projected point $\boldsymbol{x} = x^j \mathbf{A}_j$ may be given by

$$x^j = \mathbf{X} \cdot \phi_A^j \qquad \text{or} \qquad \boldsymbol{x} = (\mathbf{X} \cdot \phi_A^j)\mathbf{A}_j. \tag{4.66}$$

That is, the coefficients in the image plane are formed by projecting $\mathbf{X}$ onto the vectors formed by taking the duals of the optical planes. This is, of course, equivalent to the matrix formulation

$$\boldsymbol{x} = \begin{bmatrix} x_1 \\ x_2 \\ x_3 \end{bmatrix} = \begin{bmatrix} \phi_A^1 \\ \phi_A^2 \\ \phi_A^3 \end{bmatrix} \boldsymbol{X} = \begin{bmatrix} t_{11} & t_{12} & t_{13} & t_{14} \\ t_{21} & t_{22} & t_{23} & t_{24} \\ t_{31} & t_{32} & t_{33} & t_{34} \end{bmatrix} \begin{bmatrix} X_1 \\ X_2 \\ X_3 \\ X_4 \end{bmatrix} \equiv P\boldsymbol{X} \quad (4.67)$$

The elements of the camera matrix are therefore simply the coefficients of each optical plane in the coordinate frame of the world point. They encode the intrinsic and extrinsic camera parameters as given in equation (4.2).

Next, we consider the projection of world lines in R^4 onto the image plane. Suppose we have a world line $L = \mathbf{X}_1 \wedge \mathbf{X}_2$ joining the points $\mathbf{X}_1$ and $\mathbf{X}_2$. If $\boldsymbol{x}_1 = (\mathbf{A}_0 \wedge \mathbf{X}_1) \cap \Phi_A$ and $\boldsymbol{x}_2 = (\mathbf{A}_0 \wedge \mathbf{X}_2) \cap \Phi_A$ (i.e., the intersections of the optical rays with the image plane), then the projected line in the image plane is clearly given by

$$l = \boldsymbol{x}_1 \wedge \boldsymbol{x}_2.$$

Since we can express l in the bivector basis for the plane, we obtain

$$l = l^j L_j^A,$$

where $L_1^A = \mathbf{A}_2 \wedge \mathbf{A}_3$, etc., as defined in equation (4.58). From our previous expressions for projections given in equation (4.66), we see that we can also write l as follows:

$$l = \boldsymbol{x}_1 \wedge \boldsymbol{x}_2 = (\mathbf{X}_1 \cdot \phi_A^j)(\mathbf{X}_2 \cdot \phi_A^k) \mathbf{A}_j \wedge \mathbf{A}_k \equiv l^p L_p^A, \quad (4.68)$$

which tells us that the *line coefficients* $\{l^j\}$ are

$$\begin{aligned} l^1 &= (\mathbf{X}_1 \cdot \phi_A^2)(\mathbf{X}_2 \cdot \phi_A^3) - (\mathbf{X}_1 \cdot \phi_A^3)(\mathbf{X}_2 \cdot \phi_A^2) \\ l^2 &= (\mathbf{X}_1 \cdot \phi_A^3)(\mathbf{X}_2 \cdot \phi_A^1) - (\mathbf{X}_1 \cdot \phi_A^1)(\mathbf{X}_2 \cdot \phi_A^3) \\ l^3 &= (\mathbf{X}_1 \cdot \phi_A^1)(\mathbf{X}_2 \cdot \phi_A^2) - (\mathbf{X}_1 \cdot \phi_A^2)(\mathbf{X}_2 \cdot \phi_A^1). \end{aligned} \quad (4.69)$$

Using the identity in equation (4.36) and utilizing the fact that the join of the duals is the dual of the meet, we are then able to deduce identities of the following form for each l^j:

$$l^1 = (\mathbf{X}_1 \wedge \mathbf{X}_2) \cdot (\phi_A^2 \wedge \phi_A^3) = (\mathbf{X}_1 \wedge \mathbf{X}_2) \cdot (\phi_2^A \cap \phi_3^A)^* = L \cdot (L_1^A)^*.$$

We therefore obtain the general result,

$$l^j = L \cdot (L_j^A)^* \equiv L \cdot L_A^j, \quad (4.70)$$

where we have defined L_A^j to be the dual of L_j^A. Thus, we have once again expressed the projection of a line L onto the image plane by contracting L with the set of lines dual to those formed by intersecting the optical planes.

We can summarize the two results derived here for the projections of points ($\mathbf{X}_1$ and $\mathbf{X}_2$) and lines ($L = \mathbf{X}_1 \wedge \mathbf{X}_2$) onto the image plane:

$$
\begin{aligned}
x_1 &= (\mathbf{X}_1 \cdot \phi_A^j)\mathbf{A}_j \qquad\qquad x_2 = (\mathbf{X}_2 \cdot \phi_A^j)\mathbf{A}_j \\
l &= (L \cdot L_A^j) L_j^A \equiv l^k L_k^A .
\end{aligned}
\tag{4.71}
$$

Having formed the sets of dual planes $\{\phi_A^j\}$ and dual lines L_A^j for a given image plane, it is then conceptually very straightforward to project any point or line onto that plane.

If we express the world and image lines as bivectors, $L = \alpha_j \sigma_j + \tilde{\alpha}_j I \sigma_j$ and $L_A^p = \beta_j \sigma_j + \tilde{\beta}_j I \sigma_j$, we can write equation (4.71) as a matrix equation:

$$
\boldsymbol{l} = \begin{bmatrix} l^1 \\ l^2 \\ l^3 \end{bmatrix} = \begin{bmatrix} u_{11} & u_{12} & u_{13} & u_{14} & u_{15} & u_{16} \\ u_{21} & u_{22} & u_{23} & u_{24} & u_{25} & u_{26} \\ u_{31} & u_{32} & u_{33} & u_{34} & u_{35} & u_{36} \end{bmatrix} \begin{bmatrix} \alpha_1 \\ \alpha_2 \\ \alpha_3 \\ \tilde{\alpha}_1 \\ \tilde{\alpha}_2 \\ \tilde{\alpha}_3 \end{bmatrix} \equiv P_L \bar{\boldsymbol{l}}, \tag{4.72}
$$

where $\bar{l}$ is the vector of *Plücker coordinates* $[\alpha_1, \alpha_2, \alpha_3, \tilde{\alpha}_1, \tilde{\alpha}_2, \tilde{\alpha}_3]$ and the matrix P_L contains the β and $\tilde{beta}$'s, that is, information about the camera configuration.

When we back-project a point $\boldsymbol{x}$ or line l in the image plane, we produce their duals, that is, a line l_x or a plane ϕ_l, respectively. These back-projected lines and planes are given by the following expressions:

$$
l_x = \mathbf{A}_0 \wedge \boldsymbol{x} = (\mathbf{X} \cdot \phi_A^j) \mathbf{A}_0 \wedge \mathbf{A}_j = (\mathbf{X} \cdot \phi_A^j) \boldsymbol{L}_j^A \tag{4.73}
$$

$$
\phi_l = \mathbf{A}_0 \wedge l = (L \cdot L_A^j) \mathbf{A}_0 \wedge L_j^A = (L \cdot L_A^j) \phi_j^A . \tag{4.74}
$$

4.5.2 Geometry of two views

In this and subsequent sections we will work in projective space R^4, although a return to 3D Euclidean space will be necessary when we discuss invariants in terms of image coordinates; this will be done via the projective split. Fig. 4.3 shows a world point $\mathbf{X}$ projecting onto points $\mathbf{A}'$ and $\mathbf{B}'$ in the two image planes ϕ_A and ϕ_B, respectively.

The so-called epipoles $\boldsymbol{E}_{AB}$ and $\boldsymbol{E}_{BA}$ correspond to the intersections of the line joining the optical centers with the image planes. Since the points $\mathbf{A}_0, \mathbf{B}_0, \mathbf{A}', \mathbf{B}'$ are coplanar, we can formulate the bilinear constraint by taking advantage of the fact that the outer product of these four vectors must disappear. Thus,

$$
\mathbf{A}_0 \wedge \mathbf{B}_0 \wedge \mathbf{A}' \wedge \mathbf{B}' = 0. \tag{4.75}
$$

Now, if we let $\mathbf{A}' = \alpha_i \mathbf{A}_i$ and $\mathbf{B}' = \beta_j \mathbf{B}_j$, then equation (4.75) can be written as

$$
\alpha_i \beta_j \{\mathbf{A}_0 \wedge \mathbf{B}_0 \wedge \mathbf{A}_i \wedge \mathbf{B}_j\} = 0. \tag{4.76}
$$

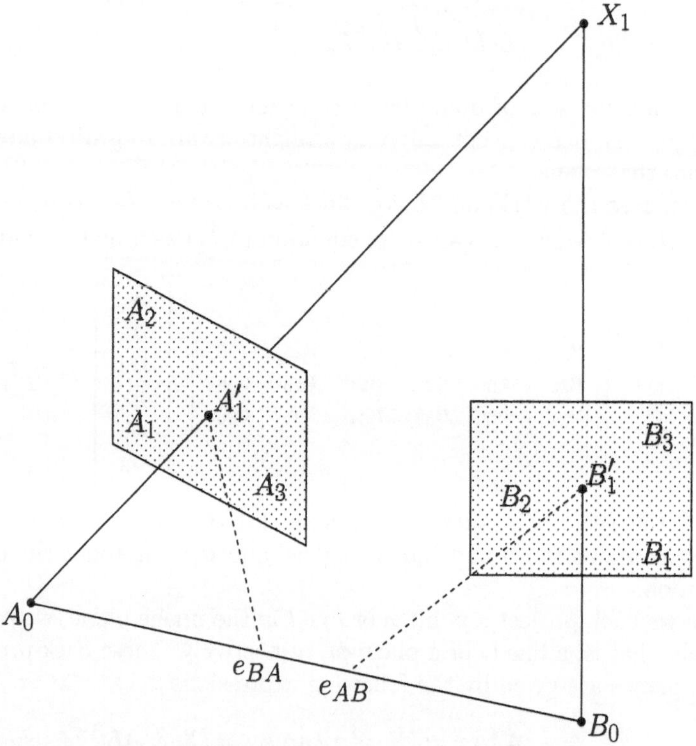

FIGURE 4.3. Sketch of binocular projection of a world point

Defining $\tilde{F}_{ij} = \{\mathbf{A}_0 \wedge \mathbf{B}_0 \wedge \mathbf{A}_i \wedge \mathbf{B}_j\} I^{-1} \equiv [\mathbf{A}_0 \mathbf{B}_0 \mathbf{A}_i \mathbf{B}_j]$ gives us

$$\tilde{F}_{ij} \alpha_i \beta_j = 0, \tag{4.77}$$

which corresponds in R^4 to the well-known relationship between the components of the *fundamental matrix* [71] or the *bilinear constraint* in E^3, F, and the image coordinates [71]. This suggests that $\tilde{F}$ can be seen as a linear function mapping two vectors onto a scalar:

$$\tilde{F}(\mathbf{A}, \mathbf{B}) = \{\mathbf{A}_0 \wedge \mathbf{B}_0 \wedge \mathbf{A} \wedge \mathbf{B}\} I^{-1}, \tag{4.78}$$

so that $\tilde{F}_{ij} = \tilde{F}(\mathbf{A}_i, \mathbf{B}_j)$. Note that viewing the fundamental matrix as a linear function means that we have a coordinate-independent description. Now, if we use the projective split to associate our point $\mathbf{A}' = \alpha_i \mathbf{A}_i$ in the image plane with its $\mathcal{E}^3$ representation $\boldsymbol{a}' = \delta_i \boldsymbol{a}_i$, where $\boldsymbol{a}_i = \frac{\mathbf{A}_i \wedge \gamma_4}{\mathbf{A}_i \gamma_4}$, it is not difficult to see that the coefficients are expressed as follows:

$$\alpha_i = \frac{\mathbf{A}' \cdot \gamma_4}{\mathbf{A}_i \cdot \gamma_4} \delta_i. \tag{4.79}$$

Thus, we are able to relate our 4D fundamental matrix $\tilde{F}$ to an *observed* fundamental matrix F in the following manner:

$$\tilde{F}_{kl} = (\mathbf{A}_k \cdot \gamma_4)(\mathbf{B}_l \cdot \gamma_4) F_{kl}, \tag{4.80}$$

so that

$$\alpha_k \tilde{F}_{kl} \beta_l = (\mathbf{A}' \cdot \gamma_4)(\mathbf{B}' \cdot \gamma_4) \delta_k F_{kl} \epsilon_l, \tag{4.81}$$

where $\boldsymbol{b}' = \epsilon_i \boldsymbol{b}_i$, with $\boldsymbol{b}_i = \frac{\mathbf{B}_i \wedge \gamma_4}{\mathbf{B}_i \gamma_4}$. F is the standard fundamental matrix that we would form from observations.

4.5.3 Geometry of three views

The so-called trilinear constraint captures the geometric relationships existing between points and lines in three camera views. Fig. 4.4 shows three image planes ϕ_A, ϕ_B, and ϕ_C with bases $\{\mathbf{A}_i\}$, $\{\mathbf{B}_i\}$, and $\{\mathbf{C}_i\}$ and optical centers $\mathbf{A}_0, \mathbf{B}_0, \mathbf{C}_0$. Intersections of two world points $\mathbf{X}_i$ with the planes occur at points $\mathbf{A}'_i, \mathbf{B}'_i, \mathbf{C}'_i$, $i = 1, 2$. The line joining the world points is $L_{12} = \mathbf{X}_1 \wedge \mathbf{X}_2$, and the projected lines are denoted by L'_A, L'_B, and L'_C.

We first define three planes:

$$\Phi'_A = \mathbf{A}_0 \wedge \mathbf{A}'_1 \wedge \mathbf{A}'_2, \quad \Phi'_B = \mathbf{B}_0 \wedge \mathbf{B}'_1 \wedge \mathbf{B}'_2, \quad \Phi'_C = \mathbf{C}_0 \wedge \mathbf{C}'_1 \wedge \mathbf{C}'_2. \tag{4.82}$$

It is clear that L_{12} can be formed by intersecting Φ'_B and Φ'_C:

$$L_{12} = \Phi'_B \cap \Phi'_C = (\mathbf{B}_0 \wedge L'_B) \cap (\mathbf{C}_0 \wedge L'_C). \tag{4.83}$$

If $L_{A_1} = \mathbf{A}_0 \wedge \mathbf{A}'_1$ and $L_{A_2} = \mathbf{A}_0 \wedge \mathbf{A}'_2$, then we can easily see that L_1 and L_2 intersect with L_{12} at $\mathbf{X}_1$ and $\mathbf{X}_2$, respectively. We therefore have

$$L_1 \wedge L_{12} = 0 \qquad \text{and} \qquad L_2 \wedge L_{12} = 0, \tag{4.84}$$

which can then be written as

$$(\mathbf{A}_0 \wedge \mathbf{A}'_i) \wedge \{(\mathbf{B}_0 \wedge L'_B) \cap (\mathbf{C}_0 \wedge L'_C)\} = 0 \quad \text{for } i = 1, 2. \tag{4.85}$$

This suggests that we should define a linear function T which maps a point and two lines onto a scalar as follows:

$$T(\mathbf{A}', L'_B, L'_C) = (\mathbf{A}_0 \wedge \mathbf{A}') \wedge \{(\mathbf{B}_0 \wedge L'_B) \cap (\mathbf{C}_0 \wedge L'_C)\}. \tag{4.86}$$

Now, using the line bases of the planes B and C in a similar manner as was used for plane A in equation (4.58), we can write

$$\mathbf{A}' = \alpha_i \mathbf{A}_i, \quad L'_B = l^B_j L^B_j \quad L'_C = l^C_k L^C_k. \tag{4.87}$$

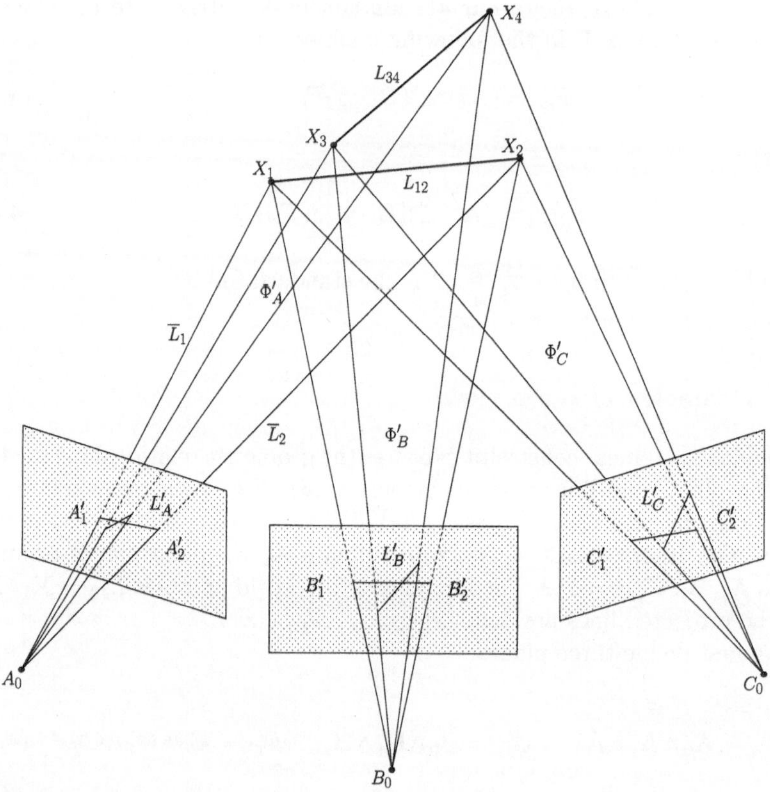

FIGURE 4.4. Model of the trinocular projection of the visual 3D space

If we define the components of a tensor as $T_{ijk} = T(\mathbf{A}_i, L_j^B, L_k^C)$, and if $\mathbf{A}', L'_B$, and L'_C are all derived from projections of the same two world points, then equation (4.85) tells us that we can write

$$T_{ijk}\alpha_i l_j^B l_k^C = 0. \tag{4.88}$$

T is the *trifocal tensor*[95, 45] and equation (4.88) is the *trilinear constraint.* In [95, 42] this constraint was arrived at by consideration of camera matrices; here, however, equation (4.88) is arrived at from purely geometric considerations, namely, that two planes intersect in a line, which in turn intersects with another line. To see how we relate the three projected *lines*, we express the line in image plane ϕ_A joining $\mathbf{A}'_1$ and $\mathbf{A}'_2$ as the intersection of the plane joining $\mathbf{A}_0$ to the world line L_{12} with the image plane $\Phi_A = \mathbf{A}_1 \wedge \mathbf{A}_2 \wedge \mathbf{A}_3$:

$$L'_A = \mathbf{A}'_1 \wedge \mathbf{A}'_2 = (\mathbf{A}_0 \wedge L_{12}) \cap \Phi_A. \tag{4.89}$$

Considering L_{12} as the meet of the planes $\Phi'_B \vee \Phi'_C$ and using the expansions of L'_A, L'_B, and L'_C given in equation (4.87), we can rewrite this equation as

$$l_i^A \boldsymbol{L}_i^A = \Big((\mathbf{A}_0 \wedge \boldsymbol{A}_i) \wedge l_j^B l_k^C \{(\mathbf{B}_0 \wedge L_j^B) \cap (\mathbf{C}_0 \wedge L_k^C)\}\Big) \cap \Phi_A. \tag{4.90}$$

Using the expansion of the meet given in equation (4.52), we have

$$l_i^A L_i^A = [(\mathbf{A}_0 \wedge \mathbf{A}_i) \wedge l_j^B l_k^C \{(\mathbf{B}_0 \wedge L_j^B) \cap (\mathbf{C}_0 \wedge L_k^C)\}] L_i^A, \qquad (4.91)$$

which, when we equate coefficients, gives

$$l_i^A = T_{ijk} l_j^B l_k^C. \qquad (4.92)$$

Thus, we obtain the familiar equation which relates the projected lines in the three views.

4.5.4 Geometry of n-views

If we have n-views, let us choose four of these views and denote them by A, B, C, and N. As before, we assume that $\{\mathbf{A}_j\}$, $\{\mathbf{B}_j\}$, ... etc., $j = 1, 2, 3$ define the image planes.

Let $\Phi_{Ai} = \mathbf{A}_0 \wedge \mathbf{A}_i \wedge \mathbf{A}'$, $\Phi_{Bi} = \mathbf{B}_0 \wedge \mathbf{B}_i \wedge \mathbf{B}'$, etc., where $\mathbf{A}'$, $\mathbf{B}'$, etc., are the projections of a world point P onto the image planes. The expression $\Phi_{Aj} \vee \Phi_{Bk}$ represents a line passing through the world point P, as does the equation $\Phi_{Cl} \cap \Phi_{Nm}$. Since these two lines intersect, we have the condition

$$\{\Phi_A j \cap \Phi_B k\} \wedge \{\Phi_C l \cap \Phi_N m\} = 0. \qquad (4.93)$$

Consider also the world line $L = \mathbf{X}_1 \wedge \mathbf{X}_2$ which projects down to l_a, l_b, l_c, l_n in the four image planes. We know from the previous sections that it is possible to write L in terms of these image lines as the meet of two planes in various ways—for example,

$$\begin{aligned} L &= (\mathbf{A}_0 \wedge l_a) \cap (\mathbf{B}_0 \wedge l_b) & (4.94)\\ L &= (\mathbf{C}_0 \wedge l_c) \cap (\boldsymbol{N}_0 \wedge l_n). & (4.95) \end{aligned}$$

Now, since $L \wedge L = 0$, we can consider $l_a = \ell_a^i L_i^A$, etc., and then write

$$\ell_a^i \ell_b^j \ell_c^k \ell_n^m [(\mathbf{A}_0 \wedge L_i^A) \cap (\mathbf{B}_0 \wedge L_j^B)] \wedge [(\mathbf{C}_0 \wedge L_k^C) \cap (\boldsymbol{N}_0 \wedge L_m^N)] = 0, \qquad (4.96)$$

which can be further expressed as

$$\ell_a^i \ell_b^j \ell_c^k \ell_n^m Q_{ijkm} = 0. \qquad (4.97)$$

Here, Q is the so-called *quadrifocal tensor* and equation 4.97 is the quadrilinear constraint recently discussed in [45]. The above constraint in terms of lines is straightforward, but it is also possible to find a relationship between point coordinates and Q. To do this, we expand equation (4.93) as follows:

$$\alpha_r \beta_s \delta_t \eta_u \{[(\mathbf{A}_0 \wedge L_{jr}^A) \cap (\mathbf{B}_0 \wedge L_{ks}^B)] \wedge [(\mathbf{C}_0 \wedge L_{lt}^C) \cap (\boldsymbol{N}_0 \wedge L_{mu}^N)]\} = 0, \qquad (4.98)$$

where we have used the notation $L_{jr}^A = \mathbf{A}_j \wedge \mathbf{A}_r \equiv \epsilon_{ijr} L_i^A$. Thus, we can also write the above equation as

$$\alpha_r \beta_s \delta_t \eta_u \epsilon_{i_1 jr} \epsilon_{i_2 ks} \epsilon_{i_3 lt} \epsilon_{i_4 mu} Q_{i_1 i_2 i_3 i_4} = 0 \qquad (4.99)$$

for any $\{i, j, k, m\}$.

4.6 Conclusion

This chapter has outlined the use of geometric algebra as a framework for analysis and computation in computer vision. In particular, the framework for projective geometry was described and the analysis of tensorial relations between multiple camera views was presented in a wholly geometric fashion. The projective geometry operations of meet and join are easily expressed analytically and easily computed in geometric algebra. Indeed, it is the ease with which we can perform the algebra of incidence (intersections of lines, planes, etc.) that simplifies many of the otherwise complex tensorial relations. The concept of duality has been discussed and used specifically in projecting down from the world to image planes; in geometric algebra, duality is a particularly simple concept and one in which the nonmetric properties of the inner product become apparent.

4.7 Exercises

5.1. Compute in P^2 the intersecting point of the lines $\boldsymbol{A} = \boldsymbol{x}_1 \wedge \boldsymbol{x}_2$ and $\boldsymbol{B} = \boldsymbol{y}_1 \wedge \boldsymbol{y}_2$. The homogeneous coordinates of the involved points are $\boldsymbol{x}_1 = (3, 1, -1)$, $\boldsymbol{x}_2 = (-1, 1, 1)$, $\boldsymbol{y}_1 = (2, -1, 1)$, and $\boldsymbol{y}_2 = (-2, 0, 1)$.

5.2. Points and planes are in P^3. Find in P^3 the relative positions of the points $\boldsymbol{P} = (-2, -4, -4, 1)$ and $\boldsymbol{Q} = (2, -4, 5, 1)$, respective to the plane $\boldsymbol{E} = \boldsymbol{A}_1 \wedge \boldsymbol{A}_2 \wedge \boldsymbol{A}_3$, where $\boldsymbol{A}_1 = (2, -1, 1, -6)$, $\boldsymbol{A}_2 = (1, 1, -1, 0)$, and $\boldsymbol{A}_3 = (-1, 0, 0, 4)$. Explain these results. (*Hint*: The join $\boldsymbol{P} \wedge \boldsymbol{E} = dI$ spans a quatrivector, where the scalar d corresponds to the Hesse distance or foot. Thus, you must compute the brackets $[\boldsymbol{PE}]$ and $[\boldsymbol{QE}]$. When the bracket is positive, the point is at the right, and when it is negative, the point is at the left.)

5.3. In P^3 compute the relative orientation of the lines $\boldsymbol{L}_1 = \boldsymbol{A}_1 \wedge \boldsymbol{A}_2$ and $\boldsymbol{L}_2 = \boldsymbol{A}_3 \wedge \boldsymbol{A}_4$, where $\boldsymbol{A}_1 = (2, 1, -3, -1)$, $\boldsymbol{A}_2 = (1, 3, 5, 2)$, $\boldsymbol{A}_3 = (1, 2, 1, 4)$, and $\boldsymbol{A}_4 = (-3, -1, 2, 4)$. (*Hint*: The join $\boldsymbol{L}_1 \wedge \boldsymbol{L}_2 = dI$ spans a quatrivector, where the scalar d corresponds to the Hesse distance or foot. Thus, you must compute the bracket $[\boldsymbol{L}_1 \boldsymbol{L}_2] > 0$ and interpret your result using the right-hand rule.)

5.4. In P^3 compute the intersection of the following planes: $\boldsymbol{E}_1 = \boldsymbol{A}_1 \wedge \boldsymbol{A}_2 \wedge \boldsymbol{A}_3$ and $\boldsymbol{E}_2 = \boldsymbol{B}_1 \wedge \boldsymbol{B}_2 \wedge \boldsymbol{B}_3$, where $\boldsymbol{A}_1 = (2, 1, -3, -1)$, $\boldsymbol{A}_2 = (1, 3, 5, 2)$, $\boldsymbol{A}_3 = (1, 2, 1, 4)$, and $\boldsymbol{B}_1 = (4, 2, -6, -2)$, $\boldsymbol{B}_2 = (4, 3, 5, 1)$, $\boldsymbol{B}_3 = (3, 6, 3, 12)$.

5.5. In P^2 compute the resulting intersecting point $\boldsymbol{p}$ of the intersecting lines $\boldsymbol{a} \wedge \boldsymbol{b}$ and the line passing by the point $\boldsymbol{c}$ which lies off the line $\boldsymbol{a} \wedge \boldsymbol{b}$ for the following points: $\boldsymbol{a} = (2, 3, 1)$, $\boldsymbol{b} = (10, 10, 1)$, and $\boldsymbol{c} = (5, 9, 1)$. (*Hint*: First compute the line passing by point $\boldsymbol{c}$ using the direction orthogonal to the line $\boldsymbol{a}\wedge\boldsymbol{b}$; then compute the meet of these lines.)

5.6. Prove the Simpson rule using the join of three projected points. If the projecting point $\boldsymbol{p}$ lies at the circumference, the join of the projected points is zero. Take three arbitrary points lying on a unit circumference and a fourth one nearby. Use CLICAL for your computations. (*Hint*: First compute the projected points as the meet of three lines passing by the point $\boldsymbol{p}$ orthogonal to the triangle sides. The triangle is formed by three arbitrary points lying on the circumference.)

5.7. Prove the Pascal theorem using the incidence algebra in P^2. Given six points lying in a conic, compute six intersecting lines using the join operation. The meet of these lines should give three intersecting points, and the join of these three intersecting points should be zero. Use Clifford 4.0 and any six points belonging to a conic of your choice.

5.8. Prove the Desargues theorem using the algebra of incidence. Let $\boldsymbol{x}_1$, $\boldsymbol{x}_2$, $\boldsymbol{x}_3$ and $\boldsymbol{y}_1$, $\boldsymbol{y}_2$, $\boldsymbol{y}_3$ be the vertices of two triangles in P^2, and suppose that the meets of the lines fulfill the equations $(\boldsymbol{x}_1\wedge\boldsymbol{x}_2)\cap(\boldsymbol{y}_1\wedge\boldsymbol{y}_2) = \boldsymbol{z}_3$, $(\boldsymbol{x}_2\wedge\boldsymbol{x}_3)\cap(\boldsymbol{y}_2\wedge\boldsymbol{y}_3) = \boldsymbol{z}_1$, and $(\boldsymbol{x}_3\wedge\boldsymbol{x}_1)\cap(\boldsymbol{y}_3\wedge\boldsymbol{y}_1) = \boldsymbol{z}_2$. Then the join of these points $\boldsymbol{z}_1\wedge\boldsymbol{z}_2\boldsymbol{z}_3=0$ if and only if a point $\boldsymbol{p}$ exists such that $\boldsymbol{x}_1\wedge\boldsymbol{y}_1\wedge\boldsymbol{p} = \boldsymbol{x}_2\wedge\boldsymbol{y}_2\wedge\boldsymbol{p} = \boldsymbol{x}_3\wedge\boldsymbol{y}_3\wedge\boldsymbol{p} =0$. In this problem, use Clifford 4.0 and define two triangles of your choice.

5.9. A point $\boldsymbol{p}$ lies on the circumcircle of an arbitrary triangle with vertices $\boldsymbol{x}_1$, $\boldsymbol{y}_1$, and $\boldsymbol{z}_1$. From the point $\boldsymbol{p}$ draw three perpendiculars to the three sides of the triangle to meet the circle at points $\boldsymbol{x}_2$, $\boldsymbol{y}_2$, and $\boldsymbol{z}_2$, respectively. Using incidence algebra, show that the lines $\boldsymbol{x}_1\wedge\boldsymbol{x}_2$, $\boldsymbol{y}_1\wedge\boldsymbol{y}_2$, and $\boldsymbol{z}_1\wedge\boldsymbol{z}_2$ are parallel.

5.10. Consider a world point $\boldsymbol{X} \in P^3$ projected onto two image planes (see Fig. 4.3) . Show that the bilinear constraint can be expressed as $\alpha_i^T \tilde{F}_{ij}\beta_j=0$, where α_i^T and β_j are tensor notations. (*Hint*: Use the geometric constraint $\boldsymbol{A}_0\wedge\boldsymbol{B}_0\wedge\boldsymbol{A}'\wedge\boldsymbol{B}'=0$, where $\boldsymbol{A}_0$ and $\boldsymbol{B}_0$ are the optical centers of the images and $\boldsymbol{A}' = \alpha_i\boldsymbol{A}_i$ and $\boldsymbol{B}' = \beta_j\boldsymbol{B}_j$ are the image points spanned using three arbitrary image points $\boldsymbol{A}_i$ or $\boldsymbol{B}_i$. The epipolar plane is given by $\boldsymbol{A}_0\wedge\boldsymbol{B}_0\wedge\boldsymbol{A}'$.)

5.11. Consider two non-intersecting world lines $\boldsymbol{L}_{12}$ and $\boldsymbol{L}_{34}$. Their projecting lines intersect in the points α_i and β_j. Show that α_i lies on the epipolar line passing by β_j.

5.12. Consider a world line $\boldsymbol{L}_{12} \in P^3$ projected onto three image planes (see Fig. 4.4). The projected line onto the first image plane Φ_A is given by

$$l_i^A\boldsymbol{L}_{A_i} = \left[\boldsymbol{A}_0\wedge\left(l_j^B l_k^C\{(\boldsymbol{B}_0\wedge\boldsymbol{L}_j^B)\cap(\boldsymbol{C}_0\wedge\boldsymbol{L}_k^C)\}\right)\right]\cap\Phi_A. \qquad (4.100)$$

Geometrically, this equation means that the optical planes $\boldsymbol{B}_0 \wedge l_j^B \boldsymbol{L}_j^B$ and $\boldsymbol{C}_0 \wedge l_j^C \boldsymbol{L}_j^C$ intersect in the line $\boldsymbol{L}_{12}$. Now the join operation of $\boldsymbol{L}_{12}$ with $\boldsymbol{A}_0$ build the optical plane which intersects the image plane Φ_A by the line $l_{A_i} \boldsymbol{L}_{A_i}$ (linear combination of three arbitrary image lines $\boldsymbol{L}_{A_i}$). Expand the equation to get the coefficients l_i^A in terms of the trilinear constraint or trifocal tensor as follows:

$$l_i^A = T_{ijk} l_j^B l_k^C .$$

5.13. Write two sets of equations for the Pascal theorem, one set involving two cameras and the second set involving three. Note that the brackets relate the cameras via the bilinear or trilinear constraints. See the following chapter for a discussion of conics and the Pascal theorem.

Part II

PRACTICAL APPLICATIONS

5. Computing the Kinematics of Robot Manipulators

5.1 Introduction

This chapter presents the formulation of robot manipulator kinematics within the geometric algebra framework. In this algebraic system the 3D Euclidean motion of points, lines, and planes can be advantageously represented using the algebra of motors. The computational complexity of direct and indirect kinematics and other problems concerning robot manipulators are dependent on the robot's degrees of freedom as well on its geometric characteristics. Our approach makes possible a direct algebraic formulation of the concrete problem in such a way that it reflects the underlying geometric structure. This is achieved by describing parts of the problem based on motor representations of points, lines, and planes where necessary. The chapter presents the formulation and computation of closed-form solutions of direct and indirect kinematics for standard robot manipulators and a simple example of a grasping task. The flexible method presented here widens the current standard point or line representation–based approaches for the treatment of problems related to robot manipulators.

5.2 Elementary Transformations of Robot Manipulators

The study of the rigid motion of objects in 3D space plays an important role in robotics. In order to linearize the rigid motion of the Euclidean space, homogeneous coordinates are normally utilized. That is why in the geometric algebra framework we choose the special or degenerated geometric algebra to extend the algebraic system from 3D Euclidean space to 4D space. In this system we can nicely model the motion of points, lines, and planes with computational advantages and geometric insight. Let us start with a description of the basic elements of robot manipulators in terms of the special or degenerated geometric algebra $\mathcal{G}^+_{3,0,1}$ or motor algebra. The most basic parts of a robot manipulator are revolute joints, prismatic joints, connecting links, and the end-effectors. In the following subsections we will treat the kinematics of the prismatic and revolute manipulator parts using the 4D geometric algebra $\mathcal{G}^+_{3,0,1}$ and will illustrate an end-effector grasping task.

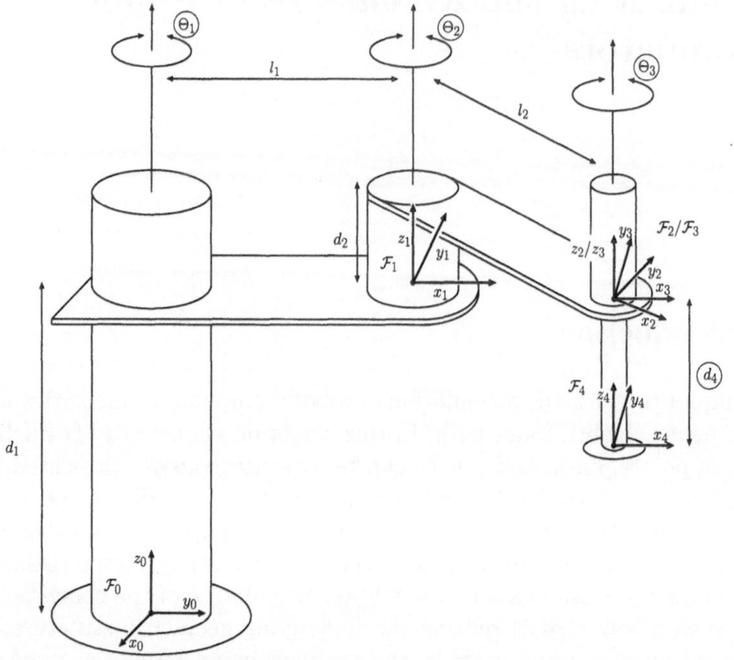

FIGURE 5.1. SCARA-type manipulator according to DH parameters given in Table 5.1 (variable parameters are circled)

5.2.1 The Denavit–Hartenberg parameterization

The computation of direct or inverse kinematics requires both an exact description of the robot manipulator's structure and its configuration. The descriptive approach used most often is known as the Denavit–Hartenberg (DH) procedure [27]. It is based on a uniform description of the position of the reference coordinate system of a particular joint relative to the next joint in consideration. Fig. 5.3.a shows how coordinate frames are attached to a joint of a robot manipulator. Table 5.1 presents the specifications of two robot manipulators, the SCARA and the Stanford manipulators , as shown in Figures 5.1 and 5.2, respectively.

This tells us whether the joint is for rotation (revolute) or for translation (prismatic). The transformation of the reference coordinate system between two joints will be called a joint-transition . Fig. 5.3.b shows the involved screws in a joint-transition according to the Denavit–Hartenberg parameters . The frame, or reference coordinate system, related to the i-th joint is attached at the end of this link and it is notated $\mathcal{F}_i$.

In Table 5.1 the parameter "v" indicates that the involved variable of the joint is variable, and the parameter "c" indicates that it is constant.

The position and orientation of the end-effector in relation to the reference coordinate system of the robot basis can be computed by linking all

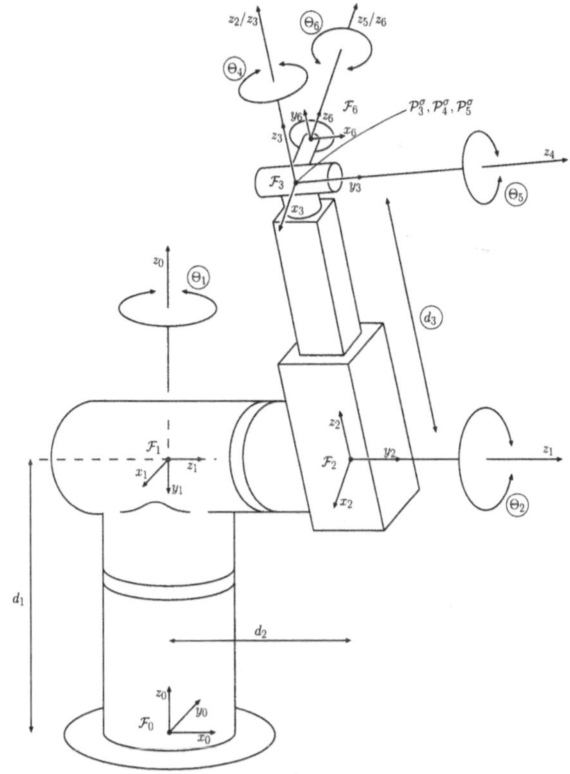

FIGURE 5.2. Stanford-type manipulator according to DH parameters in Table 5.1 (variable parameters are encircled)

Robot type	link	Revolute θ_i	v/c	Prismatic d_i	v/c	Twist angle α_i	Link length l_i
SCARA	1	θ_1	v	d_1	c	0	l_1
	2	θ_2	v	d_2	c	0	l_2
	3	θ_3	v	0		0	0
	4	0		d_4	v	0	0
Stanford	1	θ_1	v	d_1	c	-90 deg	0
	2	θ_2	v	d_2	c	90 deg	0
	3	0		d_3	v	0	0
	4	θ_4	v	0		-90 deg	0
	5	θ_5	v	0		90 deg	0
	6	θ_6	v	d_6	c	0	0

TABLE 5.1. Kinematic configuration of two robotic manipulators

joint-transitions. In this way, we are able to get straightforwardly the *direct kinematics.*

Conversely, in the case of the inverse kinematics, given the position and orientation of the end-effector, we must find values of the variable parame-

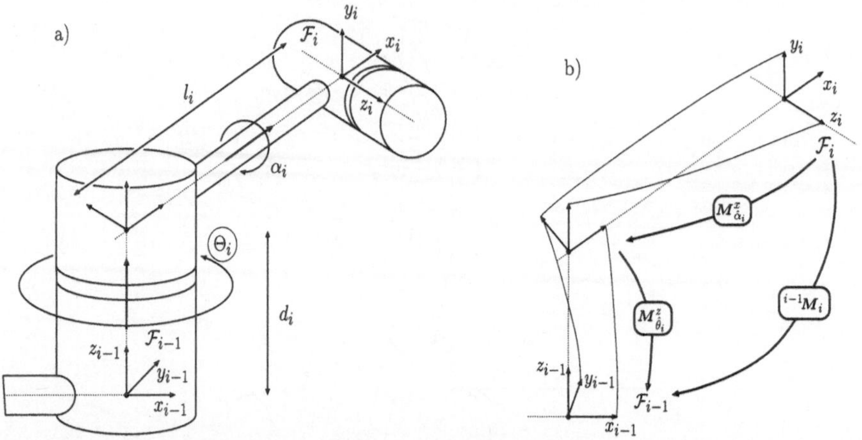

FIGURE 5.3. Motor description of a manipulator joint: (a) i-th joint of a robot manipulator and attached coordinate frames according to Denavit–Hartenberg; the encircled θ_i is the variable parameter; (b) transformation from frame $\mathcal{F}_i$ to $\mathcal{F}_{i-1}$ (motor ${}^{i-1}\boldsymbol{M}_i$ consists of two screw transformations, $\boldsymbol{M}^x_{\hat{\alpha}_i}$ and $\boldsymbol{M}^z_{\hat{\theta}_i}$)

ters of the joint-transitions which satisfy this requirement. In the following sections we will provide more details for the computation of the direct and inverse kinematics of robot manipulators.

5.2.2 Representations of prismatic and revolute transformations

The transformation of any point, line, or plane between coordinate systems $\mathcal{F}_{i-1}$ and $\mathcal{F}_i$ is revolute when the involved degree of freedom is only a variable angle θ_i, and it is prismatic when the degree of freedom is only a variable length d_i. The transformation motor ${}^{i-1}\boldsymbol{M}_i$ between $\mathcal{F}_i$ and $\mathcal{F}_{i-1}$ consists of a sequence of two screw transformations, one fixed (i.e., $\boldsymbol{M}^x_{\hat{\alpha}_i}$) and another variable (i.e., $\boldsymbol{M}^z_{\hat{\theta}_i}$) (see Fig. 5.3.b). Note that we use dual angles

$$\hat{\theta}_i = \theta_i + I d_i \tag{5.1}$$

$$\hat{\alpha}_i = \alpha_i + I l_i, \tag{5.2}$$

see [7]. In the revolute case, the latter equation uses as a variable parameter the angle θ_i and in the prismatic case the displacement d_i is the variable parameter. The transformation reads

$$\begin{aligned} {}^{i-1}\boldsymbol{M}_i &= \boldsymbol{M}^z_{\hat{\theta}_i}\boldsymbol{M}^x_{\hat{\alpha}_i} = \boldsymbol{T}^z_{d_i}\boldsymbol{R}^z_{\theta_i}\boldsymbol{T}^x_{l_i}\boldsymbol{R}^x_{\alpha_i} \\ &= (1+\frac{I}{2}\begin{pmatrix}0\\0\\d_i\end{pmatrix})\boldsymbol{R}^z_{\theta_i}(1+\frac{I}{2}\begin{pmatrix}l_i\\0\\0\end{pmatrix})\boldsymbol{R}^x_{\alpha_i}. \end{aligned} \tag{5.3}$$

For the sake of clarity the dual bivectors of the translators are given as a column vector, which makes the variable parameters explicit.

Since ${}^{i-1}\boldsymbol{M}_i \, {}^{i-1}\widetilde{\boldsymbol{M}}_i = 1$, we obtain

$$
{}^{i}\boldsymbol{M}_{i-1} \;=\; \widetilde{\boldsymbol{M}}^{x}_{\hat{\alpha}_i}\widetilde{\boldsymbol{M}}^{z}_{\hat{\theta}_i} = \widetilde{\boldsymbol{T}}^{x}_{l_i}\widetilde{\boldsymbol{R}}^{x}_{\alpha_i}\widetilde{\boldsymbol{T}}^{z}_{d_i}\widetilde{\boldsymbol{R}}^{z}_{\theta_i}\,. \tag{5.4}
$$

Be aware that for the rest of the chapter ${}^{j}\boldsymbol{M}_i$ will denote a motor transformation from $\mathcal{F}_i$ to $\mathcal{F}_j$.

We will now give general expressions for the transformation of points, lines, and planes using a single parameter, θ_i or d_i, respectively, as the variable and two fixed parameters, α_i and l_i. For the joint depicted in Fig. 5.3.b, a revolute transformation will take place only when θ_i varies and a prismatic transformation only when d_i varies. Now, taking a point $\boldsymbol{X}$ represented in the frame $\mathcal{F}_{i-1}$, we can describe its transformation from $\mathcal{F}_{i-1}$ to $\mathcal{F}_i$ using the motor algebra [7], with either θ_i or d_i as the variable parameter. We will call this transformation a *forward transformation.*

The multivector representation of point $\boldsymbol{X}$ related to the frame $\mathcal{F}_i$ will be expressed as ${}^{i}\boldsymbol{X}$, with

$$
\begin{aligned}
{}^{i}\boldsymbol{X} &= {}^{i}\boldsymbol{M}_{i-1}\, {}^{i-1}\boldsymbol{X}\, {}^{i}\overline{\widetilde{\boldsymbol{M}}}_{i-1} = \widetilde{\boldsymbol{M}}^{x}_{\hat{\alpha}_i}\widetilde{\boldsymbol{M}}^{z}_{\hat{\theta}_i}\, {}^{i-1}\boldsymbol{X}\, \overline{\boldsymbol{M}}^{z}_{\hat{\theta}_i}\overline{\boldsymbol{M}}^{x}_{\hat{\alpha}_i} \\
&= \widetilde{\boldsymbol{T}}^{x}_{l_i}\widetilde{\boldsymbol{R}}^{x}_{\alpha_i}\widetilde{\boldsymbol{T}}^{z}_{d_i}\widetilde{\boldsymbol{R}}^{z}_{\theta_i}\, {}^{i-1}\boldsymbol{X}\, \boldsymbol{R}^{z}_{\theta_i}\widetilde{\boldsymbol{T}}^{z}_{d_i}\boldsymbol{R}^{x}_{\alpha_i}\widetilde{\boldsymbol{T}}^{x}_{l_i} \\
&= 1 + I\, {}^{i}\boldsymbol{x}\,,
\end{aligned} \tag{5.5}
$$

where ${}^{i}\boldsymbol{x}$ is a bivector representing the 3D position of $\boldsymbol{X}$ referred to $\mathcal{F}_i$. A transformation in the reverse sense will be called a *backward transformation.* In this case, a point $\boldsymbol{X}$ referenced in the frame $\mathcal{F}_i$ is transformed to the frame $\mathcal{F}_{i-1}$, as follows:

$$
\begin{aligned}
{}^{i-1}\boldsymbol{X} &= {}^{i-1}\boldsymbol{M}_i\, {}^{i}\boldsymbol{X}\, {}^{i-1}\overline{\widetilde{\boldsymbol{M}}}_i = \boldsymbol{M}^{z}_{\hat{\theta}_i}\boldsymbol{M}^{x}_{\hat{\alpha}_i}\, {}^{i}\boldsymbol{X}\, \overline{\widetilde{\boldsymbol{M}}}^{x}_{\hat{\alpha}_i}\overline{\widetilde{\boldsymbol{M}}}^{z}_{\hat{\theta}_i} \\
&= 1 + I\, {}^{i-1}\boldsymbol{x}\,.
\end{aligned} \tag{5.6}
$$

Note that the motor applied from the right side is not purely conjugated as is the case with the line. The same will be also true for a plane [7].

Consider a line $\boldsymbol{L}$ represented in the frame $\mathcal{F}_{i-1}$ by ${}^{i-1}\boldsymbol{L} = {}^{i-1}\boldsymbol{n} + I\, {}^{i-1}\boldsymbol{m}$, where $\boldsymbol{n}$ and $\boldsymbol{m}$ are bivectors indicating the orientation and moment of the line, respectively. We can write the forward transformation of this line related to the frame $\mathcal{F}_i$ according to [7]

$$
\begin{aligned}
{}^{i}\boldsymbol{L} &= {}^{i}\boldsymbol{M}_{i-1}\, {}^{i-1}\boldsymbol{L}\, {}^{i}\widetilde{\boldsymbol{M}}_{i-1} = \widetilde{\boldsymbol{M}}^{x}_{\hat{\alpha}_i}\widetilde{\boldsymbol{M}}^{z}_{\hat{\theta}_i}\, {}^{i-1}\boldsymbol{L}\, \boldsymbol{M}^{z}_{\hat{\theta}_i}\boldsymbol{M}^{x}_{\hat{\alpha}_i} \\
&= {}^{i}\boldsymbol{n} + I\, {}^{i}\boldsymbol{m}\,.
\end{aligned} \tag{5.7}
$$

Its backward transformation reads

$$
\begin{aligned}
{}^{i-1}\boldsymbol{L} &= {}^{i-1}\boldsymbol{M}_i\, {}^{i}\boldsymbol{L}\, {}^{i-1}\widetilde{\boldsymbol{M}}_i = \boldsymbol{M}^{z}_{\hat{\theta}_i}\boldsymbol{M}^{x}_{\hat{\alpha}_i}\, {}^{i}\boldsymbol{L}\, \widetilde{\boldsymbol{M}}^{x}_{\hat{\alpha}_i}\widetilde{\boldsymbol{M}}^{z}_{\hat{\theta}_i} \\
&= {}^{i-1}\boldsymbol{n} + I\, {}^{i-1}\boldsymbol{m}\,.
\end{aligned} \tag{5.8}
$$

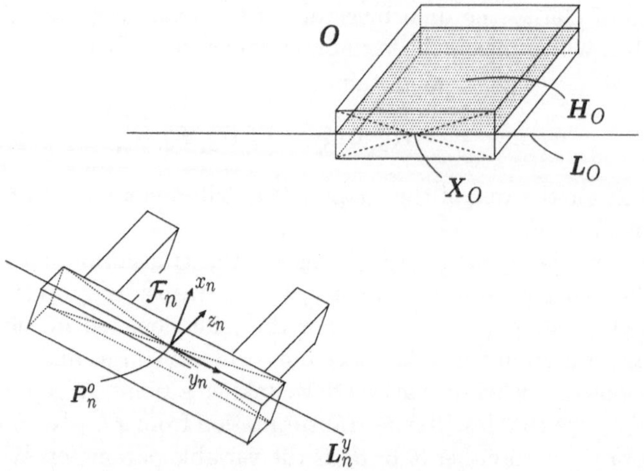

FIGURE 5.4. Two-finger grasper approaching an object

Finally, the forward transformation of a plane $\boldsymbol{H}$ represented in $\mathcal{F}_{i-1}$ reads

$$\begin{aligned} {}^{i}\boldsymbol{H} &= {}^{i}\boldsymbol{M}_{i-1}\, {}^{i-1}\boldsymbol{H}\, {}^{i}\widetilde{\overline{\boldsymbol{M}}}_{i-1} = \widetilde{\boldsymbol{M}}^{x}_{\hat{\alpha}_i} \widetilde{\boldsymbol{M}}^{z}_{\hat{\theta}_i}\ {}^{i-1}\boldsymbol{H}\ \overline{\boldsymbol{M}}^{z}_{\hat{\theta}_i} \overline{\boldsymbol{M}}^{x}_{\hat{\alpha}_i} \\ &= {}^{i}\boldsymbol{n} + I\, {}^{i}d_H\,; \end{aligned} \tag{5.9}$$

and, as above, its backward transformation equation is

$$\begin{aligned} {}^{i-1}\boldsymbol{H} &= {}^{i-1}\boldsymbol{M}_i\, {}^{i}\boldsymbol{H}\, {}^{i-1}\widetilde{\overline{\boldsymbol{M}}}_i = \boldsymbol{M}^{z}_{\hat{\theta}_i} \boldsymbol{M}^{x}_{\hat{\alpha}_i}\ {}^{i}\boldsymbol{H}\ \widetilde{\overline{\boldsymbol{M}}}^{x}_{\hat{\alpha}_i} \widetilde{\overline{\boldsymbol{M}}}^{z}_{\hat{\theta}_i} \\ &= {}^{i-1}\boldsymbol{n} + I\, {}^{i-1}d_H\,. \end{aligned} \tag{5.10}$$

5.2.3 Grasping by using constraint equations

In this subsection we will illustrate grasping as a manipulation-related task *grasping operation* that involves the positioning of a two-finger grasper in front of a static object. Fig. 5.4 shows the grasper and the considered object $\boldsymbol{O}$. The manipulator must moves the grasper near to the object, and together they must fulfill some conditions in order to grasp the object firmly. To determine the overall transformation ${}^{0}\boldsymbol{M}_n$, which moves the grasper into an appropriate grasping position, we claim that ${}^{0}\boldsymbol{M}_n$ must fulfill the three constraints below. In order to formulate these constraints, we can take advantages of the point, line, and plane representations of the motor algebra. In the following explanation, we assume that the representations of geometric entities attached to the object $\boldsymbol{O}$ in frame $\mathcal{F}_0$ are known.

Attitude condition: The grasping movement of the two fingers should be in the reference plane $\boldsymbol{H}_O$ of $\boldsymbol{O}$—that is, the yz-plane of the end-effector frame $\mathcal{F}_n$ should be equal to the reference plane $\boldsymbol{H}_O$. The *attitude condition* can be simply formulated in terms of a plane equation, as follows:

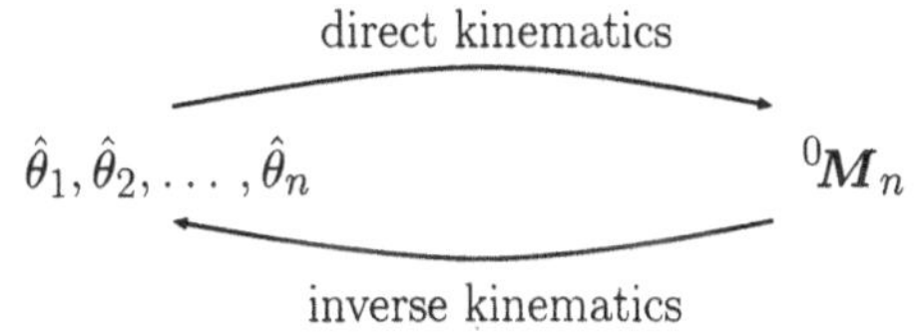

FIGURE 5.5. Direct and inverse kinematics

$$ {}^0\boldsymbol{M}_n \, {}^n\boldsymbol{H}_n^{yz} \, {}^0\widetilde{\boldsymbol{M}}_n - {}^0\boldsymbol{H}_O \approx 0 , \tag{5.11}$$

where ${}^n\boldsymbol{H}_n^{yz} = (1,0,0)^T + I\,0 = (1,0,0)^T$ (see Fig. 5.4).

Alignment condition: After the application of the motor ${}^0\boldsymbol{M}_n$, the grasper and the object should be in a parallel alignment — that is, the direction of the y-axis and the line $\boldsymbol{L}_O$ should be the same. The *alignment condition* can be simply expressed in terms of a line equation,

$$ \langle {}^0\boldsymbol{M}_n \, {}^n\boldsymbol{L}_n^y \, {}^0\widetilde{\boldsymbol{M}}_n \rangle_d - \langle {}^0\boldsymbol{L}_O \rangle_d \approx 0 , \tag{5.12}$$

where ${}^n\boldsymbol{L}_n^y = (0,1,0)^T + I(0,0,0)^T = (0,1,0)^T$ and $\langle \boldsymbol{L} \rangle_d$ denotes the direction components of line $\boldsymbol{L}$.

Touching condition: The motion ${}^0\boldsymbol{M}_n$ should also guarantee that the grasper is in the correct grasping position—that is, the origin $\boldsymbol{P}_n^o$ of the end-effector frame $\mathcal{F}_n$ should touch the reference point $\boldsymbol{X}_O$ of $\boldsymbol{O}$. The formulation of this constraint in our framework is

$$ {}^0\boldsymbol{M}_n \, {}^n\boldsymbol{P}_n^o \, {}^0\widetilde{\boldsymbol{M}}_n - {}^0\boldsymbol{X}_O \approx 0 . \tag{5.13}$$

With these three conditions, we can obtain constraints for the components of ${}^0\boldsymbol{M}_n$, and we can determine ${}^0\boldsymbol{M}_n$ numerically. The next step is to determine the variable joint parameters of the robot manipulator which lead to the position and orientation of the end-effector frame $\mathcal{F}_n$ described by ${}^0\boldsymbol{M}_n$. This problem is called the inverse kinematics problem of robot manipulators and will be treated in Section 5.4.

5.3 Direct Kinematics of Robot Manipulators

The determination of direct kinematics involves the computation of the position and orientation of the end-effector or frame $\mathcal{F}_n$ given the parameters of the joint-transitions (see Fig. 5.5). In this section we will show how the direct kinematics can be computed when we use as geometric objects points, lines, or planes. The notation we use for points, lines, and planes is shown in Fig. 5.6. The direct kinematics for the general case of a manipulator with n joints can be written as

$$ {}^0\boldsymbol{M}_n = {}^0\boldsymbol{M}_1 {}^1\boldsymbol{M}_2 {}^2\boldsymbol{M}_3 \cdots {}^{n-1}\boldsymbol{M}_n = \prod_{i=1}^{n} {}^{i-1}\boldsymbol{M}_i . \tag{5.14}$$

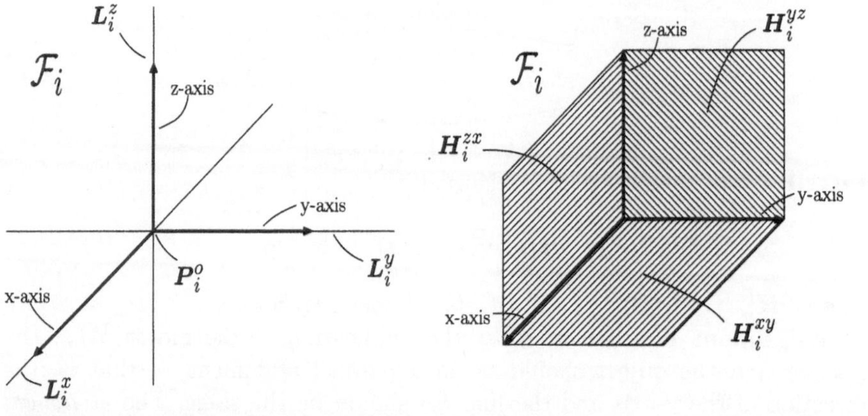

FIGURE 5.6. Notations for origin, coordinate axis, and coordinate planes for frame-specific entities

We can formulate straightforwardly the direct kinematics in terms of point, line, or plane representations as follows:

$$
\begin{aligned}
{}^0\boldsymbol{X} &= {}^0\boldsymbol{M}_n\, {}^n\boldsymbol{X}\, {}^0\widetilde{\boldsymbol{M}}_n = \prod_{i=1}^{n} {}^{i-1}\boldsymbol{M}_i\, {}^n\boldsymbol{X} \prod_{i=1}^{n} {}^{n-i}\widetilde{\boldsymbol{M}}_{n+1-i}\,, \\
{}^0\boldsymbol{L} &= \prod_{i=1}^{n} {}^{i-1}\boldsymbol{M}_i\, {}^n\boldsymbol{L} \prod_{i=1}^{n} {}^{n-i}\widetilde{\boldsymbol{M}}_{n+1-i}\,, \\
{}^0\boldsymbol{H} &= \prod_{i=1}^{n} {}^{i-1}\boldsymbol{M}_i\, {}^n\boldsymbol{H} \prod_{i=1}^{n} {}^{n-i}\widetilde{\boldsymbol{M}}_{n+1-i}\,.
\end{aligned} \tag{5.15}
$$

Now, let us write the motor ${}^0\boldsymbol{M}_4$ for the direct kinematics for points, lines, and planes in the form of equation (5.15) for the SCARA manipulator specified by the Denavit–Hartenberg parameters of Table 5.1. First, using equation (5.14) with n=4, we can easily express the required motor ${}^0\boldsymbol{M}_4$, as follows:

$$
\begin{aligned}
{}^0\boldsymbol{M}_4 &= {}^0\boldsymbol{M}_1{}^1\boldsymbol{M}_2{}^2\boldsymbol{M}_3{}^3\boldsymbol{M}_4 = (\boldsymbol{M}^z_{\hat{\theta}_1}\boldsymbol{M}^x_{\hat{\alpha}_1})\cdots(\boldsymbol{M}^z_{\hat{\theta}_4}\boldsymbol{M}^x_{\hat{\alpha}_4}) \\
&= (\boldsymbol{T}^z_{d_1}\boldsymbol{R}^z_{\theta_1}\boldsymbol{T}^x_{l_1}\boldsymbol{R}^x_{\alpha_1})\cdots(\boldsymbol{T}^z_{d_4}\boldsymbol{R}^z_{\theta_4}\boldsymbol{T}^x_{l_4}\boldsymbol{R}^x_{\alpha_4}) \\
&= (1+\frac{I}{2}\begin{pmatrix}0\\0\\d_1\end{pmatrix})\boldsymbol{R}^z_{\theta_1}(1+\frac{I}{2}\begin{pmatrix}l_1\\0\\0\end{pmatrix})(1+\frac{I}{2}\begin{pmatrix}0\\0\\d_2\end{pmatrix}) \\
&\quad \boldsymbol{R}^z_{\theta_2}(1+\frac{I}{2}\begin{pmatrix}l_2\\0\\0\end{pmatrix})\boldsymbol{R}^z_{\theta_3}(1+\frac{I}{2}\begin{pmatrix}0\\0\\d_4\end{pmatrix})\,.
\end{aligned} \tag{5.16}
$$

Note that translators with zero translation and rotors with zero angle become 1.

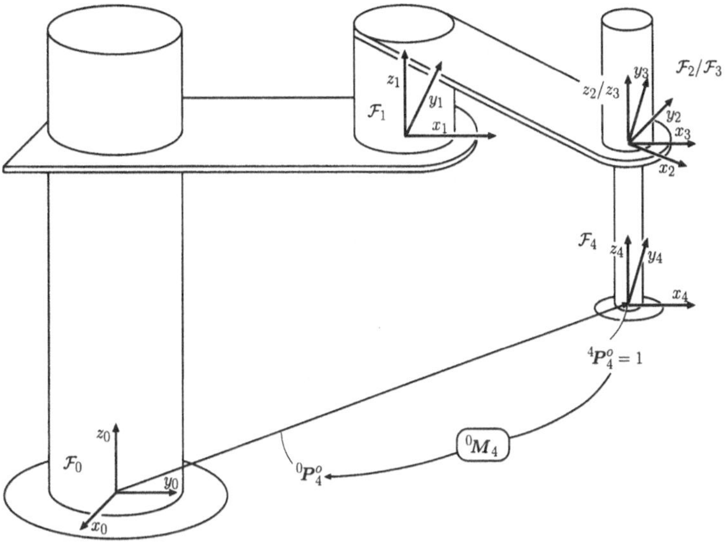

FIGURE 5.7. Representation ${}^0\boldsymbol{P}_4^o$ of $\boldsymbol{P}_4^o$ in frame $\mathcal{F}_0$ is computed using ${}^0\boldsymbol{M}_4$

Applying the motor ${}^0\boldsymbol{M}_4$ from the left and ${}^0\widetilde{\overline{\boldsymbol{M}}}_4$ from the right for point and plane equations, and the motor ${}^0\boldsymbol{M}_4$ from the left and ${}^0\widetilde{\boldsymbol{M}}_4$ from the right for line equations, as indicated by equation (5.15), we derive the direct kinematics equations of points, lines, and planes for the SCARA robot manipulator.

5.3.1 MAPLE program for motor algebra computations

Since the nature of our approach requires symbolic computation, we chose the MAPLE computer package to develop a comfortable program for computations in the frame of different geometric algebras. To employ the program, we simply have to specify the vector basis of the selected geometric algebra. The program also employs a variety of useful algebraic operators to carry out computations involving reversion, Clifford conjugations, inner and wedge operations, rotations, translations, motors, extraction of the i-blade of a multivector, etc. Here, as a first illustration, we use the program for computations in the motor algebra framework $\mathcal{G}_{3,0,1}^+$ to compute the direct kinematic equation of the origin $\boldsymbol{P}_4^o$ of $\mathcal{F}_4$ for the SCARA manipulator specified by the Denavit–Hartenberg parameters of Table 5.1. Fig. 5.7 shows the frames and the point $\boldsymbol{P}_4^o$ referred to $\mathcal{F}_0$. The final result of the computer calculation is

$$ {}^0\boldsymbol{P}_4^o = {}^0\boldsymbol{M}_4\, {}^4\boldsymbol{P}_4^o\, {}^0\widetilde{\overline{\boldsymbol{M}}}_4 = {}^0\boldsymbol{M}_4 \left(1 + I \begin{pmatrix} 0 \\ 0 \\ 0 \end{pmatrix}\right) {}^0\widetilde{\overline{\boldsymbol{M}}}_4 $$

$$= \quad 1 + I \begin{pmatrix} l_2 \cos(\theta_1 + \theta_2) + l_1 \cos(\theta_1) \\ l_2 \sin(\theta_1 + \theta_2) + l_1 \sin(\theta_1) \\ d_1 + d_2 + d_4 \end{pmatrix} . \qquad (5.17)$$

5.4 Inverse Kinematics of Robot Manipulators

Since calculations for the inverse kinematics are more complex than those for direct kinematics, our aim should be to find a systematic approach that will exploit the point, line, and plane motor algebra representations. Unfortunately, the procedure for the computation of the inverse kinematics is not amenable to a general formulation as in the case of the direct kinematics equation (5.14). That is why we are compelled to choose a real robot manipulator and compute its inverse kinematics in order to show all the characteristics of the computational assumptions.

The Stanford robot manipulator is well known among researchers concerned with the design of strategies for the symbolic computation of the inverse kinematics. According to Table 5.1, the variable parameters to be computed are θ_1, θ_2, θ_4, θ_5, θ_6, and d_3. Using the Stanford robot manipulator, we will show that the motor algebra approach gives us the freedom to switch between the point, line, or plane representation, according to the geometrical circumstances. This is one of the most important advantages of our motor algebra approach.

Mechanically, the Stanford manipulator can be divided into two basic components. The first comprises joints 1, 2, and 3 and is dedicated to the task of general positioning. The second comprises joints 4, 5, and 6, and is dedicated to the wrist-like orientation of the end-effector. Since the philosophy of our approach relies on the application of point, line, or plane representation where it is needed, we must first evaluate, for any given case, which of these three representations is suitable for the joint-transitions. In this way, a better geometric insight is guaranteed and the solution method is more easily developed. The first three joints of the Stanford manipulator are used to position the origin of the coordinate frame $\mathcal{F}_3$. Therefore, we apply a point representation to describe this part of the problem. The last three joints are used to achieve the desired orientation of the end-effector frame. For the formulation of this subproblem, we use a line and a plane representation because these entities allow us to model orientations.

5.4.1 The rendezvous method

The next important step is to represent the motor transformations from the beginning of a chain of joint-transitions to their completion, and vice versa, as depicted in Fig. 5.8. As a result, we gain a set of equations for each meeting point. In each of these points, the forward equation is equivalent to the backward equation. We use these equalities as a guide in the computation

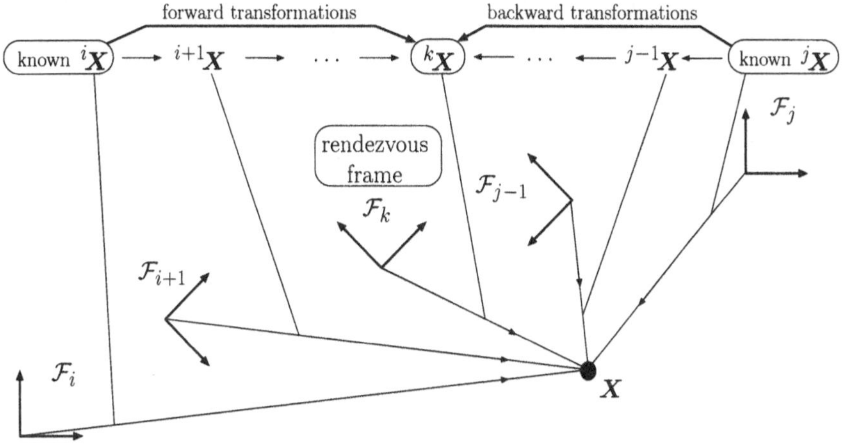

FIGURE 5.8. Rendezvous method: If ${}^{i}\boldsymbol{X}$ and ${}^{j}\boldsymbol{X}$ are known, we can compute ${}^{k}\boldsymbol{X}$ for each $i \leq k \leq j$ in one of two different ways—(1) by successive forward transformations of ${}^{i}\boldsymbol{X}$, and (2) by successive backward transformation of ${}^{j}\boldsymbol{X}$

of the unknowns. We will call this procedure the *rendezvous method.* This simple idea has proved to be very useful as a strategy for the solution of the inverse kinematics.

5.4.2 Computing θ_1, θ_2, and d_3 using a point

In the case of the Stanford manipulator , the orientation and position of frame $\mathcal{F}_6$ uniquely determines the position of frame $\mathcal{F}_3$. An explanation for this relation follows.

The position of frame $\mathcal{F}_3$ with respect to $\mathcal{F}_0$ is described by the multivector representation ${}^{0}\boldsymbol{P}_3^o$ of $\boldsymbol{P}_3^o$ in $\mathcal{F}_0$. By successive forward transformation applied on ${}^{3}\boldsymbol{P}_3^o = 1$, we find the representation ${}^{6}\boldsymbol{P}_3^o$ of $\boldsymbol{P}_3^o$ in $\mathcal{F}_6$ by

$$ {}^{6}\boldsymbol{P}_3^o = {}^{6}\boldsymbol{M}_3 \; {}^{3}\boldsymbol{P}_3^o \; {}^{6}\widetilde{\overline{\boldsymbol{M}}}_3 = 1 - I \begin{pmatrix} 0 \\ 0 \\ d_6 \end{pmatrix} . \tag{5.18} $$

Now we can compute ${}^{0}\boldsymbol{P}_3^o$ by

$$ \begin{aligned} {}^{0}\boldsymbol{P}_3^o &= {}^{0}\boldsymbol{M}_6 \; {}^{6}\boldsymbol{P}_3^o \; {}^{0}\widetilde{\overline{\boldsymbol{M}}}_6 = {}^{0}\boldsymbol{M}_6 \; (1 - I \begin{pmatrix} 0 \\ 0 \\ d_6 \end{pmatrix}) \; {}^{0}\widetilde{\overline{\boldsymbol{M}}}_6 \\ &= 1 + I \begin{pmatrix} P_x \\ P_y \\ P_z \end{pmatrix} . \end{aligned} \tag{5.19} $$

Note that ${}^{0}\boldsymbol{M}_6$ is given. The vector $(P_x, P_y, P_z)^T$ describes the position of the origin $\boldsymbol{P}_3^o$ of frame $\mathcal{F}_3$ in frame $\mathcal{F}_0$ for a given overall transformation ${}^{0}\boldsymbol{M}_6$.

Now we can apply the rendezvous method, since we know the representation of P_3^o in the two different frames $\mathcal{F}_0$ and $\mathcal{F}_3$ (see Fig. 5.9).

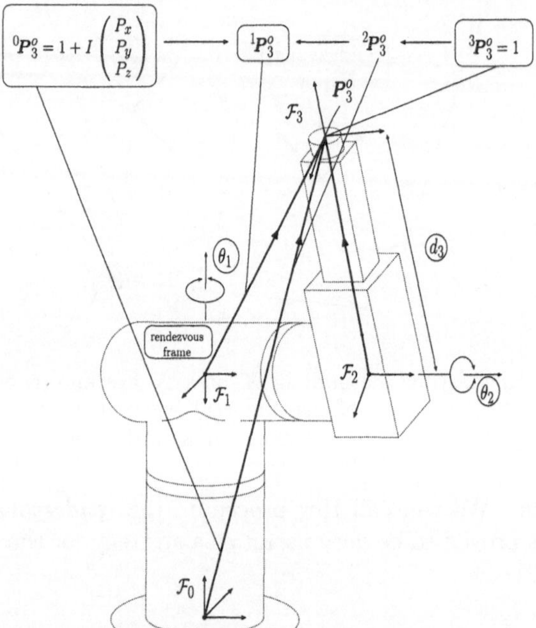

FIGURE 5.9. The rendezvous method applied to P_3^o in order to determine the equations shown in Table 5.2 (the equations of rendezvous frame $\mathcal{F}_1$ are chosen to compute the variable parameters θ_1, θ_2, and d_3)

By applying successive forward transformations, we obtain

$$\begin{aligned} {}^1P_3^o &= {}^1M_0\, {}^0P_3^o\, {}^1\widetilde{M}_0 , \\ {}^2P_3^o &= {}^2M_1\, {}^1P_3^o\, {}^2\widetilde{M}_1 , \\ {}^3P_3^o &= {}^3M_2\, {}^2P_3^o\, {}^3\widetilde{M}_2 . \end{aligned} \tag{5.20}$$

These computations were carried out with our MAPLE program, which calculated the lefthand sides of the four groups of equations in Table 5.2.

On the other hand, by applying successive backward transformations to the origin of $\mathcal{F}_3$ given by

$$ {}^3P_3^o = 1 + I\begin{pmatrix} 0 \\ 0 \\ 0 \end{pmatrix} = 1 , \tag{5.21}$$

we get

$$
\begin{aligned}
{}^{2}\boldsymbol{P}_3^o &= {}^{2}\boldsymbol{M}_3\ {}^{3}\boldsymbol{P}_3^o\ {}^{2}\widetilde{\boldsymbol{M}}_3 = 1 + I\begin{pmatrix} 0 \\ 0 \\ d_3 \end{pmatrix}, \\
{}^{1}\boldsymbol{P}_3^o &= {}^{1}\boldsymbol{M}_2\ {}^{2}\boldsymbol{P}_3^o\ {}^{1}\widetilde{\boldsymbol{M}}_2 = 1 + I\begin{pmatrix} d_3\sin(\theta_2) \\ -d_3\cos(\theta_2) \\ d_2 \end{pmatrix}, \\
{}^{0}\boldsymbol{P}_3^o &= {}^{0}\boldsymbol{M}_1\ {}^{1}\boldsymbol{P}_3^o\ {}^{0}\widetilde{\boldsymbol{M}}_1 = 1 + I\begin{pmatrix} d_3\sin(\theta_2)\cos(\theta_1) - d_2\sin(\theta_1) \\ d_3\sin(\theta_2)\sin(\theta_1) + d_2\cos(\theta_1) \\ d_3\cos(\theta_2) + d_1 \end{pmatrix}.
\end{aligned}
\tag{5.22}
$$

These equations correspond to the righthand sides of the four groups of equations in Table 5.2. For simplicity, we have used the abbreviations s_i for $\sin(\theta_i)$ and c_i for $\cos(\theta_i)$.

Frame	Eq.	Forward		Backward
$\mathcal{F}_0$	1	P_x	=	$d_3s_2c_1 - d_2s_1$
	2	P_y	=	$d_3s_2c_1 + d_2c_1$
	3	P_z	=	$d_3c_2 + d_1$
$\mathcal{F}_1$	1	$P_ys_1 + P_xc_1$	=	d_3s_2
	2	$d_1 - P_z$	=	$-d_3c_2$
	3	$P_yc_1 - P_xs_1$	=	d_2
$\mathcal{F}_2$	1	$-P_zs_2 + d_1s_2 + P_xc_1c_2 + P_ys_1c_2$	=	0
	2	$d_2 - P_yc_1 + P_xs_1$	=	0
	3	$P_zc_2 - d_1c_2 + P_xc_1s_2 + P_ys_1s_2$	=	d_3
$\mathcal{F}_3$	1	$-P_zs_2 + d_1s_2 + P_xc_1c_2 + P_ys_1c_2$	=	0
	2	$d_2 - P_yc_1 + P_xs_1$	=	0
	3	$P_zc_2 - d_1c_2 + P_xc_1s_2 + P_ys_1s_2 - d_3$	=	0

TABLE 5.2. Rendezvous equations obtained for $\boldsymbol{P}_3^o$ regarding frames $\mathcal{F}_0, \mathcal{F}_1, \mathcal{F}_2$, and $\mathcal{F}_3$

Using the third equation of the rendezvous frame $\mathcal{F}_1$, we compute

$$\theta_1 = \arctan_2(x_{1/2}, y_{1/2}), \tag{5.23}$$

where

$$x_{1/2} = \frac{d_2 - P_y y_{1/2}}{-P_x}, \qquad y_{1/2} = \frac{P_y d_2 \pm P_x\sqrt{P_x^2 + P_y^2 - d_2^2}}{P_x^2 + P_y^2}, \tag{5.24}$$

and

$$\arctan_2(x, y) = \begin{cases} \arctan(\frac{x}{y}) & : \ y > 0 \\ \frac{\pi}{2} & : \ y = 0 \text{ and } x > 0 \\ \text{undefined} & : \ y = 0 \text{ and } x = 0 \\ -\frac{\pi}{2} & : \ y = 0 \text{ and } x < 0 \\ \arctan(\frac{x}{y}) + \pi & : \ y < 0\,. \end{cases} \tag{5.25}$$

This gives two values for θ_1. Now, let us look for d_3 and θ_2. For that, we consider the first and second equation of the rendezvous frame $\mathcal{F}_1$. With $a_{1/2} = P_y x_{1/2} + P_x y_{1/2}$ and $b = P_z - d_1$, we obtain two values for d_3. Since for the Stanford manipulator d_3 must be positive, we choose

$$d_{3_{1/2}} = \sqrt{a_{1/2}^2 + b^2} \,. \tag{5.26}$$

Using this value in equations 1 and 2, we compute straightforwardly,

$$\theta_2 = \arctan_2\Big(\frac{a_{1/2}}{d_{3_{1/2}}}, \frac{b}{d_{3_{1/2}}}\Big) \,. \tag{5.27}$$

5.4.3 Computing θ_4 and θ_5 using a line

These variables will be computed using the joint-transition from $\mathcal{F}_3$ to $\mathcal{F}_6$. Given the geometric characteristics of the manipulator, an appealing option is to use the line representation to set up an appropriate equation system. The representation ${}^0\boldsymbol{L}_6^z$ of the line $\boldsymbol{L}_6^z$ in frame $\mathcal{F}_0$ can be computed using ${}^0\boldsymbol{M}_6$:

$${}^0\boldsymbol{L}_6^z = {}^0\boldsymbol{M}_6 \, {}^6\boldsymbol{L}_6^z \, {}^0\widetilde{\boldsymbol{M}}_6 = {}^0\boldsymbol{M}_6 \left(\begin{pmatrix} 0 \\ 0 \\ 1 \end{pmatrix} + I \begin{pmatrix} 0 \\ 0 \\ 0 \end{pmatrix} \right) {}^0\widetilde{\boldsymbol{M}}_6 \,. \tag{5.28}$$

Since the z-axis of the $\mathcal{F}_6$ frame crosses the origin of $\mathcal{F}_3$, we can see that the z-axis line related to this frame has zero moment. Thus, we can claim that L_6^z in the $\mathcal{F}_3$ frame is

$${}^3\boldsymbol{L}_6^z = {}^3\boldsymbol{M}_0 \, {}^0\boldsymbol{L}_6^z \, {}^3\widetilde{\boldsymbol{M}}_0 = \begin{pmatrix} A_x \\ A_y \\ A_z \end{pmatrix} + I \begin{pmatrix} 0 \\ 0 \\ 0 \end{pmatrix} \,. \tag{5.29}$$

Note that ${}^3\boldsymbol{M}_0$ is known since we have already computed θ_1, θ_2, and d_3.

Now, applying successively forward transformations, as follows:

$$\begin{aligned} {}^4\boldsymbol{L}_6^z &= {}^4\boldsymbol{M}_3 \, {}^3\boldsymbol{L}_6^z \, {}^4\widetilde{\boldsymbol{M}}_3 \,, \\ {}^5\boldsymbol{L}_6^z &= {}^5\boldsymbol{M}_4 \, {}^4\boldsymbol{L}_6^z \, {}^5\widetilde{\boldsymbol{M}}_4 \,, \\ {}^6\boldsymbol{L}_6^z &= {}^6\boldsymbol{M}_5 \, {}^5\boldsymbol{L}_6^z \, {}^6\widetilde{\boldsymbol{M}}_5 \,, \end{aligned} \tag{5.30}$$

we obtain the lefthand sides of the four groups of equations in Table 5.3. The z-axis line $\boldsymbol{L}_6^z$ of $\mathcal{F}_6$ represented in $\mathcal{F}_6$ has zero moment, and can therefore be expressed as

$${}^6L_6^z = \begin{pmatrix} 0 \\ 0 \\ 1 \end{pmatrix} + I \begin{pmatrix} 0 \\ 0 \\ 0 \end{pmatrix} . \tag{5.31}$$

Next, applying successive backward transformations, we obtain

$$\begin{aligned} {}^{5}\boldsymbol{L}_6^z &= {}^{5}\boldsymbol{M}_6\, {}^{6}\boldsymbol{L}_6^z\, {}^{5}\widetilde{\boldsymbol{M}}_6 \,, \\ {}^{4}\boldsymbol{L}_6^z &= {}^{4}\boldsymbol{M}_5\, {}^{5}\boldsymbol{L}_6^z\, {}^{4}\widetilde{\boldsymbol{M}}_5 \,, \\ {}^{3}\boldsymbol{L}_6^z &= {}^{3}\boldsymbol{M}_4\, {}^{4}\boldsymbol{L}_6^z\, {}^{3}\widetilde{\boldsymbol{M}}_4 \,. \end{aligned} \tag{5.32}$$

Using our MAPLE program, we then compute the righthand sides of the four groups of equations in Table 5.3.

Fr.	Eq.	Forward		Backw.
	1	A_x	=	$-c_4 s_5$
$\mathcal{F}_3$	2	A_y	=	$-s_4 s_5$
	3	A_z	=	$-c_5$
	1	$A_y s_4 + A_x c_4$	=	$-s_5$
$\mathcal{F}_4$	2	A_z	=	$-c_5$
	3	$A_y c_4 - A_x s_4$	=	0
	1	$-A_z s_5 + A_x c_4 c_5 + A_y s_4 c_5 c_6$	=	0
$\mathcal{F}_5$	2	$A_y c_4 - A_x s_4$	=	0
	3	$-A_z c_5 - A_x c_4 s_5 - A_y s_4 s_5$	=	1
	1	$A_x s_4 s_6 - A_y c_4 s_6 + A_y s_4 c_5 c_6 + A_x c_4 c_5 c_6 - A_z s_5 c_6$	=	0
$\mathcal{F}_6$	2	$-A_x s_4 c_6 + A_y c_4 c_6 + A_y s_4 c_5 c_6 + A_x c_4 c_5 s_6 - A_z s_5 s_6$	=	0
	3	$-A_z c_5 - A_x c_4 s_5 - A_y s_4 s_5$	=	1

TABLE 5.3. Rendezvous equations obtained for $\boldsymbol{L}_6^z$ regarding frames $\mathcal{F}_3, \mathcal{F}_4, \mathcal{F}_5$, and $\mathcal{F}_6$

Finally, we will consider the equations of rendezvous frame $\mathcal{F}_4$. Using the third equation of the Table 5.3, we compute

$$\theta_4 = \arctan_2(x_{1/2}, y_{1/2}) \,, \tag{5.33}$$

where

$$x_{1/2} = -\frac{A_y y_{1/2}}{-Ax} = \pm \frac{A_y}{\sqrt{A_x^2 + A_y^2}} \,, \qquad y_{1/2} = \pm \frac{A_x}{\sqrt{A_x^2 + A_y^2}} \,. \tag{5.34}$$

This results in two values for θ_4, which when substituted into the first and second equation of the Table 5.3 helps us to find two solutions for θ_5:

$$\theta_5 = \arctan_2(s_5, c_5) = \arctan_2\Big((-A_y s_4 - A_x c_4), -A_z\Big) \,. \tag{5.35}$$

5.4.4 Computing θ_6 using a plane representation

Since θ_1, θ_2, d_3, θ_4, and θ_5 are now known, we can compute the motor ${}^{5}\boldsymbol{M}_0$. The yz-plane $\boldsymbol{H}_6^{yz}$ represented in $\mathcal{F}_6$ has a Hesse distance of zero; thus,

$$ {}^{6}\boldsymbol{H}_6^{yz} = \begin{pmatrix} 1 \\ 0 \\ 0 \end{pmatrix} + I0 = \begin{pmatrix} 1 \\ 0 \\ 0 \end{pmatrix} . \tag{5.36} $$

The transformation of this plane to $\mathcal{F}_0$ reads

$$ {}^{0}\boldsymbol{H}_6^{yz} = {}^{0}\boldsymbol{M}_6 \, {}^{6}\boldsymbol{H}_6^{yz} \, {}^{0}\widetilde{\boldsymbol{M}}_6 = {}^{0}\boldsymbol{M}_6 \begin{pmatrix} 1 \\ 0 \\ 0 \end{pmatrix} {}^{0}\widetilde{\boldsymbol{M}}_6 . \tag{5.37} $$

Now we compute ${}^{5}\boldsymbol{H}_6^{yz}$:

$$ {}^{5}\boldsymbol{H}_6^{yz} = {}^{5}\boldsymbol{M}_0 \, {}^{0}\boldsymbol{H}_6^{yz} \, {}^{5}\widetilde{\boldsymbol{M}}_0 = \begin{pmatrix} N_x \\ N_y \\ N_z \end{pmatrix} + I \, {}^{5}d_{H_6^{yz}} . \tag{5.38} $$

The orientation bivector $(N_x, N_y, N_z)^T$ describes the orientation of the yz-plane of frame $\mathcal{F}_6$ in frame $\mathcal{F}_5$, given the values of the joint variables $\theta_1, \theta_2, \theta_4, \theta_5$, and d_3. By applying forward transformation from $\mathcal{F}_5$ to $\mathcal{F}_6$, we obtain

$$ {}^{6}\boldsymbol{H}_6^{yz} = {}^{6}\boldsymbol{M}_5 \, {}^{5}\boldsymbol{H}_6^{yz} \, {}^{6}\widetilde{\boldsymbol{M}}_5 . \tag{5.39} $$

Then, using our MAPLE program, we calculate the lefthand sides of the two groups of equations in Table 5.4. Since the values for θ_1, θ_2, d_3, θ_4, and θ_5 are not unique, we will obtain different values for the equations. By applying ${}^{5}\boldsymbol{M}_6$ to ${}^{6}\boldsymbol{H}_6^{yz}$, we next obtain the righthand sides of the two groups of equations in Table 5.4:

$$ \begin{aligned} {}^{5}\boldsymbol{H}_6^{yz} &= {}^{5}\boldsymbol{M}_6 \, {}^{6}\boldsymbol{H}_6^{yz} \, {}^{5}\widetilde{\boldsymbol{M}}_6 = {}^{5}\boldsymbol{M}_6 \begin{pmatrix} 1 \\ 0 \\ 0 \end{pmatrix} {}^{5}\widetilde{\boldsymbol{M}}_6 \\ &= \begin{pmatrix} \sin(\theta_6) \\ \cos(\theta_6) \\ 0 \end{pmatrix} . \end{aligned} \tag{5.40} $$

Frame	Eq.	Forward		Backward
$\mathcal{F}_5$	1	N_x	=	c_6
	2	N_y	=	s_6
	3	N_z	=	0
$\mathcal{F}_6$	1	$N_y s_6 + N_x c_6$	=	1
	2	$N_x s_6 - N_y c_6$	=	0
	3	N_z	=	0

TABLE 5.4. Rendezvous equations obtained for $\boldsymbol{H}_6^{yz}$ regarding frames $\mathcal{F}_5$ and $\mathcal{F}_6$

Finally, we will consider the equations of the rendezvous frame $\mathcal{F}_5$. Using the first and second equations in the Table 5.4, we can compute θ_6 by

$$\theta_6 = \arctan_2(s_6, c_6) = \arctan_2(N_x, N_y) . \tag{5.41}$$

Note that since there are two values for θ_4 and two values for θ_5, there is more than one solution for θ_6.

5.4.5 Inverse kinematic using the 3D affine plane

In this subsection we compute the inverse kinematic of a robot manipulator using the framework of the 3D affine plane (see Chapter 3). On the one hand, one can use a geometric algebra $\mathcal{G}_{p,q,0}$ with Minkowski metric for computations of projective geometry and the algebra of incidence, as is the case for computer vision problems (see Chapter 4). On the other hand, one can use a degenerated algebra for computations involving rigid motions, as is often the case in the field of robotics (see, e.g., our use of the motor algebra $\mathcal{G}^+_{3,0,1}$ in subsection 5.4 or the Clifford algebra $\mathcal{G}_{3,0,1}$ in [91]). In a more general way, the 3D affine plane allows calculations which can involve both 3D rigid transformations and the meet and join operations of the algebra of incidence.

Note that in this section we assume that the projection P_A back to the affine plane is always carried out, and thus we need not make it explicit in the formulas. In the procedure, after the equations to compute the angles θ_i have been found, simple dual trigonometric relations can then be used to determine the angles. In order to show the methodology at a symbolic level, we will avoid showing these trigonometric computation details.

The transformation M_t of a robot manipulator which takes the end-effector from its home position to a configuration determined by the n-degrees of freedom of the joint angles $\theta_1, \theta_2, ..., \theta_n$, is given by

$$M_t = M_1 M_2 M_3 ... M_n, \tag{5.42}$$

where the screw versor of a joint $M_i = T_i R_i$ is dependent on the angle θ_i.

The task of *inverse kinematics* is to calculate the angles θ_i for a given final configuration of the end-effector. Robot manipulators are equipped with a single parallel revoluted axis as well as intersecting axes. The latter can be located at the end-effector or at the home position. Two typical configurations are illustrated in Fig. 5.10.a,b. The mechanical characteristics of the robot manipulators can be used to simplify the computations—by considering either the invariant plane ϕ^h, in the case of three parallel revoluted line axes (see Fig. 5.10.a), or the invariant point p^h, in the case of the intersecting revoluted line axis (see Fig. 5.10.b).

We can solve the inverse kinematics problem by breaking it up into a series of separate equations, using the strategy suggested by Selig [91] (see Chapter 5). We will illustrate the procedure for a robot with 6 degrees of freedom. First, we rearrange the terms of equation (5.42):

$$M_2 M_3 M_4 = \widetilde{M}_1 M_t \widetilde{M}_6 \widetilde{M}_5. \tag{5.43}$$

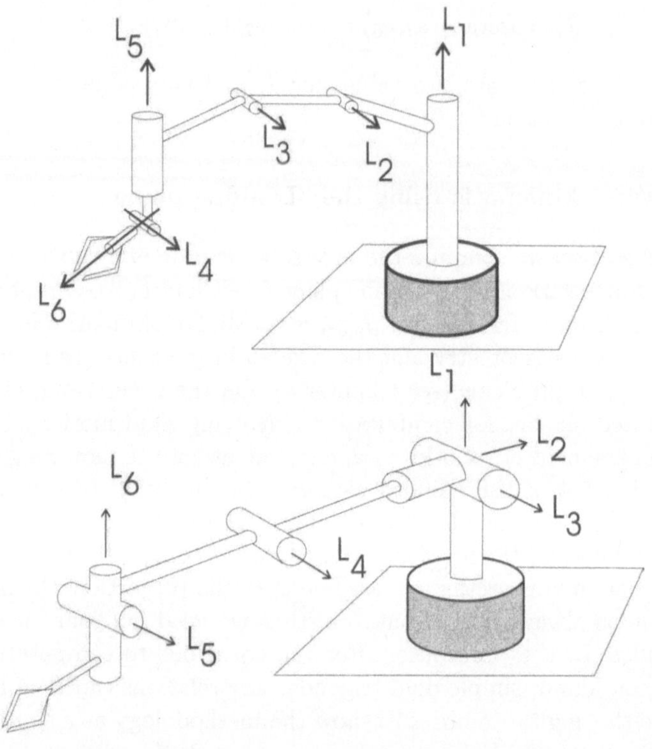

FIGURE 5.10. Robot manipulators: (a) (top) intersect revoluted line axes at the end- effector; or (b) (bottom) at the home position

In the case of three parallel joints, we can isolate them by considering the common perpendicular plane ϕ^h which satisfies the equation

$$\phi^h = M_2M_3M_4\,\phi^h\,\widetilde{M}_4\widetilde{M}_3\widetilde{M}_2 = \widetilde{M}_1M_t(\widetilde{M}_6(\widetilde{M}_5\,\phi^h\,M_5)M_6)\widetilde{M}_tM_1. \quad (5.44)$$

In the case of a meeting point p^h, we can isolate the three coincident joints as follows:

$$p^h = M_2M_3M_4\,p^h\,\widetilde{M}_4\widetilde{M}_3\widetilde{M}_2 = \widetilde{M}_1M_t\widetilde{M}_6\widetilde{M}_5\,p^h\,M_5\widetilde{M}_6\widetilde{M}_tM_1. \quad (5.45)$$

In this way, we have separated the problem into two systems of equations:

$$\widetilde{M}_tM_1\,\phi^h\,\widetilde{M}_1M_t = \widetilde{M}_6\widetilde{M}_5\,\phi^h\,M_5M_6 \quad (5.46)$$

or

$$\widetilde{M}_tM_1\,p^h\,\widetilde{M}_1M_t = \widetilde{M}_6\widetilde{M}_5\,p^h\,M_5M_6, \quad (5.47)$$

$$M_2M_3M_4 = M_1M_t\widetilde{M}_6\widetilde{M}_5 = M'. \quad (5.48)$$

We can now compute for θ_1, θ_5, θ_6 with the help of either equation (5.46) (see Fig. 5.10.a) or equation (5.47) (see Fig. 5.10.b). Then, by using these results and equation (5.48), we can solve for θ_2, θ_3, θ_4.

Let us demonstrate how the procedure works for the case of three intersecting revoluted joint axes in the common plane at the end-effector (see Fig. 5.10.a). When the plane ϕ_b^h (perpendicular to the line axes l_2, l_3, and l_4) is rotated about the end-joint, the point p_i^h on the line axis of the revoluted end-joint l_6^h remains invariant. Using a *meet* operation and equation (5.46), the angle θ_6 can be eliminated:

$$\begin{aligned} p_i^h &= (\widetilde{M}_t M_1 \,\phi^h\, \widetilde{M}_1 M_t) \cap l_6^h = (\widetilde{M}_6 \widetilde{M}_5 \,\phi^h\, M_5 M_6) \cap l_6^h \\ &= (\widetilde{M}_5 \,\phi^h\, M_5) \cap l_6^h. \end{aligned} \tag{5.49}$$

In the case of a robot manipulator in the home position, the revoluted joint axes are the manipulator basis. Equation (5.47) shows that the point p^h is an invariant for the parallel fourth and fifth line axes. Thus, we can use the equation

$$M_6 \widetilde{M}_t \,p^h\, M_t \widetilde{M}_6 = \widetilde{M}_5 \widetilde{M}_4 \,p^h\, M_4 M_5 \tag{5.50}$$

to solve for the angles θ_4 and θ_5. Using the line l_5 and p^h, we get the invariant plane,

$$\phi_i^h = M_6 \widetilde{M}_t \,p^h\, M_t \widetilde{M}_6 \wedge l_5. \tag{5.51}$$

The 3D coordinates of this plane are known in advance and correspond to the plane $x - z$ or e_{32}; thus, equation (5.51) allows us to solve for the angle θ_6. Having determined angle θ_6, we can now use equations (5.50) to complete the calculation of θ_4 and θ_5.

Now consider the three coincident line axes l_1^h, l_2^h, l_3^h given in Fig. 5.10.b. We can isolate the angle θ_2 by considering the invariant relation based on the meet of two of these lines. Thus,

$$(M_2 \, l_3^h \, \widetilde{M}_2) \cap l_1^h = (M' \, l_3^h \, \widetilde{M}') \cap l_1^h = p_0^h, \tag{5.52}$$

where $M' = M_1 M_2 M_3$ and p_0^h is the invariant intersecting point. When the lines are parallel, as shown in Fig. 5.10.a, we can use the same invariant relation, but now we consider the intersecting point to be at infinity, so that $M' = M_2 M_3 M_4$.

5.5 Conclusion

This chapter presented the application of the algebra of motors for the treatment of the direct and inverse kinematics of robot manipulators. When dealing with 3D rigid motion, it is usual to use homogeneous coordinates in the 4D space to linearize this nonlinear 3D transformation. With the same effect, we model the prismatic and revolute motion of points, lines, and planes using motors which are equivalent to screws. In our approach, we can also use the representation of planes, and this expands the useful geometric language for the treatment of robotic problems. In addition, we illustrate the use of the 3D affine plane for computing inverse kinematics, taking advantage of incidence algebra operations to simplify computations that use intersections and unions of points, lines, and planes under rigid motion.

The chapter has shown the flexibility of the motor algebra approach for the solution of the direct and inverse kinematics of robot manipulators. To solve for the robot's inverse kinematics, we have shown that, depending on our needs, we can use representations either of points, lines, or planes, which help to enormously reduce the complexity of the computation without losing geometric insight. Similarly, the use of incidence algebra in the affine plane framework allows us to define geometric constraints, or flags, by taking advantage of meet and joint operations, thereby allowing easy identification of the most important geometric objects involved.

Thus, the main contribution of this chapter has been to show that our approach offers more flexibility while at the same time preserving geometric insight during computation. The author believes that the versatility of the geometric algebra framework offers an alternative approach to the increasingly complex of application of multilink mechanisms.

6. Image Processing

6.1 Introduction

This chapter is devoted to low-level image processing, applying geometric algebra techniques. We will show that using this mathematical system it is possible to develop powerful algorithms for image filtering, pattern recognition, feature detection, image segmentation, texture analysis, and image analysis in frequency domain. These techniques are fundamental for automated visual inspection, robot guidance, medical imaging, and analysis of image sequences, as well as for satellite and aerial photogrammetry.

The development of algorithms for artificial perception benefits from psychophysical experimentation. Results indicate that human vision may operate in two distinct modes: *attentive vision* and *preattentive vision* [58]. Attentive vision involves a level of cognitive processing which is beyond the scope of this volume. In preattentive visual mode, human beings perceive scenes instantaneously over a large visual field and are able to discriminate between different visual patterns. This visual capacity relies on parallel preattentive feature-extraction and -processing. Psychophysical experiments have shown the importance of specific basic visual cues for such bottom-up processing. This chapter, therefore, presents a variety of techniques for the detection of basic geometric features like textons, edges, lines, corners, and key points.

First, the quaternionic Fourier transform is explained, and together with quaternionic Gabor filters, it is applied for phase analysis. The quaternionic phase concept helps us to disentangle the symmetry of 2D signals. Various illustrations of the use of the quaternionic phase concept will show the power of analysis in the quaternionic frequency domain. The design and application of Lie perceptrons working in the affine plane for key points detection is also presented. This approach is stimulated by certain evidence of the human visual system. On the other hand, in an effort to elucidate the relationship between geometry and color, in the final section we present a study of edge detectors which process the R, G, and B color channels separately.

6.2 Image Analysis in the Frequency Domain

A chapter devoted to image analysis would be not complete if it lacked an analysis in the frequency domain, and so here we present the *quaternionic Fourier transform* (QFT) and the quaternionic Gabor filters. During the 1990s a number of different attempts were made to use the algebra of quaternions for computations in the frequency domain. Chernov [21] used quaternions to speed up the evaluation of the 2D discrete, complex-valued, Fourier transform. Ell [31] introduced the QFT and applied it to the analysis of 2D linear, time-invariant, partial-differential systems. He used the ψ phase component of the polar representation of the QFT, equation (6.19), as an indicator of the stability of the system. Later on, Blow focused on the development of a quaternionic phase concept and clarified many theoretical and practical aspects of the QFT [15]. Using the Clifford algebra framework, he also showed that the highest level of the hierarchy of harmonic transformations is occupied by the n-dimensional Clifford Fourier transform. Sangwine [92] utilized the QFT for color image processing, assigning the individual RGB components to the quaternion imaginary components. The images are thus transformed holistically, as opposed to the more simplified approach in which each color channel is separately transformed utilizing the 2D Fourier transform. The following subsections, presenting the QFT and quaternionic Gabor filters, are based upon Blow's results [15].

6.2.1 Quaternionic Fourier transform

Like the 2D Fourier transform and the Hartley transform, the quaternionic Fourier transform (QFT) is a linear and invertible transformation. The QFT is limited to 2D signals. Clifford algebra Fourier transforms (CFTs) can deal with transformations of higher-dimensional signals. The complex Fourier transform and the QFT can be seen as special cases of CFTs. The *2D Fourier transform* (FT) is given by

$$\begin{aligned} F_c(u) &= \int_{-\infty}^{\infty}\int_{-\infty}^{\infty} T(i2\pi ux) f(\boldsymbol{x}) T(i2\pi vy) d^2\boldsymbol{x} \\ &= \int_{-\infty}^{\infty}\int_{-\infty}^{\infty} e^{(-i2\pi ux)} f(\boldsymbol{x}) e^{(-i2\pi vy)} d^2\boldsymbol{x}, \end{aligned} \qquad (6.1)$$

where $\boldsymbol{x} = (x, y)$, $\boldsymbol{u} = (u, v)$, and $f(\boldsymbol{x})$ is a 2D-real-valued function. $T(i2\pi ux)$ and $T(i2\pi vy)$ are Fourier kernels applied to both axes of the 2D signal. If we assign, instead, Fourier kernels which depend upon the quaternion bases $i = \sigma_1\sigma_2$ and $j = \sigma_2\sigma_3$ ($ij = -k = \sigma_1\sigma_3$), we then get a straightforward expression for the QFT,

$$F_q(u) = \int_{-\infty}^{\infty}\int_{-\infty}^{\infty} T(i2\pi ux) f(\boldsymbol{x}) T(j2\pi vy) d^2\boldsymbol{x}$$

$$F_q(u) = \int_{-\infty}^{\infty}\int_{-\infty}^{\infty} e^{(-i2\pi ux)} f(\boldsymbol{x}) e^{(-j2\pi vy)} d^2\boldsymbol{x}, \tag{6.2}$$

where $\boldsymbol{x} = (x, y)$, $\boldsymbol{u} = (u, v)$, and $f(\boldsymbol{x})$ is a real-, complex-, or quaternion-valued 2D function.

The *inverse quaternionic Fourier transform* (IQFT) is given by

$$\begin{aligned} f(\boldsymbol{x}) &= \int_{-\infty}^{\infty}\int_{-\infty}^{\infty} \tilde{T}(i2\pi ux) F_q(u) \tilde{T}(j2\pi vy) d^2\boldsymbol{u} \\ &= \int_{-\infty}^{\infty}\int_{-\infty}^{\infty} e^{(i2\pi ux)} F_q(\boldsymbol{u}) e^{(j2\pi vy)} d^2\boldsymbol{u}, \end{aligned} \tag{6.3}$$

where $T(i2\pi ux)\tilde{T}(i2\pi ux)$=1 and $T(j2\pi vy)\tilde{T}(j2\pi vy)$=1.

Let us now give the concept of *Hermitian function* in the quaternionic domain. As an extension of the Hermitian function $f : I\!R \to \boldsymbol{C}$ with $f(x) = f^*(-x)$ for every $x \in I\!R$, we regard $f : I\!R^2 \to I\!H$ as a quaternionic Hermitian function if it fulfills the following nontrivial involution rules [21]:

$$\begin{aligned} f(-x, y) &= -jf(x, y)j = \mathcal{T}_j(f(x, y)), \\ f(x, -y) &= -if(x, y)i = \mathcal{T}_i(f(x, y)), \\ f(-x, -y) &= -if(-x, y)i = -i(-jf(x, y)j)i = (-i-j)f(x, y)(ji) \\ &= -kf(x, y)k = \mathcal{T}_k(f(x, y)). \end{aligned} \tag{6.4}$$

The concept of quaternionic Hermitian function is very useful for the computation of the inverse QFT using the quaternionic analytic signal.

6.2.2 2D analytic signals

This subsection discusses different points of views found in the literature concerning the fundamental concept of the analytical signal of 2D signals. The reader can find a detailed analysis of this issue in [15, 37]. The particular formulation of the 2D analytical signal used influences the final representation of the signal in the four quadrants of the frequency domain. Thus, in order to recover the entire real 2D signal using the inverse Fourier transform, one must take this final representation into account. The same thought process applies when one computes the magnitude and phase of the 2D signal.

The analytical signal of a 2D signal is given by

$$\begin{aligned} f_A(\boldsymbol{x}) &= f(\boldsymbol{x}) \star (\delta^2(\boldsymbol{x}) + \frac{i}{\pi^2 xy}) \\ &= f(\boldsymbol{x}) + if(\boldsymbol{x}) \star (\frac{i}{\pi^2 xy}) = f(\boldsymbol{x}) + if_{H_i}(\boldsymbol{x}), \end{aligned} \tag{6.5}$$

where $f_{H_i}(\boldsymbol{x})$ is called the total *Hilbert transform* [103] and the symbol $\star$ stands for a 2D convolution operation. In the frequency domain, the signal is split among the four quadrants according to the following equation:

$$F_A(\boldsymbol{u}) = F(\boldsymbol{u})\Big(1 - isign(u)sign(v)\Big) \tag{6.6}$$

(see Fig. 6.1.a).

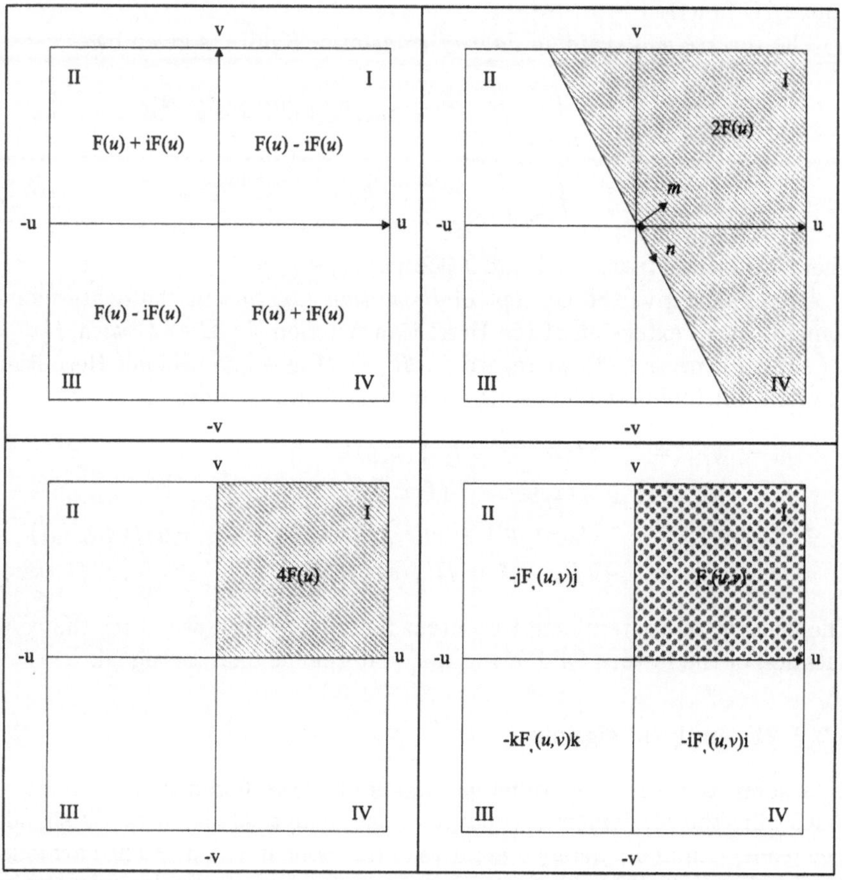

FIGURE 6.1. 2D analytic signals in the frequency domain: (a) standard 2D analytical signal $F_A(\boldsymbol{u})$, (b) partial analytical signal $F_{A_p}(\boldsymbol{u})$, (c) Hahn's 2D analytical signal $F_{A_{h1}}(\boldsymbol{u})$, and (d) quaternionic 2D analytical signal

The *partial analytical signal* locates the signal energy in the frequency domain on one side of a reference line indicated by the normal unit vector of the line $\boldsymbol{m} = (cos(\theta), sin(\theta))$, which is perpendicular to the line direction $\boldsymbol{n}$. The partial analytical signal in spatial domain is given by the equation

$$f_{A_p}(\boldsymbol{x}) = f(\boldsymbol{x}) \star \Big(\delta(\boldsymbol{x}\cdot\boldsymbol{m}) + \frac{i}{\pi\boldsymbol{x}\cdot\boldsymbol{m}}\Big)\delta(\boldsymbol{x}\cdot\boldsymbol{n}), \tag{6.7}$$

and in frequency domain by the equation

$$F_{A_p}(\boldsymbol{u}) = F(\boldsymbol{u})\Big(1 + sign(\boldsymbol{u}\cdot\boldsymbol{m})\Big) \tag{6.8}$$

(see Fig. 6.1.b).

In another approach, Hahn [40, 41] introduced the following notion of the analytic signal:

$$\begin{aligned} f_{A_h 1}(\boldsymbol{x}) &= f(\boldsymbol{x}) \star \Big(\delta(x) + \frac{i}{\pi x}\Big)\Big(\delta(y) + \frac{i}{\pi y}\Big) \\ &= f(\boldsymbol{x}) - f(\boldsymbol{x}) \star \Big(\frac{1}{\pi^2 xy}\Big) + i f(\boldsymbol{x}) \star \Big(\frac{\delta(y)}{\pi x}\Big) + i f(\boldsymbol{x}) \star \Big(\frac{\delta(x)}{\pi y}\Big) \\ &= f(\boldsymbol{x}) - f_{H_i}(\boldsymbol{x}) + i\Big(f_{H_{i_a}}(\boldsymbol{x}) + f_{H_{i_b}}(\boldsymbol{x})\Big), \end{aligned} \tag{6.9}$$

where $f_{H_i}(\boldsymbol{x})$ is the total Hilbert transform and $f_{H_{i_a}}(\boldsymbol{x})$, $f_{H_{i_b}}(\boldsymbol{x})$ are partial Hilbert transforms which only reference the x- and y-axes, respectively. In the frequency domain, the analytical signal is localized only in the first quadrant and is multiplied four times according to

$$F_{A_h 1}(\boldsymbol{u}) = \Big(1 + sign(u)\Big)\Big(1 + sign(v)\Big)F(\boldsymbol{u}), \tag{6.10}$$

(see Fig. 6.1.c). In this approach, owing to the Hermitian symmetry, only one-half of the plane of the frequency spectrum is redundant, so that a second analytical signal with its spectrum located in the second quadrant is required:

$$\begin{aligned} f_{A_h 2}(\boldsymbol{x}) &= f(\boldsymbol{x}) + f_{H_i}(\boldsymbol{x}) - i\Big(f_{H_{i_a}}(\boldsymbol{x}) - f_{H_{i_b}}(\boldsymbol{x})\Big), \\ F_{A_h 2}(\boldsymbol{u}) &= \Big(1 + sign(-u)\Big)\Big(1 + sign(v)\Big)F(\boldsymbol{u}). \end{aligned} \tag{6.11}$$

The entire 2D real signal can only be recovered by taking into account both analytic signals, $F_{A_h 1}$ and $F_{A_h 2}$ (for more details, see [41]).

As Fig. 6.1.d shows, the QFT of a 2D real signal is a quaternionic hermitian and thus the total information of the signal is not lost. This suggests that the quaternionic analytical signal may be defined by modifying the Hahn's equation (6.9), utilizing instead the quaternion basis

$$\begin{aligned} f_{A_q}(\boldsymbol{x}) &= f(\boldsymbol{x}) \star \Big(\delta(x) + \frac{i}{\pi x}\Big)\Big(\delta(y) + \frac{j}{\pi y}\Big) \\ &= f(\boldsymbol{x}) + i f(\boldsymbol{x}) \star \Big(\frac{1}{\pi^2 xy}\Big) + j f(\boldsymbol{x}) \star \Big(\frac{\delta(y)}{\pi x}\Big) + ij f(\boldsymbol{x}) \star \Big(\frac{\delta(x)}{\pi y}\Big) \\ &= f(\boldsymbol{x}) + i f_{H_{i_a}}(\boldsymbol{x}) + j f_{H_{i_b}}(\boldsymbol{x}) - k f_{H_i}(\boldsymbol{x}), \end{aligned} \tag{6.12}$$

where $f_{H_{i_a}}(\boldsymbol{x})$ and $f_{H_{i_b}}(\boldsymbol{x})$ are the partial Hilbert transforms and $f_{H_i}(\boldsymbol{x})$ is the total Hilbert transform. In the frequency domain, the quaternionic analytical signal is given by

$$F_{A_q}(\boldsymbol{u}) = \Big(1 + sign(u)\Big)\Big(1 + sign(v)\Big)F_q(\boldsymbol{u}) \tag{6.13}$$

(see Fig. 6.1.d).

We will now show that we can indeed obtain $f(x,y)$ by utilizing the first quadrant of the frequency spectrum $F_q(u,v)$ four times. To do so, we employ the simple property of quaternions, $Re(\boldsymbol{q}) = Re(-i\boldsymbol{q}i) = Re(-j\boldsymbol{q}j) = Re(-k\boldsymbol{q}k)$, such that

$$\begin{aligned}
f(x,y) &= 4Re\Big(\int_0^\infty\int_0^\infty e^{(i2\pi ux)}F_q(\boldsymbol{u})e^{(j2\pi vy)}d^2\boldsymbol{u}\Big)\\
&= Re\Big(\int_0^\infty\int_0^\infty e^{(i2\pi ux)}F_q(\boldsymbol{u})e^{(j2\pi vy)}d^2\boldsymbol{u}\Big)\\
&\quad +Re\Big(\int_0^\infty\int_0^\infty e^{(i2\pi ux)} - iF_q(\boldsymbol{u})ie^{(j2\pi vy)}d^2\boldsymbol{u}\Big)\\
&\quad +Re\Big(\int_0^\infty\int_0^\infty e^{(i2\pi ux)} - jF_q(\boldsymbol{u})je^{(j2\pi vy)}d^2\boldsymbol{u}\Big)\\
&\quad +Re\Big(\int_0^\infty\int_0^\infty e^{(i2\pi ux)} - kF_q(\boldsymbol{u})ke^{(j2\pi vy)}d^2\boldsymbol{u}\Big)\\
&= Re\Big(\int_0^\infty\int_0^\infty e^{(i2\pi ux)}F_q(\boldsymbol{u})e^{(j2\pi vy)}d^2\boldsymbol{u}\Big)\\
&\quad +Re\Big(\int_0^\infty\int_0^\infty e^{(i2\pi ux)}F_q(u,-v)e^{(j2\pi vy)}d^2\boldsymbol{u}\Big)\\
&\quad +Re\Big(\int_0^\infty\int_0^\infty e^{(i2\pi ux)}F_q(-u,v)e^{(j2\pi vy)}d^2\boldsymbol{u}\Big)\\
&\quad +Re\Big(\int_0^\infty\int_0^\infty e^{(i2\pi ux)}F_q(-u,-v)e^{(j2\pi vy)}d^2\boldsymbol{u}\Big)\\
&= Re\Big(\int_0^\infty\int_0^\infty e^{(i2\pi ux)}F_q(\boldsymbol{u})e^{(j2\pi vy)}dudv\Big)\\
&\quad +Re\Big(\int_{-\infty}^0\int_0^\infty e^{(i2\pi ux)}F_q(u,v)e^{(j2\pi vy)}dudv\Big)\\
&\quad +Re\Big(\int_0^\infty\int_{-\infty}^0 e^{(i2\pi ux)}F_q(u,v)e^{(j2\pi vy)}dudv\Big)\\
&\quad +Re\Big(\int_{-\infty}^0\int_{-\infty}^0 e^{(i2\pi ux)}F_q(u,v)e^{(j2\pi vy)}dudv\Big)\\
&= Re\Big(\int_{-\infty}^\infty\int_{-\infty}^\infty e^{(i2\pi ux)}F_q(\boldsymbol{u})e^{(j2\pi vy)}dudv\Big). \qquad (6.14)
\end{aligned}$$

Note that Hahn's approach to the analytical signal fails to recover a 2D complex Hermitian signal using the first quadrant of the the frequency spectrum. That is why Hahn introduced two complex signals for each of the real 2D signal equations, (6.10) and (6.11). By contrast, using the quaternionic analytical signal the entire real 2D signal can be recovered from the first quadrant of the frequency spectrum. This is due to the Hermitian symmetry properties of the quaternionic analytical signal. Fig. 6.2 shows the complex and quaternionic Fourier transforms of a 2D signal.

FIGURE 6.2. Analysis in frequency domain: (upper row) (a) 2D signal, (b) real and imaginary parts of FT, (c) magnitude and phase of FT; (lower row) (d) real and imaginary parts of QFT, (e) magnitude and phases of QFT

6.2.3 Properties of the QFT

Next, we will give some relevant properties of the QFT. We start with a treatment of the symmetries of 2D signals using the Fourier and Hartley transforms.

Symmetry properties

A 2D signal can be split into even and odd parts with respect to the two axes:

$$f(\boldsymbol{x}) = f_{ee}(\boldsymbol{x}) + f_{oo}(\boldsymbol{x}) + f_{eo}(\boldsymbol{x}) + f_{oe}(\boldsymbol{x}), \tag{6.15}$$

where the subindexes e (for even) and o (for odd) are related to the x-axis and y-axis, respectively. This split depends on the selected origin and image orientation. Since the 2D Fourier transform has real and imaginary parts, it is not possible to disentangle the four components of equation (6.15), as the following computation shows:

$$\begin{aligned} F(\boldsymbol{u},\boldsymbol{v}) &= \int_{-\infty}^{\infty}\Big(\int_{-\infty}^{\infty} e^{-i2\pi ux} f(x,y)dx\Big) e^{-i2\pi vy} dy \\ &= \int_{-\infty}^{\infty}\Big(\int_{-\infty}^{\infty} (cos(2\pi ux) - isin(2\pi ux)) f(x,y)dx\Big) e^{-i2\pi vy} dy \\ &= \int_{-\infty}^{\infty} (H_e - iH_o)\Big(cos(2\pi vy) - isin(2\pi vy)\Big) dy \\ &= (H_{ee} - H_{oo}) - i(H_{oe} + H_{eo}) \in \boldsymbol{C}. \end{aligned} \tag{6.16}$$

The elements of equation (6.15) are intermixed within the real and imaginary parts of this equation. In contrast, by computing the QFT following the quaternion multiplication $ij = -k$, we obtain

$$\begin{aligned} F_q(\boldsymbol{u},\boldsymbol{v}) &= \int_{-\infty}^{\infty}\Big(\int_{-\infty}^{\infty} e^{-i2\pi ux} f(x,y)dx\Big) e^{-j2\pi vy} dy \\ &= \int_{-\infty}^{\infty}\Big(\int_{-\infty}^{\infty} (cos(2\pi ux) - isin(2\pi ux)) f(x,y)dx\Big) e^{-j2\pi vy} dy \\ &= \int_{-\infty}^{\infty} (H_e - iH_o) e^{-j2\pi vy} dy \\ &= \int_{-\infty}^{\infty} (H_e - iH_o)\Big(cos(2\pi vy) - jsin(2\pi vy)\Big) dy \\ &= \int_{-\infty}^{\infty} \Big(H_e cos(2\pi vy) - iH_o cos(2\pi vy) - jH_e sin(2\pi vy) + \\ &\qquad +(ij)H_o sin(2\pi vy)\Big) dy \\ &= H_{ee} - iH_{oe} - jH_{eo} - kH_{oo} \in \mathbb{H}. \end{aligned} \tag{6.17}$$

Note that here the QFT separates the four components of equation (6.15) by projecting them into the orthonormal quaternionic basis. By contrast, the Hartley transform (HT) cannot split these parts, as the following computation shows:

$$\begin{aligned} H(\boldsymbol{u}) &= \int_{-\infty}^{\infty}\int_{-\infty}^{\infty} f(\boldsymbol{x})\Big\{cos(2\pi \boldsymbol{u}\cdot\boldsymbol{x}) + sin(2\pi \boldsymbol{u}\cdot\boldsymbol{x})\Big\} d^2\boldsymbol{x} \\ &= \int_{-\infty}^{\infty}\int_{-\infty}^{\infty} f(\boldsymbol{x})\Big\{cos(2\pi ux)cos(2\pi vy) - sin(2\pi ux)sin(2\pi vy) + \\ &\qquad +cos(2\pi ux)sin(2\pi vy) + sin(2\pi ux)cos(2\pi vy)\Big\} d^2\boldsymbol{x} \\ &= H_{ee}(\boldsymbol{u}) + H_{oo}(\boldsymbol{u}) + H_{eo}(\boldsymbol{u}) + H_{oe}(\boldsymbol{u}) \in R. \end{aligned} \tag{6.18}$$

Polar representation of the QFT

The polar representation of the QFT is given by

$$F_q(\boldsymbol{u}) = \Big|F_q(\boldsymbol{u})\Big| e^{i\phi(\boldsymbol{u})} e^{k\psi(\boldsymbol{u})} e^{k\theta(\boldsymbol{u})}, \tag{6.19}$$

and the evaluation of its phase follows the quaternion rules given in subsection 1.6.2. This kind of representation is very helpful for image analysis if we use the phase concept.

Shift property

With regard to the polar representation of the QFT, it is appropriate to mention the shift property of the QFT:

$$\begin{aligned} F_q(\boldsymbol{u})_T &= \int_{-\infty}^{\infty}\int_{-\infty}^{\infty} e^{(-i2\pi ux)} f(\boldsymbol{x}-\boldsymbol{d}) e^{(-j2\pi vy)} d^2\boldsymbol{x} \\ &= e^{(-i2\pi ud_1)} F_q(\boldsymbol{u}) e^{(-j2\pi ud_2)} \\ &= \Big|F_q(\boldsymbol{u})_T\Big| e^{i(\phi(\boldsymbol{u})-2\pi ud_1)} e^{k\psi(\boldsymbol{u})} e^{j(\chi(\boldsymbol{u})-2\pi vd_2)}. \end{aligned} \tag{6.20}$$

Modulation

The modulation of the 2D signal causes a shifting in the 2D frequency space, which is the result of the modulation in the space domain of the 2D signal from both sides by two orthogonal carriers with frequencies u_0 and v_0:

$$f_m(x,y) = e^{(i2\pi u_0 x)} f(x,y) e^{(j2\pi v_0 y)}. \tag{6.21}$$

By taking the QFT of $f_m(x,y)$, we obtain

$$F_q\Big\{f_m(x,y)\Big\}(u,v) = F_q(u-u_0, v-v_0). \tag{6.22}$$

Convolution

Consider the real 2D signals $f1$ and $f2$ with their quaternionic Fourier transforms $F1_q$ and $F2_q$, respectively. The convolution of these 2D signals can be carried out in the frequency domain as a sort of multiplication of their QFTs. This can be easily proved, by either integrating with respect to the Fourier kernel $e^{-(j2\pi yv)}$:

$$\begin{aligned} F_q &= \int_{-\infty}^{\infty}\int_{-\infty}^{\infty} e^{-(i2\pi xu)} \Big(f_1(\boldsymbol{x}) \star f_2(\boldsymbol{x})\Big) e^{-(j2\pi yv)} d^2\boldsymbol{x} \\ &= \int_{-\infty}^{\infty}\int_{-\infty}^{\infty} e^{-(i2\pi xu)} \Big(\int_{-\infty}^{\infty}\int_{-\infty}^{\infty} f_1(\boldsymbol{x}') f_2(\boldsymbol{x}-\boldsymbol{x}') d^2\boldsymbol{x}'\Big) e^{-(j2\pi yv)} d^2\boldsymbol{x} \\ &= \int_{-\infty}^{\infty}\int_{-\infty}^{\infty} e^{-(i2\pi x'u)} f_1(\boldsymbol{x}') F_{2q}(\boldsymbol{u}) e^{-(j2\pi y'v)} d^2\boldsymbol{x}' \\ &= \int_{-\infty}^{\infty}\int_{-\infty}^{\infty} e^{-(i2\pi x'u)} f_1(\boldsymbol{x}') cos(-2\pi y'v) F_{2q}(\boldsymbol{u}) d^2\boldsymbol{x}' \\ &\quad + \int_{-\infty}^{\infty}\int_{-\infty}^{\infty} e^{-(i2\pi x'u)} f_1(\boldsymbol{x}') j sin(-2\pi y'v) \Big(-jF_{2q}(\boldsymbol{u})j\Big) d^2\boldsymbol{x}' \\ &= F_{1q_e}(\boldsymbol{u}) F_{2q}(\boldsymbol{u}) + F_{1q_o}(\boldsymbol{u}) \Big(-jF_{2q}(\boldsymbol{u})j\Big) \\ &= F_{1q_e}(\boldsymbol{u}) F_{2q}(\boldsymbol{u}) + F_{1q_o}(\boldsymbol{u}) \mathcal{T}_j(F_{2q}(\boldsymbol{u})), \end{aligned} \tag{6.23}$$

or by integrating with respect to the Fourier kernel $e^{-(i2\pi xv)}$:

$$
\begin{aligned}
F_q &= F_{1q}(\boldsymbol{u})F_{2q_e}(\boldsymbol{u}) + \Big(-iF_{1q}(\boldsymbol{u})i\Big)F_{2q_o}(\boldsymbol{u}) \\
&= F_{1q}(\boldsymbol{u})F_{2q_e}(\boldsymbol{u}) + \mathcal{T}_i(F_{1q}(\boldsymbol{u}))F_{2q_o}(\boldsymbol{u}). \qquad (6.24)
\end{aligned}
$$

Note that if one of the functions is even with respect to at least one of the kernel arguments, the convolution is then equal to the product of the individual spectra,

$$F_q = F_{1q}(\boldsymbol{u})F_{2q}(\boldsymbol{u}). \qquad (6.25)$$

6.2.4 Discrete QFT

As with the method to discretize the FT and its inverse, we can proceed similarly with the QFT and its inverse. Given a discrete two-dimensional signal of size $M \times N$ with quaternionic components $f_{mn} \in \mathbb{H}$, the *discrete quaternionic Fourier transform* (DQFT) and the *inverse discrete quaternionic Fourier transform* (IDQFT) are given, respectively, by

$$F_{q_{uv}} = \sum_{m=0}^{M-1}\sum_{n=0}^{N-1} e^{(-\frac{i2\pi um}{M})} f_{mn} e^{(-\frac{j2\pi vn}{N})},$$

$$f_{mn} = \frac{1}{MN}\sum_{m=0}^{M-1}\sum_{n=0}^{N-1} e^{(\frac{i2\pi um}{M})} F_{q_{uv}} e^{(\frac{j2\pi vn}{N})}. \qquad (6.26)$$

The reader can then easily implement a computer program to determine the QFT and IQFT. Using the fast Fourier transform (FFT), we first compute the one-dimensional DFT of f_{mn} in a row-wise sense, as follows:

$$f_{un} = \sum_{m=0}^{M-1} e^{(-\frac{i2\pi um}{M})} f_{mn} = Real(f_{un}) + Imag(f_{un}). \qquad (6.27)$$

This spectrum f_{un} is then divided into real and imaginary parts, which in turn are now transformed in a column-wise sense, once again using a one-dimensional DFT, to give

$$F_{uvr} = \sum_{n=0}^{N-1} \Big(Real(f_{un})\Big) e^{(-\frac{i2\pi vn}{M})} \qquad (6.28)$$

$$F_{uvi} = \sum_{n=0}^{N-1} \Big(Imag(f_{un})\Big) e^{(-\frac{i2\pi vn}{M})}. \qquad (6.29)$$

Using these results, we can finally compose the DQFT:

$$
\begin{aligned}
F_{uvq} &= Real(F_{uvr}) + iReal(F_{uvi}) + \\
&\quad + jImag(F_{uvr}) + kImag(F_{uvi}). \qquad (6.30)
\end{aligned}
$$

Note that the first, row-wise computation outputs complex numbers (equation (6.27)), and that the second, column-wise computation rotates their real and imaginary parts spatially by 90 degrees. In this way, the procedure yields the orthogonal bivector components of the DQFT of equation (6.30). This method is an implementation of the procedure to build quaternions from complex numbers, namely, by using the *doubling technique* [110]. Current FFT routines and hardware can be re-utilized with few changes to implement a fast quaternionic Fourier transform (FQFT). The reader can find more details about the implementation of an FQFT in [33].

6.3 Image Analysis Using the Phase Concept

In the field of image processing, Gabor filters have proved to be a very useful bandpass filters with the beneficial property that they are optimally localized both in space and in the frequency domain [35]. Applications for Gabor filters include pattern recognition, classification, texture analysis, local phase estimation, and frequency estimation. In the following subsections, the 2D Gabor filter and the phase concept are explained in detail.

6.3.1 2D Gabor filters

A two-dimensional *complex Gabor filter* is a *linear shift-invariant* filter with the impulse response of a a complex carrier modulated by a Gauss function:

$$h_c(\boldsymbol{x}; \boldsymbol{u}_0, \sigma, \alpha, \phi) = g(x', y')exp(2\pi i(u_0 x + v_0 y)). \tag{6.31}$$

Here, the Gauss function is given by

$$g(x, y) = Cexp\Big(-\frac{x^2 + (\alpha y)^2}{\sigma^2}\Big), \tag{6.32}$$

where α is the aspect radio and $C = \frac{\alpha}{2\pi\sigma^2}$ the normalizing factor so that $\int_{I\!R} g(x, y)dxdy = 1$. The coordinates of $g(x', y')$ have been rotated about the origin

$$\begin{pmatrix} x' \\ y' \end{pmatrix} = \begin{pmatrix} \cos\theta & \sin\theta \\ -\sin\theta & \cos\theta \end{pmatrix} \begin{pmatrix} x \\ y \end{pmatrix}. \tag{6.33}$$

In frequency domain, the 2D Gabor filter has the following transfer function:

$$\begin{aligned} h_c(\boldsymbol{x}; \boldsymbol{u}_0, \sigma, \alpha, \phi) &\rightarrow H_c(\boldsymbol{u}; \boldsymbol{u}_0, \sigma, \alpha, \phi) \\ H_c(\boldsymbol{u}; \boldsymbol{u}_0, \sigma, \alpha, \phi) &= exp(-2\pi^2\sigma^2[(u' - u_0')^2 + (v' - v_0')^2/\alpha]). \end{aligned} \tag{6.34}$$

Fig. 6.3 shows a complex Gabor filter whose center in frequency and orientation are given by $f_0 = \sqrt{u_0^2 + v_0^2}$ and $\theta = atan(\frac{v_0}{u_0})$, respectively. Choosing

$\theta = \phi$, the principal axis of the Gauss function is aligned with the orientation of ϕ.

Now, by assigning two orthogonal complex carriers to the axes of the 2D signal we can further extend the complex Gabor filter into the quaternionic Gabor filter:

$$\begin{aligned} h_q(\boldsymbol{x}; \boldsymbol{u}_0, \sigma, \alpha, \phi = 0) &= g(\boldsymbol{x}; \sigma, \alpha) exp(i 2\pi u_0 x) exp(j 2\pi v_0 y) \\ &= g(\boldsymbol{x}; \sigma, \alpha) exp(i \frac{s_1 w_1 x}{\sigma}) exp(j \frac{s_2 \alpha w_2 y}{\sigma}). \end{aligned} \quad (6.35)$$

Note that the complex carriers are dependent on the quaternion bases i and j and that for simplicity we do not use a rotated Gauss function.

The transfer function of a quaternionic Gabor filter is a direct interpretation of the modulation theorem of the quaternionic Fourier transform (QFT) explained in Section 6.2. It consists of a shifted Gaussian function in the quaternionic frequency domain,

$$\begin{aligned} h_q(\boldsymbol{x}; \boldsymbol{u}_0, \sigma, \alpha, \phi = 0) &\rightarrow H_q(\boldsymbol{u}; \boldsymbol{u}_0, \sigma, \alpha, \phi = 0) \\ H_q(\boldsymbol{u}; \boldsymbol{u}_0, \sigma, \alpha, \phi = 0) &= exp(-2\pi^2 \sigma^2 [(u - u_0)^2 + (v - v_0)^2 / \alpha^2]), \end{aligned} \quad (6.36)$$

by which the greater amount of the Gabor filter's energy is preserved for positive frequencies u_0 and v_0 in the upper-right quadrant. In this regard, the convolution of a real image with a quaternionic Gabor filter approximates a quaternionic analytic signal. Fig. 6.3 presents two examples of quaternion Gabor filters.

Fig. 6.4 presents a convolved medical image using a 50×50-pixel Gabor filter with σ_1=7, σ_2=2, s_1=2, s_2=2, and α=90 degrees, and Fig. 6.5 a convolved medical image using a 50×50-pixel Gabor filter with σ_1=7, σ_2=2, s_1=2, s_2=2, and α=67.5 degrees.

6.3.2 The phase concept

The *local quaternionic phase* of a two-dimensional signal can be measured using the angular phase of the filter response of a quaternionic Gabor filter. The evaluation of the angular phase is carried out according to the rules of the quaternion phase presented in subsection 1.6.2.

The phase concept can be used for 3D reconstruction using interferometry techniques. Fig. 6.6 shows the measurement of the phase change of 3D objects: a cube and a bell shape form which were illuminated with a light grid. In order to complete the whole 3D object representation, we can use a stereoscopic system to get the 3D information of some key points of the illuminated object and together with the unwrapped phase we can compute for each phase object point its corresponding 3D value.

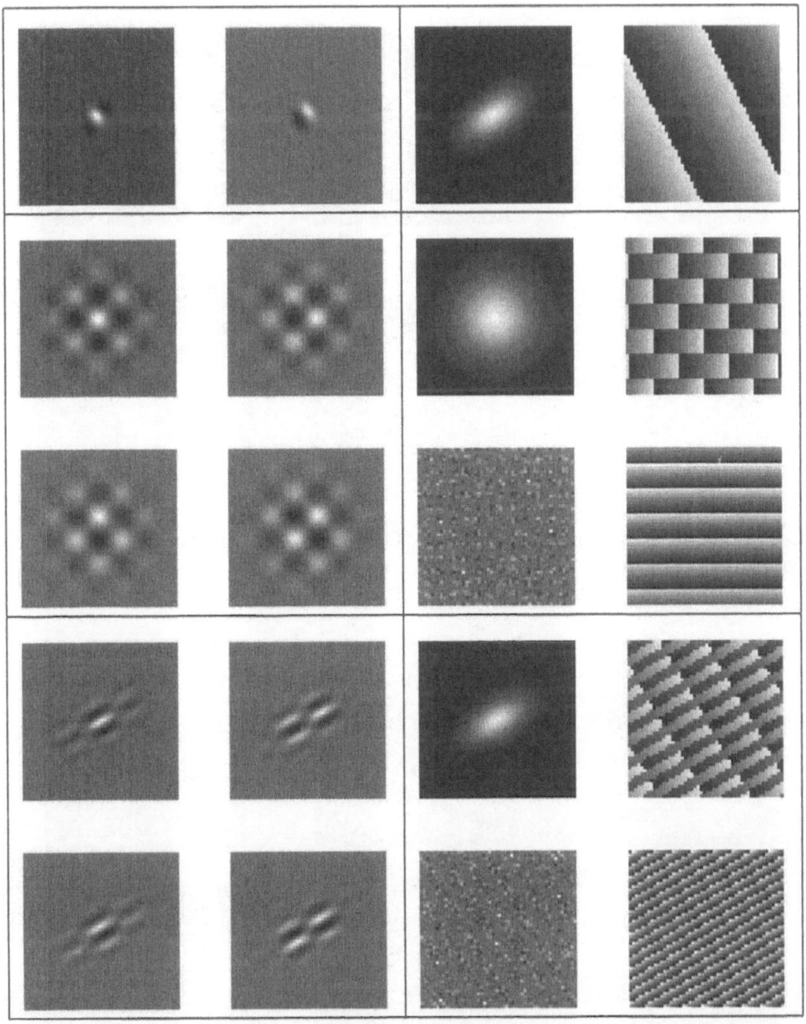

FIGURE 6.3. Complex and quaternion Gabor filters: (upper left) real and imaginary parts (r,i) of a complex Gabor 50×50-pixel filter with σ_1=8, σ_2=4, $s = 2$, and α=30 degrees; (upper right) magnitude and phase (ϕ) for this filter; (middle left) real and imaginary parts (i,j,k) of a quaternionic Gabor 50×50-pixel filter with σ_1=10, σ_2=10, $s_1 = 4$, $s_2 = 4$, and α=0; (middle right) magnitude and phases (ϕ, ψ, and θ) for this filter; (lower left) real and imaginary parts (i,j,k) of a quaternionic 50×50-pixel Gabor filter with σ_1=8, σ_2=4, s_1=2, s_2=4, and α=30 degrees; (lower right) magnitude and phases (ϕ, ψ, and θ) for this filter

6.4 Lie Filters in the Affine Plane

This section carries out the computations in the affine plane $\mathcal{A}_{e_3}(\mathcal{N}^2)$ for image analysis. We utilize the Lie algebra of the affine plane explained in

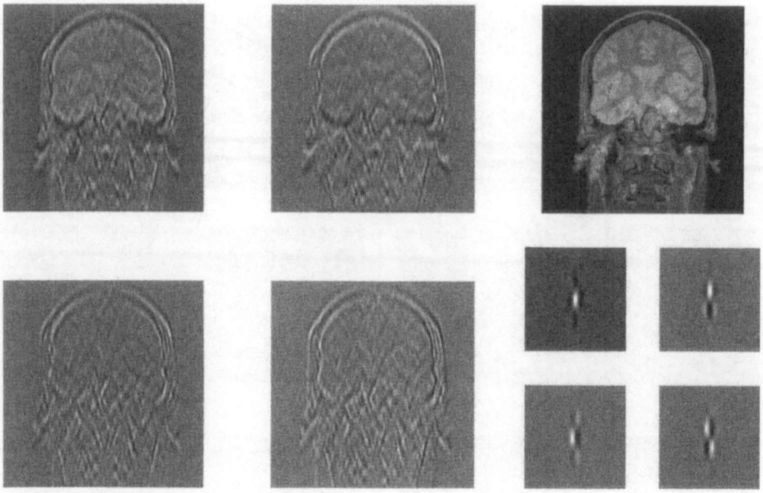

FIGURE 6.4. Real and imaginary parts of convolved quaternionic image using qgabor(50,7,2,2,2,90)

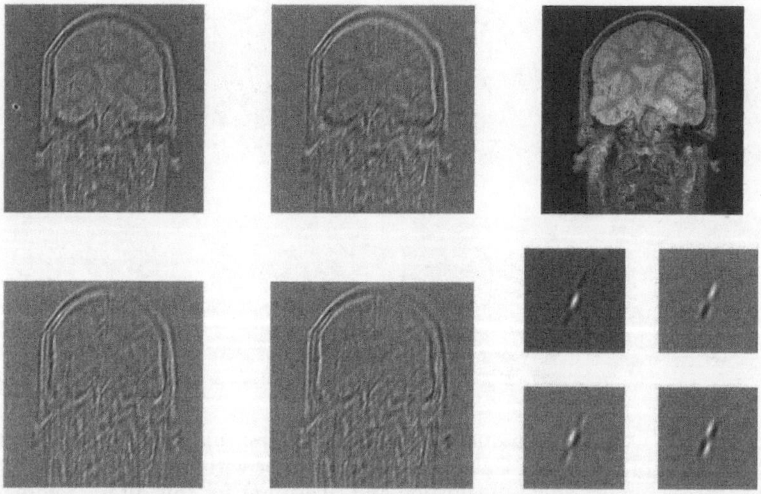

FIGURE 6.5. Real and imaginary parts of convolved quaternionic image using qgabor(50,7,2,2,2,67.5)

Chapter 3 for the design of image filters to detect visual invariants. As an illustration, we apply these filters for the recognition of hand gestures.

6.4.1 The design of an image filter

In the experiment, we used simulated images of the *optical flow* for two motions, a rotational and a translational motion (see Fig. 6.7.a), and a dilation

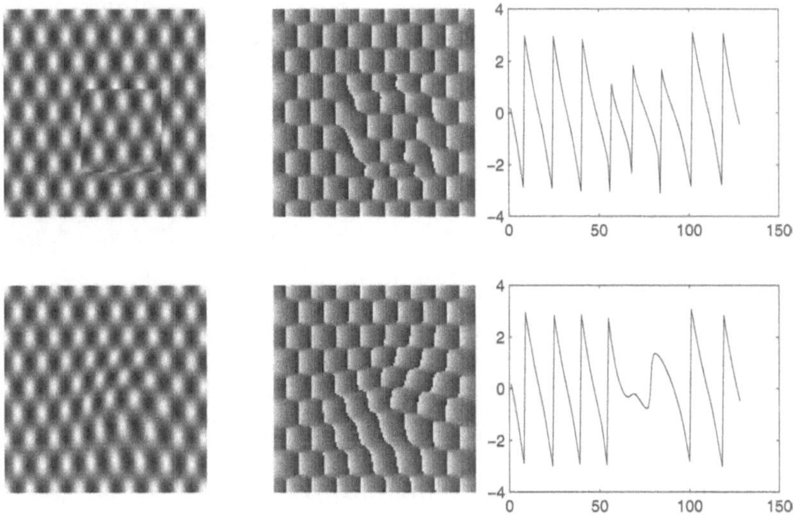

FIGURE 6.6. Left images: original 150 × 150 images which are convolved with qgabor(25,7,7,2,2,90). Middle images: one of phase images. Right images: phase changes modulo 2π along the row 64.

and a translational motion (see Fig. 6.8.a). The experiment uses only bivector computations to determine the type of motion, the axis of rotation, and/or the center of the dilation.

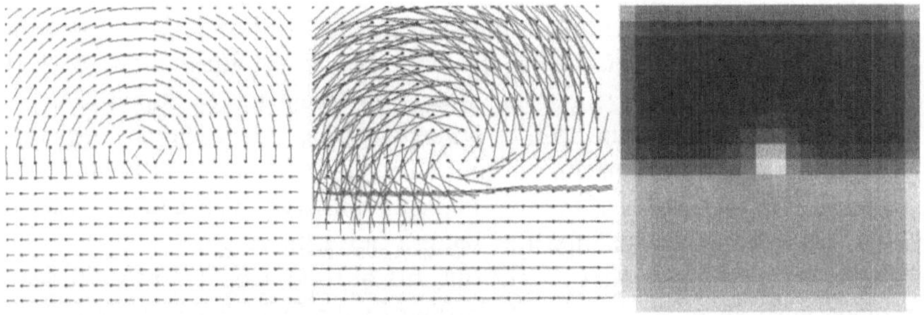

FIGURE 6.7. Detection of visual invariants: (a) rotation (L_r) and translational flow (L_x) fields; (b) convolving via geometric product with a Gaussian kernel; (c) magnitudes of the convolution

To study the motions in the affine plane, we used the Lie algebra of bivectors in the geometric algebra $\mathcal{A}_{e_3}(\mathcal{N}^2)$. The computations were carried out with the help of a computer program which we wrote in C^{++}. Each *flow vector* at any point $\mathbf{x}$ of the image was coded $\mathbf{x} = xe_1 + ye_2 + e_3 \in \mathcal{N}^3$. At each point of the flow image, we applied the commutator product of the six bivectors of the equation (3.70). Using the resultant coefficients of the

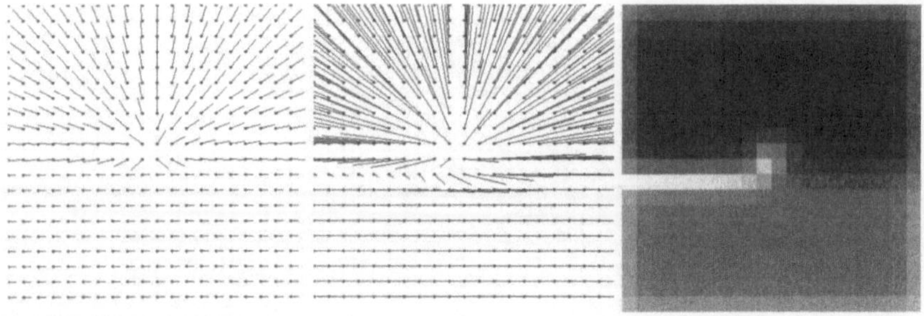

FIGURE 6.8. Detection of visual invariants: (a) expansion (L_s) and translational flow (L_x) fields; (b) convolving via the geometric product with a Gaussian kernel; (c) magnitudes of the convolution

vectors, the computer program calculated which type of differential invariant or motion was present.

Fig. 6.7.b shows the result of convolving, via the geometric product, the bivector with a *Gaussian kernel* of size 5×5. Fig. 6.7.c presents this result using the output of the kernel. The white center of the image indicates the lowest magnitude. Fig. 6.8 shows the results for the case of a flow which is expanding. Comparing Fig. 6.7.c with Fig. 6.8.c, we note the duality of the differential invariants; the centerpoint of the rotation is invariant, and the invariant of the expansion is a line.

6.4.2 Recognition of hand gestures

Another interesting application, suggested by the seminal paper of Hoffman [55], is to recognize a gesture using the key points of an image along with the previous Lie operators arranged in a detection structure, as depicted in Fig. 6.9. These Lie filters may be seen to be *perceptrons*, which play an important role in image preprocessing in the human visual system. It is believed [55] that during the first years of human life, some kinds of Lie operators combine to build the higher-dimensional Lie algebra SO(4,1).

In this sense, we assume that the outputs of the Lie operators are linearly combined with an *outstar output* according to the following equation:

$$\begin{aligned} O_\alpha(x,y) &= w_1\mathcal{L}_x(x,y) + w_2\mathcal{L}_y(x,y) + w_3\mathcal{L}_r(x,y) + \\ &\quad + w_4\mathcal{L}_s(x,y) + w_5\mathcal{L}_b(x,y) + w_6\mathcal{L}_B(x,y), \quad (6.37) \end{aligned}$$

where the weights w_i can be adjusted if we apply a supervised training procedure. If the desired feature or key point α at the point (i,y) is detected, the output $O_\alpha(x,y)$ goes to zero.

Fig. 6.10.a shows hand gestures given to a robot. By applying the Lie perceptrons arrangement to the hand region (see Fig. 6.10.b), a robot can detect whether it should *follow*, *stop*, or *move in circles*. Table 6.1 presents the weights w_i necessary for detecting the three gestures. Detection tolerance is computed as follows:

$$O_\alpha(x,y) \leq min + \frac{(max - min)Tolerance}{100} \rightarrow detection\, of\, a\, feature\, type,$$

where *min* and *max* correspond to the minimal and maximal Lie operator outputs.

Hand gesture	$\mathcal{L}_x$	$\mathcal{L}_y$	$\mathcal{L}_r$	$\mathcal{L}_s$	$\mathcal{L}_b$	$\mathcal{L}_B$	*Tolerance*
fingertip	0	0	9	−4	11	−9	10%
stop	0	0	−3	1	1	4	10%
fist	0	0	−2	2	2	−1	10%

TABLE 6.1. Weights of the Lie perceptrons arrangement for the detection of hand gestures

6.5 Color Image Processing

This section presents procedures for edge detection using color image processing. According to the literature [61], color images may be processed by merely extending approaches for gray-level image processing, that is, by separately applying the three components of the color image and then combining

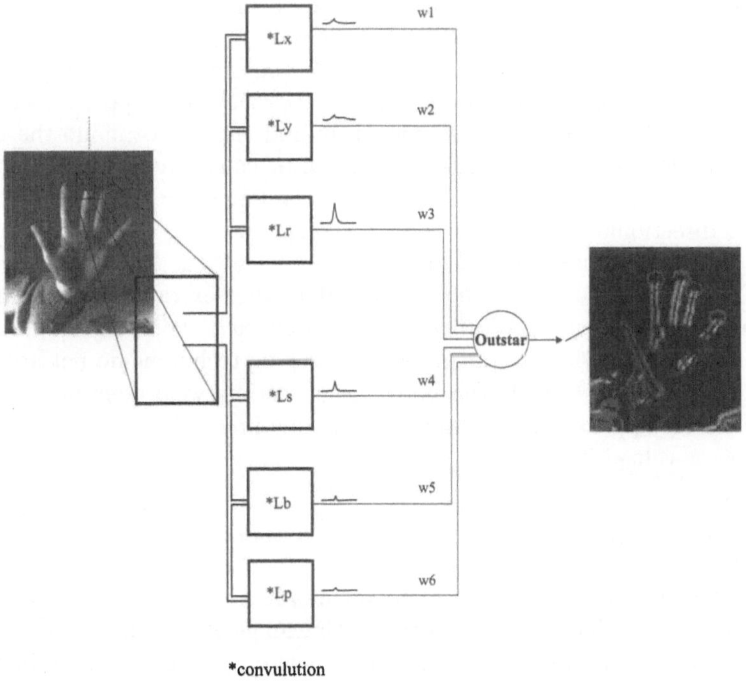

FIGURE 6.9. Lie perceptrons arrangement for feature detection

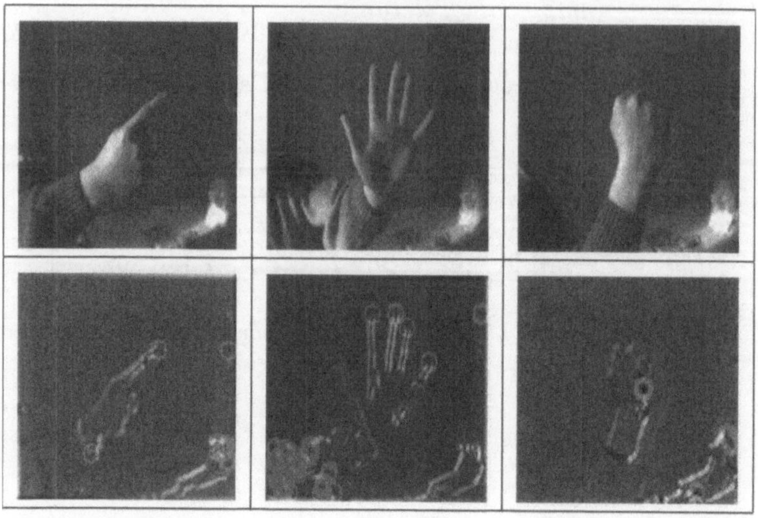

FIGURE 6.10. Gestures detection: (a) (top images) gestures for robot guidance (follow, stop, and explore); and (b) (lower images) detected gestures by the robot vision system using Lie operators

the results.. But extending the techniques of gray-level image processing to color-image processing has certain inherent limitations. For example, edge-detection of gray-level images involves finding in the image function either the maxima of the first derivative or the zero-crossings of the second derivative, but it is difficult to extend this derivative approach because the color image is a vector-valuedfunction. A naive approach is to apply Sobel masks to the three color channels independently and then to combine the results using a logical operation. This approach can be contrasted with the more sophisticated approach of Cumani [24], who computes the zero-crossing in the second directional derivative of the color image, which is thereby represented as a two-dimensional vector field.

There is some evidence, however, that feature extraction in the human visual system does not project color onto three axes [106], and so approaches that employ extensions of the gray-level imaging technique do not appear to follow the human model. In the following subsections we present methods that more closely approximate the human model by processing the color image as a bivector-valued function.

6.5.1 Rotor edge detector

Since the color image has three components, it can be represented as a continuous vector-valued function in the Euclidean geometric algebra $\mathcal{G}_{3,0,0}$. The color information $(r, g, b)^T$ of the color image $\boldsymbol{c}_{m,n}$ is amenable to be represented as a bivector spanned by the bivector basis

$$c_{m,n} = r_{m,n}\sigma_2\sigma_3 + g_{m,n}\sigma_3\sigma_1 + b_{m,n}\sigma_1\sigma_2 \tag{6.38}$$

For edge detection, we convolve the masks $\boldsymbol{m}_L(x,y)$ and $\boldsymbol{m}_R(x,y)$ of size $(2X+1)$ and $(2Y+1)$ with the image $g(m,n)$ of dimension $M \times N$, using the geometric product. The convolution equation is given by

$$\hat{c}(m,n) = \sum_{x=-X}^{X} \sum_{y=-Y}^{Y} m_L(x,y)\; c(m-x \; mod\, M, n-y \; mod\, N)\; m_R(x,y) \tag{6.39}$$

The masks introduced by Sangwine [92] resemble Prewitt's masks. These masks have as entries instead of real-number rotors:

$$m_{H_L} = \begin{bmatrix} \boldsymbol{R} & \boldsymbol{R} & \boldsymbol{R} \\ 0 & 0 & 0 \\ \tilde{\boldsymbol{R}} & \tilde{\boldsymbol{R}} & \tilde{\boldsymbol{R}} \end{bmatrix}, \quad m_{H_R} = \begin{bmatrix} \tilde{\boldsymbol{R}} & \tilde{\boldsymbol{R}} & \tilde{\boldsymbol{R}} \\ 0 & 0 & 0 \\ \boldsymbol{R} & \boldsymbol{R} & \boldsymbol{R} \end{bmatrix} \quad horizontal \tag{6.40}$$

$$m_{V_L} = \begin{bmatrix} \boldsymbol{R} & 0 & \tilde{\boldsymbol{R}} \\ \boldsymbol{R} & 0 & \tilde{\boldsymbol{R}} \\ \boldsymbol{R} & 0 & \tilde{\boldsymbol{R}} \end{bmatrix}, \quad m_{V_R} = \begin{bmatrix} \tilde{\boldsymbol{R}} & 0 & \boldsymbol{R} \\ \tilde{\boldsymbol{R}} & 0 & \boldsymbol{R} \\ \tilde{\boldsymbol{R}} & 0 & \boldsymbol{R} \end{bmatrix} \quad vertical \tag{6.41}$$

$$m_{D_L} = \begin{bmatrix} \tilde{\boldsymbol{R}} & \tilde{\boldsymbol{R}} & 0 \\ \tilde{\boldsymbol{R}} & 0 & \boldsymbol{R} \\ 0 & \boldsymbol{R} & \boldsymbol{R} \end{bmatrix}, \quad m_{D_R} = \begin{bmatrix} \boldsymbol{R} & \boldsymbol{R} & 0 \\ \boldsymbol{R} & 0 & \tilde{\boldsymbol{R}} \\ 0 & \tilde{\boldsymbol{R}} & \tilde{\boldsymbol{R}} \end{bmatrix} \quad diagonal. \tag{6.42}$$

According to equation (1.29), the rotors $\boldsymbol{R} \in \mathcal{G}_{3,0,0}$ are given by

$$\boldsymbol{R} = s\, e^{\boldsymbol{n}\frac{\pi}{4}} = s\Big(cos(\frac{\pi}{4}) + \boldsymbol{n}\, sin(\frac{\pi}{4})\Big), \tag{6.43}$$

where $\boldsymbol{n} = (\sigma_2\sigma_3 + \sigma_3\sigma_1 + \sigma_1\sigma_2)/\sqrt{3}$ and the scale factor $s = \sqrt{6}$. The application of the masks m_{H_L} and m_{H_R} on a point (m,n) of the image yields

$$\begin{aligned} \hat{c}(m,n) &= \tilde{\boldsymbol{R}}(c_{m-1,n-1} + c_{m-1,n} + c_{m-1,n+1})\boldsymbol{R} + \\ &\qquad + \boldsymbol{R}(c_{m+1,n-1} + c_{m+1,n} + c_{m+1,n+1})\tilde{\boldsymbol{R}} \\ &= \tilde{\boldsymbol{R}} c_u \boldsymbol{R} + \boldsymbol{R} c_l \tilde{\boldsymbol{R}}, \end{aligned} \tag{6.44}$$

where c_u and c_l are the upper and lower rows of the subimage of size 3×3 with different colors.

Fig. 6.11.a shows a color vector c split in its orthogonal components, with a projection $c_{\|}$ parallel to the axis of the gray values and another $c_{\perp}$ perpendicular. The effect of the masks in homogeneous or non-homogeneous color regions differs substantially. Let us analyze both cases in detail. Given a homogenous domain with color c, after the convolution, we get

$$\begin{aligned} \hat{c}(m,n) &= \tilde{\boldsymbol{R}}c\boldsymbol{R} + \boldsymbol{R}c\tilde{\boldsymbol{R}} + \tilde{\boldsymbol{R}}c\boldsymbol{R} + \boldsymbol{R}c\tilde{\boldsymbol{R}} + \tilde{\boldsymbol{R}}c\boldsymbol{R} + \boldsymbol{R}c\tilde{\boldsymbol{R}} \\ &= 3\tilde{\boldsymbol{R}}c\boldsymbol{R} + 3\boldsymbol{R}c\tilde{\boldsymbol{R}} \\ &= 3\tilde{\boldsymbol{R}}(c_{\|} + c_{\perp})\boldsymbol{R} + 3\boldsymbol{R}(c_{\|} + c_{\perp})\tilde{\boldsymbol{R}} \end{aligned}$$

$$
\begin{aligned}
&= 6s^2 c_{\|} + 3\tilde{\boldsymbol{R}} c_{\perp} \boldsymbol{R} + 3\boldsymbol{R} c_{\perp} \tilde{\boldsymbol{R}} \\
&= c_{\|} + 3\tilde{\boldsymbol{R}} c_{\perp} \boldsymbol{R} + 3\boldsymbol{R} c_{\perp} \tilde{\boldsymbol{R}} \\
&= c_{\|} + 3\tilde{\boldsymbol{R}} c_{\perp} \boldsymbol{R} - 3\tilde{\boldsymbol{R}} c_{\perp} \boldsymbol{R} \\
&= c_{\|}. \qquad (6.45)
\end{aligned}
$$

Here, it is considered that $\tilde{\boldsymbol{R}} c_{\perp} \boldsymbol{R}$ rotates the color c in $\frac{\pi}{2}$ and that $\boldsymbol{R} c_{\perp} \tilde{\boldsymbol{R}}$ rotates the color in $-\frac{\pi}{2}$, with the result that homogeneous color regions are mapped to gray values (see Fig. 6.11.b).

In the second case, when the masks are applied to a non-homogeneous region, the perpendicular components of both colors in general do not cancel each other, and the resulting edge image is colored (see Fig. 6.11.c).

We conclude that edges between regions, the perpendicular components of which are equal, and that produce values only along the gray axis, will not be detected. When two regions are of dissimilar colors, the points of the resulting edge will be of a different color, which in same cases will resemble closely antagonic colors.

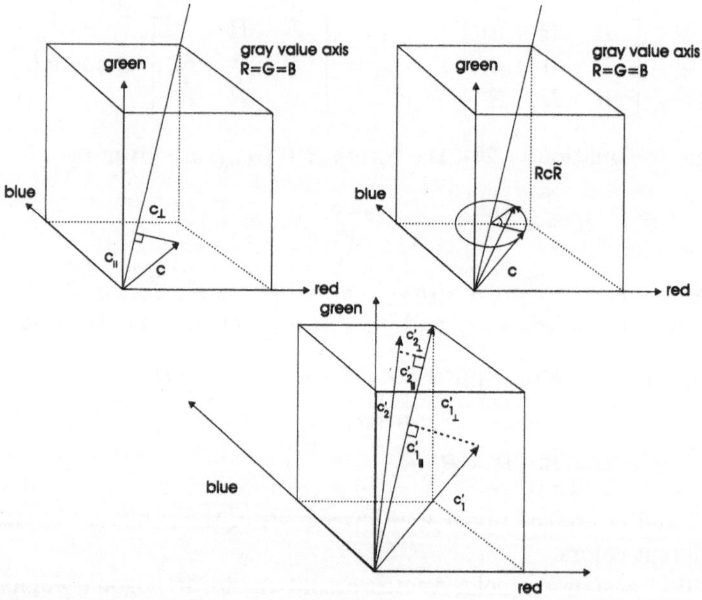

FIGURE 6.11. Color edge detection: (a) color vector; (b) Sangwine's edge detector; (c) modified Sangwine's edge detector.

6.5.2 Modified rotor edge detector

Sangwine's edge detector, described in a previous subsection, requires that the rotors rotate the bivectors at an angle of $\frac{\pi}{2}$. We claim that this edge detector can be improved by making the rotation angle dependent upon the color points within the mask. However, this modification should maintain the properties for homogeneous or non-homogeneous regions explained in the previous subsection.

For this purpose, for the rotor

$$\boldsymbol{R} = s\, e^{\boldsymbol{n}\alpha(c_1,c_2)}, \tag{6.46}$$

we choose a function $\varphi : \mathcal{R}^3 \times \mathcal{R}^3 \to \mathcal{R}$, so that the angle

$$\alpha(c_1, c_2) = \frac{\pi}{4}(1 - \varphi(c_1, c_2)) \tag{6.47}$$

varies according to the different colors c_1, c_2 of the neighbor regions. The function φ should fulfill the following properties:

- φ is symmetric, i.e. $\varphi(c_1, c_2) = \varphi(c_2, c_1)$ for all $c_1,\ c_2 \in \mathcal{R}^3$
- $\varphi(c, c)$=0 for all $c \in \mathcal{R}^3$.

The second property guarantees that homogeneous regions are mapped onto gray values.

Given $c_1 = c_{1_\parallel} + c_{1_\perp}$, $c_2 = c_{2_\parallel} + c_{2_\perp} \in \mathcal{R}^3$, the function

$$\begin{aligned} \varphi(c_1, c_2) &= \varphi(\frac{c_1}{|c_1|}, \frac{c_2}{|c_2|}) = \varphi(\hat{c}_1, \hat{c}_2) \\ &= \lambda_\parallel |\hat{c}_{1_\parallel} - \hat{c}_{2_\parallel}| + \lambda_\perp |\hat{c}_{1_\perp} - \hat{c}_{2_\perp}|, \end{aligned} \tag{6.48}$$

where $\lambda_\parallel$, $\lambda_\perp \in \mathcal{R}$, clearly fulfills the two required properties. This function was used in our modified rotor edge detector.

Fig. 6.12 shows that performance of the rotor edge detectors is better than that of the Sobel's color edge detector. Neither edge detector, however, can compete with Cumani's, because rotor edge detectors and Sobel's use 3×3 masks and do not propagate the gradient to look for connected edges, as is the case with the Cumani edge detector. This shortcoming notwithstanding, the rotor edge detectors yield colored edges for non-homogeneous regions and suppress edges caused by shadows.

Since the modified color edge detector is a generalization of the Sangwine's rotor edge detector, we can always improve the performance of the rotor edge detectors adjusting the parameters $\lambda_\parallel$, $\lambda_\perp$.

6.6 Conclusion

This chapter has shown that low-level image processing improves if signal representation and processing are carried out in a system of rich algebraic properties like geometric algebra. In this system, an n-dimensional representation of 2D signals unveils properties which are otherwise obscured with

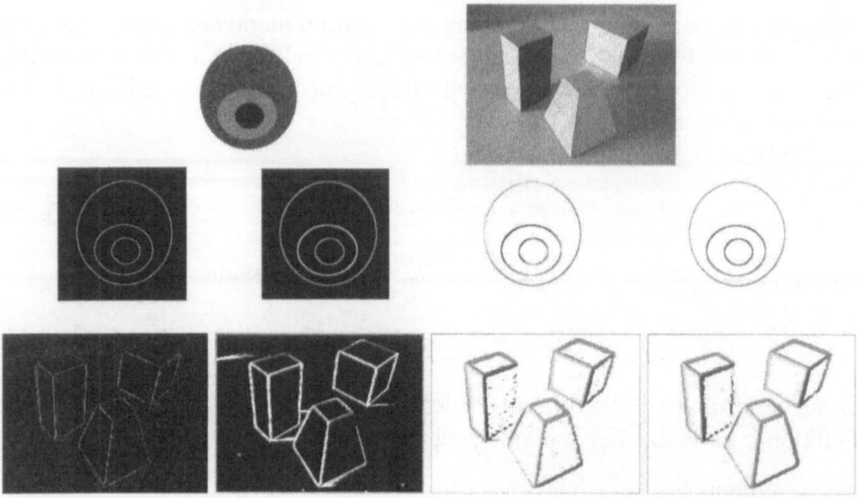

FIGURE 6.12. Comparison of color edge detectors. First row: original images. In columns outputs of the color edge detectors: (1) Cumani, (2) Sobel, (3) Sangwine, (4) modified

the use of algorithms developed by applying matrix algebra over the real or complex field. Strikingly, the bivector algebra of quaternions allows us to disentangle the symmetries of 2D signals, as in the case of the quaternionic Fourier transform. This opens up an area for the design and implementation of new filters and estimators for the analysis of signals in the quaternionic frequency domain.

The chapter also explored feature detectors using Lie perceptrons in the 2D affine plane. The filters are not only applicable to optic flow, they may also be used for the detection of key points. Combinations of Lie operators yield to complex structures for detecting more sophisticated visual geometry.

The importance of both color and geometry in image processing is highlighted when we consider edge, line, and corner detectors using color images. Since the human visual system appears not to process the R, G, and B channels of color images separately, the approaches presented here, which use compact 3D bivector representation, work in this sense.

We believe that the role of symmetry detection, texture analysis, and color image processing using powerful geometric representations enriched with the application of bivector algebras is fundamental for modern low-level image processing.

7. Applications in Computer Vision

7.1 Introduction

This chapter will demonstrate that geometric algebra provides a simple mechanism for unifying current approaches in the computation and application of projective invariants using n-uncalibrated cameras. First, we describe Pascal's theorem as a type of projective invariant, and then the theorem is applied for computing camera-intrinsic parameters. The fundamental projective invariant cross-ratio is studied in one, two, and three dimensions, using a single view and then n views. Next, by using the observations of two and three cameras, we apply projective invariants to the tasks of computing the view-center of a moving camera and to simplified visually guided grasping. The chapter also presents a geometric approach for the computation of shape and motion using projective invariants within a purely geometric algebra framework [47, 49]. Different approaches for projective reconstruction have utilized projective depth [96, 102], projective invariants [23], and factorization methods [81, 105, 107] (factorization methods incorporate projective depth calculations). We compute projective depth using projective invariants, which depend on the use of the fundamental matrix or trifocal tensor. Using these projective depths, we are then able to initiate a projective reconstruction procedure to compute shape and motion. We also apply the algebra of incidence in the development of geometric inference rules to extend 3D reconstruction.

The geometric procedures here presented contribute to the design and implementation of *perception action cycle* (PAC) systems, as depicted in Fig. 7.1.

This chapter is organized as follows: Section 2 briefly explains conics and Pascal's theorem. Section 3 demonstrates a method for computing intrinsic camera parameters using Pascal's theorem. Section 4 studies in detail the projective invariant cross-ratio in 1D, 2D, and 3D, as well as the generation of projective invariants in 3D. Section 5 presents the theory of 3D projective invariants using n-uncalibrated cameras. Section 6 illustrates the use of projective invariants for a simplified task of visually guided robot-grasping. The problem of camera self-localization is discussed in Section 7. Computation of projective depth using projective invariants in terms of the trifocal tensor is given in Section 8. The treatment of projective reconstruction and the role

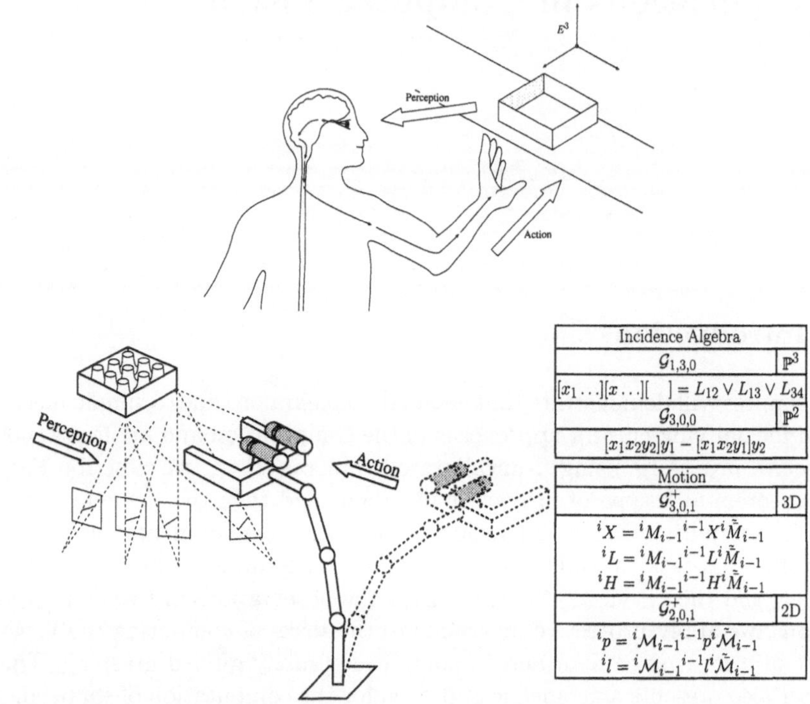

FIGURE 7.1. Abstraction of biologic and artificial PACs systems

of the algebra of incidence in completing the 3D shape is given in Section 9. Section 10 presents our conclusions.

7.2 Conics and Pascal's theorem

The role of conics and quadrics is well known in projective geometry [94]. This knowledge led to the solution of crucial problems in computer vision [75]. In the last decade, Kruppa's equations, which rely on the conic concept, have been used to compute intrinsic camera parameters [72]. In the present work, we further explore the conics concept and use Pascal's theorem to establish an equation system with clear geometric transparency. We then explain the role of conics and that of Pascal's theorem in relation to fundamental projective invariants. Our work here is based primarily on that of Hestenes and Ziegler [49], that is, on an interpretation of linear algebra together with projective geometry within a Clifford algebra framework.

In order to use projective geometry in computer vision, we utilize homogeneous coordinate representations, which allows us to embed both 3D Euclidean visual space in 3D projective space P^3 or R^4, and the 2D Euclidean space of the image plane in 2D projective space P^2 or R^3. Using the geometric algebra framework, we select for P^2 the 3D Euclidean geometric algebra $\mathcal{G}_{3,0,0}$, and for P^3 the 4D geometric algebra $\mathcal{G}_{1,3,0}$. The reader should refer to Chapter 4 for more details relating to the geometry of n cameras. Any geometric object of P^3 will be linear-projective-mapped to P^2 via a projective transformation. For example, the projective mapping of a quadric at infinity in the projective space P^3 results in a conic in the projective plane P^2.

Let us first consider a *pencil of lines* lying on the plane. Any pencil of lines may be well defined by the bivector addition of two of its lines: $\boldsymbol{l} = \boldsymbol{l}_a + s\boldsymbol{l}_b$ with $s \in R \cup \{-\infty, +\infty\}$. If two pencils of lines $\boldsymbol{l}$ and $\boldsymbol{l}' = \boldsymbol{l}'_a + s'\boldsymbol{l}'_b$ can be related one to one so that $\boldsymbol{l} = \boldsymbol{l}'$ for $s = s'$, we say that they are in projective correspondence. Using this idea, we will show that the set of intersecting points of lines in projective correspondence build a conic. Since the intersecting points $\boldsymbol{x}$ of the pencils of lines $\boldsymbol{l}$ and $\boldsymbol{l}'$ fulfill for $s = s'$ the following constraints are met:

$$\begin{aligned} \boldsymbol{x}\wedge\boldsymbol{l} &= \boldsymbol{x}\wedge\boldsymbol{l}_a + s\boldsymbol{x}\wedge\boldsymbol{l}_b = 0 \\ \boldsymbol{x}\wedge\boldsymbol{l}' &= \boldsymbol{x}\wedge\boldsymbol{l}'_a + s\boldsymbol{x}\wedge\boldsymbol{l}'_b = 0. \end{aligned} \tag{7.1}$$

The elimination of the scalar s yields a second-order geometric-product equation in $\boldsymbol{x}$,

$$(\boldsymbol{x}\wedge\boldsymbol{l}_a)(\boldsymbol{x}\wedge\boldsymbol{l}'_b) - (\boldsymbol{x}\wedge\boldsymbol{l}_b)(\boldsymbol{x}\wedge\boldsymbol{l}'_a) = 0. \tag{7.2}$$

We can also derive the parameterized conic equation, by simply computing the intersecting point $\boldsymbol{x}$ by means of the meet of the pencils of lines, as follows:

$$\boldsymbol{x} = (\boldsymbol{l}_a + s\boldsymbol{l}_b) \cap (\boldsymbol{l}'_a + s\boldsymbol{l}'_b) = \boldsymbol{l}_a \cap \boldsymbol{l}'_a + s(\boldsymbol{l}_a \cap \boldsymbol{l}'_b + \boldsymbol{l}_b \cap \boldsymbol{l}'_a) + s^2\boldsymbol{l}_b \cap \boldsymbol{l}'_b. \tag{7.3}$$

Let us, for now, define the involved lines as a wedge of points, $\boldsymbol{l}_a = \boldsymbol{a}\wedge\boldsymbol{b}$, $\boldsymbol{l}_b = \boldsymbol{a}\wedge\boldsymbol{b}'$, $\boldsymbol{l}'_a = \boldsymbol{a}'\wedge\boldsymbol{b}$, and $\boldsymbol{l}'_b = \boldsymbol{a}'\wedge\boldsymbol{b}'$, such that $\boldsymbol{l}_a \cap \boldsymbol{l}'_a = \boldsymbol{b}$ and $\boldsymbol{l}_b \cap \boldsymbol{l}'_b = \boldsymbol{b}'$ (see Fig. 7.2.a). By substituting $\boldsymbol{b}'' = \boldsymbol{l}_a \cap \boldsymbol{l}'_b + \boldsymbol{l}_b \cap \boldsymbol{l}'_a = \boldsymbol{d} + \boldsymbol{d}'$ into equation (7.3), we get

$$\boldsymbol{x} = \boldsymbol{b} + s\boldsymbol{b}'' + s^2\boldsymbol{b}', \tag{7.4}$$

which represents a nondegenerated conic for $\boldsymbol{b}\wedge\boldsymbol{b}''\wedge\boldsymbol{b}' = \boldsymbol{b}\wedge(\boldsymbol{d}+\boldsymbol{d}')\wedge\boldsymbol{b}' \neq 0$. Now, using this equation, let us recompute the original pencils of lines. By defining $\boldsymbol{l}_1 = \boldsymbol{b}''\wedge\boldsymbol{b}'$, $\boldsymbol{l}_2 = \boldsymbol{b}'\wedge\boldsymbol{b}$, and $\boldsymbol{l}_3 = \boldsymbol{b}\wedge\boldsymbol{b}''$, we can use equation (7.4) to compute the projective pencils of lines:

$$\begin{aligned} \boldsymbol{b}\wedge\boldsymbol{x} &= s\boldsymbol{b}\wedge\boldsymbol{b}'' + s^2\boldsymbol{b}\wedge\boldsymbol{b}' = s(\boldsymbol{l}_3 - s\boldsymbol{l}_2) \\ \boldsymbol{b}'\wedge\boldsymbol{x} &= \boldsymbol{b}'\wedge\boldsymbol{b} + s\boldsymbol{b}'\wedge\boldsymbol{b}'' = \boldsymbol{l}_2 - s\boldsymbol{l}_1. \end{aligned} \tag{7.5}$$

By considering the points $\boldsymbol{a}$, $\boldsymbol{a}'$, $\boldsymbol{b}$, and $\boldsymbol{b}'$ and some other point $\boldsymbol{y}$ lying in the conic depicted in Fig. 7.2.a, and by using equation (7.1) for $s = Is'$ slightly different to s', we get the bracketed expression

$$[\boldsymbol{yab}][\boldsymbol{ya'b'}] - I[\boldsymbol{yab'}][\boldsymbol{ya'b}] = 0$$
$$I = \frac{[\boldsymbol{yab}][\boldsymbol{ya'b'}]}{[\boldsymbol{yab'}][\boldsymbol{ya'b}]} \tag{7.6}$$

for some scalar $I \neq 0$. This equation is well known and represents a projective invariant, a concept which has been used quite a lot in real applications of computer vision. Sections 7.4 and 7.5 show this invariant using brackets of points, bilinearities, and the trifocal tensor (see also Bayro [9] and Lasenby [65]). We can evaluate I of equation (7.6) in terms of some other point $\boldsymbol{c}$ to develop a conic equation that can be fully expressed within brackets:

$$[\boldsymbol{yab}][\boldsymbol{ya'b'}] - \frac{[\boldsymbol{cab}][\boldsymbol{ca'b'}]}{[\boldsymbol{cab'}][\boldsymbol{ca'b}]}[\boldsymbol{yab'}][\boldsymbol{ya'b}] = 0$$

$$[\boldsymbol{yab}][\boldsymbol{ya'b'}][\boldsymbol{ab'c'}][\boldsymbol{a'bc'}] - [\boldsymbol{yab'}][\boldsymbol{ya'b}][\boldsymbol{abc'}][\boldsymbol{a'b'c'}] = 0. \tag{7.7}$$

Again, the resulting equation is well known, which tells us that any conic is uniquely determined by five points in general positions $\boldsymbol{a}$, $\boldsymbol{a}'$, $\boldsymbol{b}$ and $\boldsymbol{b}'$, and $\boldsymbol{c}$. Now, considering Fig. 7.2.b, we can identify three collinear intersecting points $\boldsymbol{\alpha}_1$, $\boldsymbol{\alpha}_2$, and $\boldsymbol{\alpha}_3$. By using the collinearity constraint and the pencils of lines in projective correspondence, we can now write a very useful equation:

$$\underbrace{((\boldsymbol{a}' \wedge \boldsymbol{b}) \cap (\boldsymbol{c}' \wedge \boldsymbol{c}))}_{\boldsymbol{\alpha}_1} \wedge \underbrace{((\boldsymbol{a}' \wedge \boldsymbol{a}) \cap (\boldsymbol{b}' \wedge \boldsymbol{c}))}_{\boldsymbol{\alpha}_2} \wedge \underbrace{((\boldsymbol{c}' \wedge \boldsymbol{a}) \cap (\boldsymbol{b}' \wedge \boldsymbol{b}))}_{\boldsymbol{\alpha}_3} = 0. \tag{7.8}$$

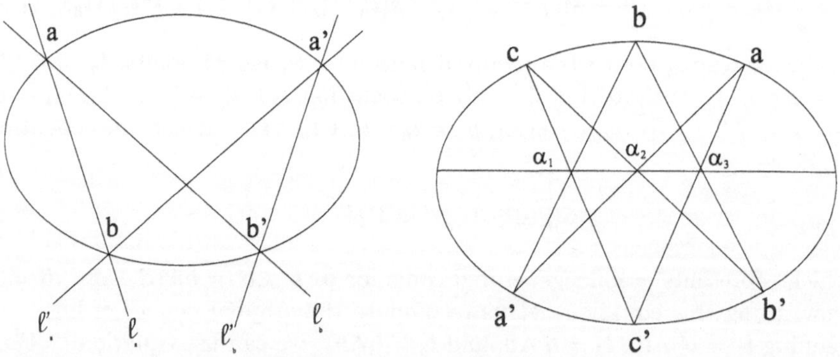

FIGURE 7.2. Pencils of lines related to a conic: (a) two projective pencils of lines used to generate the conic; (b) Pascal's theorem

This expression is a geometric formulation, using brackets, of *Pascal's theorem*, which says that the three intersecting points of the lines which connect opposite vertices of a hexagon circumscribed by a conic are collinear. Equation (7.8) will be used in the following section for computing intrinsic camera parameters.

7.3 Computing Intrinsic Camera Parameters

This section presents a technique within the geometric algebra framework for computing intrinsic camera parameters. In the previous section it was shown that equation (7.7) can be reformulated to express the constraint of equation (7.8), known as Pascal's theorem. Since Pascal's equation fulfills a property of any conic, we should also be able to use this equation to compute intrinsic camera parameters. Let us consider three intersecting points which are collinear and fulfill the parameters of equation (7.8).

Fig. (7.3) shows the first camera image, where the projected rotated points of the conic at infinity $R^T\boldsymbol{A}$, $R^T\boldsymbol{B}$, $R^T\boldsymbol{A}'$, $R^T\boldsymbol{B}'$, and $R^T\boldsymbol{C}'$ are $\boldsymbol{a} = K[R|0]R^T\boldsymbol{A} = K\boldsymbol{A}$, $\boldsymbol{b} = K[R|0]R^T\boldsymbol{B} = K\boldsymbol{B}$, $\boldsymbol{a}' = K[R|0]R^T\boldsymbol{A}' = K\boldsymbol{A}'$, $\boldsymbol{b}' = K[R|0]R^T\boldsymbol{B}' = K\boldsymbol{B}'$, and $\boldsymbol{c}' = K[R|0]\boldsymbol{C}' = K\boldsymbol{C}'$. The point

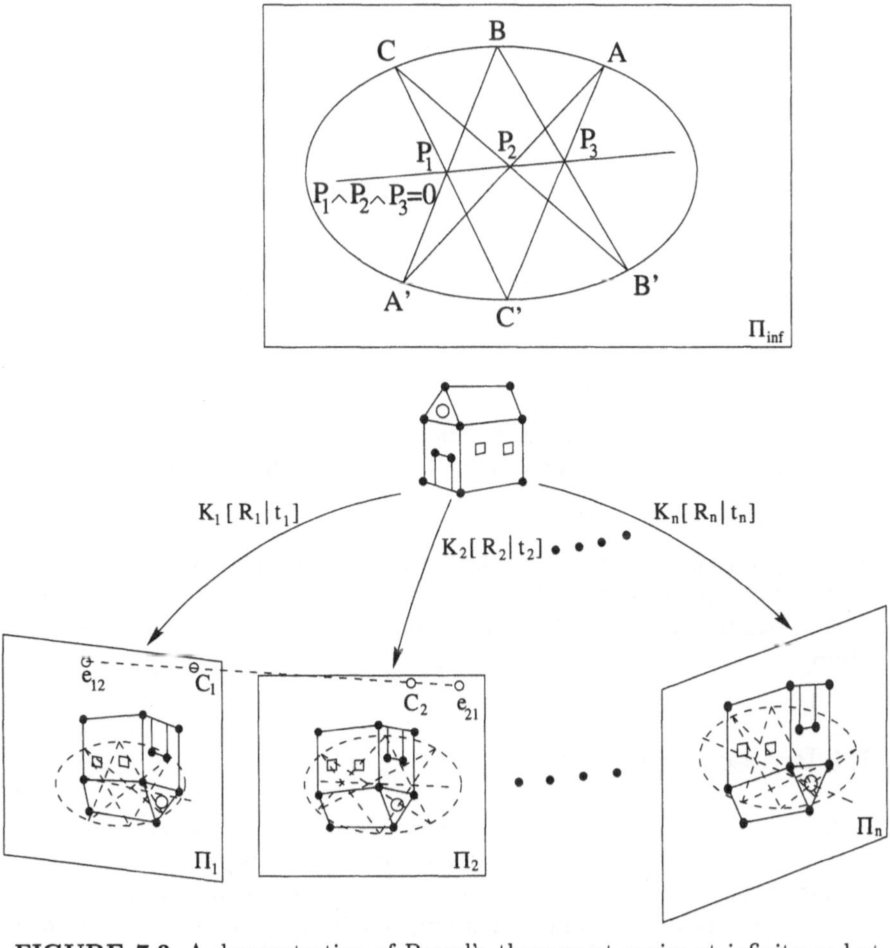

FIGURE 7.3. A demonstration of Pascal's theorem at conics at infinity and at images of n-uncalibrated cameras

$c = KK^T l_c$ is dependent upon the camera-intrinsic parameters and upon the line l_c tangent to the conic, computed in terms of the epipole $= [p_1, p_2, p_3]^T$ and a point lying at infinity upon the line of the first camera $l_c = [p_1, p_2, p_3]^T \times [1, \tau, 0]^T$. Now, using this expression for l_c, we can simplify equation (7.8) to obtain the equations for the α's in terms of brackets,

$$([a'bc']c - [a'bc]c') \wedge ([a'ab']c - [a'ac]b') \wedge ([c'ab']b - [c'ab]b') = 0 \Leftrightarrow \quad (7.9)$$

$$\begin{aligned}
&([KA'KBKC']KK^T l_c - [KA'KBKK^T l_c]KC') \wedge ([KA'KAKB']KK^T l_c - \\
&[KA'KAKK^T l_c]KB') \wedge ([KC'KAKB']KB - [KC'KAKB]KB') = 0 \\
&\Big(det(K)K([A'BC']K^T l_c - [A'BK^T l_c]C')\Big) \wedge \\
&\wedge\Big(det(K)K([A'AB']K^T l_c - [A'AK^T l_c]B')\Big) \wedge \\
&\wedge\Big(det(K)K([C'AB']B - [C'AB]B')\Big) = 0 \Leftrightarrow
\end{aligned} \tag{7.10}$$

$$\begin{aligned}
&det(K)^3 K\Big(([A'BC']K^T l_c - [A'BK^T l_c]C') \wedge ([A'AB']K^T l_c - \\
&-[A'AK^T l_c]B') \wedge ([C'AB']B - [C'AB]B')\Big) = 0 \Leftrightarrow
\end{aligned} \tag{7.11}$$

$$\begin{aligned}
&\underbrace{([A'BC']K^T l_c - [A'BK^T l_c]C')}_{\alpha_1} \wedge \underbrace{([A'AB']K^T l_c - [A'AK^T l_c]B')}_{\alpha_2} \wedge \\
&\wedge \underbrace{([C'AB']B - [C'AB]B')}_{\alpha_3} = 0.
\end{aligned} \tag{7.12}$$

Note that in equation (7.11) the scalars $det(K)^3$ and K are cancelled out, thereby simplifying the expression for the αs. The computation of the intrinsic parameters should take into account two possible situations: the intrinsic parameters remain stationary when the camera is in motion, or they will vary. By using equation (7.12), we are able to develop after one camera movement a set of eight quadratic equations, from which we can compute four intrinsic camera parameters (see [10] for the technical details of the computer algorithm).

7.4 Projective Invariants

In this section, we will use the framework established in Chapter 4 to show how standard invariants can be expressed both elegantly and concisely using geometric algebra. We begin by looking at algebraic quantities that are invariant under projective transformations, arriving at these invariants using a method which can be easily generalized from one dimension to two and three dimensions.

7.4.1 The 1D cross-ratio

The *fundamental projective invariant* of points on a line is the so-called "cross-ratio", ρ, defined as

$$\rho = \frac{AC}{BC}\frac{BD}{AD} = \frac{(t_3 - t_1)(t_4 - t_2)}{(t_4 - t_1)(t_3 - t_2)},$$

where $t_1 = |PA|$, $t_2 = |PB|$, $t_3 = |PC|$, and $t_4 = |PD|$. It is fairly easy to show that for the projection through O of the collinear points A, B, C, and D onto any line, ρ remains constant. For the 1D case, any point q on the line L can be written as $\boldsymbol{q} = t\sigma_1$ relative to P, where σ_1 is a unit vector in the direction of L. We can then move up a dimension to a 2D space, with basis vectors (γ_1, γ_2), which we will call R^2 and in which $\boldsymbol{q}$ is represented by the following vector $\mathbf{Q}$:

$$\mathbf{Q} = T\gamma_1 + S\gamma_2. \tag{7.13}$$

Note that, as before, $\boldsymbol{q}$ is associated with the bivector, as follows:

$$\boldsymbol{q} = \frac{\mathbf{Q}\wedge\gamma_2}{\mathbf{Q}\cdot\gamma_2} = \frac{T}{S}\gamma_1\gamma_2 \equiv \frac{T}{S}\sigma_1 = t\sigma_1. \tag{7.14}$$

When a point on line L is projected onto another line L', the distances t and t' are related by a projective transformation of the form

$$t' = \frac{\alpha t + \beta}{\tilde{\alpha} t + \tilde{\beta}}. \tag{7.15}$$

This nonlinear transformation in $\mathcal{E}^1$ can be made into a linear transformation in R^2 by defining the linear function $\underline{f}_1$ which maps vectors onto vectors in R^2:

$$\begin{aligned} \underline{f}_1(\gamma_1) &= \alpha_1\gamma_1 + \tilde{\alpha}\gamma_2 \\ \underline{f}_1(\gamma_2) &= \beta_1\gamma_1 + \tilde{\beta}\gamma_2. \end{aligned}$$

Consider two vectors $\mathbf{X}_1$ and $\mathbf{X}_2$ in R^2. Now form the bivector

$$S_1 = \mathbf{X}_1\wedge\mathbf{X}_2 = \lambda_1 I_2,$$

where $I_2 = \gamma_1\gamma_2$ is the pseudoscalar for R^2. We can now look at how S_1 transforms under $\underline{f}_1$:

$$S_1' = \mathbf{X}_1'\wedge\mathbf{X}_2' = \underline{f}_1(\mathbf{X}_1\wedge\mathbf{X}_2) = (\det\underline{f}_1)(\mathbf{X}_1\wedge\mathbf{X}_2). \tag{7.16}$$

This last step follows is a result of a linear function, which must map a pseudoscalar onto a multiple of itself, the multiple being the determinant of the function. Suppose that we now select four points of the line L, whose corresponding vectors in R^2 are $\{\mathbf{X}_i\}$, $i = 1, ..., 4$, and consider the ratio $\mathcal{R}_1$ of two wedge products:

$$\mathcal{R}_1 = \frac{\mathbf{X}_1 \wedge \mathbf{X}_2}{\mathbf{X}_3 \wedge \mathbf{X}_4}. \tag{7.17}$$

Then, under $\underline{f}_1$, $\mathcal{R}_1 \rightarrow \mathcal{R}_1'$, where

$$\mathcal{R}_1' = \frac{\mathbf{X}_1' \wedge \mathbf{X}_2'}{\mathbf{X}_3' \wedge \mathbf{X}_4'} = \frac{(\det \underline{f}_1)\mathbf{X}_1 \wedge \mathbf{X}_2}{(\det \underline{f}_1)\mathbf{X}_3 \wedge \mathbf{X}_4}. \tag{7.18}$$

$\mathcal{R}_1$ is therefore invariant under $\underline{f}_1$. However, we want to express our invariants in terms of distances on the 1D line. To do this, we must consider how the bivector S_1 in R^2 projects down to $\mathcal{E}^1$:

$$\begin{aligned} \mathbf{X}_1 \wedge \mathbf{X}_2 &= (T_1\gamma_1 + S_1\gamma_2) \wedge (T_2\gamma_1 + S_2\gamma_2) \\ &= (T_1 S_2 - T_2 S_1)\gamma_1\gamma_2 \\ &\equiv S_1 S_2 (T_1/S_1 - T_2/S_2) I_2 \\ &= S_1 S_2 (t_1 - t_2) I_2. \end{aligned} \tag{7.19}$$

In order to form a projective invariant which is independent of the choice of the arbitrary scalars S_i, we must now consider *ratios* of the bivectors $\mathbf{X}_i \wedge \mathbf{X}_j$ (so that $\det \underline{f}_1$ cancels), and then *multiples* of these ratios (so that the S_i's cancel). More precisely, consider the following expression:

$$Inv_1 = \frac{(\mathbf{X}_3 \wedge \mathbf{X}_1) I_2^{-1} (\mathbf{X}_4 \wedge \mathbf{X}_2) I_2^{-1}}{(\mathbf{X}_4 \wedge \mathbf{X}_1) I_2^{-1} (\mathbf{X}_3 \wedge \mathbf{X}_2) I_2^{-1}}. \tag{7.20}$$

Then, in terms of distances along the lines, under the projective transformation $\underline{f}_1$, Inv_1 goes to Inv_1', where

$$Inv_1' = \frac{S_3 S_1 (t_3 - t_1) S_4 S_2 (t_4 - t_2)}{S_4 S_1 (t_4 - t_1) S_3 S_2 (t_3 - t_2)} = \frac{(t_3 - t_1)(t_4 - t_2)}{(t_4 - t_1)(t_3 - t_2)}, \tag{7.21}$$

which is independent of the S_i's and is indeed the 1D classical projective invariant, the cross-ratio. Deriving the cross-ratio in this way allows us to easily generalize it to form invariants in higher dimensions.

7.4.2 2D generalization of the cross-ratio

When we consider points in a plane, we once again move up to a space with one higher dimension, which we shall call R^3. Let a point P in the plane M be described by the vector $\boldsymbol{x}$ in $\mathcal{E}^2$, where $\boldsymbol{x} = x\sigma_1 + y\sigma_2$. In R^3 this point will be represented by $\mathbf{X} = X\gamma_1 + Y\gamma_2 + Z\gamma_3$, where $x = X/Z$ and $y = Y/Z$. As described in Chapter 4, we can define a general projective transformation via a linear function $\underline{f}_2$ by mapping vectors to vectors in R^3, such that

$$\begin{aligned}\underline{f}_2(\gamma_1) &= \alpha_1\gamma_1 + \alpha_2\gamma_2 + \tilde{\alpha}\gamma_3 \\ \underline{f}_2(\gamma_2) &= \beta_1\gamma_1 + \beta_2\gamma_2 + \tilde{\beta}\gamma_3 \\ \underline{f}_2(\gamma_3) &= \delta_1\gamma_1 + \delta_2\gamma_2 + \tilde{\delta}\gamma_3.\end{aligned} \tag{7.22}$$

Now, consider three vectors (representing non-collinear points) $\mathbf{X}_i$, $i = 1,2,3$, in R^3, and form the trivector

$$\mathcal{S}_2 = \mathbf{X}_1 \wedge \mathbf{X}_2 \wedge \mathbf{X}_3 = \lambda_2 I_3, \tag{7.23}$$

where $I_3 = \gamma_1\gamma_2\gamma_3$ is the pseudoscalar for R^3. As before, under the projective transformation given by $\underline{f}_2$, $\mathcal{S}_2$ transforms to $\mathcal{S}_2'$, where

$$\mathcal{S}_2' = \det \underline{f}_2 \mathcal{S}_2. \tag{7.24}$$

Therefore, the ratio of any trivector is invariant under $\underline{f}_2$. To project down into $\mathcal{E}^2$, assuming that $\mathbf{X}_i\gamma_3 = Z_i(1 + \boldsymbol{x}_i)$ under the projective split, we then write

$$\begin{aligned}\mathcal{S}_2 I_3{}^{-1} &= \langle \mathbf{X}_1\mathbf{X}_2\mathbf{X}_3 I_3{}^{-1}\rangle \\ &= \langle \mathbf{X}_1\gamma_3\gamma_3\mathbf{X}_2\mathbf{X}_3\gamma_3\gamma_3 I_3{}^{-1}\rangle \\ &= Z_1Z_2Z_3\langle(1+\boldsymbol{x}_1)(1-\boldsymbol{x}_2)(1+\boldsymbol{x}_3)\gamma_3 I_3{}^{-1}\rangle,\end{aligned} \tag{7.25}$$

where the $\boldsymbol{x}_i$ represent vectors in $\mathcal{E}^2$. We can only get a scalar term from the expression within the brackets by calculating the product of a vector, two spatial vectors, and $I_3{}^{-1}$, i.e.,

$$\begin{aligned}\mathcal{S}_2 I_3{}^{-1} &= Z_1Z_2Z_3\langle(\boldsymbol{x}_1\boldsymbol{x}_3 - \boldsymbol{x}_1\boldsymbol{x}_2 - \boldsymbol{x}_2\boldsymbol{x}_3)\gamma_3 I_3{}^{-1}\rangle \\ &= Z_1Z_2Z_3\{(\boldsymbol{x}_2 - \boldsymbol{x}_1)\wedge(\boldsymbol{x}_3 - \boldsymbol{x}_1)\} I_2{}^{-1}.\end{aligned} \tag{7.26}$$

It is therefore clear that we must use multiples of the ratios in our calculations, so that the arbitrary scalars Z_i cancel. In the case of four points in a plane, there are only four possible combinations of $Z_iZ_jZ_k$ and it is not possible to cancel all the Z's by multiplying two ratios of the form $\mathbf{X}_i\wedge\mathbf{X}_j\wedge\mathbf{X}_k$ together. For five coplanar points $\{\mathbf{X}_i\}$, $i = 1, ..., 5$, however, there are several ways of achieving the desired cancellation. For example,

$$Inv_2 = \frac{(\mathbf{X}_5\wedge\mathbf{X}_4\wedge\mathbf{X}_3)I_3^{-1}(\mathbf{X}_5\wedge\mathbf{X}_2\wedge\mathbf{X}_1)I_3^{-1}}{(\mathbf{X}_5\wedge\mathbf{X}_1\wedge\mathbf{X}_3)I_3^{-1}(\mathbf{X}_5\wedge\mathbf{X}_2\wedge\mathbf{X}_4)I_3^{-1}}.$$

According to equation (7.26), we can interpret this ratio in $\mathcal{E}^2$ as

$$\begin{aligned}Inv_2 &= \frac{(\boldsymbol{x}_5 - \boldsymbol{x}_4)\wedge(\boldsymbol{x}_5 - \boldsymbol{x}_3)I_2^{-1}(\boldsymbol{x}_5 - \boldsymbol{x}_2)\wedge(\boldsymbol{x}_5 - \boldsymbol{x}_1)I_2^{-1}}{(\boldsymbol{x}_5 - \boldsymbol{x}_1)\wedge(\boldsymbol{x}_5 - \boldsymbol{x}_3)I_2^{-1}(\boldsymbol{x}_5 - \boldsymbol{x}_2)\wedge(\boldsymbol{x}_5 - \boldsymbol{x}_4)I_2^{-1}} \\ &= \frac{A_{543}A_{521}}{A_{513}A_{524}},\end{aligned} \tag{7.27}$$

where $\frac{1}{2}A_{ijk}$ is the area of the triangle defined by the three vertices $\boldsymbol{x}_i, \boldsymbol{x}_j, \boldsymbol{x}_k$. This invariant is regarded as the 2D generalization of the 1D cross-ratio.

7.4.3 3D generalization of the cross-ratio

For general points in $\mathcal{E}^3$, we have seen that we move up one dimension to compute in the 4D space R^4. For this dimension, the point $\boldsymbol{x} = x\sigma_1 + y\sigma_2 + z\sigma_3$ in $\mathcal{E}^3$ is written as $\mathbf{X} = X\gamma_1 + Y\gamma_2 + Z\gamma_3 + W\gamma_4$, where $x = X/W$, $y = Y/W$, $z = Z/W$. As before, a nonlinear projective transformation in $\mathcal{E}^3$ becomes a linear transformation, described by the linear function $\underline{f}_3$ in R^4.

Let us consider 4-vectors in R^4, $\{\mathbf{X}_i\}$, $i = 1, ..., 4$ and form the equation of a 4-vector:

$$\mathcal{S}_3 = \mathbf{X}_1 \wedge \mathbf{X}_2 \wedge \mathbf{X}_3 \wedge \mathbf{X}_4 = \lambda_3 I_4, \tag{7.28}$$

where $I_4 = \gamma_1\gamma_2\gamma_3\gamma_4$ is the pseudoscalar for R^4. As before, $\mathcal{S}_3$ transforms to $\mathcal{S}_3'$ under $\underline{f}_3$:

$$\mathcal{S}_3' = \mathbf{X}_1' \wedge \mathbf{X}_2' \wedge \mathbf{X}_3' \wedge \mathbf{X}_4' = \det \underline{f}_3 \mathcal{S}_3. \tag{7.29}$$

The ratio of any two 4-vectors is therefore invariant under $\underline{f}_3$ and we must take multiples of these ratios to ensure that the arbitrary scale factors W_i cancel. With five general points we see that there are five possibilities for forming the combinations $W_i W_j W_k W_l$. It is then a simple matter to show that one cannot consider multiples of ratios such that the W factors cancel. It is, however, possible to do this if we have six points. One example of such an invariant might be

$$Inv_3 = \frac{(\mathbf{X}_1 \wedge \mathbf{X}_2 \wedge \mathbf{X}_3 \wedge \mathbf{X}_4) I_4^{-1} (\mathbf{X}_4 \wedge \mathbf{X}_5 \wedge \mathbf{X}_2 \wedge \mathbf{X}_6) I_4^{-1}}{(\mathbf{X}_1 \wedge \mathbf{X}_2 \wedge \mathbf{X}_4 \wedge \mathbf{X}_5) I_4^{-1} (\mathbf{X}_3 \wedge \mathbf{X}_4 \wedge \mathbf{X}_2 \wedge \mathbf{X}_6) I_4^{-1}}. \tag{7.30}$$

Using the arguments of the previous sections, we can now write

$$(\mathbf{X}_1 \wedge \mathbf{X}_2 \wedge \mathbf{X}_3 \wedge \mathbf{X}_4) I_4^{-1} \equiv \\ W_1 W_2 W_3 W_4 \{(\boldsymbol{x}_2 - \boldsymbol{x}_1) \wedge (\boldsymbol{x}_3 - \boldsymbol{x}_1) \wedge (\boldsymbol{x}_4 - \boldsymbol{x}_1)\} I_3^{-1}. \tag{7.31}$$

We can therefore see that the invariant Inv_3 is the 3D equivalent of the 1D cross-ratio and consists of ratios of volumes,

$$Inv_3 = \frac{V_{1234} V_{4526}}{V_{1245} V_{3426}}, \tag{7.32}$$

where V_{ijkl} is the volume of the solid formed by the four vertices $\boldsymbol{x}_i, \boldsymbol{x}_j, \boldsymbol{x}_k, \boldsymbol{x}_l$.

Conventionally, all of these invariants are well known, but we have outlined here a general process which is straightforward and simple for generating projective invariants in any dimension.

7.4.4 Generation of 3D projective invariants

Any 3D point may be written in $\mathcal{G}_{1,3,0}$ as $\mathbf{X}_n = X_n\gamma_1 + Y_n\gamma_2 + Z_n\gamma_3 + W_n\gamma_4$, and its projected image point written in $\mathcal{G}_{3,0,0}$ as $\boldsymbol{x}_n = x_n\sigma_1 + y_n\sigma_2 + z_n\sigma_3$, where $x_n = X_n/W_n$, $y_n = Y_n/W_n$, $andz_n = Z_n/W_n$. The 3D projective basis consists of four base points and a fifth point for normalization:

$$\boldsymbol{X}_1 = \begin{pmatrix} 1 \\ 0 \\ 0 \\ 0 \end{pmatrix}, \boldsymbol{X}_2 = \begin{pmatrix} 0 \\ 1 \\ 0 \\ 0 \end{pmatrix}, \boldsymbol{X}_3 = \begin{pmatrix} 0 \\ 0 \\ 1 \\ 0 \end{pmatrix}, \boldsymbol{X}_4 = \begin{pmatrix} 0 \\ 0 \\ 0 \\ 1 \end{pmatrix}, \boldsymbol{X}_5 = \begin{pmatrix} 1 \\ 1 \\ 1 \\ 1 \end{pmatrix}.$$

Any other point $\mathbf{X}_i \in \langle \mathcal{G}_{1,3,0} \rangle_1$ can then be expressed by

$$\mathbf{X}_i = X_i \mathbf{X}_1 + Y_i \mathbf{X}_2 + Z_i \mathbf{X}_3 + W_i \mathbf{X}_4, \tag{7.33}$$

with (X_i, Y_i, Z_i, W_i) as homogeneous projective coordinates of $\mathbf{X}_i$ in the base $\{\mathbf{X}_1, \mathbf{X}_2, \mathbf{X}_3, \mathbf{X}_4, \mathbf{X}_5\}$.

The first four base points, projected to the projective plane, can be used as a projective basis of $\langle \mathcal{G}_{3,0,0} \rangle_1$ if no three of them are collinear:

$$\boldsymbol{x}_1 = \begin{pmatrix} 1 \\ 0 \\ 0 \end{pmatrix}, \quad \boldsymbol{x}_2 = \begin{pmatrix} 0 \\ 1 \\ 0 \end{pmatrix}, \quad \boldsymbol{x}_3 = \begin{pmatrix} 0 \\ 0 \\ 1 \end{pmatrix}, \quad \boldsymbol{x}_4 = \begin{pmatrix} 1 \\ 1 \\ 1 \end{pmatrix}.$$

Using this basis, we can express, in bracketed notation, the 3D projective coordinates X_n, Y_n, Z_n of any 3D point, as well as its 2D projected coordinates x_n, y_n:

$$\frac{X_n}{W_n} = \frac{[234n][1235]}{[2345][123n]}, \quad \frac{Y_n}{W_n} = \frac{[134n][1235]}{[1345][123n]}, \quad \frac{Z_n}{W_n} = \frac{[124n][1235]}{[1245][123n]}. \tag{7.34}$$

$$\frac{x_n}{w_n} = \frac{[23n][124]}{[234][12n]}, \quad \frac{y_n}{w_n} = \frac{[13n][124]}{[134][12n]}. \tag{7.35}$$

These equations show projective invariant relationships, and they can be used, for example, to compute the position of a moving camera (see subsection 7.7).

The projective structure and its projection on the 2D image can be expressed according to the following geometric constraint, as presented by Carlsson [17]:

$$\begin{pmatrix} 0 & w_5Y_5 & -y_5Z_5 & (y_5 - w_5)W_5 \\ w_5X_5 & 0 & -x_5Z_5 & (x_5 - w_5)W_5 \\ 0 & w_6Y_6 & -y_6Z_6 & (x_5 - w_5)W_5 \\ 0 & w_6Y_6 & -y_6Z_6 & (y_6 - w_6)W_6 \\ w_6X_6 & 0 & -x_6Z_6 & (x_6 - w_6)W_6 \\ 0 & w_7Y_7 & -y_7Z_7 & (y_7 - w_7)W_7 \\ w_7X_7 & 0 & -x_7Z_7 & (x_7 - w_7)W_7 \\ \cdot & \cdot & \cdot & \cdot \\ \cdot & \cdot & \cdot & \cdot \\ \cdot & \cdot & \cdot & \cdot \end{pmatrix} \begin{pmatrix} X_0^{-1} \\ Y_0^{-1} \\ Z_0^{-1} \\ W_0^{-1} \end{pmatrix} = 0, \tag{7.36}$$

where X_0, Y_0, Z_0, W_0 are the coordinates of the view-center point. Since the matrix is of rank < 4, any determinant of four rows becomes a zero. Considering $(X_5, Y_5, Z_5, W_5) = (1,1,1,1)$ as a normalizing point, and taking the determinant formed by the first four rows of equation (7.36), we get a geometric-constraint equation involving six points (see Quan [86]):

$$\begin{aligned}(w_5y_6 - x_5y_6)X_6Z_6 + (x_5y_6 - x_5w6)X_6W_6 + (x_5w_6 - y_5w6)X_6Y_6 + \\ +(y_5x_6 - w_5x6)Y_6Z_6 + (y_5w_6 - y_5x6)Y_6W_6 + \\ +(w_5x_6 - w_5y_6)Z_6W_6 = 0. \end{aligned} \tag{7.37}$$

Carlsson [17] showed that equation (7.37) can also be derived using *Plücker–Grassmann relations*, which is then computed as the *Laplace expansion* of the 4×8 rectangular matrix involving the same six points as above:

$$\begin{aligned}[\boldsymbol{X}_1, \boldsymbol{X}_2, \boldsymbol{X}_3, \boldsymbol{X}_4, \boldsymbol{X}_5, \boldsymbol{X}_5, \boldsymbol{X}_6, \boldsymbol{X}_7] = [\boldsymbol{X}_0, \boldsymbol{X}_1, \boldsymbol{X}_2, \boldsymbol{X}_3] \\ [\boldsymbol{X}_4, \mathbf{X}_5, \boldsymbol{X}_6, \boldsymbol{X}_7] - [\boldsymbol{X}_0, \boldsymbol{X}_1, \boldsymbol{X}_2, \boldsymbol{X}_4][\boldsymbol{X}_3, \boldsymbol{X}_5, \boldsymbol{X}_6, \boldsymbol{X}_7] + \\ +[\boldsymbol{X}_0, \boldsymbol{X}_1, \boldsymbol{X}_2, \boldsymbol{X}_5][\boldsymbol{X}_3, \boldsymbol{X}_4, \boldsymbol{X}_6, \boldsymbol{X}_7] - [\boldsymbol{X}_0, \boldsymbol{X}_1, \boldsymbol{X}_2, \boldsymbol{X}_6] \\ [\boldsymbol{X}_3, \mathbf{X}_4, \boldsymbol{X}_5, \boldsymbol{X}_7] + [\boldsymbol{X}_0, \boldsymbol{X}_1, \boldsymbol{X}_2, \boldsymbol{X}_7][\boldsymbol{X}_3, \boldsymbol{X}_4, \boldsymbol{X}_5, \boldsymbol{X}_6] = 0. \end{aligned} \tag{7.38}$$

By using four functions like equation (7.38) in terms of the permutations of six points as indicated by their subindices in the table below,

$\boldsymbol{X}_0$	$\boldsymbol{X}_1$	$\boldsymbol{X}_2$	$\boldsymbol{X}_3$	$\boldsymbol{X}_4$	$\boldsymbol{X}_5$	$\boldsymbol{X}_6$	$\boldsymbol{X}_7$
0	1	5	1	2	3	4	5
0	2	6	1	2	3	4	6
0	3	5	1	2	3	4	5
0	4	6	1	2	3	4	6

we get an expression in which bracketed terms having two identical points vanish:

$$\begin{aligned}[0152][1345] - [0153][1245] + [0154][1235] = 0, \\ [0216][2346] - [0236][1246] + [0246][1236] = 0, \\ [0315][2345] + [0325][1345] + [0345][1235] = 0, \\ [0416][2346] + [0426][1346] - [0436][1246] = 0. \end{aligned} \tag{7.39}$$

It is easy to prove that the bracketed terms of image points can be written in the form $[\boldsymbol{x}_i \boldsymbol{x}_j \boldsymbol{x}_k] = w_i w_j w_k [K][\boldsymbol{X}_0 \boldsymbol{X}_i \boldsymbol{X}_j \boldsymbol{X}_k]$, where [K] is the matrix of the intrinsic parameters [75]. Now, if we substitute in equation (7.39) all the brackets which have the point $\boldsymbol{X}_0$ with image points, and if we then organize all the products of brackets as a 4×4 matrix, we end up with the singular matrix

$$\begin{pmatrix} 0 & [125][1345] & [135][1245] & [145][1235] \\ [216][2346] & 0 & [236][1246] & [246][1236] \\ [315][2345] & [325][1345] & 0 & [345][1235] \\ [416][2346] & [426][1346] & [436][1246] & 0 \end{pmatrix}. \tag{7.40}$$

Here, the scalars $w_i w_j w_k[K]$ of each matrix entry cancel each other. Now, after taking the determinant of this matrix and rearranging the terms conveniently, we obtain the following useful *bracket! polynomial*:

$$
\begin{aligned}
&[125][346]\left[1236\right]\left[1246\right]\left[1345\right]\left[2345\right] - \\
&[126][345]\left[1235\right]\left[1245\right]\left[1346\right]\left[2346\right] + \\
&[135][246]\left[1236\right]\left[1245\right]\left[1346\right]\left[2345\right] - \\
&[136][245]\left[1235\right]\left[1246\right]\left[1345\right]\left[2346\right] + \\
&[145][236]\left[1235\right]\left[1246\right]\left[1346\right]\left[2345\right] - \\
&[146][235]\left[1236\right]\left[1245\right]\left[1345\right]\left[2346\right] = 0.
\end{aligned} \tag{7.41}
$$

Surprisingly, this bracketed expression is exactly the *shape constraint* for six points given by Quan [86],

$$i_1 I_1 + i_2 I_2 + i_3 I_3 + i_4 I_4 + i_5 I_5 + i_6 I_6 = 0, \tag{7.42}$$

where

$$
\begin{aligned}
i_1 &= [125][346], i_2 = [126][345], ..., i_6 = [146][235], \\
I_1 &= [1236][1246][1345][2345], I_2 = [1235][1245][1346][2346], ..., \\
I_6 &= [1236][1245][1345][2346]
\end{aligned}
$$

are the relative linear invariants in P^2 and P^3, respectively. Using the shape constraint, we are now ready to generate invariants for different purposes.

Let us illustrate this with an example (see Fig. 7.4). According to the figure, a configuration of six points indicate whether or not the end-effector is grasping properly. To test this situation, we can use an invariant generated from the constraint of equation (7.41). In this particular situation, we recognize two planes, thus $[1235] = 0$ and $[2346] = 0$. By substituting the six points into equation (7.41), we can cancel out some brackets, thereby reducing the equation to

$$
\begin{aligned}
&[125][346]\left[1236\right]\left[1246\right]\left[1345\right]\left[2345\right] - \\
&-[135][246]\left[1236\right]\left[1245\right]\left[1346\right]\left[2345\right] = 0
\end{aligned} \tag{7.43}
$$

$$[125][346]\left[1246\right]\left[1345\right] - [135][246]\left[1245\right]\left[1346\right] = 0 \tag{7.44}$$

or

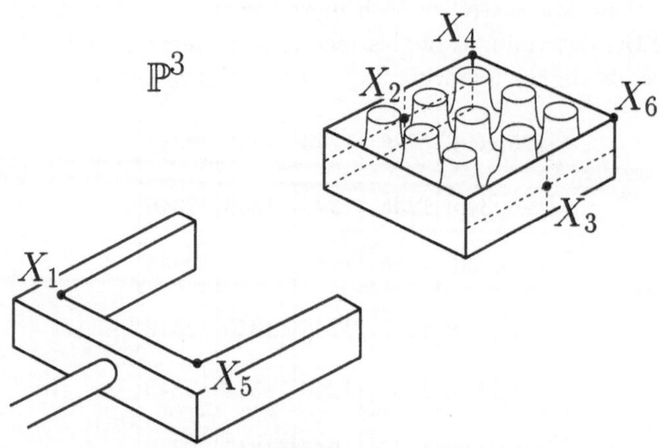

FIGURE 7.4. The action of grasping a box

$$Inv = \frac{(\mathbf{X}_1\wedge\mathbf{X}_2\wedge\boldsymbol{X}_4\wedge\mathbf{X}_5)I_4^{-1}(\boldsymbol{X}_1\wedge\mathbf{X}_3\wedge\mathbf{X}_4\wedge\mathbf{X}_6)I_4^{-1}}{(\mathbf{X}_1\wedge\mathbf{X}_2\wedge\boldsymbol{X}_4\wedge\mathbf{X}_6)I_4^{-1}(\boldsymbol{X}_1\wedge\mathbf{X}_3\wedge\mathbf{X}_4\wedge\mathbf{X}_5)I_4^{-1}} = \frac{(\boldsymbol{x}_1\wedge\boldsymbol{x}_2\wedge\boldsymbol{x}_5)I_3^{-1}(\boldsymbol{x}_3\wedge\boldsymbol{x}_4\wedge\boldsymbol{x}_6)I_3^{-1}}{(\boldsymbol{x}_1\wedge\boldsymbol{x}_3\wedge\boldsymbol{x}_5)I_3^{-1}(\boldsymbol{x}_2\wedge\boldsymbol{x}_4\wedge\boldsymbol{x}_6)I_3^{-1}}. \tag{7.45}$$

In this equation, any bracket of P^3 after the projective mapping becomes

$$(\mathbf{X}_1\wedge\mathbf{X}_2\wedge\mathbf{X}_4\wedge\mathbf{X}_5)I_4^{-1} \equiv W_1W_2W_4W_5\{(\boldsymbol{x}_2-\boldsymbol{x}_1)\wedge(\boldsymbol{x}_4-\boldsymbol{x}_1)\wedge(\boldsymbol{x}_5-\boldsymbol{x}_1)\}I_3^{-1}. \tag{7.46}$$

The constraint (7.41) ensures that the $W_iW_jW_kW_l$ constants are always canceled. Furthermore, we can interpret the invariant Inv, the equivalent of the 1D cross-ratio, as a ratio of volumes in P^3, and as a ratio of triangle areas in P^2:

$$Inv = \frac{V_{1245}V_{1346}}{V_{1246}V_{1345}} = \frac{A_{125}A_{346}}{A_{135}A_{246}}. \tag{7.47}$$

In other words, we can interpret this invariant in P^3 as the relation of 4-vectors, or volumes, which in turn are built by points lying on a quadric. After they are projected in P^2, they represent an invariant relating areas of triangles encircled by conics.

Then, utilizing this invariant, we can check whether or not the grasper is holding the box correctly. Note that by using the observed 3D points in the image, we can compute this invariant and see if the relation of the triangle areas corresponds well with the parameters for firm grasping. In other words, if the points of the grasper are located at some distance away from the object, the invariant will have a different value than will be the case if the points $\boldsymbol{X}_1$, $\boldsymbol{X}_5$ of the grasper are nearer to the points $\boldsymbol{X}_2$, $\boldsymbol{X}_3$ of the object.

7.5 3D Projective Invariants from Multiple Views

In the previous section, the projective invariant was explained within the context of homogeneous projective coordinates derived from a single image. Since, in general, objects in 3D space are observed from different positions, it would be convenient to be able to extend the projective invariant in terms of the linear constraints imposed by the geometry of two, three, or more cameras.

7.5.1 Projective invariants using two views

Let us consider a 3D *projective invariant* derived from equation (7.41):

$$\boldsymbol{Inv_3} = \frac{[\mathbf{X}_1\mathbf{X}_2\mathbf{X}_3\mathbf{X}_4][\mathbf{X}_4\mathbf{X}_5\mathbf{X}_2\mathbf{X}_6]}{[\mathbf{X}_1\mathbf{X}_2\mathbf{X}_4\mathbf{X}_5][\mathbf{X}_3\mathbf{X}_4\mathbf{X}_2\mathbf{X}_6]}. \tag{7.48}$$

The computation of the bracket

$$[1234] = (\mathbf{X}_1\wedge\mathbf{X}_2\wedge\mathbf{X}_3\wedge\mathbf{X}_4)\boldsymbol{I}_4^{-1} = ((\mathbf{X}_1\wedge\mathbf{X}_2)\wedge(\mathbf{X}_3\wedge\mathbf{X}_4))\boldsymbol{I}_4^{-1}$$

of four points from R^4, mapped onto camera-images with optical centers $\mathbf{A}_0$ and $\mathbf{B}_0$, suggests the use of a binocular model based on incidence algebra techniques, as discussed in Chapter 4. Defining the lines

$$\begin{aligned}\boldsymbol{L}_{12} &= \mathbf{X}_1\wedge\mathbf{X}_2 = (\mathbf{A}_0\wedge\boldsymbol{L}_{12}^A)\vee(\mathbf{B}_0\wedge\boldsymbol{L}_{12}^B)\\ \boldsymbol{L}_{34} &= \mathbf{X}_3\wedge\mathbf{X}_4 = (\mathbf{A}_0\wedge\boldsymbol{L}_{34}^A)\vee(\mathbf{B}_0\wedge\boldsymbol{L}_{34}^B),\end{aligned}$$

where lines $\boldsymbol{L}_{ij}^A$ and $\boldsymbol{L}_{ij}^B$ are mappings of the line $\boldsymbol{L}_{ij}$ onto the two image planes, results in the expression

$$[1234] = [\mathbf{A}_0\mathbf{B}_0\mathbf{A}'_{1234}\mathbf{B}'_{1234}]. \tag{7.49}$$

Here, $\mathbf{A}'_{1234}$ and $\mathbf{B}'_{1234}$ are the points of intersection of the lines $\boldsymbol{L}_{12}^A$ and $\boldsymbol{L}_{34}^A$ or $\boldsymbol{L}_{12}^B$ and $\boldsymbol{L}_{34}^B$, respectively. These points, lying on the image planes, can be expanded using the mappings of three points $\mathbf{X}_i$, say, $\mathbf{X}_1, \mathbf{X}_2, \mathbf{X}_3$, to the image planes. In other words, considering $\mathbf{A}_j$ and $\mathbf{B}_j$, $j = 1,2,3$, as projective bases, we can expand the vectors

$$\begin{aligned}\mathbf{A}'_{1234} &= \alpha_{1234,1}\mathbf{A}_1 + \alpha_{1234,2}\mathbf{A}_2 + \alpha_{1234,3}\mathbf{A}_3\\ \mathbf{B}'_{1234} &= \beta_{1234,1}\mathbf{B}_1 + \beta_{1234,2}\mathbf{B}_2 + \beta_{1234,3}\mathbf{B}_3.\end{aligned}$$

Then, using equation (4.81) from Chapter 4, we can express

$$[1234] = \sum_{i,j=1}^{3} \tilde{F}_{ij}\alpha_{1234,i}\beta_{1234,j} = \boldsymbol{\alpha}_{1234}^T\tilde{F}\boldsymbol{\beta}_{1234}, \tag{7.50}$$

where $\tilde{F}$ is the fundamental matrix given in terms of the projective basis embedded in R^4, and $\boldsymbol{\alpha}_{1234} = (\alpha_{1234,1}, \alpha_{1234,2}, \alpha_{1234,3})$ and $\boldsymbol{\beta}_{1234} = (\beta_{1234,1}, \beta_{1234,2}, \beta_{1234,3})$ are corresponding points.

The ratio

$$\boldsymbol{Inv_{3F}} = \frac{(\boldsymbol{\alpha}^T{}_{1234}\tilde{F}\boldsymbol{\beta}_{1234})(\boldsymbol{\alpha}^T{}_{4526}\tilde{F}\boldsymbol{\beta}_{4526})}{(\boldsymbol{\alpha}^T{}_{1245}\tilde{F}\boldsymbol{\beta}_{1245})(\boldsymbol{\alpha}^T{}_{3426}\tilde{F}\boldsymbol{\beta}_{3426})} \tag{7.51}$$

is therefore seen to be an invariant using the views of two cameras [16]. Note that equation (7.51) is invariant for whichever values of the γ_4 components of the vectors $\mathbf{A}_i, \mathbf{B}_i, \mathbf{X}_i$, etc., are chosen. If we attempt to express the invariant of equation (7.51) in terms of what we actually observe, we may be tempted to express the invariant in terms of the homogeneous Cartesian image coordinates $\boldsymbol{a}_i's$, $\boldsymbol{b}_i's$ and the fundamental matrix F calculated from these image coordinates. In order to avoid this, it is necessary to transfer the computations of equation (7.51) carried out in R^4 to R^3. Thus, if we define $\tilde{F}$ by

$$\tilde{F}_{kl} = (\mathbf{A}_k \cdot \gamma_4)(\mathbf{B}_l \cdot \gamma_4)F_{kl} \tag{7.52}$$

and consider the relationships $\boldsymbol{\alpha}_{ij} = \frac{\mathbf{A}'_i \cdot \gamma_4}{\mathbf{A}_j \cdot \gamma_4}\boldsymbol{a}_{ij}$ and $\boldsymbol{\beta}_{ij} = \frac{\mathbf{B}'_i \cdot \gamma_4}{\mathbf{B}_j \cdot \gamma_4}\boldsymbol{b}_{ij}$, we can claim

$$\boldsymbol{\alpha}_{ik}\tilde{F}_{kl}\boldsymbol{\beta}_{il} = (\mathbf{A}'_i \cdot \gamma_4)(\mathbf{B}'_i \cdot \gamma_4)\boldsymbol{a}_{ik}F_{kl}\boldsymbol{b}_{il}. \tag{7.53}$$

If F is subsequently estimated by some method, then $\tilde{F}$ as defined in equation (7.52) will also act as a *fundamental matrix* or *bilinear constraint* in R^4. Now, let us look again at the invariant $\boldsymbol{Inv_{3F}}$. As we demonstrated ealier, we can write the invariant as

$$\boldsymbol{Inv_{3F}} = \frac{(\boldsymbol{a}^T{}_{1234}F\boldsymbol{b}_{1234})(\boldsymbol{a}^T{}_{4526}F\boldsymbol{b}_{4526})\phi_{1234}\phi_{4526}}{(\boldsymbol{a}^T{}_{1245}F\boldsymbol{b}_{1245})(\boldsymbol{a}^T{}_{3426}F\boldsymbol{b}_{3426})\phi_{1245}\phi_{3426}}, \tag{7.54}$$

where $\phi_{pqrs} = (\mathbf{A}'_{pqrs} \cdot \gamma_4)(\mathbf{B}'_{pqrs} \cdot \gamma_4)$. Therefore, we see that the ratio of the terms $\boldsymbol{a}^T F \boldsymbol{b}$, which resembles the expression for the invariant in R^4 but uses only the observed coordinates and the estimated fundamental matrix, will not be an invariant. Instead, we need to include the factors ϕ_{1234}, etc., which do not cancel. They are formed as follows (see [9]): Since $\boldsymbol{a}'_3$, $\boldsymbol{a}'_4$, and $\boldsymbol{a}'_{1234}$ are collinear, we can write $\boldsymbol{a}'_{1234} = \mu_{1234}\boldsymbol{a}'_4 + (1 - \mu_{1234})\boldsymbol{a}'_3$. Then, by expressing $\mathbf{A}'_{1234}$ as the intersection of the line joining $\mathbf{A}'_1$ and $\mathbf{A}'_2$ with the plane through $\mathbf{A}_0, \mathbf{A}'_3, \mathbf{A}'_4$, we can use the projective split and equate terms, so that

$$\frac{(\mathbf{A}'_{1234} \cdot \gamma_4)(\mathbf{A}'_{4526} \cdot \gamma_4)}{(\mathbf{A}'_{3426} \cdot \gamma_4)(\mathbf{A}'_{1245} \cdot \gamma_4)} = \frac{\mu_{1245}(\mu_{3426} - 1)}{\mu_{4526}(\mu_{1234} - 1)}. \tag{7.55}$$

Note that the values of μ are readily obtainable from the images. The factors $\mathbf{B}'_{pqrs} \cdot \gamma_4$ are found in a similar way, so that if $\boldsymbol{b}'_{1234} = \lambda_{1234}\boldsymbol{b}'_4 + (1 - \lambda_{1234})\boldsymbol{b}'_3$, etc., the overall expression for the invariant becomes

$$
\begin{aligned}
\boldsymbol{Inv_{3F}} &= \frac{(\boldsymbol{a}_{1234}^T F \boldsymbol{b}_{1234})(\boldsymbol{a}_{4526}^T F \boldsymbol{b}_{4526})}{(\boldsymbol{a}_{1245}^T F \boldsymbol{b}_{1245})(\boldsymbol{a}_{3426}^T F \boldsymbol{b}_{3426})} \cdot \\
&\quad \frac{\mu_{1245}(\mu_{3426}-1)\ \lambda_{1245}(\lambda_{3426}-1)}{\mu_{4526}(\mu_{1234}-1)\ \lambda_{4526}(\lambda_{1234}-1)}. \qquad (7.56)
\end{aligned}
$$

In conclusion, given the coordinates of a set of six corresponding points in two image planes, where these six points are projections of arbitrary world points in general position, we can form 3D projective invariants, provided we have some estimate of F.

7.5.2 Projective invariant of points using three uncalibrated cameras

The technique used to form the 3D projective invariants for two views can be straightforwardly extended to give expressions for invariants of three views. Considering four world points $\mathbf{X}_1, \mathbf{X}_2, \mathbf{X}_3, \mathbf{X}_4$ or two lines $\mathbf{X}_1 \wedge \mathbf{X}_2$ and $\mathbf{X}_3 \wedge \mathbf{X}_4$ projected onto three camera planes, we can write

$$
\begin{aligned}
\mathbf{X}_1 \wedge \mathbf{X}_2 &= (\mathbf{A}_0 \wedge \boldsymbol{L}_{12}^A) \cap (\mathbf{B}_0 \wedge \boldsymbol{L}_{12}^B) \\
\mathbf{X}_3 \wedge \mathbf{X}_4 &= (\mathbf{A}_0 \wedge \boldsymbol{L}_{34}^A) \cap (\mathbf{C}_0 \wedge \boldsymbol{L}_{34}^C).
\end{aligned}
$$

Once again, we can combine the above expressions so that they give an equation for the 4-vector $\mathbf{X}_1 \wedge \mathbf{X}_2 \wedge \mathbf{X}_3 \wedge \mathbf{X}_4$,

$$
\begin{aligned}
\mathbf{X}_1 \wedge \mathbf{X}_2 \wedge \mathbf{X}_3 \wedge \mathbf{X}_4 &= ((\mathbf{A}_0 \wedge \boldsymbol{L}_{12}^A) \cap (\mathbf{B}_0 \wedge \boldsymbol{L}_{12}^B)) \wedge ((\mathbf{A}_0 \wedge \boldsymbol{L}_{34}^A) \cap (\mathbf{C}_0 \wedge \boldsymbol{L}_{34}^C)) \\
&= (\mathbf{A}_0 \wedge \mathbf{A}_{1234}) \wedge ((\mathbf{B}_0 \wedge \boldsymbol{L}_{12}^B) \cap (\mathbf{C}_0 \wedge \boldsymbol{L}_{34}^C)). \qquad (7.57)
\end{aligned}
$$

Then, by rewriting the lines $\boldsymbol{L}_{12}^B$ and $\boldsymbol{L}_{34}^C$ in terms of the line coordinates, we get $\boldsymbol{L}_{12}^B = \sum_{j=1}^{3} l_{12,j}^B \boldsymbol{L}_j^B$ and $\boldsymbol{L}_{34}^C = \sum_{j=1}^{3} l_{34,j}^C \boldsymbol{L}_j^C$. As has been shown in Chapter 4, the components of the *trifocal tensor* (which takes the place of the fundamental matrix for three views) can be written in geometric algebra as

$$
\tilde{T}_{ijk} = [(\mathbf{A}_0 \wedge \mathbf{A}_i) \wedge ((\mathbf{B}_0 \wedge \boldsymbol{L}_j^B) \cap (\mathbf{C}_0 \wedge \boldsymbol{L}_k^C))], \qquad (7.58)
$$

so that by using equation (7.57) we can derive

$$
[\mathbf{X}_1 \wedge \mathbf{X}_2 \wedge \mathbf{X}_3 \wedge \mathbf{X}_4] = \sum_{i,j,k=1}^{3} \tilde{T}_{ijk} \alpha_{1234,i} l_{12,j}^B l_{34,k}^C = \tilde{T}(\boldsymbol{\alpha}_{1234}, \boldsymbol{L}_{12}^B, \boldsymbol{L}_{34}^C). \quad (7.59)
$$

The invariant $\boldsymbol{Inv_3}$ can then be expressed as

$$
\boldsymbol{Inv_{3T}} = \frac{\tilde{T}(\boldsymbol{\alpha}_{1234}, \boldsymbol{L}_{12}^B, \boldsymbol{L}_{34}^C)\tilde{T}(\boldsymbol{\alpha}_{4526}, \boldsymbol{L}_{25}^B, \boldsymbol{L}_{26}^C)}{\tilde{T}(\boldsymbol{\alpha}_{1245}, \boldsymbol{L}_{12}^B, \boldsymbol{L}_{45}^C)\tilde{T}(\boldsymbol{\alpha}_{3426}, \boldsymbol{L}_{34}^B, \boldsymbol{L}_{26}^C)}. \qquad (7.60)
$$

Note that the factorization must be done so that the same line factorizations occur in both the numerator and denominator. We have thus developed an expression for invariants in three views that is a direct extension of the expression for invariants using two views. In calculating the above invariant from observed quantities, we note, as before, that some correction factors will be necessary: equation (7.60) is given above in terms of R^4 quantities. Fortunately, this correction is quite straightforward. By extrapolating from the results of the previous section, we simply consider the $\boldsymbol{\alpha}'s$ terms in equation (7.60) as unobservable quantities, and conversely the line terms, such as $\boldsymbol{L}^B_{12}, \boldsymbol{L}^C_{34}$, are indeed observed quantities. As a result, the expression must be modified, by using to some extent the coefficients computed in the previous section. Thus, for the unique four combinations of three cameras their invariant equations can be expressed as

$$\boldsymbol{Inv_{3T}} = \frac{T(\boldsymbol{a}_{1234}, \boldsymbol{l}^B_{12}, \boldsymbol{l}^C_{34})T(\boldsymbol{a}_{4526}, \boldsymbol{l}^B_{25}, \boldsymbol{l}^C_{26})\ \mu_{1245}(\mu_{3426}-1)}{T(\boldsymbol{a}_{1245}, \boldsymbol{l}^B_{12}, \boldsymbol{l}^C_{45})T(\boldsymbol{a}_{3426}, \boldsymbol{l}^B_{34}, \boldsymbol{l}^C_{26})\ \mu_{4526}(\mu_{1234}-1)}. \tag{7.61}$$

7.5.3 Comparison of the projective invariants

Invariants using F				Invariants using T			
0.000	0.590	0.670	0.460	0.000	0.590	0.310	0.630
	0	0.515	0.68		0	0.63	0.338
		0.59	0			0.134	0.67
			0.69				0.29

0.063	0.650	0.750	0.643	0.044	0.590	0.326	0.640
	0.67	0.78	0.687		0	0.63	0.376
		0.86	0.145			0.192	0.67
			0.531				0.389

0.148	0.600	0.920	0.724	0.031	0.100	0.352	0.660
	0.60	0.96	0.755		0.031	0.337	0.67
		0.71	0.97			0.31	0.67
			0.596				0.518

0.900	0.838	0.690	0.960	0.000	0.640	0.452	0.700
	0.276	0.693	0.527		0.063	0.77	0.545
		0.98	0.59			0.321	0.63
			0.663				0.643

FIGURE 7.5. Distance matrices showing performance of invariants after increasing Gaussian noise σ (σ=0.005, 0.015, 0.025, and 0.04)

This section presents simulations for the computation of invariants (implemented in Maple) using synthetic data, as well as computations using real images.

The computation of the bilinearity matrix F and the trilinearity focal tensor T was done using a linear method. We believe that for test purposes, this method is reliable. Four different sets of six points $S_i = \{\boldsymbol{X}_{i1}, \boldsymbol{X}_{i2}, \boldsymbol{X}_{i3}, \boldsymbol{X}_{i4}, \boldsymbol{X}_{i5}, \boldsymbol{X}_{i6}\}$, where $i = 1, ..., 4$, were considered in the simulation and the only three possible invariants were computed for each set $\{I_{1,i}, I_{2,i}, I_{3,i}\}$. Then, the invariants of each set were represented as 3D vectors ($\mathbf{v}_i = [I_{1,i}, I_{2,i}, I_{3,i}]^T$). For the first group of images, we computed four of these vectors that corresponded to four different sets of six points, using two images for the F case and three images for the T case. For the second group of images, we computed the same four vectors , but we used two new images for the F case or three new images for the T case. The comparison of the invariants was done using Euclidean distances of the vectors $d(\mathbf{v}_i, \mathbf{v}_j) = (1 - |\frac{\mathbf{v}_i \cdot \mathbf{v}_j}{||\mathbf{v}_i|| ||\mathbf{v}_j||}|)^{\frac{1}{2}}$, which is the same method used in [44].

Since in $d(\mathbf{v}_i, \mathbf{v}_j)$ we normalize the vectors $\mathbf{v}_i$ and $\mathbf{v}_j$, the distance $d(\mathbf{v}_i, \mathbf{v}_j)$ for any of them lies between 0 and 1, and the distance does not vary when $\mathbf{v}_i$ or $\mathbf{v}_j$ is multiplied by a non-zero constant. Fig. 7.5 shows a comparison table where each (i, j)-th entry represents the distance $d(\mathbf{v}_i, \mathbf{v}_j)$ between the invariants of set S_i, which are the points extracted from the first group of images, and those of set S_j, the points from the second group of images. In the ideal case, the diagonal of the distance matrices should be zero, which means that the values of the computed invariants should remain constant regardless of which group of images they were used for. The entries off the diagonal are comparisons for vectors composed of different coordinates ($\mathbf{v}_i = [I_{1,i}, I_{2,i}, I_{3,i}]^T$), and thus are not parallel. Accordingly, these entries should be larger than zero, and if they are very large, the value of $d(\mathbf{v}_i, \mathbf{v}_j)$ should be approximately 1. The figure clearly shows that the performance of the invariants based on trilinearities is much better than that of the invariants based on bilinearities, since the diagonal values for T are in general closer to zero than is the case for F, and since T entries off the diagonal are in general bigger values than is the case for F entries.

In the case of real images, we used a sequence of images taken by a moving robot equipped with a binocular head. Fig. 7.6 shows these images for the left and right eye, respectively. We took image couples, one from the left and one from the right, for the invariants using F, and two from the left and one from the right for the invariants using T. From the image, we selected thirty-eight points semi-automatically, and from these we chose six sets of points. In each set, the points are in general position. Three invariants of each set were computed and comparison tables were constructed in the same manner as for the tables of the previous experiment (see Fig. 7.7).

The data show once again that computing the invariants using a trilinear approach is much more robust than using a bilinear approach, a result which is also borne out in theory.

FIGURE 7.6. Image sequence taken during navigation by the binocular head of a mobile robot (left camera images are shown in upper row; right camera images in lower row)

using F

0.04	0.79	0.646	0.130	0.679	0.89
	0.023	0.2535	0.278	0.268	0.89
		0.0167	0.723	0.606	0.862
			0.039	0.808	0.91
				0.039	0.808
					0.039

using T

0.021	0.779	0.346	0.930	0.759	0.81
	0.016	0.305	0.378	0.780	0.823
		0.003	0.83	0.678	0.97
			0.02	0.908	0.811
				0.008	0.791
					0.01

FIGURE 7.7. Distance matrices show the performance of the computed invariants using bilinearities (top) and trilinearities (bottom) for the image sequence

7.6 Visually guided grasping

This section presents a practical use of projective invariants using three views. The results will show that despite a certain noise sensitivity in the projective invariants, they can be used for various tasks regardless of camera calibration or coordinate system.

We will apply simple geometric rules using meet or join operations, invariants, and points at infinity to the task of grasping, as depicted in Fig. 7.8.a. The grasping procedure uses only image points and consists basically of four steps.

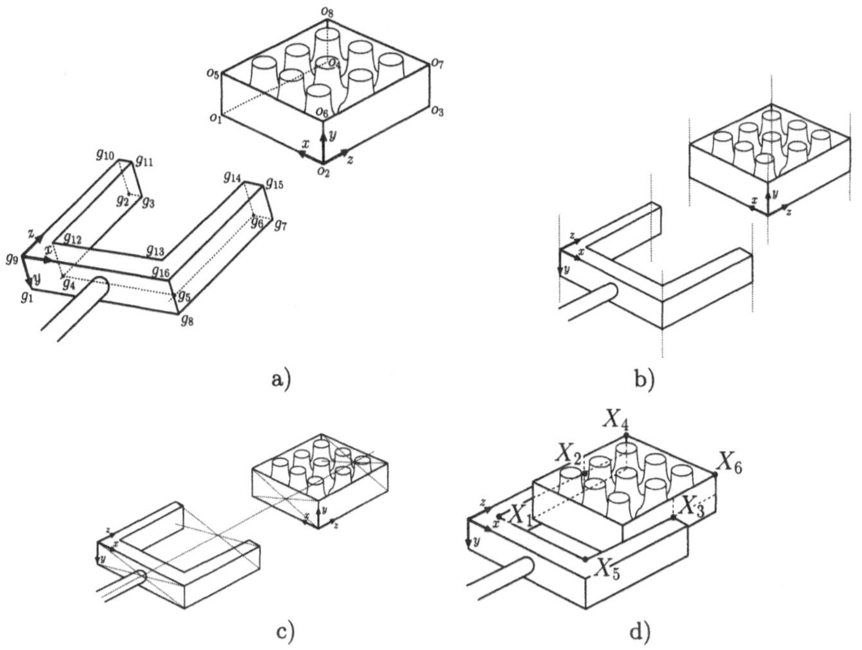

FIGURE 7.8. Grasping an object: (a) arbitrary starting position; (b) parallel orienting; (c) centering; (d) grasping and holding

7.6.1 Parallel orienting

Let us assume that the 3D points of Fig. 7.8 are observed by three cameras A, B, C. The mapped points in the three cameras are $\{\boldsymbol{o}_{A_i}\}$, $\{\boldsymbol{g}_{A_i}\}$, $\{\boldsymbol{o}_{B_i}\}$, $\{\boldsymbol{g}_{B_i}\}$, and $\{\boldsymbol{o}_{C_i}\}$, $\{\boldsymbol{g}_{C_i}\}$. In the projective 3D space P^3, the three points at infinity $\boldsymbol{V_x}, \boldsymbol{V_y}, \boldsymbol{V_z}$ for the orthogonal corners of the object can be computed as the meet of two parallel lines. Similarly, in the images planes, the *points at infinity* $\boldsymbol{v_x}, \boldsymbol{v_y}, \boldsymbol{v_z}$ are also computed as the meet of the two projected parallel lines:

$$
\begin{aligned}
\boldsymbol{V}_x &= (\boldsymbol{O}_1 \wedge \boldsymbol{O}_2) \cap (\boldsymbol{O}_5 \wedge \boldsymbol{O}_6) \rightarrow \boldsymbol{v}_{j_x} = (\boldsymbol{o}_{j_1} \wedge \boldsymbol{o}_{j_2}) \cap (\boldsymbol{o}_{j_5} \wedge \boldsymbol{o}_{j_6}), \\
\boldsymbol{V}_y &= (\boldsymbol{O}_1 \wedge \boldsymbol{O}_5) \cap (\boldsymbol{O}_2 \wedge \boldsymbol{O}_6) \rightarrow \boldsymbol{v}_{j_y} = (\boldsymbol{o}_{j_1} \wedge \boldsymbol{o}_{j_5}) \cap (\boldsymbol{o}_{j_2} \wedge \boldsymbol{o}_{j_6}), \\
\boldsymbol{V}_x &= (\boldsymbol{O}_1 \wedge \boldsymbol{O}_4) \cap (\boldsymbol{O}_2 \wedge \boldsymbol{O}_3) \rightarrow \boldsymbol{v}_{j_z} = (\boldsymbol{o}_{j_1} \wedge \boldsymbol{o}_{j_4}) \cap (\boldsymbol{o}_{j_2} \wedge \boldsymbol{o}_{j_3}), (7.62)
\end{aligned}
$$

where $j \in \{A, B, C\}$. The parallelism in the projective space P^3 can be checked in two ways. First, if the orthogonal edges of the grasper are parallel with the edges of the object, then

$$
(\boldsymbol{G}_1 \wedge \boldsymbol{G}_8) \wedge \boldsymbol{V}_x = 0, \quad (\boldsymbol{G}_1 \wedge \boldsymbol{G}_9) \wedge \boldsymbol{V}_y = 0, \quad (\boldsymbol{G}_1 \wedge \boldsymbol{G}_2) \wedge \boldsymbol{V}_z = 0. \quad (7.63)
$$

In this case, the conditions of equation (7.63), using the points obtained from a single camera, can be expressed as

$$[\boldsymbol{g}_{i_1}\boldsymbol{g}_{i_8}\boldsymbol{v}_{i_x}] = 0, \qquad [\boldsymbol{g}_{i_1}\boldsymbol{g}_{i_9}\boldsymbol{v}_{i_y}] = 0, \qquad [\boldsymbol{g}_{i_1}\boldsymbol{g}_{i_2}\boldsymbol{v}_{i_z}] = 0. \tag{7.64}$$

The second way to check the parallelism in the projective space P^3 is to note whether the perpendicular planes of the grasper and those of the object are parallel. If they are, then

$$[\boldsymbol{G}_1\boldsymbol{G}_8\boldsymbol{O}_1\boldsymbol{O}_2] = 0, \quad [\boldsymbol{G}_{15}\boldsymbol{G}_{16}\boldsymbol{O}_5\boldsymbol{O}_8] = 0, \quad [\boldsymbol{G}_{12}\boldsymbol{G}_{13}\boldsymbol{O}_3\boldsymbol{O}_4] = 0. \tag{7.65}$$

In this case, the conditions of equation (7.65) can be expressed in terms of image coordinates by using either the points obtained from two cameras (the bilinear constraint) or those obtained from three cameras (the trifocal tensor):

$$\begin{aligned}
\boldsymbol{x}^T_{j_{g_1 g_8 o_1 o_2}} F_{ij} \boldsymbol{x}_{i_{g_1 g_8 o_1 o_2}} &= 0,\\
\boldsymbol{x}^T_{j_{g_{15} g_{16} o_5 o_8}} F_{ij} \boldsymbol{x}_{i_{g_{15} g_{16} o_5 o_8}} &= 0,\\
\boldsymbol{x}^T_{j_{g_{12} g_{13} o_3 o_4}} F_{ij} \boldsymbol{x}_{i_{g_{12} g_{13} o_3 o_4}} &= 0, \qquad (7.66)\\
T_{ijk} \boldsymbol{x}_{i_{g_1 g_8 o_1 o_2}} \boldsymbol{l}_{j_{g_1 g_8}} \boldsymbol{l}_{k_{o_1 o_2}} &= 0,\\
T_{ijk} \boldsymbol{x}_{i_{g_{15} g_{16} o_5 o_8}} \boldsymbol{l}_{j_{g_{15} g_{16}}} \boldsymbol{l}_{k_{o_5 o_8}} &= 0,\\
T_{ijk} \boldsymbol{x}_{i_{g_{12} g_{13} o_3 o_4}} \boldsymbol{l}_{j_{g_{12} g_{13}}} \boldsymbol{l}_{k_{o_3 o_4}} &= 0. \qquad (7.67)
\end{aligned}$$

If the trinocular geometry is known, it is always more accurate to use equations (7.67).

7.6.2 Centering

After an initial movement the grasper should be parallel to and centered in front of the object (see Fig. 7.8.b). The center points of the grasper and object can be computed as follows:

$$\boldsymbol{C}_o = (\boldsymbol{O}_1 \wedge \boldsymbol{O}_6) \cap (\boldsymbol{O}_2 \wedge \boldsymbol{O}_5), \qquad \boldsymbol{C}_g = (\boldsymbol{G}_1 \wedge \boldsymbol{G}_{16}) \cap (\boldsymbol{G}_8 \wedge \boldsymbol{G}_9). \tag{7.68}$$

We can then check whether the line crossing through these center points eventually encounters the point at infinity $\boldsymbol{V}_z$, which is the intersecting point of the parallel lines $\boldsymbol{O}_{j_1} \wedge \boldsymbol{O}_{j_4}$ and $\boldsymbol{O}_{j_2} \wedge \boldsymbol{O}_{j_3}$. For that, we use the constraint which posits that a point is true if it lies on a line such that

$$\boldsymbol{C}_o \wedge \boldsymbol{C}_g \wedge \boldsymbol{V}_z = 0. \tag{7.69}$$

This equation, computed using the image points of a single camera, is given by

$$[\boldsymbol{c}_{i_o}\boldsymbol{c}_{i_g}\boldsymbol{v}_{i_z}] = 0. \tag{7.70}$$

7.6.3 Grasping

We can evaluate the exactitude of grasping when the plane of the grasper touches the plane of the object. This can be done by checking the following coplanar plane condition:

$$[\boldsymbol{C}_o \boldsymbol{C}_g \boldsymbol{o}_1 \boldsymbol{o}_2] = 0. \tag{7.71}$$

Since we want to use image points, we can compute this bracket straightforwardly by using the points obtained from either two or three cameras, employing, respectively, either the bilinear or the trilinear constraint:

$$\begin{aligned} \boldsymbol{x}^T_{j_{c_o c_g o_1 o_2}} F_{ij} \boldsymbol{x}_{i_{c_o c_g o_1 o_2}} &= 0, \\ T_{ijk} \boldsymbol{x}_{i_{c_o c_g o_1 o_2}} \boldsymbol{l}_{j_{c_o c_g}} \boldsymbol{l}_{k_{o_1 o_2}} &= 0. \end{aligned} \tag{7.72}$$

If the epipolar or trinocular geometry is known, it is always more accurate to use equation (7.72).

7.6.4 Holding the object

The final step is to hold the object correctly (see Fig. 7.8.d). This can be checked using the invariant in terms of the trifocal tensor given by equation (7.61). In this particular problem, an example of a perfect condition would be if the invariant had an approximate value of $\frac{3}{4}$, which would then change to perhaps $\frac{6}{8}$ or $\frac{5}{6}$ when the grasper is distanced a bit from the control point $\boldsymbol{X}_2$, $\boldsymbol{X}_3$. Note, too, that the invariant elegantly relates volumes, indicating a particular relationship between the points of the grasper and those of the object.

7.7 Camera Self-localization

We will now use equation (7.34) to compute the 3D coordinates for a moving, uncalibrated camera. For this problem, we first select as a projective basis five fixed points in 3D space, $\boldsymbol{X}_1$, $\boldsymbol{X}_2$, $\boldsymbol{X}_3$, $\boldsymbol{X}_4$, $\boldsymbol{X}_5$, and we consider the unknown point $\boldsymbol{X}_6$ to be the optical center of the moving camera (see Fig. 7.7). Assuming that the camera does not move on a plane, the projection of the optical center $\boldsymbol{X}_6$ of the first camera position should correspond to the epipole in any of the subsequent views.

We can now compute the moving optical center using points from either two cameras,

$$I_x^F = \frac{X_6}{W_6} = \frac{(\boldsymbol{\delta}^T{}_{2346} \boldsymbol{F} \boldsymbol{\epsilon}_{2346})(\boldsymbol{\delta}^T{}_{1235} \boldsymbol{F} \boldsymbol{\epsilon}_{1235})}{(\boldsymbol{\delta}^T{}_{2345} \boldsymbol{F} \boldsymbol{\epsilon}_{2345})(\boldsymbol{\delta}^T{}_{1236} \boldsymbol{F} \boldsymbol{\epsilon}_{1236})} \frac{\mu_{2345}\lambda_{2345}\mu_{1236}\lambda_{1236}}{\mu_{2346}\lambda_{2346}\mu_{1235}\lambda_{1235}}, \tag{7.73}$$

or three cameras,

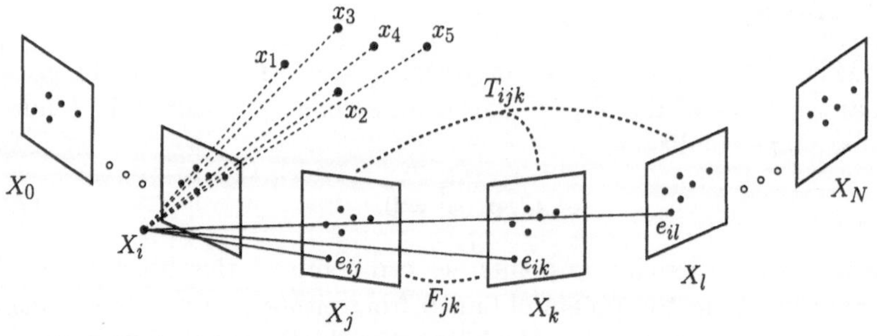

FIGURE 7.9. Computing the view-centers of a moving camera

$$\begin{aligned} I_x^T &= \frac{X_6}{W_6} \qquad (7.74) \\ &= \frac{(\boldsymbol{T}_{ijk}^{ABC}\alpha_{2346,i}l^B{}_{23,j}l^C{}_{46,k})(\boldsymbol{T}_{mnp}^{ABC}\alpha_{1235,m}l^B{}_{12,n}l^C{}_{35,p})}{(\boldsymbol{T}_{qrs}^{ABC}\alpha_{2345,q}l^B{}_{23,r}l^C{}_{45,s})(\boldsymbol{T}_{tuv}^{ABC}\alpha_{1236,t}l^B{}_{12,u}l^C{}_{36,v})} \frac{\mu_{2345}\mu_{1236}}{\mu_{2346}\mu_{1235}}. \end{aligned}$$

Similarly, by permuting the six points, as in equation (7.35), we compute I_y^F, I_y^T and I_z^F, I_z^T. The compensating coefficients for the invariants I_y and I_z vary due to the permuted points. We also simulated the computation of the invariants by increasing noise. Fig. 7.7 shows the deviation of the true optical center for three consecutive positions of a moving camera, using two views and three views, repectively.

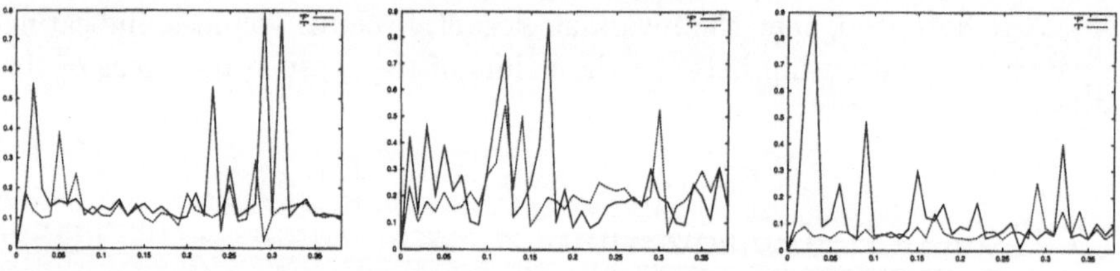

FIGURE 7.10. Computing performance of any three view-centers using F (higher spikes) and T (lower spikes); range of additive noise, 0–0.4 pixels

The figure demonstrates that trinocular computation renders more accurate results than binocular computation. The Euclidean coordinates of the optical centers are calculated by applying a transformation, which relates the projective basis to its a priori Euclidean basis.

7.8 Projective Depth

In a geometric sense *projective depth* can be defined as the relation between the distance from the view-center of a 3D point $\boldsymbol{X}_i$ and the focal distance f, as depicted in Fig. 7.11.

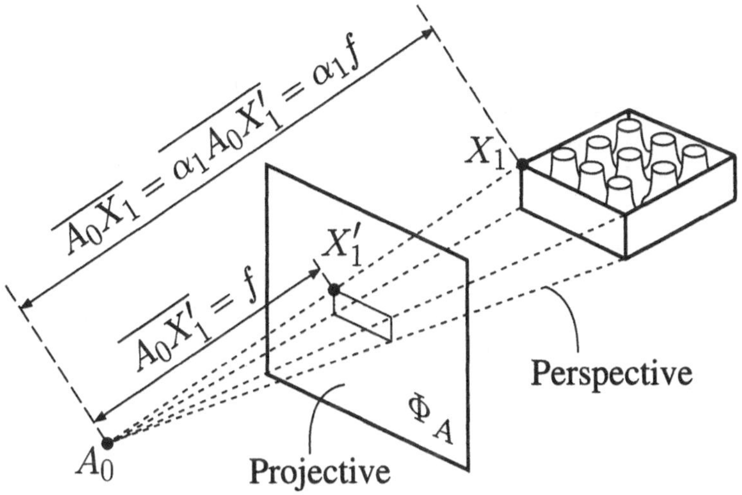

FIGURE 7.11. Geometric interpretation of projective depth

We can derive projective depth from a projective mapping of 3D points. According to the pinhole model explained in Chapter 4, the coordinates of any point in the image plane are obtained from the projection of the 3D point to the three optical planes ϕ_A^1, ϕ_A^2, ϕ_A^3. They are spanned by a trivector basis $\gamma_i, \gamma_j, \gamma_k$ and the coefficients t_{ij}. This projective mapping in a matrix representation reads as

$$\begin{aligned} \lambda \boldsymbol{x} &= \begin{bmatrix} x \\ y \\ 1 \end{bmatrix} = \begin{bmatrix} \phi_A^1 \\ \phi_A^2 \\ \phi_A^3 \end{bmatrix} \boldsymbol{X} = \begin{bmatrix} t_{11} & t_{12} & t_{13} & t_{14} \\ t_{21} & t_{22} & t_{23} & t_{24} \\ t_{31} & t_{32} & t_{33} & t_{34} \end{bmatrix} \begin{bmatrix} X \\ Y \\ Z \\ 1 \end{bmatrix} \\ &= \begin{bmatrix} f & 0 & 0 \\ 0 & f & 0 \\ 0 & 0 & 1 \end{bmatrix} \begin{bmatrix} r_{11} & r_{12} & r_{13} & t_x \\ r_{21} & r_{22} & r_{23} & t_y \\ r_{31} & r_{32} & r_{33} & t_z \\ 0 & 0 & 0 & 1 \end{bmatrix} \begin{bmatrix} X \\ Y \\ Z \\ 1 \end{bmatrix}, \end{aligned} \tag{7.75}$$

where the projective scale factor is called λ . Note that the projective mapping is further expressed in terms of a f, rotation, and translation components. Let us attach the world coordinates to the view-center of the camera. The resultant projective mapping becomes

$$\lambda \boldsymbol{x} = \begin{bmatrix} f & 0 & 0 & 0 \\ 0 & f & 0 & 0 \\ 0 & 0 & 1 & 0 \end{bmatrix} \begin{bmatrix} X \\ Y \\ Z \\ 1 \end{bmatrix} \equiv P\boldsymbol{X}. \tag{7.76}$$

We can then straightforwardly compute

$$\lambda = Z. \tag{7.77}$$

The method for computing the projective depth ($\equiv \lambda$) of a 3D point appears simple using invariant theory, i.e., using equation (7.34). For this computation, we select a basis system, taking four 3D points in general position $\boldsymbol{X}_1$, $\boldsymbol{X}_2$, $\boldsymbol{X}_3$, $\boldsymbol{X}_5$, and the optical center of camera at the new position as the four point $\boldsymbol{X}_4$, and $\boldsymbol{X}_6$ as the 3D point which has to be reconstructed. This process is shown in Fig. 7.12.

Since we are using mapped points, we consider the *epipole* (mapping of the current view-center) to be the fourth point and the mapped sixth point to be the point with unknown depth. The other mapped basis points remain constant during the procedure.

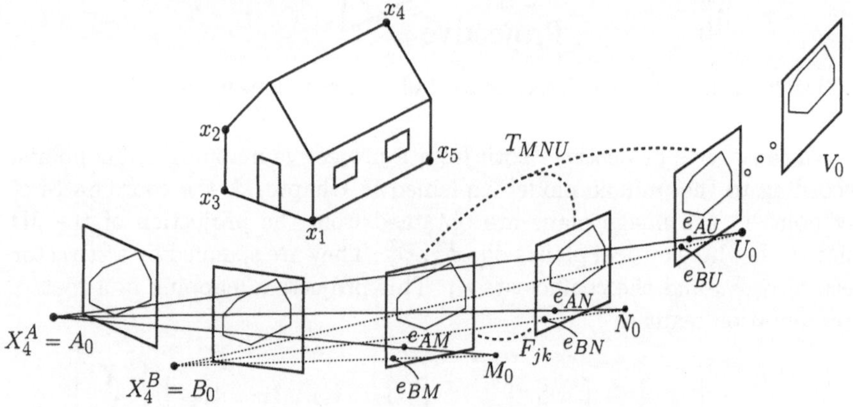

FIGURE 7.12. Computing the projective depths of n cameras

According to equation (7.34), the tensor-based expression for the computation of the third coordinate, or projective depth, of a point $\boldsymbol{X}_j$ ($= \boldsymbol{X}_6$) is given by

$$\lambda_j = \frac{Z_j}{W_j} = \frac{T(\boldsymbol{a}_{124j}, \boldsymbol{l}^B_{12}, \boldsymbol{l}^C_{4j}) T(\boldsymbol{a}_{1235}, \boldsymbol{l}^B_{12}, \boldsymbol{l}^C_{35})}{T(\boldsymbol{a}_{1245}, \boldsymbol{l}^B_{12}, \boldsymbol{l}^C_{45}) T(\boldsymbol{a}_{123j}, \boldsymbol{l}^B_{12}, \boldsymbol{l}^C_{3j})} \cdot \frac{\mu_{1245}\mu_{123j}}{\mu_{124j}\mu_{1235}}. \tag{7.78}$$

In this way, we can successively compute the projective depths λ_{ij} of the j-points relating to the i-camera. We will use λ_{ij} in section 7.9, in which we employ the join-image concept and singular value decomposition (SVD) for *singular value decomposition* 3D reconstruction.

Since this type of invariant can also be expressed in terms of the quadrifocal tensor [66], we are also able to compute projective depth based on four cameras.

7.9 Shape and Motion

The orthographic and paraperspective *factorization method for shape and motion* using the affine camera model was developed by Tomasi, Kanade, and Poelman [81, 105]. This method works for cameras viewing small and distant scenes, and thus for all scale factors of projective depth λ_{ij}=1. In the case of perspective images, the scale factors λ_{ij} are unknown. According to Triggs [107], all λ_{ij} satisfy a set of consistency reconstruction equations of the so-called *join − image*. One way to compute λ_{ij} is by using the epipolar constraint. If we use a matrix representation, this is given by

$$F_{ik}\lambda_{ij}\boldsymbol{x}_{ij} = \boldsymbol{e}_{ik} \wedge \lambda_{kj}\boldsymbol{x}_{kj}, \tag{7.79}$$

which, after computing an inner product with $\boldsymbol{e}_{ik} \wedge x_{kj}$, gives the relation of projective depths for the j-point between camera i and k:

$$\lambda'_{kj} = \frac{\lambda_{kj}}{\lambda_{ij}} = \frac{(\boldsymbol{e}_{ik} \wedge \boldsymbol{x}_{kj})F_{ik}\boldsymbol{x}_{ij}}{||\boldsymbol{e}_{ik} \wedge \boldsymbol{x}_{kj}||^2}. \tag{7.80}$$

Considering the i-camera as a reference, we can normalize λ_{kj} for all k-cameras and use λ'_{kj} instead. If that is not the case, we can normalize between neighbor images in a chained relationship [107].

In section 7.8, we presented a better procedure for the computing of λ_{ij} involving three cameras. An extension of equation (7.80), however, in terms of the trifocal or quadrifocal tensor is awkward and unpractical.

7.9.1 The join-image

The *Join-image* $\mathcal{J}$ is nothing more than the intersections of optical rays and planes with points or lines in 3D projective space, as depicted in Fig. 7.13. The interrelated geometry can be linearly expressed by the fundamental matrix and trifocal and quadrifocal tensors. The reader will find more information about these linear constraints in Chapter 4.

In order to take into account the interrelated geometry, the *projective reconstruction* procedure should bring together all the data of the individual images in a geometrically coherent manner. We do this by considering the points $\boldsymbol{X}_j$ for each i-camera,

$$\lambda_{ij}\boldsymbol{x}_{ij} = P_i\boldsymbol{X}_j, \tag{7.81}$$

as the i-row points of a matrix of rank 4. For m cameras and n points, the $3m \times n$ matrix $\mathcal{J}$ of the join-image is given by

$$\mathcal{J} = \begin{pmatrix} \lambda_{11}\boldsymbol{x}_{11} & \lambda_{12}\boldsymbol{x}_{12} & \lambda_{13}\boldsymbol{x}_{13} & . & . & . & \lambda_{1n}\boldsymbol{x}_{1n} \\ \lambda_{21}\boldsymbol{x}_{21} & \lambda_{22}\boldsymbol{x}_{22} & \lambda_{23}\boldsymbol{x}_{23} & . & . & . & \lambda_{2n}\boldsymbol{x}_{2n} \\ \lambda_{31}\boldsymbol{x}_{31} & \lambda_{32}\boldsymbol{x}_{32} & \lambda_{33}\boldsymbol{x}_{33} & . & . & . & \lambda_{3n}\boldsymbol{x}_{3n} \\ . & . & . & . & . & . & . \\ . & . & . & . & . & . & . \\ . & . & . & . & . & . & . \\ \lambda_{m1}\boldsymbol{x}_{m1} & \lambda_{m2}\boldsymbol{x}_{m2} & \lambda_{m3}\boldsymbol{x}_{m3} & . & . & . & \lambda_{mn}\boldsymbol{x}_{mn} \end{pmatrix}. \quad (7.82)$$

For the affine reconstruction procedure, the matrix is of rank 3. The matrix $\mathcal{J}$ of the join-image is therefore amenable to a singular value decomposition for the computation of the shape and motion [81, 105].

7.9.2 The SVD method

The application of SVD to $\mathcal{J}$ gives

$$\mathcal{J}_{3m\times n} = U_{3m\times r} S_{r\times r} V^T_{n\times r}, \quad (7.83)$$

where the columns of matrix $V^T_{n\times r}$ and $U_{3m\times r}$ constitute the orthonormal base for the input (co-kernel) and output (range) spaces of $\mathcal{J}$. In order to get a decomposition in motion and shape of the projected point structure, $S_{r\times r}$ can be absorbed into both matrices, $V^T_{n\times r}$ and $U_{3m\times r}$, as follows:

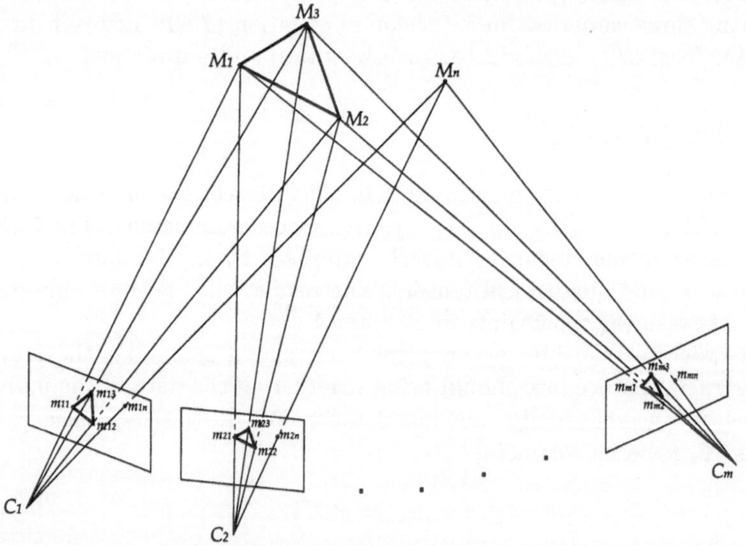

FIGURE 7.13. Geometry of the join-image

$$\mathcal{J}_{3m\times n} = (U_{3m\times r}S^{\frac{1}{2}}_{r\times r})(S^{\frac{1}{2}}_{r\times r}V^T_{n\times r}) = \begin{pmatrix} P_1 \\ P_2 \\ P_3 \\ \cdot \\ \cdot \\ \cdot \\ P_m \end{pmatrix}_{3m\times 4} (\boldsymbol{X}_1\boldsymbol{X}_2\boldsymbol{X}_3 ... \boldsymbol{X}_n)_{4\times n}. \tag{7.84}$$

Using this method to divide $S_{r\times r}$ is not unique. Since the rank of $\mathcal{J}$ is 4, we should use the first four biggest singular values for $S_{r\times r}$. The matrices P_i correspond to the projective mappings or *motion* from the projective space to the individual images, and $\boldsymbol{X}_j$ represents the point structure or *shape*. We can test our approach by using a simulation program written in Maple. Using the method described in Section 7.8, we first compute the projective depth of the points of a wire house observed with nine cameras, and we then use SVD to obtain the house's shape and motion. The reconstructed house, after the Euclidean readjustment for the presentation, is shown in Fig. 7.14.

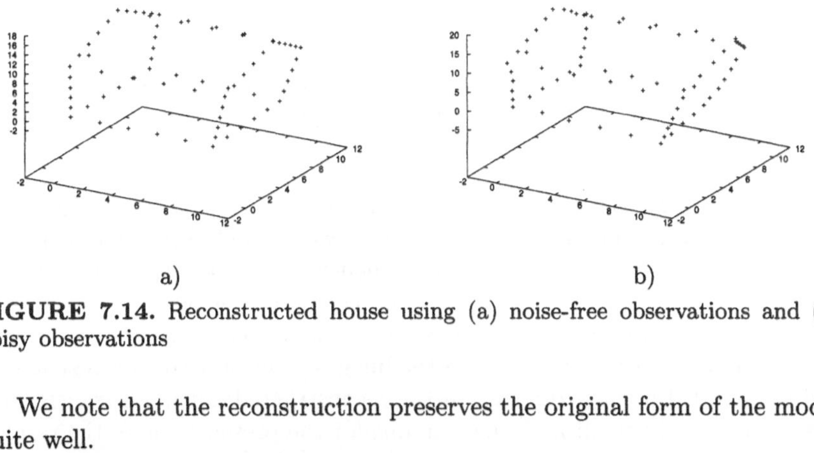

a) b)

FIGURE 7.14. Reconstructed house using (a) noise-free observations and (b) noisy observations

We note that the reconstruction preserves the original form of the model quite well.

In the following section, we will show how to improve the shape of the reconstructed model by using the geometric expressions $\cap$ (meet) and $\wedge$ (join) from the algebra of incidence along with particular tensor-based invariants.

7.9.3 Completion of the 3D shape using invariants

Projective structure can be improved in one of two ways: (1) by adding points on the images, expanding the join- image, and then applying the SVD procedure; or (2) after the reconstruction is done, by computing new or occluded 3D space points. Both approaches can use, on the one hand, geometric inference rules based on symmetries, or on the other, concrete knowledge about

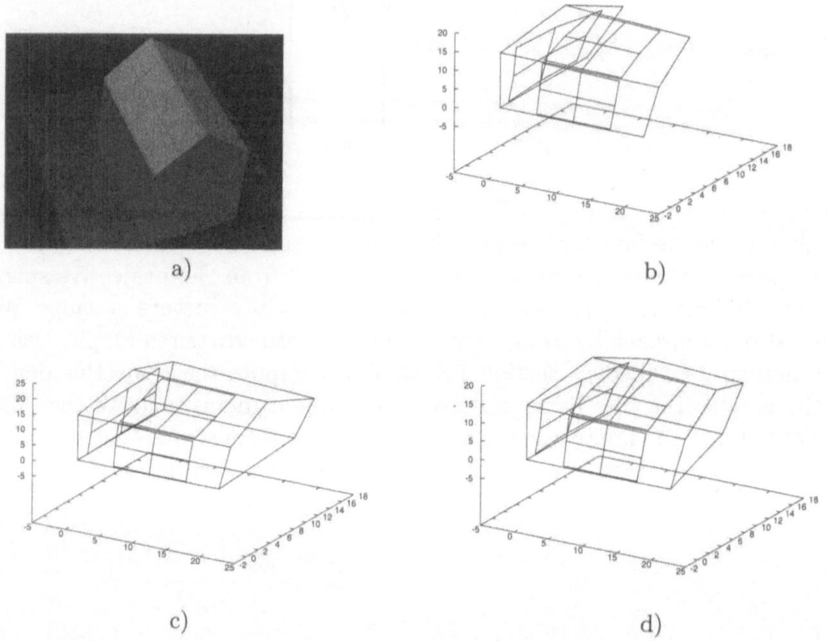

FIGURE 7.15. 3D reconstruction using three images: (a) one of the three images; (b) reconstructed incomplete house using three images; (c) extending the join-image; (d) completing in the 3D space

the object. Using three real views of a similar model house with its rightmost lower corner missing (see Fig. 7.15.b), we computed in each image the virtual image point of this 3D point. Then we reconstructed the scene, as shown in Fig. 7.15.c. We also tried using geometric incidence operations to complete the house, employing space points as depicted in Fig. 7.15.d. The figures show that creating points in the images yields a better reconstruction of the occluded point. Note that in the reconstructed image we transformed the projective shape into a Euclidean one for the presentation of the results. We also used lines to connect the reconstructed points but only so as to make the form of the house visible. Similarly, we used the same procedures to reconstruct the house using nine images, see Fig. 7.16.a-d.

The figure shows that the resulting reconstructed point is virtually the same in both cases, which allows us to conclude that for a limited number of views the join- image procedure is preferable, but for the case of several images, an extension of the point structure in the 3D space is preferable.

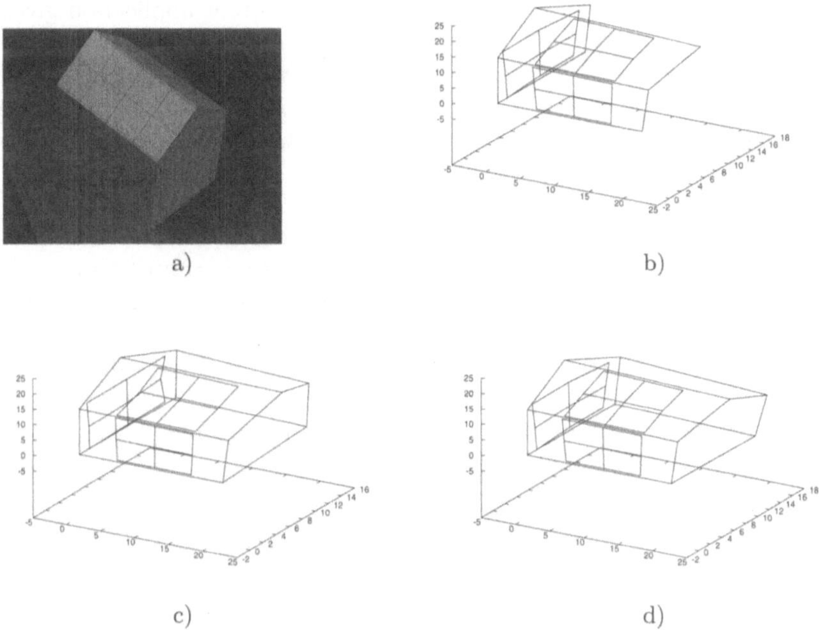

FIGURE 7.16. 3D reconstruction using nine images: (a) one of the nine images; (b) reconstructed incomplete house using nine images; (c) extending the join-image; (d) completing in the 3D space

7.10 Conclusion

In this chapter, we presented the theory of projective invariants and its application for n-uncalibrated cameras within a geometric algebra framework. We first showed how projective invariants can be used to compute the view-center of a moving camera. We also developed geometric rules for a task of visually guided grasping. Our purpose here was to motivate the reader to apply invariants from a geometric point of view and take advantage of the power of the algebra of incidence.

Next, using a trifocal tensor-based projective invariant, we developed a method for the computation of projective depths, which in turn were used to initiate an SVD procedure for the projective reconstruction of shape and motion. Further, we applied the rules of incidence algebra to complete the reconstruction, for example, in the critical case of occluded points.

The main contribution of this chapter is that we were able to demonstrate a simple way to unify current approaches for the computation and application of projective invariants using n-uncalibrated cameras. We formulated Pascal's theorem as a projective invariant of conics. This invariant was then used to solve the camera calibration problem. Simple illustrations, such as camera self-localization and visually guided grasping, show the potential of the use of projective invariants, points at infinity, and geometric rules developed using the algebra of incidence. The most important application given is the projective reconstruction of shape and motion. Remarkably, the use of trifocal, tensor-based, projective invariants allows for the computing of the projective depths required for the initialization of the SVD procedure to compute shape and motion. In this way, we were able to link the use of n-views-based projective invariants with SVD projective reconstruction methods.

The bracket algebra involved in the computation of the presented projective invariants is noise sensitive. We believe that to compute as we did is a promising approach for high-level geometric reasoning, especially if better ways to cope with the noise can be found. One promising approach, which should be explored further, might be to express the bracket equations as polynomials and then to look for their Gröbner basis. This helps to calculate the exact number of real solutions which satisfy certain geometric constraints arising from physical conditions.

8. Rigid Motion Estimation Using Line Observations

8.1 Introduction

This chapter is dedicated to the estimation of 3D Euclidean transformation using motor algebra. Two illustrations of estimation procedures are given: the first uses a batch approach for the estimation of the unknown 3D transformation between the coordinate reference systems of a robot neck, or arm, and of a digital camera. This problem is called the hand–eye problem and it is solved using a motion-of-lines model. The second illustration uses a recursive estimation method based on Kalman filter techniques. After introducing the motor extended Kalman filter (MEKF), we estimate 3D rigid motion using the MEKF and 3D lines gained by a visual robot system. These two approaches show that the task of estimating 3D rigid motion is easier using motor algebra because the motion-of-lines model is linear. This chapter benefits by work done in colaboration with Daniilidis and Zang [8, 12, 26].

8.2 Batch Estimation Using SVD Techniques

In this section we will illustrate the use of motor algebra for solving an exemplary task of visually guided robotics. We choose the so- called hand–eye calibration problem. This kind of task may be found in the area of visually guided robotics, where cameras are attached to robot arms or mounted on a vehicle and they have to be directed toward a goal. On the one hand, the cameras capture visual cues in the 3D visual space and employ their own world reference coordinate system. On the other hand, the robot arm or vehicle moves relative to a reference coordinate system. If we compute the intrinsic and extrinsic parameters through the camera's movements, we can find the geometrical relationship between the camera position and the world coordinates. The position of the robot arm or vehicle, on the other hand, is always known, owing to the angular position of the step motors of the device, which are permanently controlled by the computer. The problem of hand–eye calibration arises when we try to determine the group transformation between the reference coordinates of the mechanical device and the coordinate frame of the camera.

An abstraction of the geometry of a camera mounted on a robot arm is depicted in Fig. 8.1. The classical way to describe the hand–eye problem in

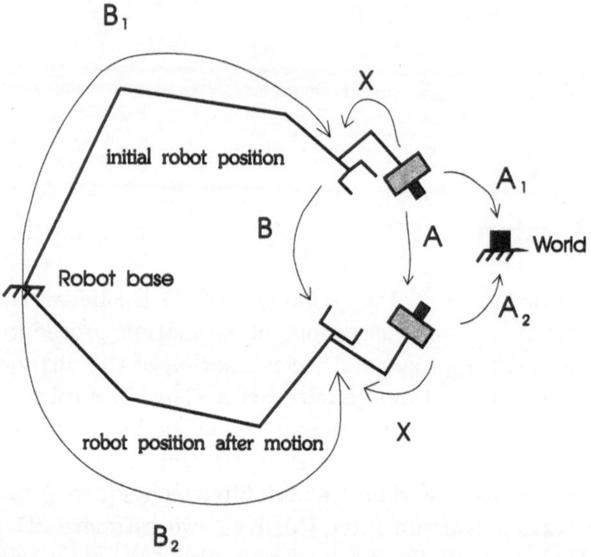

FIGURE 8.1. Abstraction of the hand–eye system

mathematical terms is by using transformation matrices. This problem was originally formulated by Shiu and Ahmad [97] and Tsai and Lenz [108] as a matrix equation of a Euclidean transformation:

$$\mathrm{AX}=\mathrm{XB}, \tag{8.1}$$

where the matrices $\mathrm{A} = \mathrm{A}_1\ \mathrm{A}_2^{-1}$ and $\mathrm{B} = \mathrm{B}_1\mathrm{B}_2^{-1}$ express the elimination of the transformation between hand–base and world. From equation (8.1), the following matrix equation and a vector equation can be derived by splitting the Euclidean transformation into rotation and translation components:

$$\mathrm{R}_A\mathrm{R}_X = \mathrm{R}_X\mathrm{R}_B \tag{8.2}$$

$$(\mathrm{R}_A - \mathrm{I})\mathrm{t}_X = \mathrm{R}_X\mathrm{t}_B - \mathrm{t}_A. \tag{8.3}$$

In the literature we find a variety of methods to estimate the rotation matrix R_X from equation (8.2) (see the survey by Wang [112]), most of which first estimate the rotation matrix decoupled from the translation component. Tsai and Lenz showed that to solve the problem at least two motions are required, with rotations having no parallel axes [108]. The most relevant approaches employ either the axis and the angle of rotation [97, 108], quaternions [22], dual quaternions [39] or a canonical matrix representation [68].

Horaud and Dornaika [56] were the first to apply a nonlinear method to compute R_X and t_X simultaneously. In their work, they showed the instability of the computation of the matrices A_i, given the projective matrices $M_i = SA_i = SR_{A_i}St_{A_i}$, where S is the matrix of the camera-intrinsic parameters. Let us assume that the matrix of the intrinsic parameters S remains constant during camera motion and that one extrinsic calibration A_2 is known. By introducing $N_i = SR_{A_i}$ and $n_i = St_{A_i}$ and replacing $X = A_2Y$, we get as the hand–eye unknown Y. Thus, equation (8.1) can be reformulated as

$$A_2^{-1}\, A_1\, Y = YB. \tag{8.4}$$

Now, if $A_2^{-1}A_1$ is written as a function of the projection parameters, it is possible to obtain an expression fully independent of the intrinsic parameters S, that is,

$$A_2^{-1}A_1 = \begin{bmatrix} N_2^{-1}N_1 & N_2^{-1}(\, n_1 - n_2) \\ 0_3^T & 1 \end{bmatrix} = \begin{bmatrix} R & t \\ 0_3^T & 1 \end{bmatrix}. \tag{8.5}$$

Taking into consideration the selected matrices and relations, this result allows us to reconsider the formulation of the hand–eye problem employing the standard equation (8.1), which can then be solved using all the known methods, including the one presented in this chapter.

Another relevant contribution to the hand–eye problem was made by Chen [18]. Employing a geometric point of view, he formulated the hand–eye calibration problem using screw theory. Using this method, Chen discovered that the hand–eye transformation is fully independent of the pitch and the angle of the camera and hand motions. The unknown transformation simply depends upon the parameters which relate to the screw axis lines of the hand motion and of the camera motion. In this chapter, we will use a unitary motor that is completely isomorphic with the unit screw, and we will present an algorithm, different from the one used by Horaud and Dornaika [56], to compute rotation and translation simultaneously in a linear manner.

8.2.1 Solving AX = XB using motor algebra

In terms of motors, system equation (8.1) can be expressed as

$$\boldsymbol{M}_A \boldsymbol{M}_X = \boldsymbol{M}_X \boldsymbol{M}_B \tag{8.6}$$

or as

$$\boldsymbol{M}_A = \boldsymbol{M}_X \boldsymbol{M}_B \tilde{\boldsymbol{M}}_X, \tag{8.7}$$

where $\boldsymbol{M}_A = \boldsymbol{A} + I\boldsymbol{A}'$, $\boldsymbol{M}_B = \boldsymbol{B} + I\boldsymbol{B}'$, and $\boldsymbol{M}_X = \boldsymbol{R} + I\boldsymbol{R}'$. Next, we simplify this equation to show the motor relation between the motor line axis of the camera $\boldsymbol{L}_A$ and the motor line axis of the hand $\boldsymbol{L}_B$.

We can isolate the scalar part of $\boldsymbol{M}_A$ by using the grade operator $\langle \boldsymbol{M}_A \rangle_0 \equiv \langle \boldsymbol{M}_A \rangle$, according to equation (2.24), and we can then use the previous equation to get

$$\begin{aligned}
\langle \boldsymbol{M}_A \rangle &= \frac{1}{2}(\boldsymbol{M}_X \boldsymbol{M}_B \tilde{\boldsymbol{M}}_X + \boldsymbol{M}_X \tilde{\boldsymbol{M}}_B \tilde{\boldsymbol{M}}_X) \\
&= \frac{1}{2}\boldsymbol{M}_X(\boldsymbol{M}_B + \tilde{\boldsymbol{M}}_B)\tilde{\boldsymbol{M}}_X = \boldsymbol{M}_X \langle \boldsymbol{M}_B \rangle \tilde{\boldsymbol{M}}_X \\
&= \boldsymbol{M}_X \tilde{\boldsymbol{M}}_X \langle \boldsymbol{M}_B \rangle = \langle \boldsymbol{M}_B \rangle. \qquad (8.8)
\end{aligned}$$

Thus, we are able to equalize the scalar parts of $\boldsymbol{M}_A$ and $\boldsymbol{M}_B$, and then, using equation (2.6), we obtain

$$cos(\frac{\theta_A}{2} + I\frac{d_A}{2}) = cos(\frac{\theta_B}{2} + I\frac{d_B}{2}), \qquad (8.9)$$

which may also be written by separating the real and dual terms:

$$\begin{aligned}
cos(\frac{\theta_A}{2}) &= cos(\frac{\theta_B}{2}) \\
d_A sin(\frac{\theta_A}{2}) &= d_B sin(\frac{\theta_B}{2}). \qquad (8.10)
\end{aligned}$$

In this way, we are sure that only the bivector terms of $\boldsymbol{M}_A$ and $\boldsymbol{M}_B$ will contribute to the computation of the unknown $\boldsymbol{M}_X$. Finally, using equation (2.6), the hand–eye equation reduces to

$$\begin{aligned}
sin(\frac{\theta_A}{2} + I\frac{d_A}{2})\boldsymbol{L}_A &= \boldsymbol{M}_X(sin(\frac{\theta_B}{2} + I\frac{d_B}{2})\boldsymbol{L}_B)\tilde{\boldsymbol{M}}_X \\
&= sin(\frac{\theta_B}{2} + I\frac{d_B}{2})\boldsymbol{M}_X \boldsymbol{L}_B \tilde{\boldsymbol{M}}_X. \qquad (8.11)
\end{aligned}$$

If θ_A and θ_B do not abandon the range from 0 to 360 degrees, we can neglect the sines to get the simplified expression

$$\boldsymbol{L}_A = \boldsymbol{M}_X \boldsymbol{L}_B \tilde{\boldsymbol{M}}_X, \qquad (8.12)$$

which shows that in this kind of problem formulation, the rotation and pitch of $\boldsymbol{M}_A$ and $\boldsymbol{M}_B$ are always equal throughout all the hand movements and therefore can be ignored in the computations. It will suffice to focus on only the rotation axes of the involved motors— that is, equation (8.12) is reduced to just the motion of the line axis of the hand $\boldsymbol{L}_B$ toward the line axis of the camera $\boldsymbol{L}_A$. This characteristic, known as the congruence theorem, has been pointed out by Chen [18]. However, thanks to the use of motor algebra, the proof of this theorem has now been reduced to a single step, shown by equation (8.8). This simplification of the hand–eye problem is depicted in Fig. 8.2.

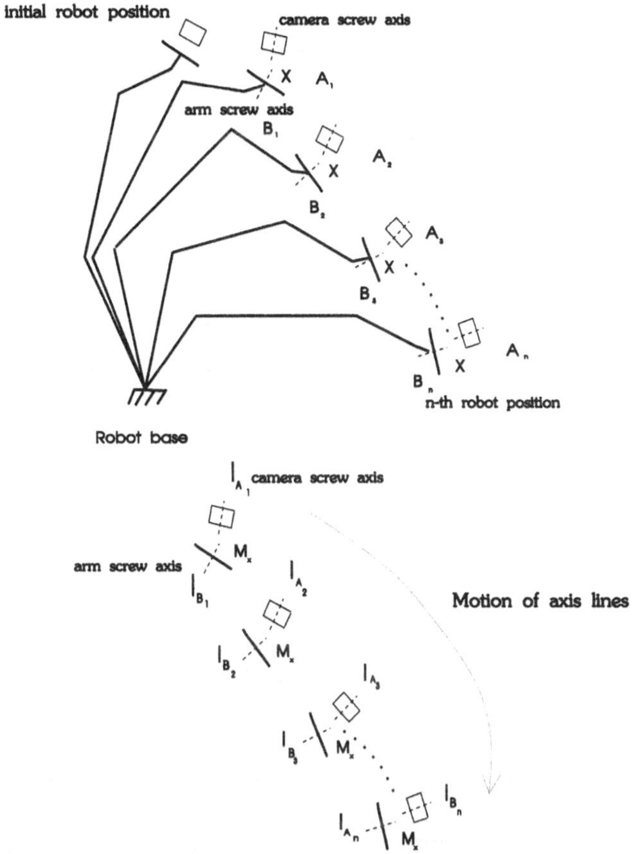

FIGURE 8.2. The hand–eye system as the motion of related axes lines

Since the hand–eye problem pertains to the motion of lines, equation (2.42) can be used to estimate the unknown 3D transformation which relates to the screw line axes of both the hand and the camera:

$$\boldsymbol{L}_A = \boldsymbol{a} + I\boldsymbol{a}' = \boldsymbol{R}\boldsymbol{b}\tilde{\boldsymbol{R}} + I(\boldsymbol{R}\boldsymbol{b}\tilde{\boldsymbol{R}}' + \boldsymbol{R}\boldsymbol{b}'\tilde{\boldsymbol{R}} + \boldsymbol{R}'\boldsymbol{b}\tilde{\boldsymbol{R}}), \qquad (8.13)$$

where $\boldsymbol{a}$, $\boldsymbol{a}'$, $\boldsymbol{b}$, and $\boldsymbol{b}'$ are spanned by bivectors. Separating real and dual terms,

$$\begin{aligned} \boldsymbol{a} &= \boldsymbol{R}\boldsymbol{b}\tilde{\boldsymbol{R}} \\ \boldsymbol{a}' &= \boldsymbol{R}\boldsymbol{b}\tilde{\boldsymbol{R}}' + \boldsymbol{R}\boldsymbol{b}'\tilde{\boldsymbol{R}} + \boldsymbol{R}'\boldsymbol{b}\tilde{\boldsymbol{R}}, \end{aligned} \qquad (8.14)$$

and multiplying from the right with motor $\boldsymbol{R}$, using the relation $\tilde{\boldsymbol{R}}\boldsymbol{R}' + \tilde{\boldsymbol{R}}'\boldsymbol{R}$ $=0$, we get the following multivector relationships:

$$\begin{aligned} \boldsymbol{a}\boldsymbol{R} - \boldsymbol{R}\boldsymbol{b} &= 0 \\ (\boldsymbol{a}'\boldsymbol{R} - \boldsymbol{R}\boldsymbol{b}') + (\boldsymbol{a}\boldsymbol{R}' - \boldsymbol{R}'\boldsymbol{b}) &= 0. \end{aligned} \qquad (8.15)$$

These equations can be expressed in a matrix consisting of the scalar and bivector terms and the outer product as follows:

$$\begin{bmatrix} \boldsymbol{a}-\boldsymbol{b} & [\boldsymbol{a}+\boldsymbol{b}]_\times & \mathbf{0}_{3\times 1} & \mathbf{0}_{3\times 3} \\ \boldsymbol{a}'-\boldsymbol{b}' & [\boldsymbol{a}'+\boldsymbol{b}']_\times & \boldsymbol{a}-\boldsymbol{b} & [\boldsymbol{a}+\boldsymbol{b}]_\times \end{bmatrix} \begin{bmatrix} \boldsymbol{R} \\ \boldsymbol{R}' \end{bmatrix} = 0, \tag{8.16}$$

where the matrix—which we will call $\boldsymbol{D}$—is a 6×8 matrix, and the vector of unknowns $(\boldsymbol{R},\boldsymbol{R}')^T$ is eight-dimensional. The notation $[\boldsymbol{a}+\boldsymbol{b}]_\times$ stands for the vector cross-product as an antisymmetric matrix. Recall that we have two constraints on the unknowns, so that the result is a unit motor with the properties

$$\boldsymbol{R}\tilde{\boldsymbol{R}} = 1 \qquad \text{and} \qquad \boldsymbol{R}\boldsymbol{R}' = 0. \tag{8.17}$$

So far, we have six equations and two constraints. However, because the unit bivectors $\boldsymbol{a}$ and $\boldsymbol{b}$ are perpendicular to the bivectors $\boldsymbol{a}'$ and $\boldsymbol{b}'$, respectively, we conclude that two of the equations are necessarily redundant. That is not a surprise, really, because we already know that at least two lines are required to estimate 3D motion from their pertinent correspondences [90]. The result is that at least two motions of the hand–eye system are required in order to compute two lines from the involved screws. Chen [18] clearly noted this fact and analyzed the uniqueness of the problem. He proved geometrically that even in the case of two parallel rotation axis lines, it is still possible to compute all the parameters up to the pitch.

8.2.2 Estimation of the hand–eye motor using SVD

We reduced the hand–eye problem to equation (8.16), which depends only on 3D bivectors. Now, for the estimation of the unknown rigid motion, we employ the singular value decomposition (SVD) method [85], which is actually a vector approach for finding singular values. We are able to use this method since we are dealing only with bivectors . If we were dealing with a simultaneous estimation of multivectors of different grade, we would, of course, extend the SVD method to encompass a multivector concept.

Let us consider that $n \geq 2$ motions are available. Employing SVD, we build the following $6n \times 8$ matrix:

$$\boldsymbol{C} = [\ \boldsymbol{D}_1^T \quad \boldsymbol{D}_2^T \quad \dots \quad \boldsymbol{D}_n^T\ ]^T. \tag{8.18}$$

Because 3D motion has six degrees of freedom, in the case of noise-free data, the greatest possible value of this matrix will be rank 6. Let us analyze this matrix in more detail. In the case of noise-free data, for which equations were calculated basically using geometric and algebraic concepts, we would expect that the null space necessarily contains at least the solution $(\boldsymbol{R}, \boldsymbol{R}')$. The solution $(\mathbf{0}_{4\times 1}, \boldsymbol{R})$ ("pure rotation") is the trivial one, and thus we are able to reaffirm that the matrix indeed has a maximum rank of 6. In the particular case where all the b-axis lines are mutually parallel, one degree of freedom remains constant; in this case, the matrix will be of rank 5.

For the solution of equation (8.18) we use the SVD method. This procedure decomposes the matrix $\boldsymbol{C}$ into three matrices, as follows: $\boldsymbol{C} = \boldsymbol{U}\boldsymbol{\Sigma}\boldsymbol{V}^T$. The columns of the $\boldsymbol{U}$ and $\boldsymbol{V}$ matrices correspond to the left and right singular vectors, respectively, and $\boldsymbol{\Sigma}$ is a diagonal matrix with singular values. Since the rank of the matrix $\boldsymbol{C}$ is 6, the last two right singular vectors $\boldsymbol{v}_7$ and $\boldsymbol{v}_8$ correspond to the two vanishing singular values which span the null space of $\boldsymbol{C}$. For convenience, these will now be expressed in terms of two 4×1 vectors, $\boldsymbol{v}_7^T = (\boldsymbol{u}_1, \boldsymbol{v}_1)^T$ and $\boldsymbol{v}_8^T = (\boldsymbol{u}_2, \boldsymbol{v}_2)^T$. Since $(\boldsymbol{R}, \boldsymbol{R}')^T$ is a null vector of $\boldsymbol{C}$, specifically $\boldsymbol{C}(\boldsymbol{R}, \boldsymbol{R}')^T = 0$, then it must be expressed as a linear combination of $\boldsymbol{v}_7$ and $\boldsymbol{v}_8$, as follows:

$$\begin{bmatrix} \boldsymbol{R} \\ \boldsymbol{R}' \end{bmatrix} = \alpha \begin{bmatrix} \boldsymbol{u}_1 \\ \boldsymbol{v}_1 \end{bmatrix} + \beta \begin{bmatrix} \boldsymbol{u}_2 \\ \boldsymbol{v}_2 \end{bmatrix}.$$

Now, taking into account the two degrees of freedom imposed by equation (8.17), we obtain two quadratic equations in α and β:

$$\alpha^2 \boldsymbol{u}_1^T \boldsymbol{u}_1 + 2\alpha\beta \boldsymbol{u}_1^T \boldsymbol{u}_2 + \beta^2 \boldsymbol{u}_2^T \boldsymbol{u}_2 = 1 \qquad (8.19)$$

$$\alpha^2 \boldsymbol{u}_1^T \boldsymbol{v}_1 + \alpha\beta(\boldsymbol{u}_1^T \boldsymbol{v}_2 + \boldsymbol{u}_2^T \boldsymbol{v}_1) + \beta^2 \boldsymbol{u}_2^T \boldsymbol{v}_2 = 0\ . \qquad (8.20)$$

If we take into consideration that $\alpha \neq 0$, and $\beta \neq 0$ and without loss of generality we assume that $\boldsymbol{u}_1^T \boldsymbol{v}_1 \neq 0$, we can set $\mu = \alpha/\beta$ and substitute in equation (8.20) to obtain two solutions for μ. We then substitute the relation $\alpha = \mu\beta$ into equation (8.19) to obtain the following quadratic expression:

$$\beta^2(\mu^2 \boldsymbol{u}_1^T \boldsymbol{u}_1 + \mu(2\boldsymbol{u}_1^T \boldsymbol{u}_2) + \boldsymbol{u}_2^T \boldsymbol{u}_2) = 1, \qquad (8.21)$$

which yields two solutions of opposite sign (this sign variation is simply an effect of sign invariance of the solution). Either term, $[\boldsymbol{R}, \boldsymbol{R}']^T$ or $[-\boldsymbol{R}, -\boldsymbol{R}']^T$, will satisfy the motion equations and the involved constraints.

Since the equation also contains μ squared, we should also consider the viability of the other two solutions. Here, we can see that the second solution for μ causes the factor on the left-hand side of equation (8.21) to disappear. This corresponds to the solution $(\boldsymbol{0}_{4\times 1}, \boldsymbol{R})$ and clearly does not satisfy the first constraint of equation (8.17). The algorithm, then, can be summarized as consisting of the following procedure:

1. Consider n hand motions $(\boldsymbol{b}_i, \boldsymbol{b}_i')$ and their corresponding camera motions $(\boldsymbol{a}_i, \boldsymbol{a}_i')$. Check to see if their scalar terms are equal (Chen's invariance theorem). By extracting the line directions and moments of the screw axes lines, construct the matrix $\boldsymbol{C}$ as in equation (8.18).

2. Apply the SVD procedure to $\boldsymbol{C}$ and check to see that two singular values are almost equal to zero. In the case of noisy data, keep the four largest singular values. Then select the related right singular vectors $\boldsymbol{v}_7$ and $\boldsymbol{v}_8$.

3. Set the coefficients for $\alpha^2 \boldsymbol{u}_1^T \boldsymbol{v}_1 + \alpha\beta(\boldsymbol{u}_1^T \boldsymbol{v}_2 + \boldsymbol{u}_2^T \boldsymbol{v}_1) + \beta^2 \boldsymbol{u}_2^T \boldsymbol{v}_2 = 0$, then solve, finding two solutions for μ.

4. Use these two values of μ to solve the equation $\beta^2(\mu^2 \boldsymbol{u}_1^T \boldsymbol{u}_1 + \mu(2\boldsymbol{u}_1^T \boldsymbol{u}_2) + \boldsymbol{u}_2^T \boldsymbol{u}_2) = 1$, and then select the solution with the largest value to compute α and then β.

5. The final solution will be $\alpha \boldsymbol{v}_7 + \beta \boldsymbol{v}_8$.

8.3 Experimental Results

In this section we test this algorithm to compare its performance with a two-step algorithm similar to the one introduced by Chou and Kamel [22]. These authors estimated quaternion rotation $\boldsymbol{q}$ directly from the equation $\boldsymbol{aq} = \boldsymbol{qb}$ and then they computed the rotation matrix R_X and solved the translation t_X component using the vector equation (8.3).

The experiments were carried out using a computer simulation. First, n hand motions $(\mathrm{R}_b, \mathrm{t}_b)$ were created and Gaussian noise with a relative standard deviation of 1% was added so as to simulate the inaccuracy of angle readings. To simulate the hand–eye scenario, we generated camera motions $(\mathrm{R}_a, \mathrm{t}_a)$, similarly adding Gaussian noise of varying standard deviation. In this case, the noise was added as absolute value to the rotation-axis direction and as relative value to both the angle and the translation. In order to compute the estimated rotor $\boldsymbol{R}$ and the translation component $\boldsymbol{t}$ between the hand and camera, the algorithm was run 1,000 times for each value of added noise. The quantification of both algorithms was done according to the root mean square (RMS) of the absolute errors in the rotation-unit rotor $\|\boldsymbol{R} - \hat{\boldsymbol{R}}\|$ and the RMS of the relative errors in the translation $\|\boldsymbol{t} - \hat{\boldsymbol{t}}\|/\|\boldsymbol{t}\|$.

For the first test, a set of 20 hand motions was prepared using different rotation axes and large rotation angles and a translation that varied from 10 to 20 mm. Fig. 8.3 compares the results of our algorithm, labeled MOTOR, and those of the two-step algorithm, labeled SEPARATE.

The upper graph shows RMS rotation error, and the lower graph shows RMS relative to translation error. Our algorithm substantially outperforms the two-step algorithm. By computing the rotation simultaneously with the translation, we were able to get a much better estimation of the rotation than was the case using a separate computation.

In the second test, we wanted to explore the estimation performance of both algorithms using zero translation. As expected, in this context the behavior of both algorithms is almost the same (see Fig. 8.4). This effect is easy to explain if we consider equation (8.16). Since the translation is zero, the dual parts of the measurements $(\boldsymbol{a}', \boldsymbol{b}')$ become zero. Therefore, the left lower block of the matrix in equation (8.16) will disappear, which obliges the separate computation of $\boldsymbol{R}$ and $\boldsymbol{R}'$.

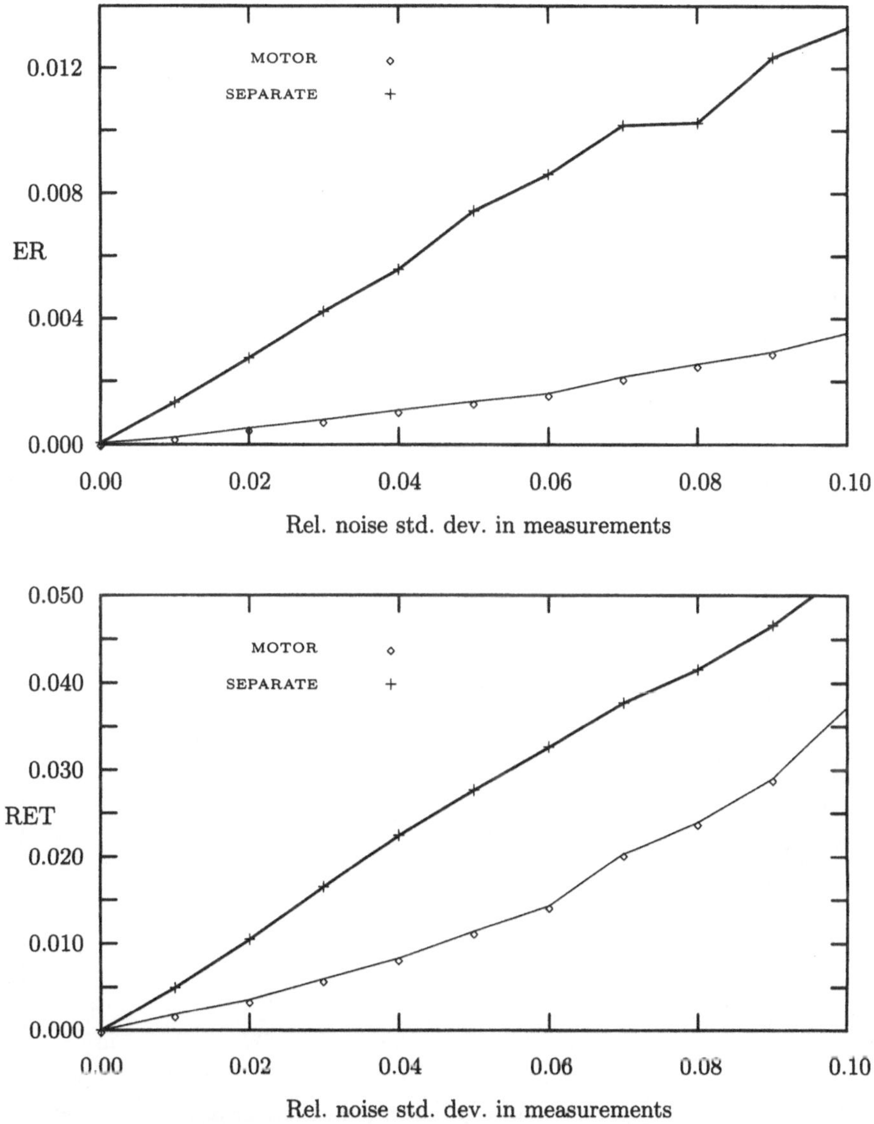

FIGURE 8.3. Behavior of the proposed algorithm (MOTOR) and of a two-step algorithm (SEPARATE) with noise variation. ER stands for error in rotation and RET for relative error in translation.

In the last experiment, we were interested in the performance of both algorithms when the noise level is kept constant and the number of motions is gradually increased. Generally speaking, one would expect much better estimation with the use of a greater number of hand and camera motions.

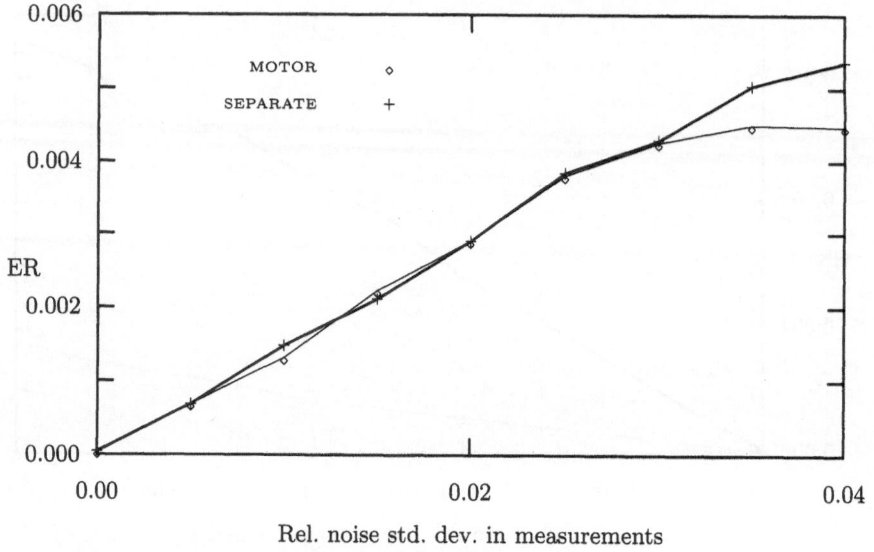

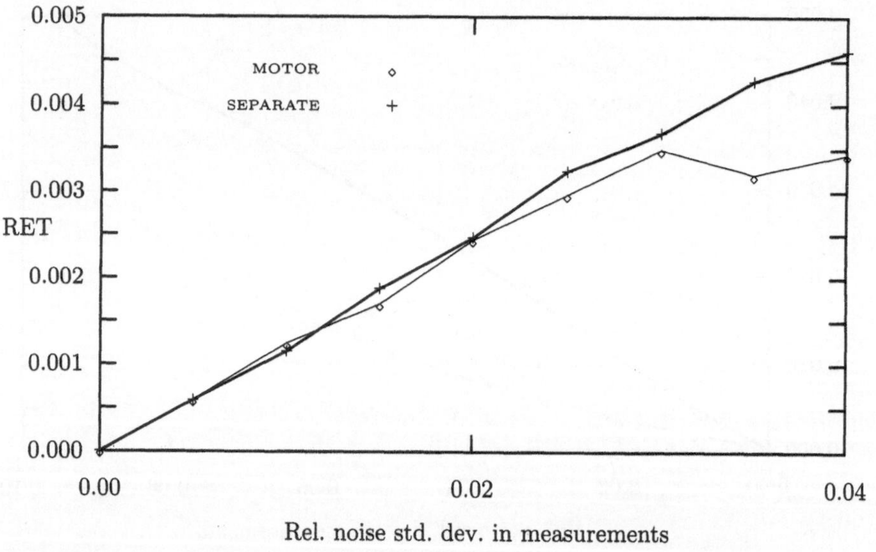

FIGURE 8.4. Performance of both algorithms in absence of translation

The noise level was kept at 5%, and the number of motions varied from 2 to 20. Fig. 8.5 shows that from the fourth motion onward our algorithm had a superior performance.

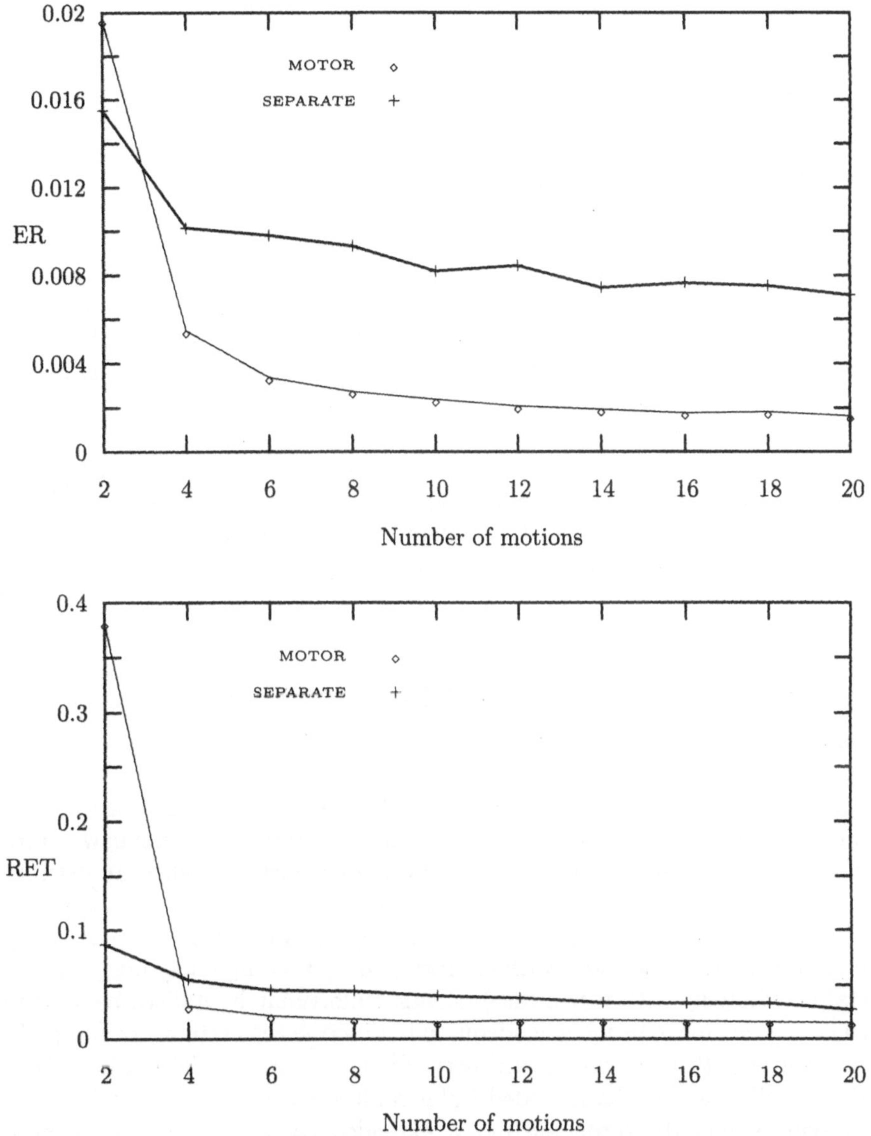

FIGURE 8.5. Errors in rotation (upper) and translation (below) as a function of the number of hand and camera motions

8.4 Discussion

This chapter proposes the Clifford, or geometric, algebra for computations in visually guided robotics. In looking for other suitable ways of representing the motion of geometric primitives, it turns out that the algebra of motors is well suited to express 3D kinematics, since its use allows us to linearize the nonlinear 3D rigid motion transformation.

In the literature it has been shown that the invariance of the angle and the pitch of the screws of the camera and hand help to reduce the complexity of the hand–eye calibration problem. We used this fundamental idea to simplify the hand–eye problem to a problem of motion of lines. For this case, we used the algebra of motors, which is indicated for problems involving the algebra of lines. The resultant simplified parameterization of the problem enabled us to establish a linear homogeneous system for calculating the motor parameters. By computing the null space using SVD and considering of a few of the constraints of dual rotors, we were able to devise a simple algorithm, one that obviates the need for nonlinear computations. In this work, it can be seen that the algebraic structure of the resultant equations helps us better to understand the performance of the algorithm.

The next section of this chapter is devoted to the application of Kalman filter techniques for the estimation of 3D rigid motion using 3D line observations. First, we will outline Kalman filter techniques and describe in detail the motor extended Kalman filter, then we will apply these techniques for 3D rigid motion estimation using observed lines captured by a robotic visual system.

8.5 Recursive Estimation Using Kalman Filter Techniques

The Kalman filter is a linear recursive algorithm that is unbiased and of minimum variance. It is employed to estimate optimally the unknown state of a linear dynamic system using noisy data which are taken at discrete real-time intervals. The extended Kalman filter (EKF) approach modifies the standard Kalman filter (used for linear systems) in order to treat noisy nonlinear systems. It starts with an initial guess, then updates this predicted state continually with new measurements. Unfortunately, if disturbances are so large that linearization is inadequate to describe the system, the filter will not converge to a reasonable estimate. First, we give a brief outline of the Kalman filter and of the extended Kalman filter; then, using this background we will explain the rotor and motor extended Kalman filters. For a more complete explanation, the reader is referred to [101].

8.5.1 The Kalman filter

Let us describe a dynamic system using a linear-difference-state equation, as follows:

$$\boldsymbol{X}_i = \boldsymbol{\Phi}_{i/i-1}\boldsymbol{X}_{i-1} + \boldsymbol{W}_i. \tag{8.22}$$

The state of the system at t_i is given by the n-dimensional vector $\boldsymbol{X}_i$. The term $\boldsymbol{\Phi}_{i/i-1}$ is an $n \times n$ transition matrix and $\boldsymbol{W}_i$ is the random error with the known first- and second-order characteristics

$$E[\boldsymbol{W}_i] = \boldsymbol{0}, \qquad i = 0, 1, ... \tag{8.23}$$
$$E[\boldsymbol{W}_i \boldsymbol{W}_j^T] = \mathcal{Q}_i \delta_{ij}, In \tag{8.24}$$

where δ_{ij} is the Kronecker delta function. The matrix $\mathcal{Q}_i$ is assumed to be extended Kalman filter (EKF).

Suppose that at each time t_i there is available an m-dimensional vector of measurement $\boldsymbol{Z}_i$ that is linearly related to the state and which is corrupted by the additive noise $\boldsymbol{V}_i$. This is the so called observation equation

$$\boldsymbol{Z}_i = \mathcal{H}_i \boldsymbol{X}_i + \boldsymbol{V}_i, \tag{8.25}$$

where $\mathcal{H}_i$ is a known $m \times n$ observation matrix, and the vector $\boldsymbol{V}_i$ a random error with the known statistics

$$E[\boldsymbol{V}_i] = \boldsymbol{0}, \qquad i = 0, 1, ... \tag{8.26}$$
$$E[\boldsymbol{V}_i \boldsymbol{V}_j^T] = \mathcal{C}_i \delta_{ij}, \tag{8.27}$$

where the matrix $\mathcal{C}_i$ is assumed to be non-negative definite [101].

Further, assume that the random processes $\boldsymbol{W}_i$ and $\boldsymbol{V}_i$ are uncorrelated, that is, for each i, j,

$$E[\boldsymbol{W}_i \boldsymbol{V}_j^T] = \mathcal{O}, \tag{8.28}$$

where $\mathcal{O}$ is the zero matrix.

Given the preceding models (8.22) and (8.25), we shall determine an estimate $\hat{\boldsymbol{X}}_i$ of the state at t_i that is a linear combination of an estimate $\hat{\boldsymbol{X}}_{i-1}$ at t_{i-1} and the data $\boldsymbol{Z}_i$ measured at time t_i. By defining an unknown $(n \times m)$ gain matrix $\mathcal{K}_i$, the estimate $\hat{\boldsymbol{X}}_i$ is given by

$$\hat{\boldsymbol{X}}_i = \boldsymbol{\Phi}_{i/i-1} \hat{\boldsymbol{X}}_{i-1} + \mathcal{K}_i [\boldsymbol{Z}_i - \mathcal{H}_i \boldsymbol{\Phi}_{i/i-1} \hat{\boldsymbol{X}}_{i-1}]. \tag{8.29}$$

The matrix $\mathcal{K}_i$ is determined so that the estimate has the minimal variance, That is, $\hat{\boldsymbol{X}}_i$ is chosen so as to minimize its mean squared error:

$$E_{MIN} = \{E[(\hat{\boldsymbol{X}}_i - \boldsymbol{X}_i)^T (\hat{\boldsymbol{X}}_i - \boldsymbol{X}_i)]\}_{MIN}. \tag{8.30}$$

Equation (8.30) is equivalent to the minimization of the trace of the state error covariance matrix $\mathcal{P}_i$, that is,

$$E_{MIN} = \{trace\ \mathcal{P}_i\}_{MIN} = \{trace\ E[(\hat{\boldsymbol{X}}_i - \boldsymbol{X}_i)(\hat{\boldsymbol{X}}_i - \boldsymbol{X}_i)^T]\}_{MIN}. \tag{8.31}$$

By substituting equation (8.25) into (8.29), and then substituting equations (8.29) and (8.22) into equation (8.31), it can be shown that the trace of the matrix $\mathcal{P}_i$ will be minimized by choosing the following optimal gain matrix $\mathcal{K}_i$,

$$\mathcal{K}_i = \mathcal{P}_{i/i-1}\mathcal{H}_i^T(\mathcal{H}_i\mathcal{P}_{i/i-1}\mathcal{H}_i^T + \mathcal{C}_i)^{-1}, \tag{8.32}$$

where $\mathcal{P}_{i/i-1}$ is the error covariance matrix

$$\mathcal{P}_{i/i-1} = \boldsymbol{\Phi}_{i/i-1}\mathcal{P}_i\boldsymbol{\Phi}_{i/i-1}^T + \mathcal{Q}_i \tag{8.33}$$

of the predicted state

$$\hat{\boldsymbol{X}}_{i/i-1} = \boldsymbol{\Phi}_{i/i-1}\hat{\boldsymbol{X}}_i. \tag{8.34}$$

With this optimal gain matrix $\mathcal{K}_i$, the matrix $\mathcal{P}_i$ reduces to

$$\mathcal{P}_i = \mathcal{P}_{i/i-1} - \mathcal{K}_i\mathcal{H}_i\mathcal{P}_{i/i-1} = (I - \mathcal{K}_i\mathcal{H}_i)\mathcal{P}_{i/i-1}. \tag{8.35}$$

Equations (8.29), (8.33), (8.32), and (8.35) constitute the Kalman filter equations for the model of the system (8.22) and that of the measurement (8.25), respectively.

From equation (8.32), we see that as the measurement error covariance matrix $\mathcal{C}_i$ approaches zero, the gain matrix $\mathcal{K}_i$ weights the residual second term of equation (8.29) more heavily:

$$\lim_{\mathcal{C}_i \to \mathcal{O}} \mathcal{K}_i = \mathcal{H}_i^{-1}. \tag{8.36}$$

On the other hand, as the estimated state error covariance $\mathcal{P}_i$ approaches zero, the gain $\mathcal{K}_i$ weights the residual second term of equation (8.29) less heavily:

$$\lim_{\mathcal{P}_i \to \mathcal{O}} \mathcal{K}_i = \mathcal{O}. \tag{8.37}$$

Another way of thinking about the control of the gain of the Kalman filter by $\mathcal{K}_i$ is to consider that as the measurement error covariance matrix $\mathcal{C}_i$ approaches zero, the actual measurement $\boldsymbol{Z}_i$ is "trusted" more and more, while the predicted state $\boldsymbol{\Phi}_{i/i-1}\hat{\boldsymbol{X}}_i$ is trusted less and less. On the other hand, as the estimated state error covariance $\mathcal{P}_i$ approaches zero the actual measurement $\boldsymbol{Z}_i$ is trusted less and less, while the predicted state $\boldsymbol{\Phi}_{i/i-1}\hat{\boldsymbol{X}}_i$ (the dynamic model) is trusted more and more.

8.5.2 The extended Kalman filter

As described previously, the Kalman filter addresses the general problem of trying to estimate the state $\boldsymbol{X}_i$ of a discrete-time controlled process that is governed by a linear stochastic difference equation. But what happens if the process and/or the relation between the measurement and the state is nonlinear? Some of the most interesting and successful applications of Kalman filtering are concerned with just these types of situations. A Kalman filter that linearizes about the current predicted state $\hat{\boldsymbol{X}}_{i/i-1}$ and measurement $\boldsymbol{Z}_i$ is called an extended Kalman filter, or EKF.

In computer vision the measurement model is usually described by a nonlinear observation equation $\boldsymbol{f}_i(\boldsymbol{Z}_{0,i}, \boldsymbol{X}_i) = \boldsymbol{0}$, where the parameter $\boldsymbol{Z}_{0,i}$ is the accurate measurement. In practice, such a measurement is affected by random errors. We assume that the measurement system is disturbed by additive white noise

$$\boldsymbol{Z}_i = \boldsymbol{Z}_{0,i} + \boldsymbol{V}_i, \tag{8.38}$$

where the statistics of noise $\boldsymbol{V}_i$ is given by equations (8.26) and (8.27).

To apply the Kalman filter technique, we must expand the nonlinear observation equation into a first-order Taylor series about $(\boldsymbol{Z}_i, \hat{\boldsymbol{X}}_{i/i-1})$,

$$\begin{aligned}\boldsymbol{f}_i(\boldsymbol{Z}_{0,i}, \boldsymbol{X}_i) &= \boldsymbol{f}_i(\boldsymbol{Z}_i, \hat{\boldsymbol{X}}_{i/i-1}) + \frac{\partial \boldsymbol{f}_i(\boldsymbol{Z}_i, \hat{\boldsymbol{X}}_{i/i-1})}{\partial \boldsymbol{Z}_{0,i}}(\boldsymbol{Z}_{0,i} - \boldsymbol{Z}_i) + \\ &\quad \frac{\partial \boldsymbol{f}_i(\boldsymbol{Z}_i, \hat{\boldsymbol{X}}_{i/i-1})}{\partial \boldsymbol{X}_i}(\boldsymbol{X}_i - \hat{\boldsymbol{X}}_{i/i-1}) + \mathcal{O}^2 = \boldsymbol{0}. \end{aligned} \tag{8.39}$$

By ignoring the second-order term $\mathcal{O}^2$, the linearized measurement equation (8.39) becomes

$$\boldsymbol{Y}_i = \boldsymbol{\mathcal{H}}_i \boldsymbol{X}_i + \boldsymbol{N}_i, \tag{8.40}$$

where $\boldsymbol{Y}_i$ is the new measurement vector, $\boldsymbol{N}_i$ is the noise vector of the new measurement, and $\boldsymbol{\mathcal{H}}_i$ is the linearized transformation matrix. The components of equation (8.40) are given by

$$\begin{aligned}\boldsymbol{Y}_i &= -\boldsymbol{f}_i(\boldsymbol{Z}_i, \hat{\boldsymbol{X}}_{i/i-1}) + \frac{\partial \boldsymbol{f}_i(\boldsymbol{Z}_i, \hat{\boldsymbol{X}}_{i/i-1})}{\partial \boldsymbol{X}_i}\hat{\boldsymbol{X}}_{i/i-1}, \\ \boldsymbol{\mathcal{H}}_i &= \frac{\partial \boldsymbol{f}_i(\boldsymbol{Z}_i, \hat{\boldsymbol{X}}_{i/i-1})}{\partial \boldsymbol{X}_i}, \\ \boldsymbol{N}_i &= \frac{\partial \boldsymbol{f}_i(\boldsymbol{Z}_i, \hat{\boldsymbol{X}}_{i/i-1})}{\partial \boldsymbol{Z}_{0,i}}(\boldsymbol{Z}_{0,i} - \boldsymbol{Z}_i), \\ E[\boldsymbol{N}_i] &= \boldsymbol{0}, \\ E[\boldsymbol{N}_i \boldsymbol{N}_i^T] &= \boldsymbol{\mathcal{C}}_{i/i-1} = \frac{\partial \boldsymbol{f}_i(\boldsymbol{Z}_i, \hat{\boldsymbol{X}}_{i/i-1})}{\partial \boldsymbol{Z}_{0,i}} \boldsymbol{\mathcal{C}}_i \frac{\partial \boldsymbol{f}_i(\boldsymbol{Z}_i, \hat{\boldsymbol{X}}_{i/i-1})}{\partial \boldsymbol{Z}_{0,i}}^T,\end{aligned}$$

where $\boldsymbol{\mathcal{C}}_i$ is given by the statistics of the measurement (8.27). This linearized equation (8.40) is a general form for the nonlinear model. We will use this form for our particular nonlinear measurement model in Section 8.6.

8.5.3 The rotor-extended Kalman filter

This subsection describes an EKF algorithm to estimate rotors or quaternions. In the static case, the measurements of points free of error satisfy the conditions

$$\begin{aligned} \boldsymbol{R}_{i+1} &= \boldsymbol{R}_i, & (8.41)\\ \boldsymbol{p}'_{0,i+1} &= \mathcal{R}(\boldsymbol{R}_{i+1})\boldsymbol{p}_{0,i+1}, & (8.42) \end{aligned}$$

where $\{\boldsymbol{p}_{0,i}\}$ and $\{\boldsymbol{p}'_{0,i}\}$ are sets of points before and after rotation, respectively, and $\boldsymbol{R}_i$ is the rotation quaternion for the i-th pair of points $p_{0,i}$ and $p'_{0,i}$. $\mathcal{R}(\boldsymbol{R})$ is the matrix representation of $\boldsymbol{R}$,

$$\mathcal{R}(\boldsymbol{R}) = \begin{pmatrix} r_1^2+r_2^2-r_3^2-r_4^2 & 2(r_2r_3+r_1r_4) & 2(r_2r_4-r_1r_3) \\ 2(r_2r_3-r_1r_4) & r_1^2-r_2^2+r_3^2-r_4^2 & 2(r_4r_3+r_1r_2) \\ 2(r_2r_4+r_1r_3) & 2(r_4r_3-r_1r_2) & r_1^2-r_2^2-r_3^2+r_4^2, \end{pmatrix}, \quad (8.43)$$

where r_j for j = 1,2,3,4 represents the four components of $\boldsymbol{R}$ which satisfy the condition

$$\| \boldsymbol{R} \| = 1. \quad (8.44)$$

Let us assume that the measurements $\{\boldsymbol{p}_{i+1}\}$ and $\{\boldsymbol{p}'_{i+1}\}$ of $\{\boldsymbol{p}_{0,i+1}\}$ and $\{\boldsymbol{p}'_{0,i+1}\}$ are corrupted by noise $\{\boldsymbol{n}_{i+1}\}$ and $\{\boldsymbol{n}'_{i+1}\}$, respectively, such that

$$\begin{aligned} \boldsymbol{p}_{i+1} &= \boldsymbol{p}_{0,i+1} + \boldsymbol{n}_{i+1} & (8.45)\\ \boldsymbol{p}'_{i+1} &= \boldsymbol{p}'_{0,i+1} + \boldsymbol{n}'_{i+1}. & (8.46) \end{aligned}$$

Here, it is assumed that the noise vectors $\{\boldsymbol{n}_{i+1}\}$ and $\{\boldsymbol{n}'_{i+1}\}$ have zero mean and the respective covariance matrices $\{\boldsymbol{C}_{i+1}\}$ and $\{\boldsymbol{C}'_{i+1}\}$ are known.

We rewrite equation (8.42) as the function $\boldsymbol{f}_{i+1}$ depending on the variables $(\boldsymbol{p}_{0,i+1}, \boldsymbol{p}'_{0,i+1}, \boldsymbol{R}_{i+1})$:

$$\boldsymbol{f}_{i+1}(\boldsymbol{p}_{0,i+1}, \boldsymbol{p}'_{0,i+1}, \boldsymbol{R}_{i+1}) = \boldsymbol{p}'_{0,i+1} - \mathcal{R}(\boldsymbol{R}_{i+1})\boldsymbol{p}_{0,i+1} = \boldsymbol{0}. \quad (8.47)$$

Expanding this equation about $(\boldsymbol{p}_{i+1}, \boldsymbol{p}'_{i+1}, \hat{\boldsymbol{R}}_{i+1/i})$ in terms of the first-order Taylor series, we get

$$\begin{aligned} \boldsymbol{f}_{i+1}(\boldsymbol{p}_{0,i+1}, \boldsymbol{p}'_{0,i+1}, \boldsymbol{R}_{i+1}) &= \boldsymbol{f}_{i+1}(\boldsymbol{p}_{i+1}, \boldsymbol{p}'_{i+1}, \hat{\boldsymbol{R}}_{i+1/i}) + \\ &+ \frac{\partial \boldsymbol{f}_{i+1}(\boldsymbol{p}_{i+1}, \boldsymbol{p}'_{i+1}, \hat{\boldsymbol{R}}_{i+1/i})}{\partial \boldsymbol{p}'_{0,i+1}}(\boldsymbol{p}'_{0,i+1} - \boldsymbol{p}'_{i+1}) + \\ &+ \frac{\partial \boldsymbol{f}_{i+1}(\boldsymbol{p}_{i+1}, \boldsymbol{p}'_{i+1}, \hat{\boldsymbol{R}}_{i+1/i})}{\partial \boldsymbol{p}_{0,i+1}}(\boldsymbol{p}_{0,i+1} - \boldsymbol{p}_{i+1}) + \quad (8.48)\\ &+ \frac{\partial \boldsymbol{f}_{i+1}(\boldsymbol{p}_{i+1}, \boldsymbol{p}'_{i+1}, \hat{\boldsymbol{R}}_{i+1/i})}{\partial \boldsymbol{R}_{i+1}}(\boldsymbol{R}_{i+1} - \hat{\boldsymbol{R}}_{i+1/i}) + \mathcal{O}^2 = \boldsymbol{0}, \end{aligned}$$

where the second-order term $\mathcal{O}^2$ can be omitted, and therefore

$$\frac{\partial \boldsymbol{f}_{i+1}(\boldsymbol{p}_{i+1}, \boldsymbol{p}'_{i+1}, \hat{\boldsymbol{R}}_{i+1/i})}{\partial \boldsymbol{p}'_{0,i+1}} = 1, \tag{8.49}$$

$$\frac{\partial \boldsymbol{f}_{i+1}(\boldsymbol{p}_{i+1}, \boldsymbol{p}'_{i+1}, \hat{\boldsymbol{R}}_{i+1/i})}{\partial \boldsymbol{p}_{0,i+1}} = -\mathcal{R}(\hat{\boldsymbol{R}}_{i+1/i}), \tag{8.50}$$

$$\frac{\partial \boldsymbol{f}_{i+1}(\boldsymbol{p}_{i+1}, \boldsymbol{p}'_{i+1}, \hat{\boldsymbol{R}}_{i+1/i})}{\partial \boldsymbol{R}_{i+1}} = \frac{\partial \mathcal{R}(\hat{\boldsymbol{R}}_{i+1/i})\boldsymbol{p}_{i+1}}{\partial \boldsymbol{R}_{i+1}}. \tag{8.51}$$

In order to compute expression (8.51), we utilize the following vectors:

$$\boldsymbol{p}_{i+1} \cong (p_1 \quad p_2 \quad p_3)^T, \tag{8.52}$$

$$\boldsymbol{R}_{i+1} \cong (r_1 \quad r_2 \quad r_3 \quad r_4)^T \tag{8.53}$$

$$\hat{\boldsymbol{R}}_{i+1/i} \cong (\hat{r}_1 \quad \hat{r}_2 \quad \hat{r}_3 \quad \hat{r}_4)^T. \tag{8.54}$$

Thus, we can write

$$\mathcal{R}(\hat{\boldsymbol{R}}_{i+1/i})\boldsymbol{p}_{i+1} =$$
$$\begin{pmatrix} \hat{r}_1^2 + \hat{r}_2^2 - \hat{r}_3^2 - \hat{r}_4^2 & 2(\hat{r}_2\hat{r}_3 + \hat{r}_1\hat{r}_4) & 2(\hat{r}_2\hat{r}_4 - \hat{r}_1\hat{r}_3) \\ 2(\hat{r}_2\hat{r}_3 - \hat{r}_1\hat{r}_4) & \hat{r}_1^2 - \hat{r}_2^2 + \hat{r}_3^2 - \hat{r}_4^2 & 2(\hat{r}_4\hat{r}_3 + \hat{r}_1\hat{r}_2) \\ 2(\hat{r}_2\hat{r}_4 + \hat{r}_1\hat{r}_3) & 2(\hat{r}_4\hat{r}_3 - \hat{r}_1\hat{r}_2) & \hat{r}_1^2 - \hat{r}_2^2 - \hat{r}_3^2 + \hat{r}_4^2 \end{pmatrix} \begin{pmatrix} p_1 \\ p_2 \\ p_3 \end{pmatrix}$$
$$= (\hat{p}'_1 \quad \hat{p}'_2 \quad \hat{p}'_3)^T = \hat{\boldsymbol{p}}'_{i+1/i}.$$

The derivative of the vector $\hat{\boldsymbol{p}}'_{i+1/i}$ with respect to a vector $\boldsymbol{R}_{i+1}$ is of the form

$$\frac{\partial \mathcal{R}(\hat{\boldsymbol{R}}_{i+1/i})\boldsymbol{p}_{i+1}}{\partial \boldsymbol{R}_{i+1}} = \frac{\partial \hat{\boldsymbol{p}}'_{i+1/i}}{\partial \boldsymbol{R}_{i+1}} = \begin{pmatrix} \frac{\partial \hat{p}'_1}{\partial r_1} & \frac{\partial \hat{p}'_1}{\partial r_2} & \frac{\partial \hat{p}'_1}{\partial r_3} & \frac{\partial \hat{p}'_1}{\partial r_4} \\ \frac{\partial \hat{p}'_2}{\partial r_1} & \frac{\partial \hat{p}'_2}{\partial r_2} & \frac{\partial \hat{p}'_2}{\partial r_3} & \frac{\partial \hat{p}'_2}{\partial r_4} \\ \frac{\partial \hat{p}'_3}{\partial r_1} & \frac{\partial \hat{p}'_3}{\partial r_2} & \frac{\partial \hat{p}'_3}{\partial r_3} & \frac{\partial \hat{p}'_3}{\partial r_4} \end{pmatrix}. \tag{8.55}$$

Now, defining a 3×4 matrix $\mathcal{H}_{i+1/i} = -\frac{\partial \mathcal{R}(\hat{\boldsymbol{R}}_{i+1/i})\boldsymbol{p}_{i+1}}{\partial \boldsymbol{R}_{i+1}}$, we can write the previous equation as

$$-\mathcal{H}_{i+1/i} \stackrel{\text{def}}{=} \frac{\partial \mathcal{R}(\hat{\boldsymbol{R}}_{i+1/i})\boldsymbol{p}_{i+1}}{\partial \boldsymbol{R}_{i+1}} = \begin{pmatrix} h_1 & h_2 & h_3 & h_4 \\ h_4 & -h_3 & h_2 & -h_1 \\ -h_3 & -h_4 & h_1 & h_2 \end{pmatrix}, \tag{8.56}$$

where

$$h_1 = 2(\hat{r}_1 p_1 + \hat{r}_4 p_2 - \hat{r}_3 p_3), \quad h_2 = 2(\hat{r}_2 p_1 + \hat{r}_3 p_2 + \hat{r}_4 p_3),$$
$$h_3 = 2(-\hat{r}_3 p_1 + \hat{r}_2 p_2 - \hat{r}_1 p_3), \quad h_4 = 2(-\hat{r}_4 p_1 + \hat{r}_1 p_2 + \hat{r}_2 p_3).$$

By first substituting (8.56) into (8.51), and then substituting the resultant equation along with equations (8.49) and (8.50) into equation (8.48), we get an expression in which the second-order terms can be omitted, as follows:

$$\begin{aligned} \mathbf{0} &= \boldsymbol{p}'_{i+1} - \boldsymbol{\mathcal{R}}(\hat{\boldsymbol{R}}_{i+1/i})\boldsymbol{p}_{i+1} + (\boldsymbol{p}'_{0,i+1} - \boldsymbol{p}'_{i+1}) - \\ & -\boldsymbol{\mathcal{R}}(\hat{\boldsymbol{R}}_{i+1/i})(\boldsymbol{p}_{0,i+1} - \boldsymbol{p}_{i+1}) + \boldsymbol{\mathcal{H}}_{i+1/i}(\boldsymbol{R}_{i+1} - \hat{\boldsymbol{R}}_{i+1/i}). \end{aligned} \tag{8.57}$$

This equation can then be further rearranged as

$$\begin{aligned} & \boldsymbol{p}'_{i+1} - \boldsymbol{\mathcal{R}}(\hat{\boldsymbol{R}}_{i+1/i})\boldsymbol{p}_{i+1} + \boldsymbol{\mathcal{H}}_{i+1/i}\hat{\boldsymbol{R}}_{i+1/i} \\ & \quad = \boldsymbol{\mathcal{H}}_{i+1/i}\boldsymbol{R}_{i+1} + (\boldsymbol{p}'_{i+1} - \boldsymbol{p}'_{0,i+1}) - \boldsymbol{\mathcal{R}}(\hat{\boldsymbol{R}}_{i+1/i})(\boldsymbol{p}_{i+1} - \boldsymbol{p}_{0,i+1}). \end{aligned} \tag{8.58}$$

The terms of this equation are now identifiable as the measurement $\boldsymbol{z}_{i+1}$ and the noise of the measurement $\boldsymbol{n}_{i+1/i}$, as follows:

$$\boldsymbol{z}_{i+1} = \boldsymbol{p}'_{i+1} - \boldsymbol{\mathcal{R}}(\hat{\boldsymbol{R}}_{i+1/i})\boldsymbol{p}_{i+1} + \boldsymbol{\mathcal{H}}_{i+1/i}\hat{\boldsymbol{R}}_{i+1/i}, \tag{8.59}$$

$$\begin{aligned} \boldsymbol{n}_{i+1/i} &= (\boldsymbol{p}'_{i+1} - \boldsymbol{p}'_{0,i+1}) - \boldsymbol{\mathcal{R}}(\hat{\boldsymbol{R}}_{i+1/i})(\boldsymbol{p}_{i+1} - \boldsymbol{p}_{0,i+1}) \\ &= \boldsymbol{n}'_{i+1} - \boldsymbol{\mathcal{R}}(\hat{\boldsymbol{R}}_{i+1/i})\boldsymbol{n}_{i+1}. \end{aligned} \tag{8.60}$$

Using these variables we can finally write the first-order linearized measurement equation more compactly:

$$\boldsymbol{z}_{i+1} = \boldsymbol{\mathcal{H}}_{i+1/i}\boldsymbol{R}_{i+1} + \boldsymbol{n}_{i+1/i}. \tag{8.61}$$

Here, $\boldsymbol{n}_{i+1/i}$ represents zero mean noise, with the covariance given by

$$\boldsymbol{\mathcal{C}}_{i+1/i} = \boldsymbol{\mathcal{C}}'_{i+1} + \boldsymbol{\mathcal{R}}(\hat{\boldsymbol{R}}_{i+1/i})\boldsymbol{\mathcal{C}}_{i+1}\boldsymbol{\mathcal{R}}^T(\hat{\boldsymbol{R}}_{i+1/i}), \tag{8.62}$$

where $\boldsymbol{\mathcal{C}}'_{i+1}$ and $\boldsymbol{\mathcal{C}}_{i+1}$ are the known covariance matrices of noise $\boldsymbol{n}'_{i+1}$ and $\boldsymbol{n}_{i+1}$, respectively.

Rotation estimation. Next, we will describe the procedure for estimating a rotation expressed as a rotor $\boldsymbol{R}$. At the beginning of the iteration, or step $i = 0$, the initial state $\hat{\boldsymbol{R}}_0$ and an initial estimation error covariance matrix $\boldsymbol{\mathcal{P}}_0$ are given. According to equation (8.41), given an estimate for $\hat{\boldsymbol{R}}^*{}_i$ and the covariance matrix $\boldsymbol{\mathcal{P}}_i$ at step i, it is reasonable to predict the next step $i+1$ in this way:

$$\hat{\boldsymbol{R}}_{i+1/i} = \hat{\boldsymbol{R}}^*{}_i, \tag{8.63}$$

$$\boldsymbol{\mathcal{P}}_{i+1/i} = \boldsymbol{\mathcal{P}}_i. \tag{8.64}$$

Taking into account the measurements $\boldsymbol{p}_{i+1}$, $\boldsymbol{p}'_{i+1}$ and the predicted state $\hat{\boldsymbol{R}}_{i+1/i}$, the new measurement $\boldsymbol{z}_{i+1}$ from equation (8.59) can be straightforwardly computed. Then the Kalman gain matrix and the estimate $\hat{\boldsymbol{R}}_{i+1}$ at step $i+1$ are computed using EKF, as follows:

$$\begin{aligned} \mathcal{K}_{i+1} &= \mathcal{P}_{i+1/i}\mathcal{H}^T_{i+1/i}(\mathcal{H}_{i+1/i}\mathcal{P}_{i+1/i}\mathcal{H}_{i+1/i} + \mathcal{C}_{i+1/i})^{-1}, & (8.65)\\ \hat{\boldsymbol{R}}_{i+1} &= \hat{\boldsymbol{R}}_{i+1/i} + \mathcal{K}_{i+1}(\boldsymbol{z}_{i+1} - \mathcal{H}_{i+1/i}\hat{\boldsymbol{R}}_{i+1/i}) \\ &= \hat{\boldsymbol{R}}_{i+1/i} + \mathcal{K}_{i+1}(\boldsymbol{p}'_{i+1} - \mathcal{R}(\hat{\boldsymbol{R}}_{i+1/i})\boldsymbol{p}_{i+1}). & (8.66) \end{aligned}$$

Prudently, $\hat{\boldsymbol{R}}_{i+1}$ must be modified to satisfy the constraint $\| \boldsymbol{R} \| = 1$:

$$\hat{\boldsymbol{R}}^*{}_{i+1} = \frac{\hat{\boldsymbol{R}}_{i+1}}{\| \hat{\boldsymbol{R}}_{i+1} \|}. \tag{8.67}$$

The updating of the error covariance matrix follows, according to

$$\mathcal{P}_{i+1} = (I - \mathcal{K}_{i+1}\mathcal{H}_{i+1})\mathcal{P}_{i+1/i}(I - \mathcal{K}_{i+1}\mathcal{H}_{i+1})^T + \mathcal{K}_{i+1}\mathcal{C}_{i+1}\mathcal{K}^T_{i+1}. \tag{8.68}$$

Note that $\mathcal{H}_{i+1}$ and $\mathcal{C}_{i+1}$ are recalculated using the current estimate $\hat{\boldsymbol{R}}^*{}_{i+1}$. As far as the implementation of the filter is concerned, the measurement error covariance matrix $\mathcal{C}_i$ might be measured prior to the operation of the filter.

8.6 The Motor Extended Kalman Filter

The use of the EKF filter in the motor algebra framework gives us the simultaneous estimation of translation and rotation. According to the literature, there are only batch methods for the simultaneous estimation of these components [7, 56]. The motor extended Kalman filter (MEKF) turns out to be a natural extension of the rotor extended Kalman filter, thanks to the multivector concept of geometric algebra. First, let us define the noisy motion equation using lines in the motor algebra framework $\mathcal{G}^+_{1,3,0}$.

The geometric features we will consider for the measurements are 3D observed lines ($\boldsymbol{L}^1$, $\boldsymbol{L}^2$,..., $\boldsymbol{L}^n$, $n \geq 2$) which belong to an object moving in the 3D space. The rigid motion parameters between any pairing of consecutive time instants $(t_0, t_1, t_2, ..., t_N)$ are described compactly by the motor $\boldsymbol{M}_i$. According to equation (2.41), the motion of any line of the object is modeled by

$$\boldsymbol{L}_i = \boldsymbol{M}_i\boldsymbol{L}_{i-1}\widetilde{\boldsymbol{M}}_i. \tag{8.69}$$

If the change of the parameters of the line in motion between the time instants t_{i-1} and t_i is described in terms of motor velocity $\boldsymbol{V}_{i/i-1}$,

$$\boldsymbol{L}_i = \boldsymbol{V}_{i/i-1}\boldsymbol{L}_{i-1}\widetilde{\boldsymbol{V}}_{i/i-1}, \tag{8.70}$$

we can then express the recursive motion equation of the line in general as follows:

$$\boldsymbol{L}_i = \boldsymbol{M}_i\boldsymbol{L}_{i-1}\widetilde{\boldsymbol{M}}_i = (\boldsymbol{V}_{i/i-1}\boldsymbol{M}_{i-1})\boldsymbol{L}_{i-1}(\widetilde{\boldsymbol{M}}_{i-1}\widetilde{\boldsymbol{V}}_{i/i-1}). \tag{8.71}$$

Thus, we obtain the ideal dynamic motion model in terms of the motors:

$$M_i = V_{i/i-1} M_{i-1}. \tag{8.72}$$

For example, suppose the motion is a screw motion with rotation of constant angular velocity ω about an axis of a known line ($L_s = \bar{r} + It_c \wedge \bar{r}$) and with constant translation velocity v_s along the axis line. If the data sampling is done at equidistant time intervals, then the time instants can be represented by integers, so the motor equation reads

$$V_{i/i-1} = V = (1 + Iv_s/2)(cos(\omega/2) + sin(\omega/2) L_s). \tag{8.73}$$

Since in real work the relation between M_{i-1} and M_i is known only approximately, the real dynamic model of the noisy 3D motion is given by

$$M_i = \mathcal{V}_{i/i-1,Ml} M_{i-1} + W_i, \tag{8.74}$$

where the statistics of W_i are given by equations (8.23) and (8.24). Note that $\mathcal{V}_{i/i-1,Ml}$ signifies the "left-multiplication matrix" of motor $\mathcal{V}_{i/i-1}$.

8.6.1 Representation of the line motion model in linear algebra

The line motion model presented in the previous section uses geometric algebra $\mathcal{G}^+_{3,0,1}$. Because the EKF computer algorithm is implemented using the techniques of linear algebra, we should also formulate the line motion model $L' = ML\tilde{M}$ within the frame of linear algebra.

Let us start by considering rotor relationships. The multiplication of two rotors U and V in geometric algebra $\mathcal{G}^+_{3,0,1}$ may be represented by

$$\begin{aligned} W &= UV = (u_0 + \boldsymbol{u})(v_0 + \boldsymbol{v}) \\ &= u_0 v_0 + \boldsymbol{u} \cdot \boldsymbol{v} + u_0 \boldsymbol{v} + v_0 \boldsymbol{u} + \boldsymbol{u} \wedge \boldsymbol{v}. \end{aligned} \tag{8.75}$$

Multiplication of these two rotors in linear algebra is represented by

$$W = \mathcal{U}_{Rl} V = \mathcal{V}_{Rr} U, \tag{8.76}$$

where $U = (u_0 \quad u_1 \quad u_2 \quad u_3)^T$, $V = (v_0 \quad v_1 \quad v_2 \quad v_3)^T$ and

$$\mathcal{U}_{Rl} = \begin{pmatrix} u_0 & -u_1 & -u_2 & -u_3 \\ u_1 & u_0 & u_3 & -u_2 \\ u_2 & -u_3 & u_0 & u_1 \\ u_3 & u_2 & -u_1 & u_0 \end{pmatrix} \tag{8.77}$$

$$\mathcal{V}_{Rr} = \begin{pmatrix} v_0 & -v_1 & -v_2 & -v_3 \\ v_1 & v_0 & -v_3 & v_2 \\ v_2 & v_3 & v_0 & -v_1 \\ v_3 & -v_2 & v_1 & v_0 \end{pmatrix}. \tag{8.78}$$

We call $\mathcal{U}_{Rl}$ the "left-multiplication matrix of rotor $\boldsymbol{U}$," and $\mathcal{V}_{Rr}$ the "right-multiplication matrix of rotor $\boldsymbol{V}$."

Multiplying $\boldsymbol{S} = \boldsymbol{U} + I\boldsymbol{U}'$ and $\boldsymbol{T} = \boldsymbol{V} + I\boldsymbol{V}'$ in geometric algebra $\mathcal{G}^+_{3,0,1}$ gives

$$\begin{aligned} \boldsymbol{Q} &= \boldsymbol{ST} = (\boldsymbol{U} + I\boldsymbol{U}')(\boldsymbol{V} + I\boldsymbol{V}') \\ &= \boldsymbol{UV} + I(\boldsymbol{UV}' + \boldsymbol{U}'\boldsymbol{V}), \end{aligned} \tag{8.79}$$

where $\boldsymbol{U}, \boldsymbol{U}', \boldsymbol{V}$, and $\boldsymbol{V}'$ are all expressed in the form of rotors. Multiplication of these two motors in terms of matrices gives

$$\boldsymbol{Q} = \mathcal{S}_{Ml}\boldsymbol{T} = \mathcal{T}_{Mr}\boldsymbol{S}, \tag{8.80}$$

where

$$\begin{aligned} \boldsymbol{S} &= (u_0 \;\; u_1 \;\; u_2 \;\; u_3 \;\; u_0' \;\; u_1' \;\; u_2' \;\; u_3')^T, \\ \boldsymbol{T} &= (v_0 \;\; v_1 \;\; v_2 \;\; v_3 \;\; v_0' \;\; v_1' \;\; v_2' \;\; v_3')^T, \\ \mathcal{S}_{Ml} &= \begin{pmatrix} \mathcal{U}_{Rl} & 0_{4\times4} \\ \mathcal{U}'_{Rl} & \mathcal{U}_{Rl} \end{pmatrix}, \quad \mathcal{T}_{Mr} = \begin{pmatrix} \mathcal{V}_{Rr} & 0_{4\times4} \\ \mathcal{V}'_{Rr} & \mathcal{V}_{Rr} \end{pmatrix}. \end{aligned} \tag{8.81}$$

In this case, we call $\mathcal{S}_{Ml}$ the "left-multiplication matrix of motor $\boldsymbol{S}$," and $\mathcal{T}_{Mr}$ the "right-multiplication matrix of motor $\boldsymbol{T}$."

To convert the line motion model of equation (2.41) to matrix algebra, we can treat the real and dual components $\boldsymbol{n}$, $\boldsymbol{m}$, $\boldsymbol{n}'$, and $\boldsymbol{m}'$ of the lines $\boldsymbol{L}$ and $\boldsymbol{L}'$ as rotors with zero scalar. By multiplying, from the right, both sides of equation (2.41) by $\boldsymbol{M}$, we get

$$\boldsymbol{L}'\boldsymbol{M} - \boldsymbol{ML} = 0. \tag{8.82}$$

This results in the following linear motion equation:

$$(\mathcal{L}'_{Ml} - \mathcal{L}_{Mr})\boldsymbol{M} = \mathcal{A}_M\boldsymbol{M} = \boldsymbol{0}, \tag{8.83}$$

This matrix representation of the line motion was suggested in [26]. The constraints of equations (1.27) and (2.19), respectively, now are

$$\boldsymbol{R}^T\boldsymbol{R} = 1, \tag{8.84}$$

$$\boldsymbol{R}^T\boldsymbol{R}' = 0, \tag{8.85}$$

with $\boldsymbol{R} = (r_0 \; r_1 \; r_2 \; r_3)^T$, $\boldsymbol{R}' = (r_0' \; r_1' \; r_2' \; r_3')^T$, and $\boldsymbol{M} = \boldsymbol{R} + I\boldsymbol{R}'$.

These properties will be used for the implementation of the MEKF algorithm in the next section.

8.6.2 Linearization of the measurement model

Considering equation (8.83), we can easily see that the relation between the measurement $\mathcal{A}_M$ and the state $\boldsymbol{M}$ is, unfortunately, nonlinear; that is why we should linearize it. Assume that the measurement $\boldsymbol{\mathcal{A}}_{\boldsymbol{M}i}$ represents the true data $\boldsymbol{\mathcal{A}}_{\boldsymbol{M}0,i}$ contaminated by measurement noise $\boldsymbol{\mathcal{N}}_{\mathcal{A}_M,i}$ with zero mean and known covariance matrix $\boldsymbol{\mathcal{C}}_{\mathcal{A}_M,i}$. Then,

$$\boldsymbol{\mathcal{A}}_{\boldsymbol{M}i} = \boldsymbol{\mathcal{A}}_{\boldsymbol{M}0,i} + \boldsymbol{\mathcal{N}}_{\mathcal{A}_M,i}. \tag{8.86}$$

Supposing that the predicted state of $\boldsymbol{M}_i$ is $\hat{\boldsymbol{M}}_{i/i}$, then according to equation (8.48), we can define a function $\boldsymbol{f}_{M,i}$ depending on the variables $(\boldsymbol{\mathcal{A}}_{\boldsymbol{M}0,i}, \boldsymbol{M}_i)$, as follows:

$$\boldsymbol{f}_{M,i}(\boldsymbol{\mathcal{A}}_{\boldsymbol{M}0,i}, \boldsymbol{M}_i) = \boldsymbol{\mathcal{A}}_{\boldsymbol{M}0,i}\boldsymbol{M}_i = \boldsymbol{0}. \tag{8.87}$$

This equation can then be expanded into a first-order Taylor series about the predicted state
$(\boldsymbol{\mathcal{A}}_{\boldsymbol{M}i}, \hat{\boldsymbol{M}}_{i/i-1})$:

$$\begin{aligned} \boldsymbol{f}_{M,i}(\boldsymbol{\mathcal{A}}_{\boldsymbol{M}0,i}, \boldsymbol{M}_i) &= \boldsymbol{f}_{M,i}(\boldsymbol{\mathcal{A}}_{M_i}, \hat{\boldsymbol{M}}_{i/i-1}) \\ &+ \frac{\partial \boldsymbol{f}_{M,i}(\boldsymbol{\mathcal{A}}_{\boldsymbol{M}i}, \hat{\boldsymbol{M}}_{i/i-1})}{\partial \boldsymbol{M}_i}(\boldsymbol{M}_i - \hat{\boldsymbol{M}}_{i/i-1}) + \\ &+ (\boldsymbol{\mathcal{A}}_{\boldsymbol{M}0,i} - \boldsymbol{\mathcal{A}}_{\boldsymbol{M}i})\frac{\partial \boldsymbol{f}_{M,i}(\boldsymbol{\mathcal{A}}_{\boldsymbol{M}i}, \hat{\boldsymbol{M}}_{i/i-1})}{\partial \boldsymbol{\mathcal{A}}_{\boldsymbol{M}0,i}} + \mathcal{O}^2 = \boldsymbol{0}. \end{aligned} \tag{8.88}$$

Now, by renaming the components

$$\frac{\partial \boldsymbol{f}_{M,i}(\boldsymbol{\mathcal{A}}_{\boldsymbol{M}i}, \hat{\boldsymbol{M}}_{i/i-1})}{\partial \boldsymbol{M}_i} = \boldsymbol{\mathcal{A}}_{\boldsymbol{M}i}, \tag{8.89}$$

$$\frac{\partial \boldsymbol{f}_{M,i}(\boldsymbol{\mathcal{A}}_{\boldsymbol{M}i}, \hat{\boldsymbol{M}}_{i/i-1})}{\partial \boldsymbol{\mathcal{A}}_{\boldsymbol{M}0,i}} = \hat{\boldsymbol{M}}_{i/i-1}, \tag{8.90}$$

then omitting the second-order terms $\mathcal{O}^2$, and, finally, by taking into account equation (8.86) for $\boldsymbol{\mathcal{A}}_{\boldsymbol{M}i+1}$, we obtain

$$\begin{aligned} \boldsymbol{\mathcal{A}}_{\boldsymbol{M}i}\hat{\boldsymbol{M}}_{i/i-1} &+ \boldsymbol{\mathcal{A}}_{\boldsymbol{M}i}(\boldsymbol{M}_i - \hat{\boldsymbol{M}}_{i/i-1}) + (\boldsymbol{\mathcal{A}}_{\boldsymbol{M}0,i} - \boldsymbol{\mathcal{A}}_{\boldsymbol{M}i})\hat{\boldsymbol{M}}_{i/i-1} = \\ &= \boldsymbol{\mathcal{A}}_{\boldsymbol{M}i}\hat{\boldsymbol{M}}_{i/i-1} + \boldsymbol{\mathcal{A}}_{\boldsymbol{M}i}(\boldsymbol{M}_i - \hat{\boldsymbol{M}}_{i/i-1}) - \boldsymbol{\mathcal{N}}_{\mathcal{A}_M,i+1}\hat{\boldsymbol{M}}_{i/i-1} \\ &= \boldsymbol{0}, \end{aligned} \tag{8.91}$$

or

$$-\boldsymbol{\mathcal{A}}_{\boldsymbol{M}i}\boldsymbol{M}_i + \boldsymbol{\mathcal{N}}_{\mathcal{A}_M,i}\hat{\boldsymbol{M}}_{i/i-1} = \boldsymbol{\mathcal{A}}_{\boldsymbol{M}i}\hat{\boldsymbol{M}}_{i/i-1} - \boldsymbol{\mathcal{A}}_{\boldsymbol{M}i}\hat{\boldsymbol{M}}_{i/i-1} = 0. \tag{8.92}$$

As a result, we can claim that the measurement equation for the MEKF at step i is given by

$$\boldsymbol{Z}_i = -\boldsymbol{\mathcal{A}}_{\boldsymbol{M}i}\boldsymbol{M}_i + \boldsymbol{\mathcal{N}}_{\mathcal{A}_M,i}\hat{\boldsymbol{M}}_{i/i-1} = \boldsymbol{\mathcal{H}}_i\boldsymbol{M}_i + \boldsymbol{N}_{Z,i} = \boldsymbol{0}, \tag{8.93}$$

where we call $\boldsymbol{\mathcal{H}}_i = -\boldsymbol{\mathcal{A}}_{M_i}$ and $\boldsymbol{N}_{Z,i} = \boldsymbol{\mathcal{N}}_{\mathcal{A}_{M,i+1}}\hat{\boldsymbol{M}}_{i/i-1}$. The covariance matrix of $\boldsymbol{N}_{Z,i}$ is $\boldsymbol{\mathcal{C}}_i$.

8.6.3 Enforcing a geometric constraint

In order to estimate the motor state, we assume first that at the beginning, or step $i = 0$, the initial state $\hat{\boldsymbol{M}}_{1/0}$ and the initial error covariance matrix of the estimate $\mathcal{P}_{1/0}$ are given. Now, according to equations (8.29, 8.33, 8.32, and 8.35), the estimation equation of the motor state is given by

$$\begin{aligned} \boldsymbol{M}_i^* &= \boldsymbol{\Phi}_{i/i-1}\hat{\boldsymbol{M}}_{i-1} + \mathcal{K}_i(\boldsymbol{Z}_i - \mathcal{H}_i\boldsymbol{\Phi}_{i/i-1}\hat{\boldsymbol{M}}_{i-1}) \\ &= \mathcal{V}_{i/i-1,Ml}\hat{\boldsymbol{M}}_{i-1} + \mathcal{K}_i(\boldsymbol{Z}_i - \mathcal{H}_i\mathcal{V}_{i/i-1,Ml}\hat{\boldsymbol{M}}_{i-1}) \\ &= (\boldsymbol{R}^{*T}_i \quad \boldsymbol{R'}^{*T}_i)^T, \end{aligned} \tag{8.94}$$

where the optimal Kalman gain matrix $\mathcal{K}_i$ is computed according to the formula

$$\mathcal{K}_i = \mathcal{P}_{i/i-1}\mathcal{H}_i^T(\mathcal{H}_i\mathcal{P}_{i/i-1}\mathcal{H}_i^T + \mathcal{C}_i)^{-1}, \tag{8.95}$$

where

$$\mathcal{P}_{i/i-1} = \boldsymbol{\Phi}_{i/i-1}\mathcal{P}_i\boldsymbol{\Phi}_{i/i-1}^T + \mathcal{Q}_i \tag{8.96}$$

and the error covariance matrix for the i-step is updated as

$$\mathcal{P}_i = \mathcal{P}_{i/i-1} - \mathcal{K}_i\mathcal{H}_i\mathcal{P}_{i/i-1} = (\boldsymbol{I} - \mathcal{K}_i\mathcal{H}_i)\mathcal{P}_{i/i-1}. \tag{8.97}$$

Now, $\boldsymbol{M}_i^*$ consists of two four-dimensional vectors $\boldsymbol{R}_i^*$ and $\boldsymbol{R}_i'^*$ which must be varied to fulfill the constraints of equations (8.84) and (8.85). In the case of equation (8.84), the modifications can be done simply by considering the unit rotor

$$\hat{\boldsymbol{R}}_i = \frac{\boldsymbol{R}_i^*}{\| \boldsymbol{R}_i^* \|}. \tag{8.98}$$

It is not that simple to satisfy the constraint of equation (8.85), however. The constraint

$$\boldsymbol{R}'^T\boldsymbol{R} = 0 \tag{8.99}$$

tells us that $\boldsymbol{R}$ must be orthogonal to the dual rotor $\boldsymbol{R}'$ and valid up to a scalar (see the role of this scalar in equation (8.104) below). Unfortunately, in practice, the rotor estimate $\boldsymbol{R}_i^*$ is usually not orthogonal to the estimated dual rotor $\boldsymbol{R'}^*_i$. Fig. 8.6 suggests clearly how to enforce this geometric constraint in order to modify the orientation of $\boldsymbol{R'}^*_i$.

In order to do so, first we consider the cosine of the angle φ between estimates $\boldsymbol{R}_i^*$ and $\boldsymbol{R}_i'^*$:

$$cos(\varphi) = \frac{\boldsymbol{R'}^{*T}_i\boldsymbol{R}_i^*}{\| \boldsymbol{R}_i'^* \| \cdot \| \boldsymbol{R}_i^* \|} \tag{8.100}$$

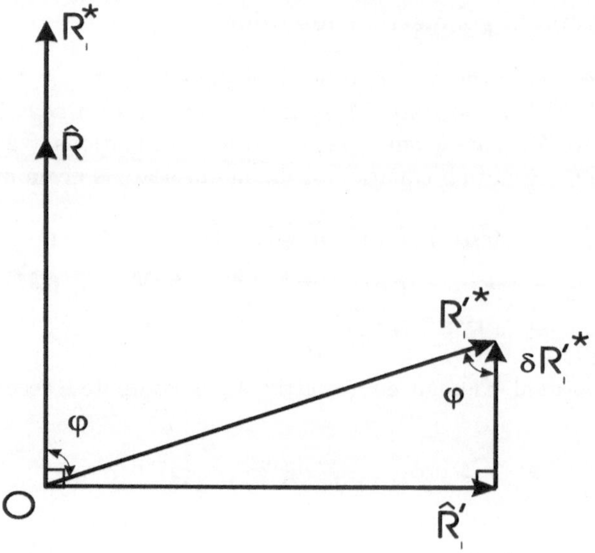

FIGURE 8.6. Constraint of orthogonality according to $\hat{\boldsymbol{R}}\hat{\boldsymbol{R}}^{'} = 0$

This equation can be simplified by using equation (8.98) and the unit rotor $\hat{\boldsymbol{R}}_i$, as follows:

$$cos(\varphi) = \frac{\boldsymbol{R}'^{*T}_{i}\hat{\boldsymbol{R}}_i}{\| \boldsymbol{R}_i'^{*} \|}. \tag{8.101}$$

Then we consider the deviation from the ideal orthogonal $\hat{\mathbf{R}}^{'}$,

$$\delta\hat{\boldsymbol{R}}_i'^{*} = \| \hat{\boldsymbol{R}}_i'^{*} \| \, cos(\varphi)\hat{\boldsymbol{R}}_i = (\boldsymbol{R}'^{*T}_{i}\hat{\boldsymbol{R}}_i)\boldsymbol{R}_i. \tag{8.102}$$

Finally, it is a straightforward matter to compute the ideal orthogonal $\hat{\boldsymbol{R}}'_i$, first we compute the unit rotor $\boldsymbol{R}_u$ orthogonal to $\hat{\boldsymbol{R}}_i$:

$$\boldsymbol{R}_u = \frac{(\boldsymbol{R}_i'^{*} - \delta\hat{\boldsymbol{R}}_i'^{*})}{\| \boldsymbol{R}_i'^{*} - \delta\hat{\boldsymbol{R}}_i'^{*} \|} = \frac{(\boldsymbol{R}_i'^{*} - (\boldsymbol{R}'^{*T}_{i}\hat{\boldsymbol{R}}_i)\hat{\boldsymbol{R}}_i)}{\| \boldsymbol{R}_i'^{*} - (\boldsymbol{R}'^{*T}_{i}\hat{\boldsymbol{R}}_i)\hat{\boldsymbol{R}}_i \|}, \tag{8.103}$$

then we multiply it times the absolute value of the estimated $\boldsymbol{R}_i'^{*}$:

$$\hat{\boldsymbol{R}}'_i = \| \boldsymbol{R}_i'^{*} \| \, \boldsymbol{R}_u. \tag{8.104}$$

In other words, we have rotated the estimated $\boldsymbol{R}_i'^{*}$ until it is orthogonal to $\hat{\boldsymbol{R}}_i$.

8.6.4 Operation of the MEKF algorithm

The processing of information using the MEKF filter can be explained very simply by considering the block diagrams presented in Fig. 8.7.a,b.

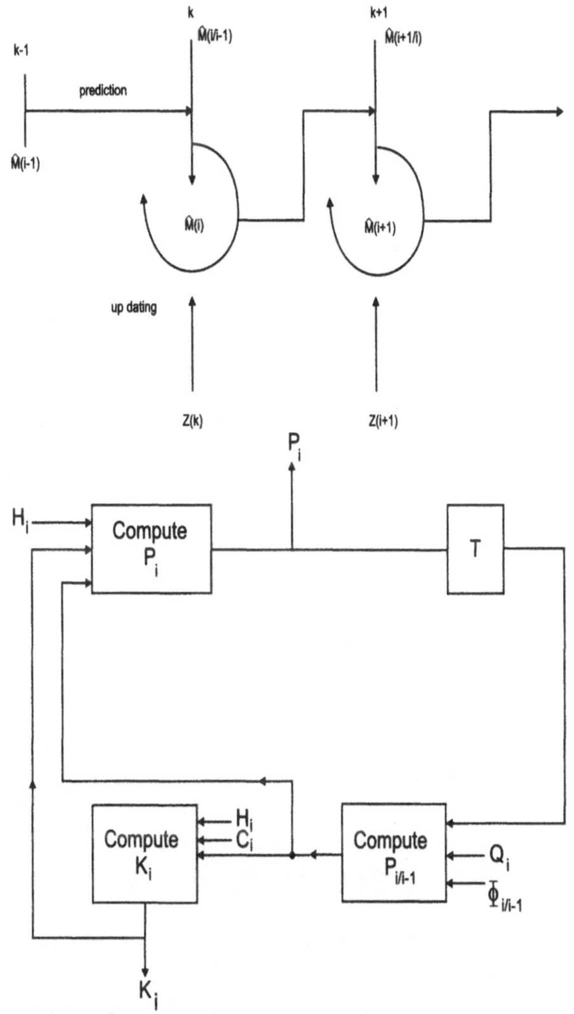

FIGURE 8.7. MEKF operation: (a) cycles of estimation and updating, and (b) Kalman gain computation

In general, during the MEKF cycle, represented by Fig. 8.7.a, the updating phase uses a prediction and a corrected input measurement to actualize a new estimate, which in turn will be modified using a geometric constraint. This cycle continues for each new measurement into infinity, but the MEKF should stabilize to the estimated proper states after only a few iterations.

The Kalman gain $\mathcal{K}_i$ can be calculated before the actual estimation is carried out since it does not depend at all on the measurement of $\boldsymbol{Z}_i$. The computation cycle for $\mathcal{K}_i$, illustrated in Fig. 8.7.b, would proceed as follows:

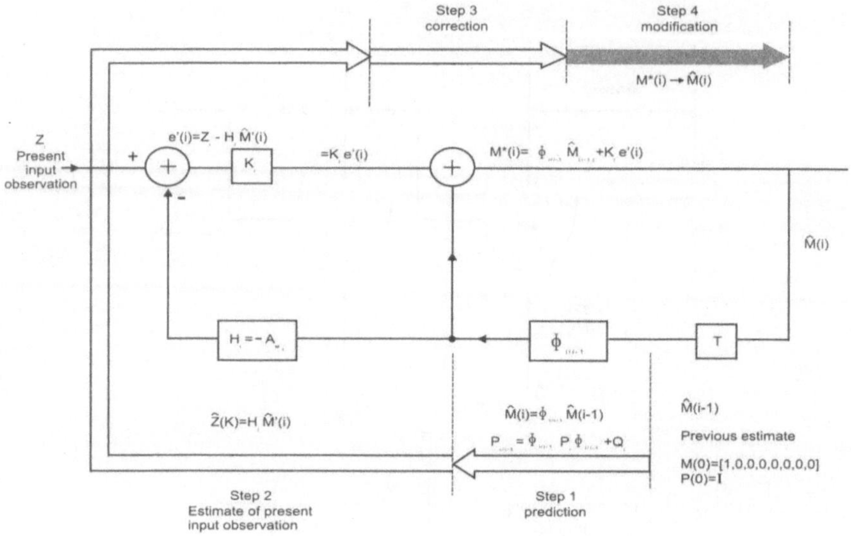

FIGURE 8.8. Representation of the MEKF algorithm

Step	Procedure
1	Given $\mathcal{P}_{i-1/i-1} = \mathcal{P}_i$, $\mathcal{Q}_i$, and $\boldsymbol{\Phi}_{i/i-1}$, then $\mathcal{P}_{i/i-1}$ is computed using equation (8.96).
2	$\mathcal{P}_{i/i-1}$, $\mathcal{H}_i$, and $\mathcal{C}_i$ are substituted in equation (8.95) to obtain $\mathcal{K}_i$, which will be used in step 3 of the MEKF algorithm.
3	$\mathcal{P}_{i/i-1}$, $\mathcal{K}_i$, and $\mathcal{H}_i$ are substituted in equation (8.97) to determine $\mathcal{P}_i$, which is stored until the time of the next measurement, when the cycle is repeated.

Now the MEKF algorithm illustrated in Fig. 8.8 will be explained. For the initialization of the MEKF, we can use for the initial time instant i the known values of $\hat{\boldsymbol{M}}_{i-1}$ and $\mathcal{P}_{i-1}$, or, if we do not know them, we can simply choose the trivial values $\hat{\boldsymbol{M}}_{i-1} = [10000000]^T$ and $\mathcal{P}_{i-1} = \boldsymbol{I}_{8\times 8}$. After the initialization, the MEKF seeks to determine $\hat{\boldsymbol{M}}_i$ for some future instant of time. The computation procedure of the MEKF would proceed as follows:

Step	Action	Procedure
1	Prediction	The estimated $\hat{\boldsymbol{M}}_{i-1}$ is propagated forward by premultiplying it by the discrete system model matrix $\boldsymbol{\Phi}_{i/i-1}$. This gives the predicted estimate $\hat{\boldsymbol{M}}_{i/i-1} = \boldsymbol{\Phi}_{i/i-1}\hat{\boldsymbol{M}}_{i-1}$. Then the measurement model $\boldsymbol{\mathcal{H}}_i = -\boldsymbol{\mathcal{A}}_{\boldsymbol{M}_i}$ is linearized.
2	Estimation	$\boldsymbol{\Phi}_{i/i-1}\hat{\boldsymbol{M}}_{i/i-1}$ is premultiplied by $\boldsymbol{\mathcal{H}}_i = -\boldsymbol{\mathcal{A}}_{\boldsymbol{M}_i}$, giving the estimated input measurement $\hat{\boldsymbol{Z}}_i = \boldsymbol{\mathcal{H}}_i\boldsymbol{\Phi}_{i/i-1}\hat{\boldsymbol{M}}_{i/i-1}$, which is then subtracted from the actual measurement $\boldsymbol{Z}_i$ to obtain the measured residual or error, $\boldsymbol{e}'_i = \boldsymbol{Z}_i - \boldsymbol{\mathcal{H}}_i\boldsymbol{\Phi}_{i/i-1}\hat{\boldsymbol{M}}_{i-1}$.
3	Correction	The error $\boldsymbol{e}'_i$ is premultiplied by the matrix $\boldsymbol{\mathcal{K}}_i$ and the result is added to $\hat{\boldsymbol{M}}_{i/i-1}$ to give the current estimate $\boldsymbol{M}^*_i$ (see equation (8.94)).
4	Modification	The component $\boldsymbol{R}'^*_i$ of the estimate $\boldsymbol{M}^*_i = (\boldsymbol{R}^{*T}_i, \boldsymbol{R}'^{*T}_i)^T$ is modified using a geometric constraint according to equation (8.104).Then the final estimate, $\hat{\boldsymbol{M}}_i = (\hat{\boldsymbol{R}}^T_i, \hat{\boldsymbol{R}}'^T_i)^T$, is stored until the next measurement is made, at which time the cycle is repeated.

The MEKF would run recursively, completing these cycles until time instant N. It is necessary to mention that Kalman filter implementation is sensitive to numerical instability, but several techniques, such as square-root filtering and the so-called U-D factorization [73], are available to overcome such problems.

8.6.5 Estimation of the relative positioning of 6a robot cnd-effector

In this experiment we applied the MEKF algorithm to estimate the relative motion between the end-joint of a Staubli RX90 robot arm and a 3D line belonging to a rigid object. The 3D line parameters were recovered during the arm movement using a stereo vision system. This approach can be used for several kinds of industrial applications, including maneuvering and grasping.

The physical setup of the experiment is shown in Fig. 8.9. The system looks to a pair of lines lying on the floor and moves in the 3D space, always conserving those lines in its field of view. The main task is to estimate automatically the relative motion between the floor lines and the system's

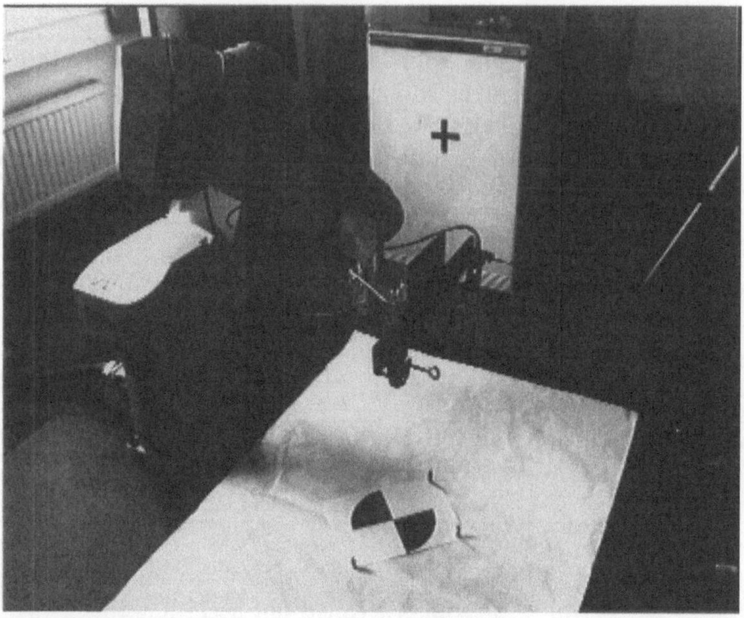

FIGURE 8.9. Physical setup of the experiment

end-joint. The visual system consists of two gray-scale CCD 640 × 480 cameras fastened to the last joint of the robot arm. The Staubli robot arm has six joints which can be controlled by six variables (x, y, z, roll, pitch, and yaw). The coordinates (x, y, z) describe the position of the tool coordinate system T of the end-joint, which refers to the global coordinate system W of the robot. The orientation of the end-joint is described by the variables (roll, pitch, yaw) in terms of Euler angles. Since in practice we require three views in order to reconstruct a 3D line, we can create a virtual third line by slightly moving the two-camera stereo system, as illustrated in Fig. 8.10. The movement of the robot arm is controlled by the relative position and orientation between the tool coordinate system T and the base system W. The camera calibration procedure obtains the projective transformation matrix $\mathbf{P}$, which relates the visual space to the image plane up to a scalar value. The coordinate system of the camera C at the end-joint is related to the tool system frame T via a certain transformation $\mathbf{X}$ which was computed using a hand–eye calibration procedure [62]. When the tool system T is transformed from T_1 to T_2 by the transformation $\mathbf{T}$, the camera system C will be transformed from C_1 to C_2 by a certain transformation $\mathbf{C}$

$$\mathbf{C} = \mathbf{X}\mathbf{T}\mathbf{X}^{-1}. \tag{8.105}$$

Since the motion of the robot arm specified by the transformation $\mathbf{T}$ is known, we can compare it with the relative motion $\mathbf{C}$. The relative motion

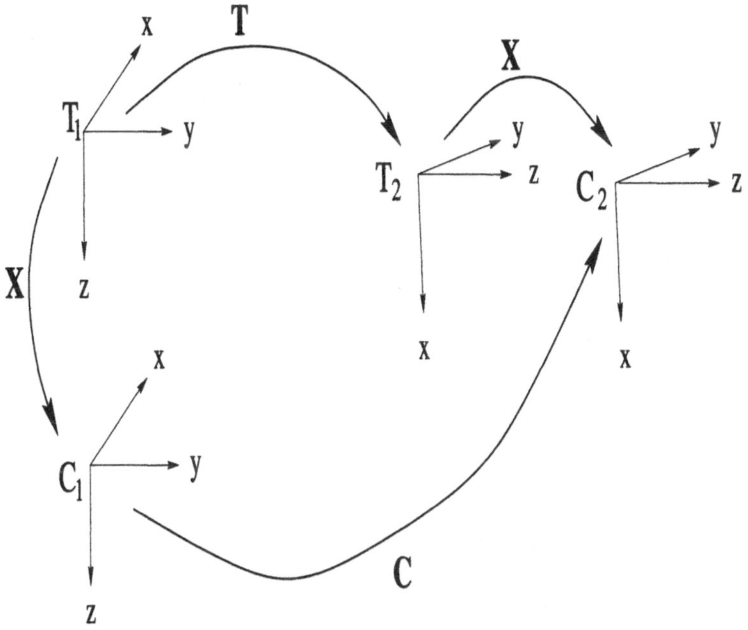

FIGURE 8.10. Relationship between the tool system T and the camera system C

of the frame W and the frame C is a screw motion with constant angular velocity $w = -\phi/90$ and constant translation velocity $\boldsymbol{v}_s = 0.2$. The axis line $\boldsymbol{L}_s$ is parallel to the z-axis of the system C and one point touching this axis line is given by the coordinates (1.5, 0, 0). In motor algebra, $\mathcal{G}^+_{3,0,1}$, the axis line, is given by

$$\boldsymbol{L}_s = \gamma_1\gamma_2 + I(1.5\gamma_2\gamma_3)\wedge(\gamma_1\gamma_2) = \gamma_1\gamma_2 + I1.5\gamma_3\gamma_1, \tag{8.106}$$

and the motor $\boldsymbol{\mathcal{V}}$ is calculated as follows:

$$\begin{aligned} \boldsymbol{V} &= (1 + I\boldsymbol{v}_{s0}/2)(cos(\omega/2) + sin(\omega/2)\boldsymbol{L}_s) \\ &= 0.9994 - 0.0349\gamma_1\gamma_2 + I(0.0035 - 0.0523\gamma_3\gamma_1 + 0.0999\gamma_1\gamma_2). \end{aligned} \tag{8.107}$$

According equation (8.72) the motor $\boldsymbol{M}_{i+1}$, expressed in terms of linear algebra, is given by

$$\boldsymbol{M}_i = \boldsymbol{\mathcal{V}}_{Ml}\boldsymbol{M}_{i-1}, \tag{8.108}$$

initialized with $\boldsymbol{M}_0 = (1\ \ 0\ \ 0\ \ 0\ \ 0\ \ 0\ \ 0\ \ 0)^T$. The reconstructed 3D lines listed in Table 8.1 were used to estimate the relative motion between the end-joint and the object on the floor using the MEKF algorithm .

The procedure followed in the experiment is summarized below.

Time	Line	A point on the line	Direction
0	1	(0.000 3.087 -2.327)	(-0.345 0.937 -0.027)
	2	(0.556 0.000 -2.250)	(0.941 0.336 0.023)
1	1	(1.125 0.000 -2.027)	(-0.404 0.914 0.013)
	2	(0.701 0.000 -2.049)	(0.915 0.401 0.029)
2	1	(1.111 0.000 -1.82)	(-0.462 0.886 0.017)
	2	(0.794 0.000 -1.83)	(0.880 0.471 0.055)
⋮			
14	1	(0.018 0.000 0.648)	(-0.971 0.236 -0.036)
	2	(1.103 0.000 0.538)	(0.241 0.965 0.103)
15	1	(-0.680 0.000 0.753)	(-0.986 0.159 -0.025)
	2	(0.000 -6.341 0.783)	(0.171 0.985 -0.003)

TABLE 8.1. Reconstructed 3D lines

Step	Procedure
1	Cameras calibration to obtain $\boldsymbol{P}$ for each camera
2	Hand–eye calibration to obtain $\boldsymbol{X}$ for each camera
3	Robot arm movement images taken at constant sample rate (see Figures 8.11 and 8.12)
4	Extraction of 2D lines from the images using Hough transform (see Figures 8.11 and 8.12)
5	3D line reconstruction using matched lines of three images (see Table 8.1)
6	Estimation of the motion using 3D line observations and the MEKF algorithm (see Figure 8.13)

The algorithm for motion estimation runs online recursively following steps 3 to 6.

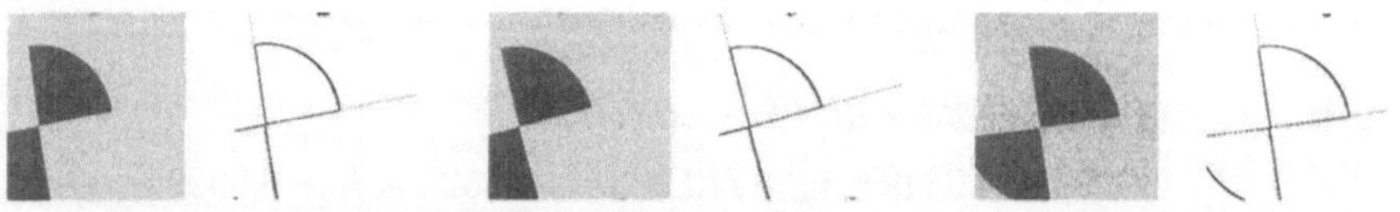

FIGURE 8.11. Stereo triplet of sample object at time $I = 0$ with its edge images overlapped by extracted 2D lines

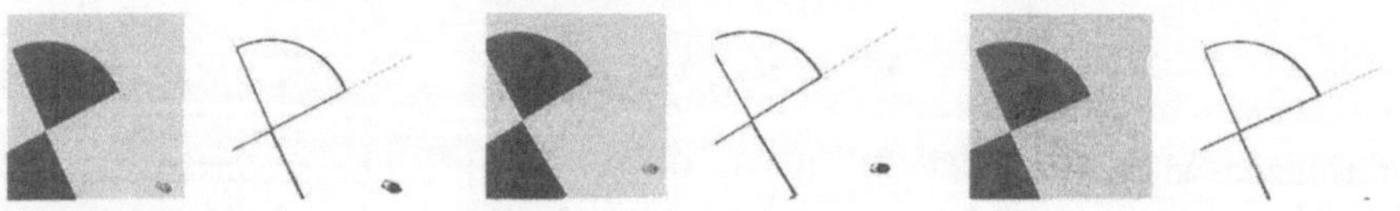

FIGURE 8.12. Stereo triplet of a sample object at time $i = 4$ with its edge images overlapped by extracted 2D lines

Fig. 8.13 presents the eight estimated parameters of the motion for fifteen instants of time. We can see clearly that after only four observations the MEKF algorithm starts to follow almost perfectly the ground truth of the eight parameters. This real experiment together with the previous simulation confirm that the MEKF algorithm is an appropriate tool for the estimation of screw transformations using line observations.

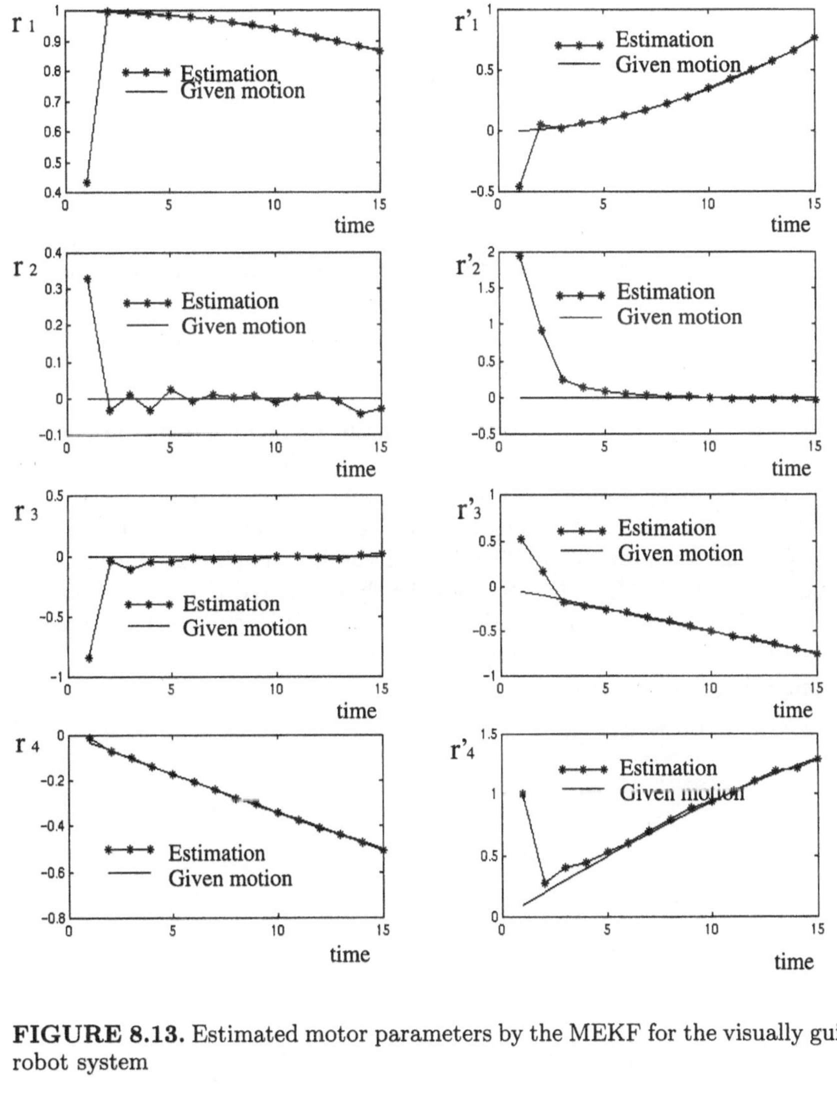

FIGURE 8.13. Estimated motor parameters by the MEKF for the visually guided robot system

8.7 Conclusion

In this chapter we modeled the motion of lines in 4D space using motor algebra. This kind of modeling linearizes 3D Euclidean rigid motion transformation. The model of motion of lines using motors is very appealing for the design of an extended Kalman filter for the motion estimation. For the design of the filter, we started with the rotor extended Kalman filter. As a natural extension of that process, we then posited the theoretical foundations for a motor extended Kalman filter (MEKF).

The MEKF algorithm has the virtue that it can estimate rotation and translation transformations simultaneously. Since most recursive algorithms in the literature compute translation and rotation transformations separately, we can claim that this is one of the most important advantages of the MEKF. Additionally, using the modeling of the lines in motor algebra we were able to linearize the nonlinear measurement model, thereby avoiding the problem of singularities. The dynamic motion model using motors as states is useful to effectively formulate and to compute the screw motion of a line as a minimal rigid entity. In the algorithm of MEKF, we modified the estimating step so that a certain geometric constraint is satisfied, which made the estimation converge faster to a proper motor state. Tests with simulated data [12] confirmed that the tuning of the MEKF parameters improved substantially the MEKF capabilities.

We presented a real application of visually guided robot manipulation. The system was efficiently calibrated using controlled robot movements and an effective hand–eye calibration method. The recovery of the parameters of the 3D lines was carried out using a stereo vision system and the techniques of Hough transform and shape filtering for the line matching. During robot maneuvering, the MEKF algorithm efficiently estimated the relative motion between its end-joint and a 3D object. These experiments confirmed that the new MEKF algorithm is an attractive online method for estimating screw motions using line observations.

9. Geometric Neuralcomputing

9.1 Introduction

It appears that for biological creatures, the external world may be internalized in terms of intrinsic geometric representations. We can formalize the relationships between the physical signals of external objects and the internal signals of a biological creature by using extrinsic vectors to represent those signals coming from the world and intrinsic vectors to represent those signals originating in the internal world. We can also assume that external and internal worlds employ different reference coordinate systems. If we consider the acquisition and coding of knowledge to be a distributed and differentiated process, we can imagine that there should exist various domains of knowledge representation that obey different metrics and that can be modeled using different vectorial bases. How it is possible that nature should have acquired through evolution such tremendous representational power for dealing with such complicated signal processing [60]. In a stimulating series of articles, Pellionisz and Llinàs [77, 78] claim that the formalization of geometrical representation seems to be a dual process involving the expression of extrinsic physical cues built by intrinsic central nervous system vectors. These vectorial representations, related to reference frames intrinsic to the creature, are covariant for perception analysis and contravariant for action synthesis. The geometric mapping between these two vectorial spaces can thus be implemented by a neural network which performs as a metric tensor [78].

Along this line of thought, we can use Clifford, or geometric, algebra to offer an alternative to the tensor analysis that has been employed since 1980 by Pellionisz and Llinàs for the perception and action cycle (PAC) theory. Tensor calculus is covariant, which means that it requires transformation laws for defining coordinate-independent relationships. Clifford, or geometric, algebra is more attractive than tensor analysis because it is coordinate-free, and because it includes spinors, which tensor theory does not. The computational efficiency of geometric algebra has also been confirmed in various challenging areas of mathematical physics [29]. The other mathematical system used to describe neural networks is matrix analysis. But, once again, geometric algebra better captures the geometric characteristics of the problem independent of a coordinate reference system, and it offers other computational advantages that matrix algebra does not, e.g., bivector representation of linear operators in the null cone, incidence relations (meet and join operations), and the conformal group in the horosphere.

Initial attempts at applying geometric algebra to neural geometry have already been described in earlier papers [4, 5, 52, 53]. In this chapter, we demonstrate that standard feedforward networks in geometric algebra are generalizable, and then provide an introduction to the use of support vector machines within the geometric algebra framework. In this way, we are able straightforwardly to generate support multivector machines in the form of either two layer networks or radial basis function networks for the processing of multivectors.

The chapter is organized as follows: Section 2 reviews the computing principles of feedforward neural networks, giving their most important characteristics. Section 3 deals with the extension of the multilayer perceptron (MLP) to complex and quaternionic MLPs. Section 4 shows that standard feedforward networks in geometric algebra are generalizable. Section 5 describes the generalized learning rule across different geometric algebras, and Section 6 presents experiments which compare geometric neural networks with real-valued MLPs. Section 7 introduces the support multivector machine, and its experimental analysis is presented in Section 8. The final section discusses the applicability of geometric feedforward neural nets and support multivector machines.

9.2 Real-Valued Neural Networks

The approximation of *nonlinear mappings* using neural networks is useful in various aspects of signal processing, such as in pattern classification, prediction, system modeling, and identification. This section reviews the fundamentals of standard real-valued feedforward architectures.

Cybenko [25] used for the approximation of a continuous function, $g(\mathbf{x})$, the superposition of weighted functions

$$y(\mathbf{x}) = \sum_{j=1}^{N} w_j \sigma_j(\mathbf{w}_j^T \mathbf{x} + \theta_j), \tag{9.1}$$

where $\sigma(.)$ is a continuous discriminatory function like a sigmoid, $w_j \in \mathcal{R}$ and $\mathbf{x}, \theta_j, \mathbf{w}_j \in \mathcal{R}^n$. Finite sums of the form of equation (9.1) are dense in $C^0(I_n)$, if $|g_k(\mathbf{x}) - y_k(\mathbf{x})| < \varepsilon$ for a given $\varepsilon > 0$ and all $\mathbf{x} \in [0,1]^n$. This is called a *density theorem* and is a fundamental concept in approximation theory and nonlinear system modeling [25, 57].

A structure with k outputs y_k, having several layers using logistic functions, is known as the *multilayer perceptron* (MLP) [89]. The output of any neuron of a hidden layer or of the output layer can be represented in a similar way,

$$o_j = f_j(\sum_{i=1}^{N_i} w_{ji}x_{ji} + \theta_j) y_k = f_k(\sum_{j=1}^{N_j} w_{kj}o_{kj} + \theta_k), \tag{9.2}$$

where $f_j(\cdot)$ is logistic and $f_k(\cdot)$ is logistic or linear. Linear functions at the outputs are often used for pattern classification. In some tasks of pattern classification, a hidden layer is necessary, whereas in some tasks of automatic control, two hidden layers may be required. Hornik [57] showed that standard multilayer feedforward networks are able accurately to approximate any measurable function to a desired degree. Thus, they can be seen as *universal approximators*. In the case of a training failure, we should attribute any error to inadequate learning, an incorrect number of hidden neurons, or a poorly defined deterministic relationship between the input and output patterns.

Poggio and Girosi [82] developed the *radial basis function* (RBF) network, which consists of a superposition of weighted Gaussian functions,

$$y_j(\mathbf{x}) = \sum_{i=1}^{N} w_{ji} G_i\big(\mathtt{D}_i(\mathbf{x} - \mathbf{t}_i)\big), \tag{9.3}$$

where y_j is the j-output, $w_{ji} \in \mathcal{R}$, G_i is a Gaussian function, $\mathtt{D}_i$ an $N \times N$ dilatation diagonal matrix, and $\mathbf{x}, \mathbf{t}_i \in \mathcal{R}^n$. The vector $\mathbf{t}_i$ is a translation vector. This architecture is supported by the regularization theory.

9.3 Complex MLP and Quaternionic MLP

An MLP is defined to be in the complex domain when its weights, activation function, and outputs are complex-valued. The selection of the activation function is not a trivial matter. For example, the extension of the sigmoid function from $\mathcal{R}$ to $\mathcal{C}$,

$$\boldsymbol{f}(\boldsymbol{z}) = \frac{1}{(1 + e^{-\boldsymbol{z}})}, \tag{9.4}$$

where $\boldsymbol{z} \in \mathcal{C}$, is not allowed, because this function is analytic and unbounded [36]; this is also true for the functions $\tanh(\boldsymbol{z})$ and $e^{-\boldsymbol{z}^2}$. We believe these kinds of activation functions exhibit problems with convergence in training due to their singularities. The necessary conditions that a complex activation $\boldsymbol{f}(\boldsymbol{z}) = a(x,y) + ib(x,y)$ has to fulfill are: $\boldsymbol{f}(\boldsymbol{z})$ must be nonlinear in x and y, the partial derivatives a_x, a_y, b_x and b_y must exist ($a_x b_y \not\equiv b_x a_y$), and $\boldsymbol{f}(\boldsymbol{z})$ must not be entire. Accordingly, Georgiou and Koutsougeras [36] proposed the formulation

$$\boldsymbol{f}(\boldsymbol{z}) = \frac{\boldsymbol{z}}{c + \frac{1}{r}|\boldsymbol{z}|}, \tag{9.5}$$

where $c, r \in \mathcal{R}^+$. These authors thus extended the traditional real-valued back-propagation learning rule to the complex-valued rule of the *complex multilayer perceptron* (CMLP).

Arena et al. [2] introduced the quaternionic multilayer perceptron (QMLP), which is an extension of the CMLP. The weights, activation functions, and outputs of this net are represented in terms of quaternions [43]. Arena et al. chose the following non-analytic bounded function

$$\begin{aligned} \boldsymbol{f}(\boldsymbol{q}) &= \boldsymbol{f}(q_0 + q_1 i + q_2 j + q_3 k) \\ &= \left(\frac{1}{1+e^{-q_0}}\right) + \left(\frac{1}{1+e^{-q_1}}\right)i + \left(\frac{1}{1+e^{-q_2}}\right)j + \left(\frac{1}{1+e^{-q_3}}\right)k, \end{aligned} \tag{9.6}$$

where $\boldsymbol{f}(\cdot)$ is now the function for quaternions. These authors proved that superpositions of such functions accurately approximate any continuous quaternionic function defined in the unit polydisc of C^n. The extension of the training rule to the CMLP was demonstrated in [2].

9.4 Geometric Algebra Neural Networks

Real, complex, and quaternionic neural networks can be further generalized within the geometric algebra framework, in which the weights, the activation functions, and the outputs are now represented using multivectors. For the real-valued neural networks discussed in section 9.2, the vectors are multiplied with the weights, using the scalar product. For geometric neural networks, the scalar product is replaced by the geometric product.

9.4.1 The activation function

The activation function of equation (9.5), used for the CMLP, was extended by Pearson and Bisset [76] for a type of Clifford MLP by applying different Clifford algebras, including quaternion algebra. We propose here an activation function that will affect each multivector basis element. This function was introduced independently by the authors [5] and is in fact a generalization of the function of Arena et al. [2]. The function for an n-dimensional multivector $\boldsymbol{m}$ is given by

$$\begin{aligned} \boldsymbol{f}(\boldsymbol{m}) = \boldsymbol{f}(&m_0 + m_i\sigma_i + m_j\sigma_j + m_k\sigma_k + \cdots + m_{ij}\sigma_i\wedge\sigma_j + \cdots + \\ &+ m_{ijk}\sigma_i\wedge\sigma_j\wedge\sigma_k + \cdots + m_n\sigma_1\wedge\sigma_2\wedge\cdots\wedge\sigma_n) \\ = (&m_0) + f(m_i)\sigma_i + f(m_j)\sigma_j + f(m_k)\sigma_k + \cdots + f(m_{ij})\sigma_i\wedge\sigma_j + \\ &+ \cdots + f(m_{ijk})\sigma_i\wedge\sigma_j\wedge\sigma_k + \cdots + f(m_n)\sigma_1\wedge\sigma_2\wedge\ldots\wedge\sigma_n, \end{aligned} \tag{9.7}$$

where $\boldsymbol{f}(\cdot)$ is written in bold to distinguish it from the notation used for a single-argument function $f(\cdot)$. The values of $f(\cdot)$ can be of the sigmoid or Gaussian type.

9.4.2 The geometric neuron

The *McCulloch–Pitts neuron* uses the scalar product of the input vector and its weight vector [89]. The extension of this model to the *geometric neuron* requires the substitution of the scalar product with the Clifford or geometric product, i.e.,

$$\mathbf{w}^T\mathbf{x}+\theta \qquad \Rightarrow \qquad \boldsymbol{w}\boldsymbol{x}+\boldsymbol{\theta}=\boldsymbol{w}\cdot\boldsymbol{x}+\boldsymbol{w}\wedge\boldsymbol{x}+\boldsymbol{\theta}. \tag{9.8}$$

Fig. 9.1 shows in detail the McCulloch–Pitts neuron and the geometric neuron. This figure also depicts how the input pattern is formatted in a specific geometric algebra. The geometric neuron outputs a richer kind of pattern.

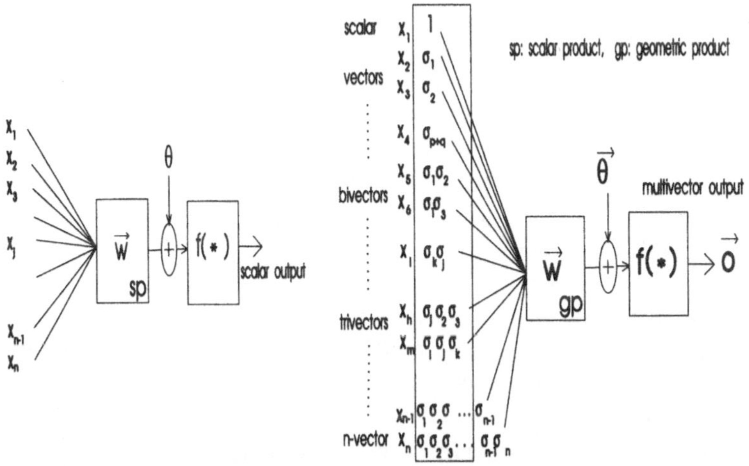

FIGURE 9.1. *McCulloch–Pitts neuron and geometric neuron*

We can illustrate this with an example in $\mathcal{G}_{3,0,0}$:

$$\begin{aligned}
\boldsymbol{o} &= \boldsymbol{f}(\boldsymbol{w}\boldsymbol{x}+\boldsymbol{\theta}) \qquad (9.9)\\
&= \boldsymbol{f}(s_0+s_1\sigma_1+s_2\sigma_2+s_3\sigma_3+s_4\sigma_1\sigma_2+s_5\sigma_1\sigma_3+s_6\sigma_2\sigma_3+s_7\sigma_1\sigma_2\sigma_3)\\
&= f(s_0)+f(s_1)\sigma_1+f(s_2)\sigma_2+f(s_3)\sigma_3+f(s_4)\sigma_1\sigma_2+\ldots+\\
&\qquad +f(s_5)\sigma_1\sigma_3+f(s_6)\sigma_2\sigma_3+f(s_7)\sigma_1\sigma_2\sigma_3,
\end{aligned}$$

where $\boldsymbol{f}$ is the activation function defined in equation (9.7), and $s_i \in \mathcal{R}$. If we use the McCulloch–Pitts neuron in the real-valued neural network, the output is simply the scalar given by

$$o=f(\sum_i^N w_i x_i+\theta). \tag{9.10}$$

The geometric neuron outputs a signal with more geometric information

$$o = f(wx + \theta) = f(w \cdot x + w \wedge x + \theta). \quad (9.11)$$

It has both a scalar product like the McCulloch–Pitts neuron,

$$f(w \cdot x + \theta) = f(s_0) \equiv f(\sum_i^N w_i x_i + \theta) \quad (9.12)$$

and also the outer product given by

$$\begin{aligned} f(w \wedge x + \theta - \theta) &= f(s_1)\sigma_1 + f(s_2)\sigma_2 + f(s_3)\sigma_3 + f(s_4)\sigma_1\sigma_2 + \ldots + \\ &\quad + f(s_5)\sigma_1\sigma_3 + f(s_6)\sigma_2\sigma_3 + f(s_7)\sigma_1\sigma_2\sigma_3. \end{aligned} \quad (9.13)$$

Note that the outer product gives the scalar cross-products between the individual components of the vector, which are nothing more than the multivector components of points or lines (vectors), planes (bivectors), and volumes (trivectors). This characteristic can be used for the implementation of geometric preprocessing in the extended geometric neural network. To a certain extent, this kind of neural network resembles the higher-order neural networks of [79]. However, an extended geometric neural network uses not only a scalar product of higher order, but also all the necessary scalar cross-products for carrying out a *geometric cross-correlation*. Fig. 9.2 shows a geometric network with its extended first layer.

In conclusion, a geometric neuron can be seen as a kind of *geometric correlation operator*, which, in contrast to the McCulloch–Pitts neuron, offers not only points but higher-grade multivectors such as planes, volumes, ... , and hyper-volumes for interpolation.

9.4.3 Feedforward geometric neural networks

Fig. 9.3 depicts standard neural network structures for function approximation in the geometric algebra framework. Here, the inner vector product has been extended to the geometric product and the activation functions are according to (9.7).

Equation (9.1) of Cybenko's model in geometric algebra is

$$y(x) = \sum_{j=1}^N w_j f(w_j \cdot x + w_j \wedge x + \theta_j). \quad (9.14)$$

The extension of the MLP is straightforward. The equations using the geometric product for the outputs of hidden and output layers are given by

$$\begin{aligned} o_j &= f_j(\sum_{i=1}^{N_i} w_{ji} \cdot x_{ji} + w_{ji} \wedge x_{ji} + \theta_j) \\ y_k &= f_k(\sum_{j=1}^{N_j} w_{kj} \cdot o_{kj} + w_{kj} \wedge o_{kj} + \theta_k). \end{aligned} \quad (9.15)$$

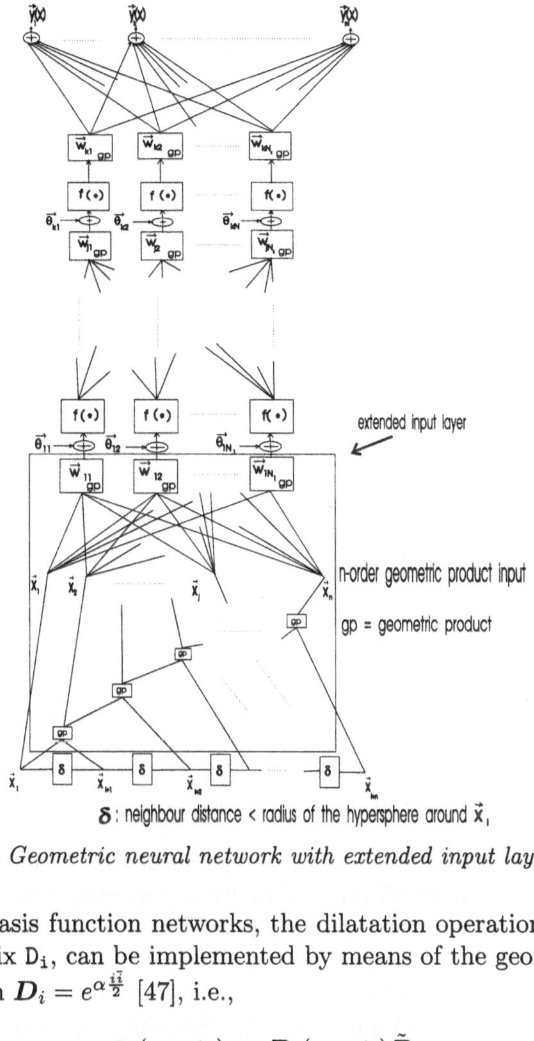

FIGURE 9.2. *Geometric neural network with extended input layer*

In radial basis function networks, the dilatation operation, given by the diagonal matrix $\mathtt{D_i}$, can be implemented by means of the geometric product with a dilation $\boldsymbol{D}_i = e^{\alpha\frac{i\bar{i}}{2}}$ [47], i.e.,

$$\mathtt{D}_i(\mathbf{x} - \mathbf{t}_i) \Rightarrow \boldsymbol{D}_i(\boldsymbol{x} - \boldsymbol{t}_i)\tilde{\boldsymbol{D}}_i \tag{9.16}$$

$$\boldsymbol{y}_k(\boldsymbol{x}) = \sum_{j=1}^{N} \boldsymbol{w}_{kj}\boldsymbol{G}_j(\boldsymbol{D}_j(\boldsymbol{x}_{ji} - \boldsymbol{t}_j)\tilde{\boldsymbol{D}}_j). \tag{9.17}$$

Note that in the case of the geometric RBF we are also using an activation function according to (9.7). Equation (9.17) with $\boldsymbol{w}_{kj} \in R$ represents the equation of an RBF architecture for multivectors of 2^n dimension, which is isomorph to a real-valued RBF network with 2^n-dimensional input vectors. In Section 9.7, we will show that we can use support vector machines for the automatic generation of an RBF network for multivector processing.

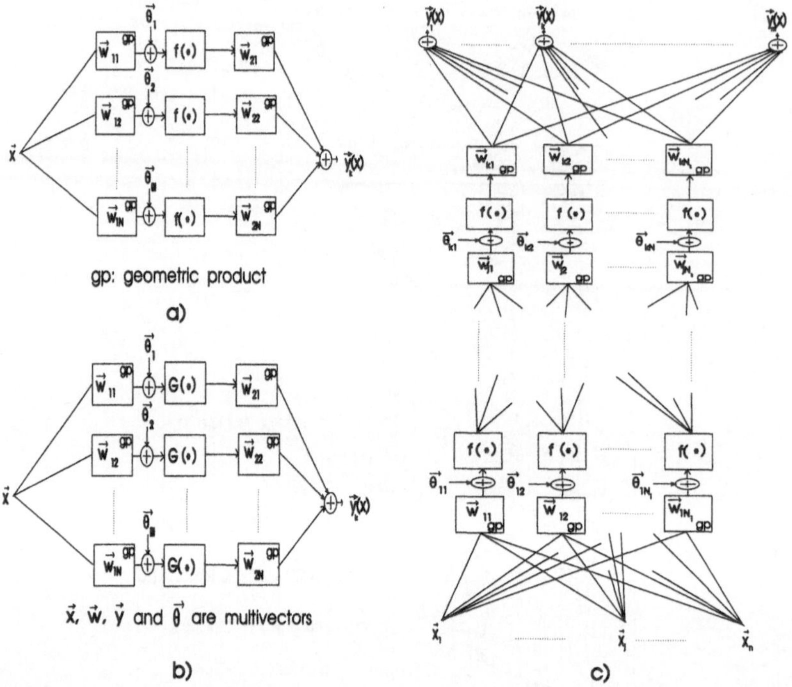

FIGURE 9.3. *Geometric network structures for approximation: (a) Cybenko's, (b) GRBF network, (c) $GMLP_{p,q,r}$*

9.4.4 Generalized geometric neural networks

One major advantage to use Clifford geometric algebra in neurocomputing is that the nets function for all types of multivectors: real, complex, double (or hyperbolic), and dual, as well as for different types of computing models, like horospheres and null cones (see [11, 54]. The chosen multivector basis for a particular geometric algebra $\mathcal{G}_{p,q,r}$ defines the signature of the involved subspaces. The signature is computed by squaring the pseudoscalar: if $I^2 = -1$, the net will use complex numbers; if $I^2 = 1$, the net will use double or hyperbolic numbers; and if $I^2 = 0$, the net will use dual numbers (a degenerated geometric algebra). For example, for $\mathcal{G}_{0,2,0}$, we can have a quaternion-valued neural network; for $\mathcal{G}_{1,1,0}$, a hyperbolic MLP; for $\mathcal{G}_{0,3,0}$, a hyperbolic (double) quaternion-valued RBF; or for $\mathcal{G}_{3,0,0}$, a net which works in the entire Euclidean three-dimensional geometric algebra; for $\mathcal{G}^+_{4,1,0}$, a net which works in the horosphere; or, finally, for $\mathcal{G}^+_{3,3,0}$, a net which uses only the bivector null cone.

The conjugation involved in the training learning rule depends on whether we are using complex, hyperbolic, or dual-valued geometric neural networks, and varies according to the signature of the geometric algebra (see equations (9.21–9.23)).

9.5 The Learning Rule

This section demonstrates the multidimensional generalization of the gradient descent learning rule in geometric algebra. This rule can be used for training the geometric MLP (GMLP) and for tuning the weights of the geometric RBF (GRBF). Previous learning rules for the real-valued MLP, complex MLP [36], and quaternionic MLP [2] are special cases of this extended rule.

9.5.1 Multidimensional back-propagation training rule

The *norm of a multivector* $\boldsymbol{x}$ for the learning rule is given by

$$|\boldsymbol{x}| = (\boldsymbol{x}|\boldsymbol{x})^{\frac{1}{2}} = \Big(\sum_{A}[\boldsymbol{x}]_A^2\Big)^{\frac{1}{2}}. \tag{9.18}$$

The geometric neural network with n inputs and m outputs approximates the target mapping function

$$\mathcal{Y}_t : (\mathcal{G}_{p,q,r})^n \rightarrow (\mathcal{G}_{p,q,r})^m, \tag{9.19}$$

where $(\mathcal{G}_{p,q,r})^n$ is the n-dimensional module over the geometric algebra $\mathcal{G}_{p,q,r}$ [76]. The error at the output of the net is measured according to the metric

$$E = \frac{1}{2}\int_{\boldsymbol{x}\in\boldsymbol{X}} |\mathcal{Y}_w - \mathcal{Y}_t|^2, \tag{9.20}$$

where $\boldsymbol{X}$ is some compact subset of the Clifford module $(\mathcal{G}_{p,q,r})^n$ involving the product topology derived from equation (9.18) for the norm and where $\mathcal{Y}_w$ and $\mathcal{Y}_t$ are the learned and target mapping functions, respectively. The *back-propagation algorithm* [89] is a procedure for updating the weights and biases. This algorithm is a function of the negative derivative of the error function (equation (9.20)) with respect to the weights and biases themselves. The computing of this procedure is straightforward, and here we will only give the main results. The updating equation for the multivector weights of any hidden j-layer is

$$\boldsymbol{w}_{ij}(t+1) = \eta\Big[\Big(\sum_{k}^{N_k}\delta_{kj}\otimes\overline{\boldsymbol{w}_{kj}}\Big)\odot\boldsymbol{F}'(\boldsymbol{net}_{ij})\Big]\otimes\overline{\boldsymbol{o}_i} + \alpha\boldsymbol{w}_{ij}(t) \tag{9.21}$$

for any k-output with a nonlinear activation function

$$\boldsymbol{w}_{jk}(t+1) = \eta\big[(\boldsymbol{y}_{k_t} - \boldsymbol{y}_{k_a})\odot\boldsymbol{F}'(\boldsymbol{net}_{jk})\big]\otimes\overline{\boldsymbol{o}_j} + \alpha\boldsymbol{w}_{jk}(t), \tag{9.22}$$

and for any k-output with a linear activation function

$$\boldsymbol{w}_{jk}(t+1) = \eta(\boldsymbol{y}_{k_t} - \boldsymbol{y}_{k_a})\otimes\overline{\boldsymbol{o}_j} + \alpha\boldsymbol{w}_{jk}(t). \tag{9.23}$$

In the above equations, $\boldsymbol{F}$ is the activation function defined in equation (9.7), t is the update step, η and α are the *learning rate* and the momentum, respectively, $\otimes$ is the Clifford or geometric product, $\odot$ is the scalar product, and $\overline{(\cdot)}$ is the *multivector anti-involution* (reversion or conjugation).

In the case of the non-Euclidean $\mathcal{G}_{0,3,0}$, $\overline{(\cdot)}$ corresponds to the simple conjugation. Each neuron now consists of p+q+r units, each for a multivector component. The biases are also multivectors and are absorbed as usual in the sum of the activation signal, here defined as $\boldsymbol{net}_{ij}$. In the learning rules, equations (9.21– 9.23), the computation of the geometric product and the anti-involution varies depending on the geometric algebra being used [83]. To illustrate, the conjugation required in the learning rule for quaternion algebra is $\bar{\boldsymbol{x}} = x_0 - x_1\sigma_1 - x_2\sigma_2 - x_3\sigma_1\sigma_2$, where $\boldsymbol{x} \in \mathcal{G}_{0,2,0}$.

9.5.2 Simplification of the learning rule using the density theorem

Given $\boldsymbol{X}$ and $\boldsymbol{Y}$ as compact subsets belonging to $(\mathcal{G}_{p,q})^n$ and $(\mathcal{G}_{p,q})^m$, respectively, and considering $\mathcal{Y}_t : \boldsymbol{X} \to \boldsymbol{Y}$ a continuous function, we are able to find some coefficients $w_1, w_2, w_3, ..., w_{N_j} \in \mathcal{R}$ and some multivectors $\boldsymbol{y}_1, \boldsymbol{y}_2, \boldsymbol{y}_3, ..., \boldsymbol{y}_{N_j} \in \mathcal{G}_{p,q}$ and $\boldsymbol{\theta}_1, \boldsymbol{\theta}_2, \boldsymbol{\theta}_3, ..., \boldsymbol{\theta}_{N_j} \in \mathcal{G}_{p,q}$ so that the following inequality $\forall \epsilon > 0$ is valid:

$$E(\mathcal{Y}_t, \mathcal{Y}_w) = sup\big[|\mathcal{Y}_t(\boldsymbol{x}) - \sum_{j=1}^{N_j} w_j \boldsymbol{f}_j(\sum_{i=1}^{N_i} \boldsymbol{w}_i \boldsymbol{x} + \boldsymbol{\theta}_i)|\boldsymbol{x} \in \boldsymbol{X}\big] < \epsilon, \quad (9.24)$$

where $\boldsymbol{f}_j$ is the multivector activation function of equation (9.7). Here, the approximation given by

$$S = \sum_{j=1}^{N_j} w_j \boldsymbol{f}_j(\sum_{i=1}^{N_i} \boldsymbol{w}_i \boldsymbol{x} + \boldsymbol{\theta}_i) \quad (9.25)$$

is the subset of the class of functions $C^0(\mathcal{G}_{p,q})$ with the norm

$$|\mathcal{Y}_t| = sup_{\boldsymbol{x} \in \boldsymbol{X}} |\mathcal{Y}_t(\boldsymbol{x})|. \quad (9.26)$$

And finally, since equation (9.24) is true, we can say that S is dense in $C^0(\mathcal{G}_{p,q})$. The density theorem presented here is the generalization of the one used for the quaternionic MLP by Arena et al. [2].

The density theorem shows that the weights of the output layer for the training of geometric feedforward networks can be real values. Therefore, the training of the output layer can be simplified, i.e., the output weight multivectors can be the scalars of the blades of k grade. This k-grade element of the multivector is selected by convenience (see equation (1.4)).

9.5.3 Learning using the appropriate geometric algebras

The primary reason for processing signals within a geometric algebra framework is to have access to representations with a strong geometric character and to take advantage of the geometric product. It is important, however, to consider the type of geometric algebra that should be used for any specific problem. For some applications, the decision to use the model of a particularly geometric algebra is straightforward. However, in other cases, without some a priori knowledge of the problem it may be difficult to assess which model will provide the best results. If our pre-existing knowledge of the problem is limited, we must explore the various network topologies in different geometric algebras. This requires some orientation in the different geometric algebras that could be used. Since each geometric algebra is either isomorphic to a matrix algebra of $\mathcal{R}$, $\mathcal{C}$, or $\mathcal{H}$, or simply the tensor product of these algebras, we must take great care in choosing the geometric algebras. Porteous [83] showed the *isomorphisms*

$$\mathcal{G}_{p+1,q} = \mathcal{R}_{p+1,q} \cong \mathcal{G}_{q+1,p} = \mathcal{R}_{q+1,p}, \tag{9.27}$$

and presented the following expressions for completing the *universal table of geometric algebras*:

$$\begin{aligned} \mathcal{G}_{p,q+4} = \mathcal{R}_{p,q+4} \cong \mathcal{R}_{p,q} \otimes \mathcal{R}_{0,4} \cong \mathcal{R}_{0,4} \cong \mathcal{H}(2) \\ \mathcal{G}_{p,q+8} = \mathcal{R}_{p,q+8} \cong \mathcal{R}_{p,q} \otimes \mathcal{R}_{0,8} \cong \mathcal{R}_{0,8} \cong \mathcal{R}(16), \end{aligned} \tag{9.28}$$

where $\otimes$ stands for the real tensor product of two algebras. Equation (9.28) is known as the periodicity theorem [83]. We can use Table 9.1, which presents the Clifford, or geometric, algebras up to dimension 16, to search for the appropriate geometric algebras. The entries of Table 9.1 correspond to the p and q of the $\mathcal{G}_{p,q}$, and each table element is isomorphic to the geometric algebra $\mathcal{G}_{p,q}$.

	q	→				
p	$\mathcal{R}$	$\mathcal{C}$	$\mathcal{H}$	${}^2\mathcal{H}$	$\mathcal{H}(2)$	$\mathcal{C}(4)$
	${}^2\mathcal{R}$	$\mathcal{R}(2)$	$\mathcal{C}(2)$	$\mathcal{H}(2)$	${}^2\mathcal{H}(2)$	$\mathcal{H}(4)$
↓	$\mathcal{R}(2)$	${}^2\mathcal{R}(2)$	$\mathcal{R}(4)$	$\mathcal{C}(4)$	$\mathcal{H}(4)$	${}^2\mathcal{H}(4)$
	$\mathcal{C}(2)$	$\mathcal{R}(4)$	${}^2\mathcal{R}(4)$	$\mathcal{R}(8)$	$\mathcal{C}(8)$	$\mathcal{H}(8)$
	$\mathcal{H}(2)$	$\mathcal{C}(4)$	$\mathcal{R}(8)$	${}^2\mathcal{R}(8)$	$\mathcal{R}(16)$	$\mathcal{C}(16)$

TABLE 9.1. Clifford or geometric algebras up to dimension 16

Examples of this table are the geometric algebras R$\cong \mathcal{G}_{0,0}$, $\mathcal{R}_{0,1} \cong \mathcal{C} \cong \mathcal{G}_{0,1}$, $\mathcal{H} \cong \mathcal{G}_{0,2}$ and $\mathcal{R}_{1,1} \cong {}^2\mathcal{R} \cong \mathcal{G}_{1,1}$, $\mathcal{C}(2) \cong \mathcal{C} \otimes \mathcal{R}(2) \cong \mathcal{G}_{3,0} \cong \mathcal{G}_{1,2}$ for the 3D space and $\mathcal{H}(2) \cong \mathcal{G}_{1,3}$ for the 4D space.

9.6 Experiments Using Geometric Feedforward Neural Networks

In this section, we present a series of experiments in order to demonstrate the capabilities of geometric neural networks. We begin with an analysis of the XOR problem by comparing a real-valued MLP with bivector-valued MLPs. In the second experiment, we used the encoder-decoder problem to analyze the performance of the geometric MLPs using different geometric algebras. In the third experiment, we used the Lorenz attractor to perform step-ahead prediction. Finally, we present a practical problem, using a neural network for 3D pose estimation, to show the importance of selecting the correct geometric algebra.

9.6.1 Learning a high nonlinear mapping

The power of using bivectors for learning is confirmed with the test using the XOR function. Fig. 9.4 shows that geometric nets $\mathrm{GMLP}_{0,2,0}$ and $\mathrm{GMLP}_{2,0,0}$ have a faster convergence rate than either the MLP or the P-QMLP—the quaternionic multilayer perceptron of Pearson [76], which uses the activation function given by equation (9.5). Fig. 9.4 shows the MLP with two- and four-

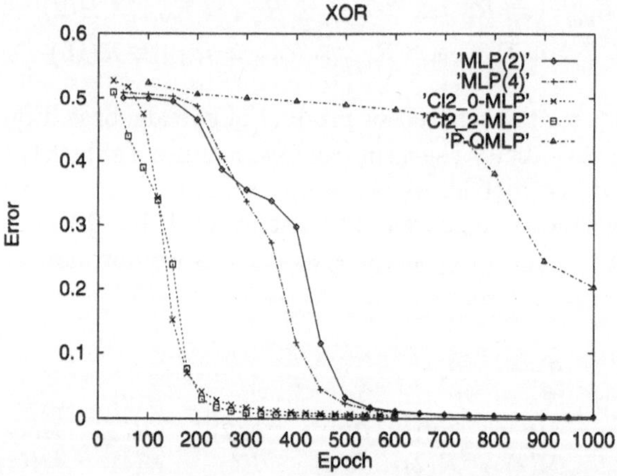

FIGURE 9.4. *Learning XOR using the MLP(2), MLP(4),* $GMLP_{0,2,0}$, $GMLP_{2,0,0}$, *and P-QMLP*

dimensional input vectors. Since the MLP(4), working also in 4D, cannot outperform the GMLP, it can be claimed that the better performance of the geometric neural network is due not to the higher dimensional quaternionic inputs but rather to the algebraic advantages of the geometric neurons of the net.

9.6.2 Encoder-decoder problem

The *encoder-decoder problem* is also an interesting benchmark test to analyze the performance of three-layer neural networks. The training input patterns are equal to the output patterns. The neural network learns in its hidden neurons a compressed binary representation of the input vectors, in such a way that the net can decode it at the output layer.

We tested real- and multivector-valued MLPs using sigmoid transfer functions in the hidden and output layers. Two different kinds of training sets, consisting of one input neuron and of multiple input neurons were used (see Table 9.2). Since the sigmoids have asymptotic values of 0 and 1, the used output training values were numbers near to 0 or 1.

Input	0.97 0.03 0.03 0.03	0.03 0.03 0.03 0.03
Output	0.97 0.03 0.03 0.03	0.03 0.03 0.03 0.03
Input	0.03 0.97 0.03 0.03	0.03 0.03 0.03 0.03
Output	0.03 0.97 0.03 0.03	0.03 0.03 0.03 0.03
Input	0.03 0.03 0.97 0.03	0.03 0.03 0.03 0.03
Output	0.03 0.03 0.97 0.03	0.03 0.03 0.03 0.03
Input	0.03 0.03 0.03 0.97	0.03 0.03 0.03 0.03
Output	0.03 0.03 0.03 0.97	0.03 0.03 0.03 0.03
Input	0.03 0.03 0.03 0.03	0.97 0.03 0.03 0.03
Output	0.03 0.03 0.03 0.03	0.97 0.03 0.03 0.03
Input	0.03 0.03 0.03 0.03	0.03 0.97 0.03 0.03
Output	0.03 0.03 0.03 0.03	0.03 0.97 0.03 0.03
Input	0.03 0.03 0.03 0.03	0.03 0.03 0.97 0.03
Output	0.03 0.03 0.03 0.03	0.03 0.03 0.97 0.03
Input	0.03 0.03 0.03 0.03	0.03 0.03 0.03 0.97
Output	0.03 0.03 0.03 0.03	0.03 0.03 0.03 0.97

Input	0.97 0.03 0.03 0.03	0.03 0.03 0.03 0.03
	0.97 0.03 0.03 0.03	0.03 0.03 0.03 0.03
	0.97 0.03 0.03 0.03	0.03 0.03 0.03 0.03
Output	0.97 0.03 0.03 0.03	0.03 0.03 0.03 0.03
Input	0.03 0.97 0.03 0.03	0.03 0.03 0.03 0.03
	0.03 0.97 0.03 0.03	0.03 0.03 0.03 0.03
	0.03 0.97 0.03 0.03	0.03 0.03 0.03 0.03
Output	0.03 0.97 0.03 0.03	0.03 0.03 0.03 0.03
	...	..
Input	0.03 0.03 0.03 0.03	0.03 0.03 0.03 0.97
	0.03 0.03 0.03 0.03	0.03 0.03 0.03 0.97
	0.03 0.03 0.03 0.03	0.03 0.03 0.03 0.97
Output	0.03 0.03 0.03 0.03	0.03 0.03 0.03 0.97

TABLE 9.2. Test of real- and multivector-valued MLPs using (top) one input and one output, and (bottom) three inputs and one output

Fig. 9.5 shows the mean square error (MSE) during the training of the G00 (working in $\mathcal{G}_{0,0,0}$, a real-valued 8–8–8 MLP, and the geometric MLPs—G30 working in $\mathcal{G}_{3,0,0}$, G03 in $\mathcal{G}_{0,3,0}$, and G301 in the degenerated algebra $\mathcal{G}^+_{3,0,1}$ (algebra of the dual quaternions). For the one-input case, the multivector-

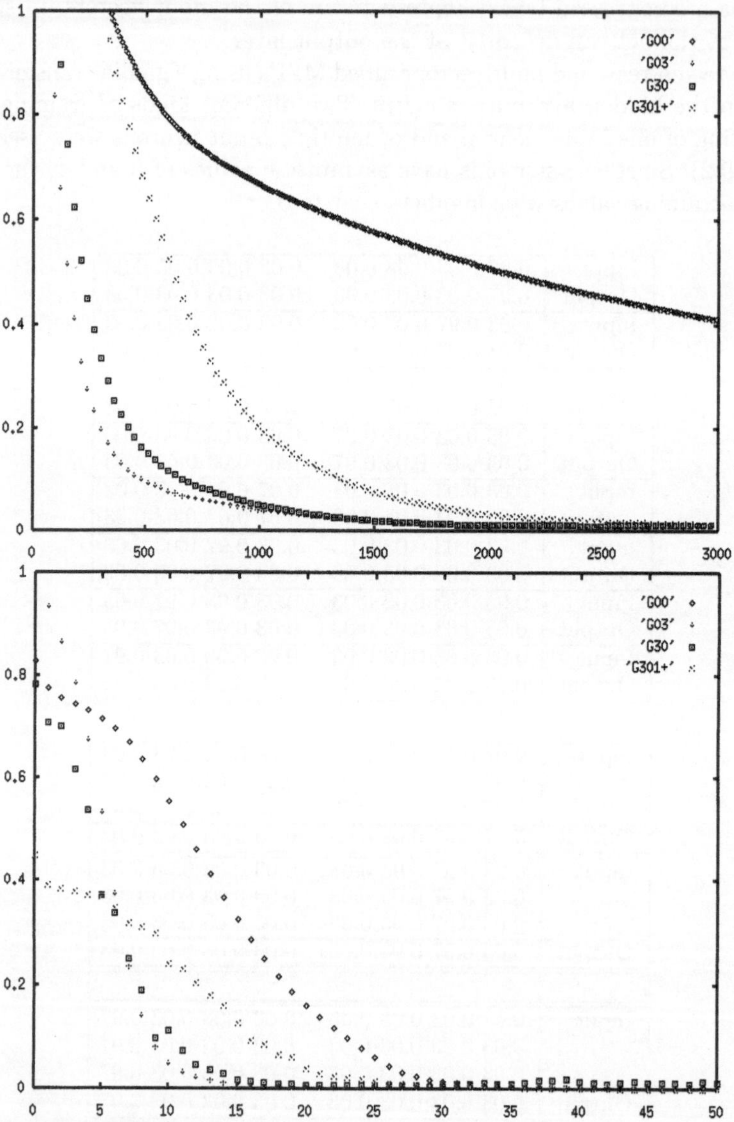

FIGURE 9.5. MSE for the encoder-decoder problem with (top) one input neuron and (bottom) three input neurons

valued MLP network is a three- layer network with one neuron in each layer, i.e., a 1–1–1 network. Each neuron has the dimension of the used geometric algebra. For example, in the figure G03 corresponds to a neural network working in $\mathcal{G}_{3,0,0}$ with eight-dimensional neurons.

For the case of multiple input patterns, the network is a three-layer network with three input neurons, one hidden neuron, and one output neuron, i.e., a 3–1–1 network. The training method used for all neural nets was the batch momentum learning rule. We can see that in both experiments, the real-valued MLP exhibits the worst performance. Since the MLP has eight inputs and the multivector-valued networks have effectivly the same number of inputs, the geometric MLPs are not being favored by a higher dimensional coding of the patterns. Thus, we can attribute the better performance of the multivector-valued MLPs solely to the benefits of the Clifford geometric products involved in the pattern processing through the layers of the neural network.

9.6.3 Prediction

Let us show another application of a geometric multilayer perceptron to distinguish the geometric information in a chaotic process. In this case, we used the well-known Lorenz attractor (σ = 3, r = 26.5, and b = 1), with initial conditions of [0,1,0] and a sample rate of 0.02 seconds. A 3–12–3 MLP and a 1–4–1 $\text{GMLP}_{0,2,0}$ were trained in the interval 12–17 seconds to perform an 8 τ step-ahead prediction. The next 750 samples unseen during training were used for the test. Fig. 9.6.a shows the error during training; note that the $\text{GMLP}_{0,2,0}$ converges faster than the MLP. It is interesting to compare the prediction capability of the nets. Figure 9.6.b,c shows that the $\text{GMLP}_{0,2,0}$ predicts better than the MLP. By analyzing the covariance parameters of the MLP [0.96815, 0.67420,0.95675] and of the $\text{GMLP}_{0,2,0}$ [0.9727, 0.93588, 0.95797], we see that the MLP requires more time to acquire the geometry involved in the second variable, and that is why the convergence is slower. The result is that the MLP loses its ability to predict well in the other side of the looping (see Fig. 9.6.b). In contrast, the geometric net is able to capture the geometric characteristics of the attractor from an early stage, so it cannot fail, even if it has to predict at the other side of the looping.

9.7 Support Vector Machines in Geometric Algebra

The *support vector machine* (SV machine) approach of Vladimir N. Vapnik [109] applies optimization methods for learning. Using SV machines, we can generate a type of two-layer network and RBF networks, as well as networks with other kernels. Our idea is to generate neural networks by using SV machines in conjunction with geometric algebra, and thereby in the neural processing of multivectors. We will call our approach the *support multivector*

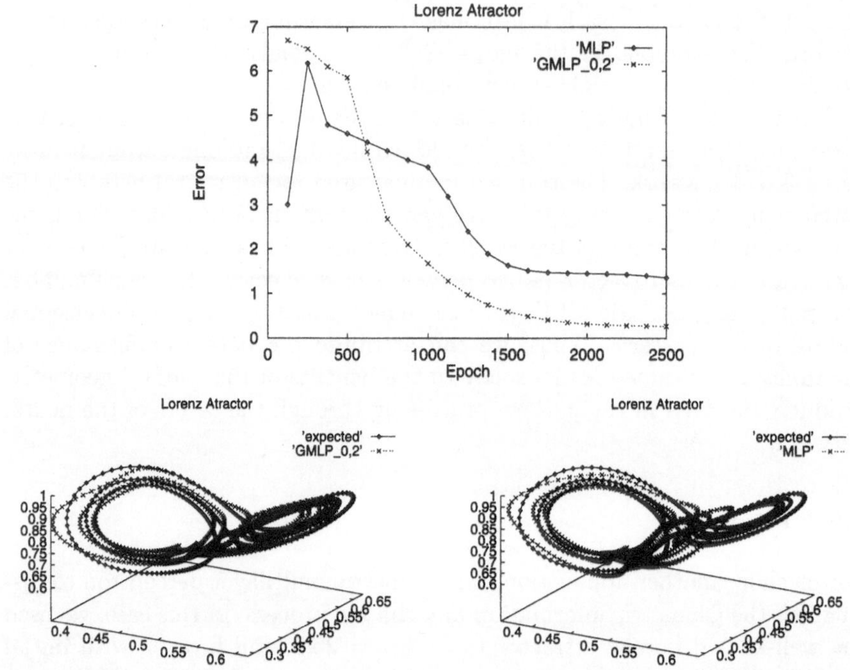

FIGURE 9.6. *(a) Training error; (b) prediction by* $GMLP_{0,2,0}$ *and expected trend; (c) prediction by MLP and expected trend.*

machine (SMVM). We shall review SV machines briefly and then explain the SMVM.

9.7.1 Support vector machines

The SV machine maps the input space R^d into a high-dimensional *feature space* H, given by $\Phi : R^d \Rightarrow H$, satisfying a Kernel $K(\boldsymbol{x}_i, \boldsymbol{x}_j) = \Phi(x_i) \cdot \Phi(x_j)$, which fulfills *Mercer's condition* [109]. The SV machine constructs an optimal hyperplane in the feature space which divides the data into two clusters.

SV machines build the mapping

$$f(\boldsymbol{x}) = sign\Big(\sum_{supportvectors} y_i \alpha_i K(\boldsymbol{x}_i, \boldsymbol{x}) - b \Big). \tag{9.29}$$

The coefficients α_i in the separable case (and analogously in the non-separable case), are found by maximizing the functional based on Lagrange coefficients:

$$W(\alpha) = \sum_{i=1}^{l} \alpha_i - \frac{1}{2} \sum_{i,j}^{l} \alpha_i \alpha_j y_i y_j K(x_i, x_j) \tag{9.30}$$

subject to the constraints $\sum_{i=1}^{l} \alpha_i y_i = 0$, where $\alpha_i \geq 0$, i=1,2,...,l. This functional coincides with the functional for finding the optimal hyperplane.

Examples of SV machines include

$$K(\boldsymbol{x}, \boldsymbol{x}_i) = [(\boldsymbol{x} \cdot \boldsymbol{x}_i) + 1]^d \quad \text{(polynomial learning machines)} \tag{9.31}$$

$$K_\gamma(|x - x_i|) = exp\{-\gamma|\boldsymbol{x} - \boldsymbol{x}_i|^2\} \quad \text{(radial basis functions machines)} \tag{9.32}$$

$$K(\boldsymbol{x}, \boldsymbol{x}_i) = S\Big(v(\boldsymbol{x} \cdot \boldsymbol{x}_i) + c\Big) \quad \text{(two-layer neural networks)} \tag{9.33}$$

9.7.2 Support multivector machines

A *support multivector machine* (SMVM) maps the multivector input space R^{2n} of $\mathcal{G}_{p,q,r}$ $(n = p + q + r)$ into a high-dimensional feature space R^{n_f} $(n_f >= 2^n)$

$$\Phi : R^{2^n} \Rightarrow R^{n_f}. \tag{9.34}$$

The SMVM constructs an optimal separating hyperplane in the *multivector feature space* by using, in the nonlinear case, the kernels

$$\sum_{m=1}^{N\,graded\,spaces} K_m(\boldsymbol{x}_{mi}, \boldsymbol{x}_{mj}) = \sum_{m=1}^{N\,graded\,spaces} \Phi(x_{mi}) \cdot \Phi(x_{mj}), \tag{9.35}$$

which fulfill Mercer's conditions. SMVMs for multivectors $\boldsymbol{x}$ of a geometric algebra $\mathcal{G}_{p,q,r}$ are implemented by the multivector mapping

$$\{y_1, y_2, ..., y_m\} = \sum_{m=1}^{N graded spaces} f_m(\boldsymbol{x}_{mi})$$

$$= \sum_{m=1}^{N\,graded\,spaces} sign\Big(\sum_{support\ vectors} y_{mi}\alpha_{mi} K(\boldsymbol{x}_{mi}, \boldsymbol{x}_m) - b_m \Big), \tag{9.36}$$

where m denotes the grade of the spaces. The coefficients α_{mi} in the separable case (and analogously in the non-separable case), are found by maximizing the functional based on Lagrange coefficients:

$$W(\alpha_i^m) = W\Big(\sum_{m=1}^{N\,graded\,spaces} \sum_{i}^{l} \alpha_{mi} \Big) = \tag{9.37}$$

$$\sum_{m=1}^{N\,graded\,spaces} \sum_{i=1}^{l} \alpha_{mi} - \frac{1}{2} \sum_{m=1}^{N\,graded\,spaces} \sum_{i,j}^{l} \alpha_{mi}\alpha_{mj} y_{mi} y_{mj} K(x_{mi}, x_{mj}),$$

subject to the constraint

$$\sum_{m=1}^{N\,graded\,spaces} \sum_{i=1}^{l} \alpha_{mi} y_{mi} = 0, \tag{9.38}$$

where $\alpha_{mi} \geq 0$, for m=1,...,N graded spaces and i=1,2,...,l. This functional coincides with the functional for finding the optimal separating hyperplane for the multivector feature space.

9.7.3 Generating SMVMs with different kernels

Using the kernel of equation (9.31) results in a multivector classifier based on a multivector polynomial of degree p. An SMVM with kernels, according to equation (9.32), constitutes a *Gaussian radial-basis function multivector* classifier. The reader can see that by using the SMVM approach we can straightforwardly generate multivector RBF networks, avoiding the complications of training that are encountered in the use of classical RBF networks. The number of the centers ($N_s = m \times 2^n$, m 2^n-dimensional multivectors), the centers themselves (s_i $i = 1, ..., N_s$), the weights (α_i s_i $i = 1, ..., N_s$), and the threshold (b) are all produced automatically by the SMVM training. This is an important contribution to the field, because in earlier work [4, 5], we have simply used extensions of the real-valued networks RBF for the so-called geometric RBF networks with classical training methods. We believe that the use of RBF–SMVM presents a promising neurocomputing tool for various applications of data coded in geometric algebra.

In the case of two-layer networks (equation (9.33)), the first layer is composed of N_{s_1} sets of weights, with each set consisting of the dimension of the data $d = m \times 2^n$ and m 2^n-dimensional multivectors, and the second layer is composed of N_{s_2} weights (the α_i). In this way, according to Cybenko's theorem [25], an evaluation simply requires the consideration of weighted sum of sigmoids, evaluated on inner products of test data with the multivector support vectors. Using our approach, we can see that the architecture (N_{s_2} weights) is found by the SMVM automatically.

9.7.4 Multivector regression

In order to generalize the linear SMVM to regression estimation, a margin is constructed in the space of the target values $m_i \in R$, $i = 1, 2, ..., 2^n$ (components of a target multivector) by using Vapnik's ϵ-insensitive loss function

$$|m_i - f_i(\boldsymbol{x})|_\epsilon := max 0, |m_i - f_i(\boldsymbol{x})| - \epsilon. \tag{9.39}$$

To estimate a linear regression

$$m_i = f_i(\boldsymbol{x}) = (\boldsymbol{w} \cdot \boldsymbol{x}) + b \tag{9.40}$$

with precision ϵ, one minimizes

$$\frac{1}{2}||\boldsymbol{w}||^2 + C \sum_{u=1}^{l} |m_{iu} - f_i(\boldsymbol{x}_u)|_\epsilon. \tag{9.41}$$

Here, $\boldsymbol{x}$, $and \boldsymbol{w}$ are multivectors of a $\mathcal{G}_{p,q,r}$.

The generalization to nonlinear regression estimation is implemented using kernel functions $k(\cdot)$ (equations (9.31–9.33)). Introducing Lagrange multipliers, we arrive at the functional of the following optimization problem; i.e., choose a priori $C > 0$, $\epsilon \geq 0$ and maximize

$$W(\boldsymbol{\alpha}, \boldsymbol{\alpha}^*) = -\epsilon \sum_{u=1}^{l} (\alpha_u^* + \alpha_u) + \sum_{u=1}^{l} (\alpha_u^* - \alpha_u) m_{iu} - \frac{1}{2} \sum_{u,v=1}^{l} (\alpha_u^* - \alpha_u)(\alpha_v^* - \alpha_v) k(\boldsymbol{x}_u, \boldsymbol{x}_v) \quad (9.42)$$

subject to $0 \leq \alpha_u, \alpha_u^* \leq C$, $u = 1, ..., l$, and $\sum_{u=1}^{l} (\alpha_u^* - \alpha_u) = 0$. The regression estimate takes the form

$$m_i = f_i(\boldsymbol{x}) = \sum_{u=1}^{l} (\alpha_u^* - \alpha_u) k(\boldsymbol{x}_u, \boldsymbol{x}) + b, \quad (9.43)$$

where m_i are the coefficients of the multivector $\boldsymbol{m} \in \mathcal{G}_{p,q,r}$.

9.8 Experimental Analysis of Support Multivector Machines

This section presents the use of the SMVM using RBF kernels to locate support multivectors, which illustrates the geometric role of the *support multivectors.* A second experiment applies SMVM to a task of robot grasping. In this experiment, the coding of data using motor algebra simplifies the complexity of the problem.

9.8.1 Finding support multivectors

In this section, we demonstrate the use of SV machines for finding support vectors in the 2D and 3D case. The chosen examples allow us to depict the feature space and show clearly to the reader how SV machines and the SMVM work. First, we took two clusters in R^2 and applied a nonlinear SVM and a nonlinear SMVM, using in both cases an RBF kernel. Fig. 9.7.a shows the original 2D data, Fig. 9.7.b the support vectors found by the SV machine, and 9.7.c the support multivectors found by the SMVM in $\mathcal{G}_{2,0,0}$. The multivectors were coded as

$$\boldsymbol{m}_i = \boldsymbol{x}_i + \frac{1}{3} \sum_{j=i}^{i+2} \boldsymbol{x}_j + (\boldsymbol{x}_i - \boldsymbol{x}_{i+1}) \wedge (\boldsymbol{x}_i - \boldsymbol{x}_{i+2}). \quad (9.44)$$

Note that for the SMVM the gained areas follow the borders of the clusters, whereas for the SV machine, some support vectors are located in the interior of the clusters.

In the next experiment, we were interested in the separation of two clouds of 3D points, as shown in Fig. 9.8.a. Note that the points of the clouds lie on a nonlinear surface. Fig. 9.8.b shows the individual support vectors found by a linear SV machine as the curvature of the data manifold changed. Similarly, Fig. 9.8.c shows the individual support multivectors found by the linear SMVM in $\mathcal{G}_{3,0,0}$. The multivectors coding the data are of the form

$$\boldsymbol{m}_i = \boldsymbol{x}_i + \frac{1}{4}\sum_{j=i}^{i+3} \boldsymbol{x}_j + (\boldsymbol{x}_i - \boldsymbol{x}_{i+1}) \wedge (\boldsymbol{x}_i - \boldsymbol{x}_{i+2}) \wedge (\boldsymbol{x}_i - \boldsymbol{x}_{i+3}), \qquad (9.45)$$

which represent pyramidal volumes. Note that the width of the volume basis follows the curvature change of the surface. This experiment shows how the SMVM captures the geometric properties of the manifold. It is interesting to note that only a linear SMVM is sufficient to find the optimal support multivector.

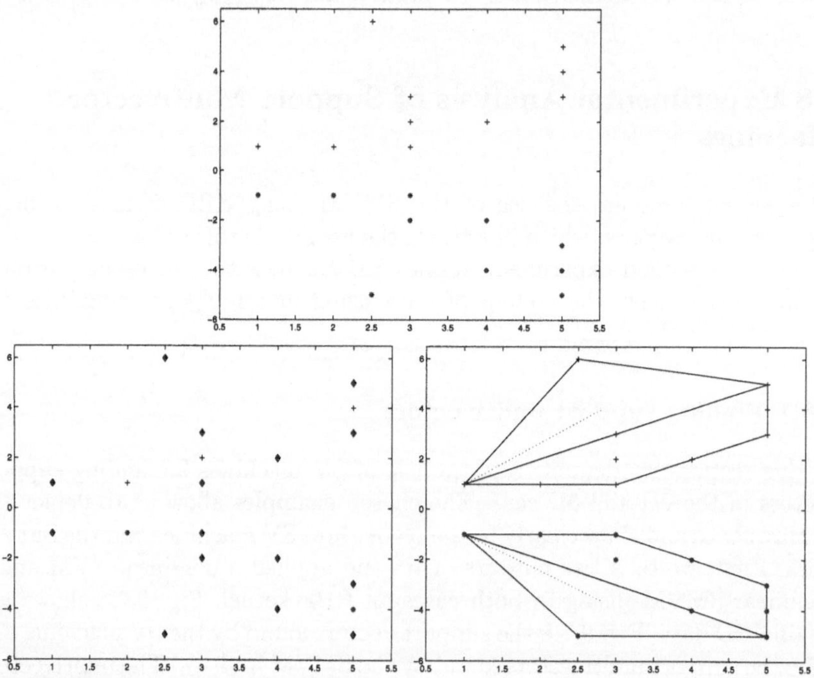

FIGURE 9.7. *2D case using RBF kernel: (a) two 2D clusters data; (b) SV machine (support vectors indicated with diamonds); (c) SMVM using $\mathcal{G}_{2,0,0}$ (support multivectors indicated by triangles).*

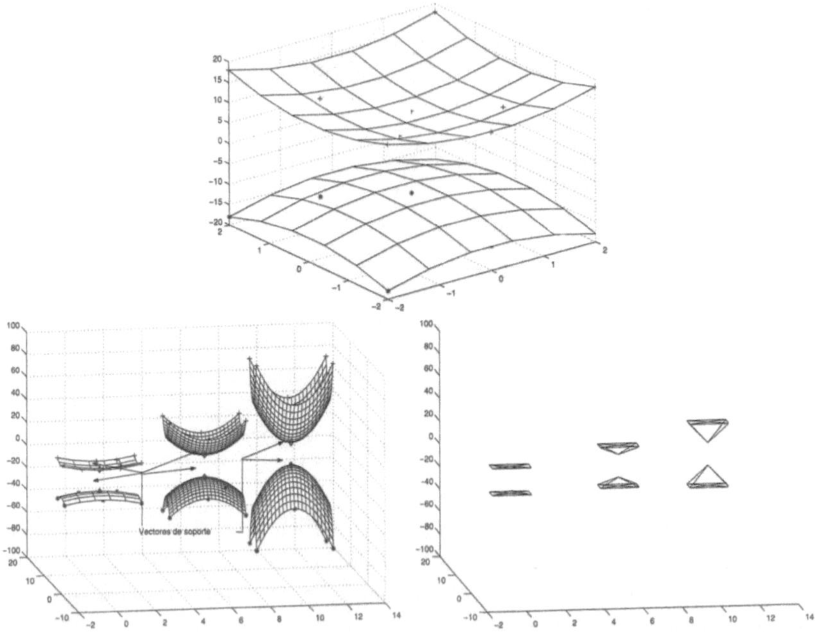

FIGURE 9.8. *3D case: (a) two 3D clusters; (b) linear SV machine lineal by change of curvature of the data surface (one support vector); (c) linear SMVM using $\mathcal{G}_{3,0,0}$ by change of curvature of the data surface (one multivector changing its shape according the surface curvature).*

9.8.2 Estimation of 3D rigid motion

In this experiment, we show the importance of input data coding and the use of the SMVM for estimation. The problem consisted of the estimation of the Euclidean motion necessary to move an object to a certain point along a 3D nonlinear curve. This can be the case when we have to move the grasper of a robot manipulator to a specific curve point. Fig..9.9 is an ideal representation of a similar task which would commonly occur on the floor of a factory. The stereo camera system records the 3D coordinates of a target position, and the SMVM estimates the motion for the grasper. For this experiment, we used simulated data. In order to linearize the model of the motion of a point, we used the geometric algebra $\mathcal{G}^+_{3,0,1}$, or *motor algebra* [8]. Working in a 4D space, we simplified the motor estimation necessary to carry out the 3D motions along the curve. We assumed that the trajectory was known, and we prepared the training data as couples of 3D position points $\boldsymbol{x}_i$. The 3D rigid motions coded in the motor algebra $\mathcal{G}^+_{3,0,1}$ were as follows:

$$\boldsymbol{P}_i = 1 + I\boldsymbol{x}_i \tag{9.46}$$

$$\boldsymbol{M}_i = \boldsymbol{T}_i \boldsymbol{R} s_i, \tag{9.47}$$

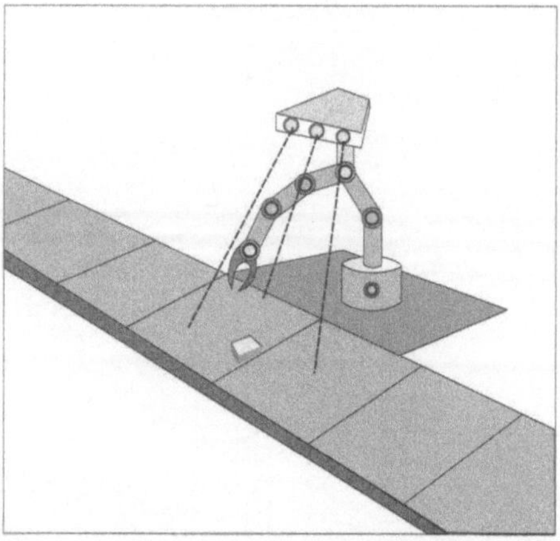

FIGURE 9.9. *Visually guided robot manipulation*

where the rotor $\boldsymbol{Rs}_i = \cos(\frac{\theta_i}{2}) + \sin(\frac{\theta_i}{2})\boldsymbol{Ls}_i$ rotate in $\theta \in R$ about the screw axis line $\boldsymbol{Ls}_i = \boldsymbol{n}_i + I\boldsymbol{m}_i$, and the translator $\boldsymbol{T}_i = 1 + I\frac{d_i \boldsymbol{n}_i}{2}$ corresponds to the sliding in the distance $d_i \in R$ along $\boldsymbol{Ls}_i$. Considering motion along a nonlinear path, we took the lines tangent to the curve to be screw lines $\boldsymbol{Ls}_i$. By using the estimated motor $\boldsymbol{M}_j^e$ for the position $\boldsymbol{P}_j$, obtained using the SMVM, we were able to move the grasper to the new position j as follows:

$$\boldsymbol{X}_j = \boldsymbol{M}_j^e \boldsymbol{X}_l \widetilde{\boldsymbol{M}}_j^e = \boldsymbol{T}_j^e \boldsymbol{R}_j^e \boldsymbol{X}_l \widetilde{\boldsymbol{R}}_j^e \boldsymbol{T}_j^e, \tag{9.48}$$

where $\boldsymbol{X}_l$ stands for any point belonging to the grasper at the last position.

The training data for the SMVM consisted of the couples $\boldsymbol{P}_i$ as input data and $\boldsymbol{M}_i$ as output data. The training was done so that the SMVM could estimate the motors $\hat{\boldsymbol{M}}_j^e$ for unseen points $\boldsymbol{P}_j$. Since the points $\boldsymbol{P}_i$ are given by the three first bivector components and the outputs by the eight motor components of $\boldsymbol{M}_i$, we used an SMVM architecture with three inputs and eight outputs. Three inputs, because the points are of the form

$$\boldsymbol{P}_j = 1 + I\boldsymbol{x}_j \equiv [1, 0, 0, 0, x_{j1}, x_{j2}, x_{j3}, 0]. \tag{9.49}$$

Thus, we were able to ignore the first component "1", because it is constant for all $\boldsymbol{P}_j$. After the training, we tested to see whether the SMVM could estimate the correct 3D rigid motion. Fig. 9.10 (top left) shows a nonlinear motion path. We selected a series of points from this curve and their corresponding motors for training the SMVM architecture. For recall mode, we chose three arbitrary points which had not been used during the training of the SMVM. The estimated motors for these points were applied to the object in order to move it to these particular positions of the curve. We can see in Fig. 9.10 that the estimated motors are very good.

Next, we trained a real-valued MLP with three input nodes, ten hidden nodes, and eight output nodes, using the same training data and a convergence error of 0.001. Fig. 9.10 (top right) shows the motion approximated by the net. We can see that the SMVM in Fig. 9.10 exhibits a slightly better performance.

Finally, we performed three similar experiments using noisy data. For this experiment, we added 0.1%, 1%, and 2% of uniform distributed noise to the three components of the position vectors and to the eight components of the motors multivectors. We trained the SMVM and MLP with these noisy data. Once again, we used a convergence error of 0.001 for the MLP.

The results presented in Fig. 9.10 confirm that the performance of the SMVM definitely surpasses that of the real-valued MLP. For the three cases of noisy data, the three estimated motors of the SMVM are better than the ones approximated by the MLP.

9.9 Conclusion

According to the literature, there are basically two mathematical systems used in neural computing: tensor algebra and matrix algebra. In contrast, the authors have chosen to use the coordinate-free system of Clifford or geometric algebra for the analysis and design of feedforward neural networks. Our work shows that real-, complex-, and quaternion-valued neural networks are simply particular cases of geometric algebra multidimensional neural networks, and that some can be generated using support multivector machines. In particular, the generation of RBF networks in geometric algebra is easier using an SMVM, which allows one to find the optimal parameters automatically. The use of SV machines within the geometric algebra framework widens their sphere of applicability and furthermore expands our understanding of their use for multidimensional learning. The experimental analysis confirms the potential of geometric neural networks for a variety of real applications using multidimensional representations.

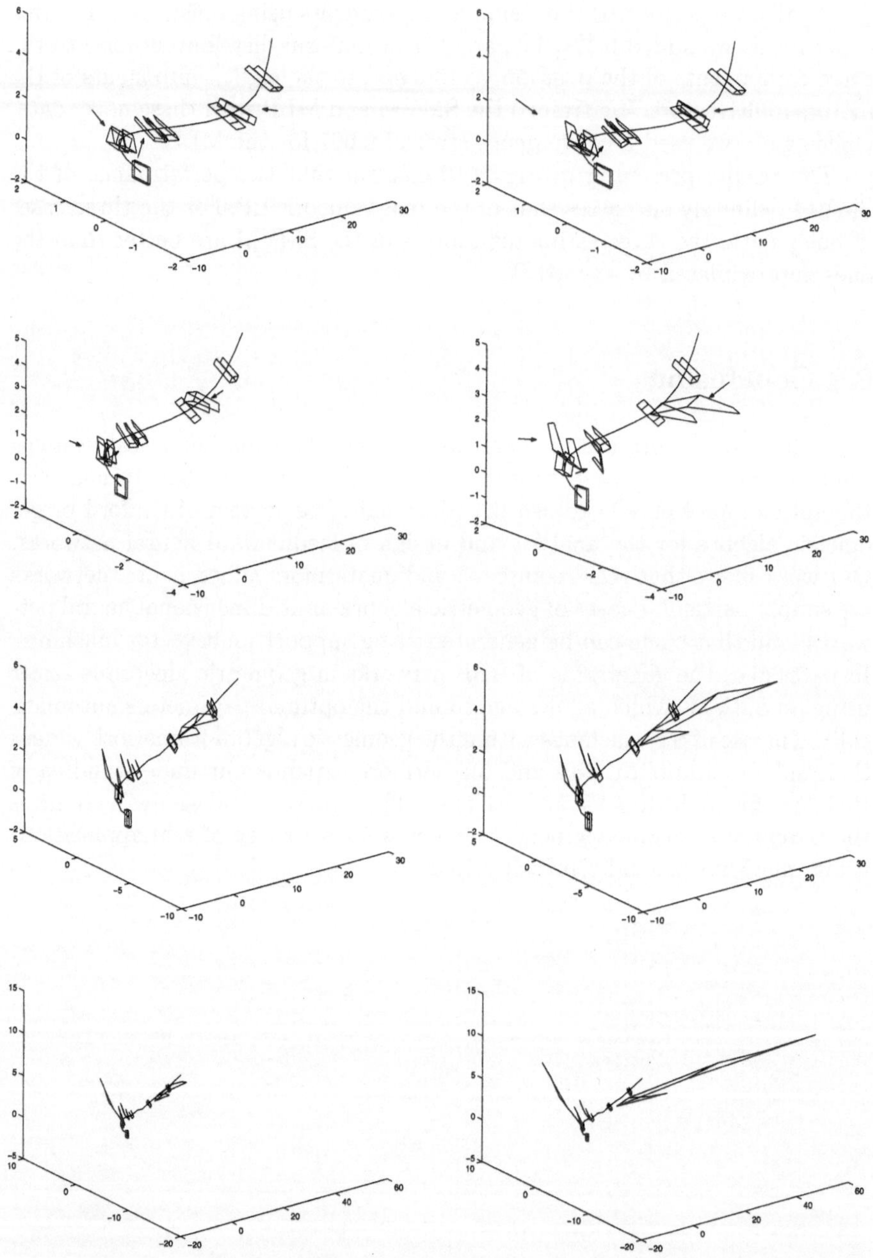

FIGURE 9.10. *Three estimated grasper positions (indicated with an arrow) using noise-free data and noisy data (0.1%, 1%, and 2%, respectively, from top to bottom): left column: estimation using an SMVM in* $\mathcal{G}_{3,0,1}$*; right column: approximation using a 3–10–8 MLP*

References

1. Ablamowicks R. CLIFFORD 4.0 Software packet using Maple for Clifford algebra computations. http://math.tntech.edu/rafal/cliff4/
2. Arena P., Caponetto R., Fortuna L., Muscato G. and Xibilia M.G. Quaternionic multilayer perceptrons for chaotic time series prediction. IEICE Trans. Fundamentals. Vol. E79-A. No. 10 October, pp. 1–6, 1996.
3. Ashdown M.A.J. 1998. Maple code for geometric algebra Available from http://www.mrao.cam.ac.uk/ maja
4. Bayro-Corrochano E. Clifford self-organizing neural network, Clifford wavelet network. *Proc. 14th IASTED Int. Conf. Applied Informatics*, Feb. 20-22, Innsbruck, Austria, pp. 271–274, 1996.
5. Bayro-Corrochano E., Buchholz S. and Sommer G. Self-organizing Clifford neural network *IEEE ICNN'96 Washington, DC*, June, pp. 120–125, 1996.
6. Bayro-Corrochano E., Lasenby J., Sommer G. Geometric algebra: A framework for computing point and line correspondences and projective structure using n uncalibrated cameras. In *IEEE Proceedings of ICPR'96 Vienna, Austria*, Vol. I, August, pp. 334–338, 1996.
7. Bayro-Corrochano E., Daniilidis K. , Sommer G. Hand-eye calibration in terms of motions of lines using geometric algebra. In *10th Scandinavian Conference on Image Analysis*, Vol. I, pp. 397–404, Lappeenranta, 1997.
8. Bayro–Corrochano E., Daniilidis K., and Sommer G. Motor algebra for 3D kinematics. The case of the hand–eye calibration. In *Int. Journal of Mathematical Imaging and Vision*, Vol. 13 (2), October 2000, pp. 79–99.
9. Bayro-Corrochano E. and Lasenby J. Geometric techniques for the computation of projective invariants using n uncalibrated cameras. In *Proceedings of the Indian Conference on Computer Vision and Image Processing*, New Delhi, India, 21–23 December, pp. 95–100, 1998.
10. Bayro-Corrochano E. and Rosenhahn B. Computing the intrinsic camera parameters using Pascal's theorem. In *Geometric Computing with Clifford Algebra*, G. Sommer (Ed.), Chapter 16, Springer Verlag, Heidelberg, 2000.
11. Bayro–Corrochano E. and Sobczyk G. Applications of Lie algebras in the geometric algebra framework. Geometric Algebra Applications with Applications in Science and Engineering. Eduardo Bayro–Corrochano and Garret Sobczyk (eds.), chap. 4. Birkhäuser, New York, 2000.
12. Bayro-Corrochano E. and Zhang Y. The motor extended Kalman filter: a geometric approach for 3D rigid motion estimation. *Journal of Mathematical Imaging and Vision*, Vol. 13(3), December 2000, pp. 205–227.
13. Belinfante J. and Kolman B. Lie Groups and Lie Algebras: With Applications and Computational Methods. *SIAM*, Philadelphia, 1972.
14. Blaschke W. Kinematik und Quaternionen. *VEB Deutscher Verlag der Wissenschaften*, Berlin, 1960.

15. Bülow T. *Hypercomplex Fourier Transforms.* PhD Thesis. Computer Science Institute, Christian Albrechts Universität zu Kiel, 1998.
16. Carlsson, S. The double algebra: an effective tool for computing invariants in computer vision. *Applications of Invariance in Computer Vision*, Lecture Notes in Computer Science 825; Proceedings of 2nd-joint Europe-US workshop, Azores, October 1993. Eds. Mundy, Zisserman and Forsyth. Springer-Verlag, 1994.
17. Carlsson, S. Symmetry in Perspective. In *Proceedings of the European Conference on Computer Vision*, Freiburg, Germany, pp. 249–263, 1998.
18. Chen H. A screw motion approach to uniqueness analysis of head-eye geometry. In *IEEE Conf. Computer Vision and Pattern Recognition*, Maui, Hawaii, June 3-6, pp. 145–151, 1991.
19. Clifford W. K. Preliminary sketch of bi-quaternions. *Proc. London Math. Soc.*, 4, pp. 381–395, 1873.
20. Clifford W. K. Applications of Grassmann's extensive algebra. *Am. J. Math.*, 1, pp. 350–358, 1878.
21. Chernov V.M. Discrete orthogonal transforms with data representation in composition algebras. In *Scandinavian Conference on Image Analysis, Uppsala, Sweden*, 1995, pp. 357-364.
22. Chou J. C. K. and Kamel M. Finding the position and orientation of a sensor on a robot manipulator using quaternions. *Intern. Journal of Robotics Research*, 10(3), pp. 240–254, 1991.
23. Csurka G. and Faugeras O. Computing three dimensional project invariants from a pair of images using the Grassmann–Cayley algebra *Journal of Image and Vision Computing*, 16, pp. 3–12, 1998.
24. Cumani A. Edge detection in multispectral images. CVGIP: Graphical Models and Image Processing, Vol. 53, pp. 40–51, 1991.
25. Cybenko G. Approximation by superposition of a sigmoidal function. *Mathematics of control, signals and systems*, Vol. 2, pp. 303–314, 1989.
26. Daniilidis K. and Bayro Corrochano E. The dual quaternion approach to hand-eye calibration. *IEEE Proceedings of the International Conference on Pattern Recognition ICPR'96*, Viena, Austria, Vol. I, pp. 318–322, August, 1996.
27. Denavit J. and Hartenberg R. S. A kinematic notation for the lower–pair mechanism based on matrices. *J. Opt. Soc. Am. A*, pp. 465–484, 1955.
28. Dodwell P. C. The Lie transformation group model of visual perception. *Perception and Psychophysics*, 34(1), pp. 1- 16, 1983.
29. Doran C.J.L. Geometric algebra and its applications to mathematical physics. *Ph.D. Thesis*, University of Cambridge, 1994.
30. Dorst L., Mann S. and Bouma T. GABLE: A Matlab tutorial for geometric algebra. available from http://www.carol.wins.uva.nl/ gable, 1999.
31. Ell T.A. Hypercomplex Spektral Transformations. PhD Thesis. University of Minnesota, 1992.
32. Faugeras, O. Stratification of three-dimensional vision: projective, affine and metric representations. *J. Opt. Soc. Am. A*, pp. 465–484, 1995.
33. Felsberg M. Signal processing using frequency domain methods in Clifford algebra. Msc. Thesis, Computer Science Institute, Christian Albrechts Universität zu Kiel, 1998.
34. Fulton W. and Harris J. Representation Theory: A First Course. Springer–Verlag, New York, 1991.
35. Gabor D. Theory of communication. *Journal of the IEE*, 93:429-457, 1946.
36. Georgiou G. M. and Koutsougeras C. Complex domain backpropagation. *IEEE Trans. on Circuits and Systems*, pp. 330–334, 1992.

37. Granlund G.H. and Knutsson H. *Signal Processing for Computer Vision.* Kluwer Academic Publishers, 1995.
38. Grassmann H. Der Ort der Hamilton'schen Quaternionen in der Ausdehnungslehre. *Math. Ann.*, 12: 375, 1877.
39. Gu Y. L. and Luh J. Y. S. Dual–number transformation and its applications to robotics. *IEEE Journal of Robotics and Automation*, Vol. RA–3, No. 6, pp. 615–623, 1987.
40. Hahn S.L. Multidimesnsional complex signals with single-orthant spectra. In Proc. IEEE, 80(8):1287-1300, 1992.
41. Hahn S.L. *Hilbert Transforms in Signal Processing.* Artech House, Boston, London, 1996.
42. Hartley, R. Lines and Points in three views – a unified approach. In *ARPA Image Understanding Workshop*, Monterey, California, 1994.
43. Hamilton, W.R. Lectures on Quaternions. Hodges and Smith, Dublin, 1853.
44. Hartley R.I. Projective Reconstruction and Invariants from Multiple Images *IEEE Trans.PAMI*, Vol 16, No.10, pp. 1036–1041, 1994.
45. Hartley, R. The Quadrifocal tensor In *ECCV98*, LNCS, Springer-Verlag, 1998.
46. Hestenes D. Space-Time Algebra. Gordon and Breach, 1966.
47. Hestenes D. and Sobczyk G. Clifford Algebra to Geometric Calculus: A Unified Language for Mathematics and Physics, 1984. D. Reidel, Dordrecht.
48. Hestenes D. New Foundations for Classical Mechanics. D. Reidel, Dordrecht, 1986.
49. Hestenes D. and Ziegler R. Projective geometry with Clifford algebra. *Acta Applicandae Mathematicae*, 23, pp. 25–63, 1991.
50. Hestenes, D. The Design of Linear Algebra and Geometry. *Acta Applicandae Mathematicae*, 23: 65–93, 1991.
51. Hestenes D. Space-Time Algebra. *Gordon and Breach*, 1966.
52. Hestenes D. Invariant body kinematics I: Saccadic and compensatory eye movements. Neural Networks, Vol. 7, pp. 65–77, 1993.
53. Hestenes D. Invariant body kinematics II: Reaching and neurogeometry. Neural Networks, Vol. 7, pp. 79–88, 1993.
54. Hestenes D. Old wine in new bottles: a new algebraic framework for computational geometry. Geometric Algebra Applications with Applications in Science and Engineering. Eduardo Bayro–Corrochano and Garret Sobczyk (eds.), chap. 1. Birkhäuser, New York, 2001.
55. Hoffman W. C. The Lie algebra of visual perception. *Journal of Mathematical Psychology*, 3, pp. 65-98, 1966.
56. Horaud R. and Dornaika F. Hand-eye calibration. *Intern. Journal of Robotics Research*, 14, pp. 195–210, 1995.
57. Hornik K. Multilayer feedforward networks are universal approximators. Neural Networks, Vol. 2, pp. 359–366, 1989.
58. Jähne B. Digitale Bildverarbeitung. Springer Verlag, Berlin, 1993.
59. Kantor I. L. and Solodovnikov A. S. Hypercomplex Numbers: An Elementary Introduction to Algebras. Springer Verlag, New York Inc., 1989.
60. Koenderink J.J. The brain: a geometry engine. Psychological Research, Vol. 52, pp. 122–127, 1990.
61. Koschan A. A comparative study on color edge detection. In *Proceedings 2nd Asian Conference on Computer Vision AC-CV'95*, Singapore, 5-8, December 1995, Vol. III, pp. 574–578.
62. Kunze, S. Ein Hand–Auge–System zur visuell basierten Lokalisierung und Identifikation von Objekten. Diploma Thesis, Christian–Albrechts–Universität zu Kiel, Institut für Informatik und Praktische Mathematik, 1999.

63. Lasenby A.N. A 4D Maple package for geometric algebra manipulations in spacetime. Available from http://www.mrao.cam.ac.uk/ clifford, 1994.
64. Lasenby J., Bayro Corrochano E.J., Lasenby A. and Sommer G. A new methodology for computing invariants in computer vision. In *IEEE Proceedings of the International Conference on Pattern Recognition, ICPR'96*, Vienna, Austria, Vol. I, pp. 393–397, August, 1996.
65. Lasenby J. and Bayro Corrochano E. Computing 3D Projective Invariants from points and lines. *In G. Sommer, K. Daniilidis, and J. Pauli, editors, Computer Analysis of Images and Patterns*, 7th Int. Conf., CAIP'97, Kiel, Springer-Verlag, Sept., pp. 82–89, 1997.
66. Laseby J. and Bayro Corrochano E. Analysis and computation of projective invariants from multiple views in the geometric algebra framework. In Special Issue on Invariants for Pattern Recognition and Classification, ed. M.A. Rodrigues. *Int. Journal of Pattern Recognition and Artificial Intelligence*, Vol 13, No. 8, December, pp. 1105–1121, 1999.
67. Li H., Hestenes D. and Rockwood A. Generalized Homogeneous Coordinates for Computational Geometry. In: G. Sommer (Ed.). Geometric Computing with Clifford Algebra, Springer Verlag, 2001.
68. Li M. and Betsis D. Hand–eye calibration. In *Proc. Int. Conf. on Computer Vision*, Boston, MA, June 20–23, pp. 40–46, 1995.
69. Lounesto P. CLICAL software paquet and user manual. Helsinki University of Technology of Mathematics, Research Report A248. 1987.
70. Lounesto P. Clifford Algebras and Spinors. Cambridge University Press, Cambridge, 1997.
71. Luong Q. T. and Faugeras O. D. The fundamental matrix: theory, algorithms, and stability analysis. Int. J. Comput. Vision 17(1), pp. 43–76, 1995.
72. Maybank S. J. and Faugeras O. D. A theory of self–calibration of a moving camera. *International Journal of Computer Vision*, 8(2), pp. 123–151, 1992.
73. Maybeck, P. Stochastic models, estimation and Control, **1**. Academic Press, New York, 1979.
74. Miller W. Lie Theory and Special Functions. Academic Press, New York, 1968.
75. Mundy J. and Zisserman A. (Eds.) Geometric Invariance in Computer Vision. MIT Press, 1992.
76. Pearson J.K. and Bisset D.L. Back Propagation in a Clifford Algebra. *Artificial Neural Networks, 2, I. Aleksander and J. Taylor (Ed.)*, pp. 413–416, 1992.
77. Pellionisz A. and Llinàs R. Tensorial approach to the geometry of brain function: cerebellar coordination via a metric tensor. Neuroscience Vol. 5, pp. 1125–1136, 1980.
78. Pellionisz A. and Llinàs R. Tensor network theory of the metaorganization of functional geometries in th central nervous system. Neuroscience Vol. 16, No. 2, pp. 245–273, 1985.
79. Perantonis S.J. and Lisboa P.J.G. Translation, rotation, and scale invariant pattern recognition by high-order neural networks and moment classifiers. IEEE Trans. on Neural Networks, Vol. 3, No. 2, March, pp. 241–251, 1992.
80. Perwass, C.B.U. Applications of geometric algebra in computer vision. Ph.D. Thesis, University of Cambridge, 2000.
81. Poelman C.J. and Kanade T. A paraperspective factorization method for shape and motion recovery. In J–O. Eklundh, editor, *European Conference on Computer Vision*, Stockholm, pp. 97–108, 1994.
82. Poggio T. and Girosi F. Networks for approximation and learning. *IEEE Proc.*, Vol. 78, No. 9, 1481:1497, Sept. 1990.
83. Porteous R.I. 1995. Clifford Algebras and the Classical Groups. *Cambridge University Press*, Cambridge.

84. Pozo J.M. and Sobczyk G. Realizations of the conformal group. *Geometric Algebra with Applications in Science and Engineerings.* . E. Bayro–Corrochano and G. Sobczyk (eds.), chap. 3. Birkhäuser, New York, 2001.
85. Press W. H., Teukolsky S. A., Vetterling W.T. and Flannery B.P. Numerical Recipes in C. Cambridge University Press. 1994.
86. Quan L. Invariants of 6 points from 3 uncalibrated images. In *Proc. of the European Conference of Computer Vision*, Vol. II, pp. 459–470, 1994.
87. Riesz M. Clifford Numbers and Spinors. Lecture Series No. 38, University of Maryland, 1958. Reprinted as facsimile (eds. : E.F. Bolinder and P. Lounesto) by Kluwer, Dordrecht, The Netherlands, 1993.
88. Rooney J. On the three types of complex number and planar transformations. *Environment and Planning B*, Vol. 5, pp. 89–99, 1978.
89. Rumelhart D.E. and McClelland J.L. Parallel Distributed Processing: Explorations in the Microestructure of Cognition. 2 Vols. Cambridge: MIT Press, 1986.
90. Sabata R. and Aggarwal J. K. Estimation of motion from a pair of range images: a review. *CVGIP: Image Understanding*, 54, pp. 309–324, 1991.
91. Selig J. M. Clifford algebra of points, lines and planes. South Bank University, School of Computing, Information Technology and Maths, Technical Report SBU–CISM–99–06, 1999.
92. Sangwine S.J. Fourier transforms of colour images using quaternion or hypercomplex numbers. *Electronic Letters*, 32(21): 1979–1980, 1996.
93. Selig J. Robotics kinematics and flags. appea *In Advances in Geometric Algebra with Applications in Science and Engineering. Automatic theorem proving, computer vision, quantum and neural computing and robotics.* E. Bayro–Corrochano and G. Sobczyk (eds.), chap. 12. Birkhäuser, New York, 2000.
94. Semple J.G. and Kneebone G.T. *Algebraic Projective Geometry.* Oxford University Press, Oxford. Reprinted by Oxford Science Publications, 1985.
95. Shashua A. and Werman M. Trilinearity of three perspective views and its associated tensor. In proceedings of *ICCV'95*, MIT, 1995.
96. Shashua, A. Projective structure from uncalibrated images: structure from motion and recognition PAMI, 16(8), pp. 778–790, August, 1994.
97. Shiu Y.C. and Ahmad S. Calibration of wrist-mounted robotic sensors by solving homogeneous transform equations of the form $AX = XB$. *IEEE Trans. Robotics and Automation*, 5, pp. 16–27, 1989.
98. Sobczyk G. The Generalized Spectral Decomposion of a Linear Operator. *The College Mathematics Journal*, 28:1, pp. 27–38, 1997.
99. Sobczyk G. Spectral integral domains in the classroom, *Aportaciones Matemáticas*, Serie Comunicaciones 20, pp. 169–188, 1997.
100. Sobczyk G. Universal geometric algebra. In *Advances in Geometric Algebra with Applications in Science and Engineering.* . E. Bayro–Corrochano and G. Sobczyk (eds.), Chap. 2, Birkhäuser, New York, 2001.
101. Sorenson, H. W. Kalman filtering techniques *In Advances in Control Systems Theory and Applications*, Edited by C. T. Leondes, Vol. 3, Academic Press, pp. 218–292, 1966.
102. Sparr G. Kinetic depth. In *Proc. of the European Conference of Computer Vision*, Vol. II, pp. 471–482, 1994.
103. Stark H. An extension of the Hilbert transform product theorem. *Proc. IEEE*, 59: 1359–1360, 1971.
104. Study E. Geometrie der Dynamen. Leipzig 1903.
105. Tomasi C. and Kanade T. Shape and motion from image streams under orthography: a factorization method. *Int. J. Computer Vision*, 9(2), pp. 137–154, 1992.

106. Tomasi C. Color edge detection with the compass operator. In *IEEE Conference on Computer Vision and Pattern Recognition '99*, Volume 2, June, pp. 160–166, 1999.
107. Triggs, W. Matching Constraints and the Joint Image. In *IEEE Computer Society Press, Proceedings of the Int. Conference of Computer Vision ICCV'95*, Boston, pp. 338–343, 1995.
108. Tsai R. Y. and Lenz R. K. A new technique for fully autonomous and efficient 3D robotics hand/eye calibration. *IEEE Trans. Robotics and Automation*, 5, pp. 345–358, 1989.
109. Vapnik V. Statistical Learning Theory. Wiley, New York, 1998.
110. Yaglom M. Complex Numbers in Geometry. Academic Press, Leicester, 1968.
111. Zhang Z. and Faugeras O. 3–D Dynamic Scene Analysis. Springer Verlag, 1992.
112. Wang C. Extrinsic calibration of a vision sensor mounted on a robot. *IEEE Trans. Robotics and Automation*, pp. 161–175, 1992.

Index